NO USELESS MOUTH

NO USELESS MOUTH

WAGING WAR AND FIGHTING HUNGER IN THE AMERICAN REVOLUTION

RACHEL B. HERRMANN

CORNELL UNIVERSITY PRESS
Ithaca and London

First published 2019 by Cornell University Press

Library of Congress Cataloging-in-Publication Data

Names: Herrmann, Rachel B., author.
Title: No useless mouth : waging war and fighting hunger in the American Revolution / Rachel B. Herrmann.
Description: Ithaca : Cornell University Press, 2019. | Includes bibliographical references and index.
Identifiers: LCCN 2018060505 (print) | LCCN 2019001071 (ebook) | ISBN 9781501716133 (pdf) | ISBN 9781501716126 (ret) | ISBN 9781501716119 (pbk. ; alk. paper)
Subjects: LCSH: United States—History—Revolution, 1775–1783—Indians. | United States—History—Revolution, 1775–1783—African Americans. | Food security—United States—History—18th century. | Food security—Nova Scotia—History—18th century. | Food security—Sierra Leone—History—18th century. | Indians of North America—Food—History—18th century. | African Americans—Food—History—18th century. | Nova Scotia—History—1763–1867. | Sierra Leone—History—To 1896.
Classification: LCC E269.I5 (ebook) | LCC E269.I5 H47 2019 (print) | DDC 973.3—dc23
LC record available at https://lccn.loc.gov/2018060505

Cover image: *Plan of Civilization*, unidentified artist (n.d.). Courtesy of the Greenville County Museum of Art. Museum purchase with funds from the Museum Association's 1990 and 1991 Collectors Groups and the 1989, 1990 and 1991 Museum Antiques Shows, sponsored by Elliott, Davis & Company, CPAs Corporate Benefactors: Ernst and Young; Fluor Daniel; Mr. and Mrs. Alester G. Furman III; Mr. and Mrs. M. Dexter Hagy; Thomas P. Hartness; Mr. and Mrs. E. Erwin Maddrey II; Mary M. Pearce; Mr. and Mrs. John D. Pellett, Jr.; Mr. W. Thomas Smith; Mr. and Mrs. Edward H. Stall; Eleanor and Irvine Welling.

This one's for the archive rats and primary source enthusiasts

Contents

NO USELESS MOUTH

Introduction

Why the Fight against Hunger Mattered

During a July 1791 treaty negotiation, Timothy Pickering, a key figure in the development of early U.S. food policy, misremembered past instances of Native and non-Native hunger while giving a "history lesson." At this meeting on the Tioga River (which ran between present-day Pennsylvania and New York), Pickering met a group of Senecas, one of the six tribes of the Iroquois Confederacy. "When the white people came to this Island, the Indians lived chiefly by hunting and fishing," he explained to Cornplanter, one of the Iroquois negotiators. On this "island" of North America, "the white people immediately began to till the ground, to grow corn, wheat, and other grain . . . and to raise abundance of cattle, sheep and hogs." In the past, Pickering explained, "the Indians continued to follow hunting and fishing, growing only a little corn. They were often in want of food," and "exposed to great hardships."[1]

Pickering met Cornplanter and the other Senecas in the midst of a fight against hunger that began before colonists arrived in North America and ended in the 1810s. In 1791 Pickering was a newcomer to Iroquois diplomacy. He had only been working as a negotiator for a year, and the learning curve had been steep.[2] He started his job during a momentous shift in relations between Natives and non-Natives, when the United States, after a decade of weakness and uncertainty, was trying to gain the upper hand in its dealings with Indians. As a result, his speech to Cornplanter conveyed an inaccurate historical picture.

Cornplanter, for his part, likely knew that Pickering was misinterpreting the actions of seventeenth-century English colonists, who had taken a while to become farmers. Their domesticated animals had died on the ships that traveled to North America. They had spent their first months in Virginia searching for inedible commodities, and in Virginia and New England they had turned into useless mouths dependent on Indians for farmed vegetables, gathered berries, and hunted venison. Contrary to Pickering's claims, it was the English colonists, not the Indians, who had struggled to overcome hunger. It was odd for Pickering to make this speech to Native treaty participants, especially to one named Cornplanter, because the Iroquois had grown corn in abundance long before encountering non-Natives.[3]

The Seneca negotiator sitting across from Pickering was known by several names. To Indians he was Gyantwahia or Kayéthwahkeh, which translates approximately to "where it is planted." To non-Natives he was Cornplanter, John O'Bail, John Abeel, or John Abiel.[4] He had a reputation for effective speechmaking and would have been familiar with his tribe's spoken history. These contemporary creation stories described the fall of Sky Woman onto the back of a turtle and told of how, with the help of other animals, she had constructed an island on the turtle's back. Sky Woman had a daughter. Some Iroquois said the daughter's son, Thaluhyawaku, learned to plant corn. Others said that, while still in the womb, Thaluhyawaku's twin brother, Tawiskalu, maliciously decided to leave his mother's body through her side. This birth killed Sky Woman's daughter, but her early death yielded unexpected bounty in the corn, beans, and squash that sprang forth from the grave.[5] Corn production was intrinsic to the Iroquois past and present.

Yet Pickering's account minimized the history of Iroquois farming and thus erased systematic Indian hunger prevention. Pickering shared his tale because the U.S. government wanted the Iroquois to become farmers. Cornplanter, as his name suggests, could already farm, but he listened to this lesson on the benefits of agriculture because he was trying to maneuver to retain land in his dealings with the new United States.

Hunger's important role in Pickering's false history should be unsurprising, considering that people had long reckoned with it for various environmental and man-made reasons. In the early modern period, cities under siege could expect to be starved out, and they suffered more quickly during times of crop failure or unanticipated changes in the weather. Famine resulted from extended periods of hunger and was evident in instances of actual deaths, food riots, high prices, property crime, and rising migration.[6] During the eighteenth century most British people suffered from hunger, but not famine. In North America, some European observers perceived Native Americans as ravenous, while others thought them better able to deal with dearth. At the same time, slave masters deprived enslaved people of food because they hoped to keep them weak and compliant.

No Useless Mouth is a book about how Native Americans, non-Natives, and people of African descent experienced hunger before, during, and after the American Revolutionary War (1775–1783). It historicizes efforts to create, avoid, and withstand hungriness so as to better understand the moments in time when Native Americans and formerly enslaved peoples gained enough power to shape food policies of hunger prevention and creation, rather than just suffering from the ill effects of new initiatives that men like Pickering envisioned. This book's exploration of the many different contexts of hunger during the era of the American Revolution uncovers how these Native and black revolutionaries acquired so much power—and why they ultimately lost it.

Enduring, ignoring, creating, and preventing hunger were all ways to exercise power during the American Revolution. Hunger prompted violence *and* forged ties; it was a weapon of war and a tool of diplomacy. In North America, Cherokee, Creek, Delaware, Iroquois (Haudenosaunee), Miami, and Shawnee Indians grew and destroyed foodstuffs during the Revolutionary War, which forced their British and American allies to hunger with them, and to furnish provisions that accommodated Native tastes. By the 1810s the United States had learned how to prevent Indian hunger, to weaponize food aid, and to deny Indians the power gained by enduring and ignoring scarcity.

Indians won leverage during the Revolutionary War itself. People of African descent gained some power by creating white hunger during the Revolutionary War, but more so as formerly enslaved communities, primarily after leaving the new United States and migrating to British colonies in Nova Scotia and then Sierra Leone. At the end of the war, British officials in North America chose to transport formerly enslaved refugees to Nova Scotia. In the country that is now called Canada these black colonists were relatively powerless, but they witnessed white colonists' use of food laws to assert authority. Once abolitionists in England turned their attention toward ending the transatlantic slave trade by founding a self-governing black antislavery colony in Sierra Leone, and relocated black colonists from Nova Scotia to Africa, former slaves won the right to fight hunger directly. But after white officials in Sierra Leone realized that colonists' hunger-prevention efforts gave them too much freedom, black colonists lost their hunger-preventing rights. Black revolutionaries managed for a short time to challenge the power regimes in place during the late eighteenth century.

This book similarly challenges how we think about the American Revolution. Its title comes from a 1780 letter by General Frederick Haldimand, the governor of Quebec, at a time when Britain's Indian allies were living through a refugee crisis in British forts. When Haldimand wrote that "no useless Mouth, which can possibly be sent away" could be allowed to remain at these strongholds, he hoped that only Native warriors would spend the winter with British soldiers. Indians tested this assumption that only Native fighters were useful by supplying their own communities and refusing and destroying their allies' provisions, and they proved their usefulness again by fostering the spread of hunger among enemy soldiers and civilians alike. Like Haldimand, historians are accustomed to thinking about white colonists as an increasingly powerful group, Natives as increasingly weak, and enslaved people as individuals with relatively little power.[7] No Useless Mouth turns these narratives on their heads. It instead finds more rather than less power in Indian communities from the 1770s to the 1790s. It offers a new chronology of the eventual decline in Native power against the U.S. government. I highlight a more condensed but strikingly similar chronology of power relations for formerly enslaved people. And I trace myriad, useful efforts to fight hunger before the more widely studied humanitarian initiatives of the nineteenth century.[8]

The Revolutionary War was fought just as much on Indian terms as it was on British and American ones, and Indians continued to drive U.S. food policies after the conflict. Famine-deterrence initiatives evolved through U.S. cooperation with Native Americans, and similar efforts emerged among formerly enslaved communities as black men and women moved out of the United States and across the ocean once the war concluded. All parties were at various times producers, consumers, and destroyers of food, which means that a study of hunger offers an opportunity to understand not only the big moments of power shifts in land cessions and trade negotiations, but also the smaller day-to-day activities that engendered them. In other words, hunger exposes the contingency of power relations in the late eighteenth and early nineteenth centuries.

"I hope you will have taken effectual methods to secure you an abundant supply of provisions. That seems to be the pivot upon which all your operations turn." Secretary of War Henry Knox sent this advice to General "Mad" Anthony Wayne in 1794, near the end of a decade-long war between the United States and a confederated force of Delaware, Miami, and Shawnee Indians— but he might have urged similar preparations during the Revolutionary War. The conflict between the new United States and these Indians was a direct result of the Revolutionary War, in which both Knox and Wayne also fought. Throughout the latter half of the eighteenth century, all military considerations turned on the quest for food and the consequences of its absence, hunger.

The position of all negotiating parties during times of war and peace cannot be understood without knowing whether they were hungry and to what degree. If Native Americans were less hungry than historians have admitted, for example, or if formerly enslaved black colonists were legally empowered to fight hunger themselves, then both groups possessed more authority than scholars have supposed. The American Revolution becomes an era characterized at various points by resilience, resistance, conflict, continuity, and change.[9]

This reinterpretation requires taking a long view of the revolutionary period. Beginning it in the late 1750s, during the Seven Years' War, and ending it in the 1810s encompasses a sixty-year period when diplomatic practices were most in flux. Such disruption allowed Native Americans during the Revolutionary War to emphasize and shape food-related negotiations, while enabling them—now joined by formerly enslaved Africans—to participate in the animal theft and crop destruction that had characterized the seventeenth and early eighteenth centuries. This narrative continues through the 1780s and 1790s because Native Americans and U.S. officials worked together to formulate U.S. hunger-prevention strategies, and because it was also during the 1790s when ex-bondpeople earned the political and legal right to fight hunger on their own terms. By the 1810s, however, Indians and formerly enslaved people had lost their battles against hunger.

My periodization has been driven by my teaching on the American Revolution in a system of higher education that does not require both halves of the undergraduate U.S. history survey (which usually runs from 1492 to 1865 or 1877, and then from 1865 or 1877 to the present).[10] I differentiate the Revolutionary War from the American Revolution. The former stretched from 1775 or 1776 (depending on whether the start of the war begins at Lexington and Concord or with the Declaration of Independence) to 1783 with the signing of the Treaty of Paris by Great Britain and the United States. The longer timescale of the American Revolution assumes that to appreciate the full effects of the war, scholars must look back to the 1750s and forward to the 1830s. After all, the war's chronological boundaries were largely irrelevant to the Indians and enslaved peoples who participated in it. And the end of the war was just the beginning of newly emancipated black colonists' struggle for political rights in the British Empire.

This periodization also addresses several interpretive problems that need to be solved in retelling the history of Native Americans' and enslaved peoples' involvement in the American Revolution. These problems appear in histories of food and hunger, U.S. foreign relations, and the American empire. Historians of foreign relations have omitted Native Americans, jumped from covering

Indian affairs in the 1790s to discussing Indian affairs in the 1830s, or missed the continuities between British and American Indian policies because they privilege the history of the United States after the end of the Revolutionary War.[11]

This elision has meant that power relations between the 1780s and 1810s, centered around food and hunger, have been either misinterpreted or omitted entirely.[12] Such a decision risks assuming that Indians possessed little leverage against the United States, and misses important continuities and changes in British and then American interactions with Native Americans from the 1750s through the 1820s. U.S. officials persuaded Native Americans to attend treaties by working hard to replicate colonial-era British diplomacy, but they did so during a time when food diplomacy had grown indispensable, and when mistakes in practicing it invited major consequences. Federal U.S. Indian agents agonized about the violent insecurity that arose during times of famine in Indian towns and villages, and warned that if the federal government could not provide food aid, it needed to prepare for war. In *No Useless Mouth* I make clear that colonial and postrevolutionary Indian affairs must be analyzed as foreign affairs, and that diplomats' efforts to address Native hunger informed these daily interactions between Natives and non-Natives from the 1750s to the 1810s. Reexamining these food-related negotiations has the effect of exposing the untenable position of the United States during the 1780s and 1790s, and explaining the steps it took to intervene in Native hunger-prevention efforts from the 1790s onward.

In addition to histories of U.S. foreign relations is the scholarship on the American empire during this period, which blames settler colonists for expanding that empire by seizing land from Native Americans—as Americans did in 1779 when they moved into Iroquois houses after John Sullivan's summer campaign against them.[13] Studies of the American Revolution agree that after the war, the U.S. government quickly constituted its own "Empire of Liberty." Historians disagree about whether this decision was radical or not, and they struggle to assign responsibility for the American empire's consolidation. They concur that squatters, unscrupulous traders, and individuals in the interior of the continent drove the formulation of policy at the federal level, such as the government's decision in 1787 to create the Northwest Ordinance for organizing new territory beyond the Appalachian Mountains.[14] But they have yet to fully describe the federal and Native negotiations that enabled these settler colonial land grabs. This book makes clear that Indians could not lose their land to settler colonists until they had lost the fight against hunger with the federal government.[15]

As a concept, settler colonialism is deficient in several respects: first, because the idea of *settlement* should not be used to describe exclusively non-Native behavior; second, because Indian affairs were foreign affairs; third, because Natives actively shaped U.S. policies; and finally, because scholars have not yet clarified whether their definitions of eighteenth-century settler colonialism describe a staggered process of land seizures or a daily milieu of oppression. Indians, like non-Natives, were settled folks; they produced corn, pork, and beef on land to which they periodically returned, hunted for game in predictable patterns and locations, and did not recognize the government's right to sell their territory.[16] Using the word *settler* to critique non-Native behavior thus creates a false dichotomy between Indians and non-Indians, and reproduces the language of eighteenth-century land grabbers.

Further, in a structure of settler colonialism, the colony is separate from but still tied to the mother country; internally rather than internationally focused; the behavior of settler colonists dictates policy back in the metropole; and colonialism is something that happens to indigenous peoples. After the Revolutionary War, however, the federal government had severed relations with Great Britain, viewed Indians as separate nations with whom it conducted foreign policy, and responded to *and* anticipated the behavior of its land-hungry non-Native inhabitants.[17] Native Americans did not passively experience these policies and landgrabs; they intervened to shape policy and critiqued illegal land cessions. It was inaccurate ideas about Native crop and meat production and anxiety about the results of Native hunger that gave rise to the fiction that Indians improperly used their land and therefore required less of it. During the 1790s, U.S. officials—including Timothy Pickering—mischaracterized Native hunger-prevention efforts with the explicit purpose of legitimizing a food policy that facilitated the federal government's acquisition of Native land. In this book, settler colonialism consolidated the territory of the American empire while, simultaneously, the U.S. government enacted a federal Indian food policy that met the expectations of Native Americans *and* its settler colonists.

No Useless Mouth's exploration of the relationship between empire, Native American history, and U.S. foreign relations also requires a reconsideration of the political economy of the late eighteenth and early nineteenth centuries. Before the Revolutionary War, the mercantilism of the British Empire had restricted North American colonists' abilities to trade outside of established British imperial networks. Freedom to trade after the war enabled the United States to make trade agreements with other nations, including Indian nations. However, tensions remained between those who wanted unrestrained foreign and domestic exchange, and economic nationalists who believed that the U.S. government had to intervene in the economy by fixing prices and wages and enacting trade barriers through protectionist legislation. This debate over trade policy colored U.S.-Indian commercial relations as it became less clear where

Indian nations fell within the U.S. commercial orbit. Native Americans in North America wanted the ability to practice unrestricted trade with the United States, but also with British, French, and Spanish officials in North America. They also asked the U.S. government to fix prices for the deerskins they sold in a rapidly evolving fur trade; powerful Indians pushed for economic policies that allowed them to trade freely while enjoying the benefits of protectionism.[18]

To understand how these histories of empire and foreign relations fit together with histories of slavery, scholars must reexamine how enslaved and formerly enslaved people traded, produced, stole, transported, and regulated foodstuffs. The historians who have recognized that the institution of slavery (and its expansion) contradicted eighteenth-century authors' claims that the Empire of Liberty was a peaceful empire have been less invested in tracking the contradictions of black imperialism abroad.[19] Others have not considered the importance of black runaways in shaping foreign policy between British and American officials during the war itself. When British forces invited enslaved Africans to run away and join them in the fight against rebel American colonists, and to then steal food from the plantations of former masters, they initiated a chain of events that would lead some British military leaders to reinterpret retaliatory food deprivation as American acts of war against Britain. When the war ended, the exodus of former slaves from the United States to present-day Canada caused considerable disagreement between British and American military leaders. When formerly enslaved people tried to fight hunger in Sierra Leone, they did so by enacting protectionist legislation that elevated their foodstuffs over those grown and prepared by Africans. The white Sierra Leone Council failed to anticipate the tensions that black colonists' antihunger regulations would create between colonists and Africans—whom black politicians characterized as foreigners whose buying practices merited different pricing policies.

This broad reinterpretation of hunger-prevention initiatives as domestic and foreign policy tells a very different story from histories of single food commodities, which explain how these commodities changed history.[20] Scholars have undertaken important work on food and power, but the era of the American Revolution remains largely unexplored. Histories of food from the sixteenth to the twentieth century have also been less interested in hunger.[21] General surveys of hunger pay insufficient attention to North America, or argue that hunger became preventable only during the mid-nineteenth century onward. It would be easy to assume that state hunger prevention was an achievement only of the mid-nineteenth or even twentieth century.[22] U.S. officials, Native Americans, British officials, and formerly enslaved black colonists clearly tried to prevent hunger in the late eighteenth century, demonstrating that although many of the tactics for fighting hunger remained the same as the colonial period's, the composition of the groups who battled scarcity and the power they lost and gained changed significantly.

Three key behaviors changed and were, in turn, changed by evolving ideas about hunger. Detailing these behaviors should help readers understand how the American Revolution both fostered continuity and changed hunger-prevention initiatives, consequently destabilizing power relationships. These modes of behavior—*food diplomacy*, *victual warfare*, and *victual imperialism*—exist on a spectrum between accommodation and violence because it is impossible to talk about hunger without considering peaceful and aggressive food exchange and destruction. Depending on context, some degree of accommodation and some degree of violence was possible. Diplomacy usually accompanies discussions of war, and, indeed, eighteenth-century diplomats often undertook negotiations to prevent past violence from spiraling into cycles of revenge. They also understood that diplomacy was crucial in stopping future conflicts.

On the more peaceful end of this scale, then, is *food diplomacy*, defined as the sharing of, or collective abstention from, grain, meat, or alcohol in order to create or maintain alliances. In this book I characterize food diplomacy so as to include a shared experience of hunger because Native Americans attached so many meanings to the idea of starvation and because the absence of food thus informed food-sharing activities.[23] Various terms describe similar pursuits: gastrodiplomacy, culinary diplomacy, political gastronomy, and food aid. Food diplomacy is the best option for the revolutionary period. Gastrodiplomacy conjures images of statesmen negotiating over grand meals, and misses the ordinary people who participated in the Revolutionary War. Gastronomy is about delicate eating, while the word culinary references kitchens.[24] Food aid is distributed to civilians in reaction to a crisis, so it was part of revolutionary customs, but the phrase is not broad enough to describe all forms of cooperative exchange, such as distributions of rations to Indian warriors.[25] Food diplomacy encompasses the political culture of eighteenth-century diplomacy that extended beyond protocol and court etiquette, such as the alliance-making of government officials, the forest diplomacy of Native war and peace chiefs, and the maneuvering of traders. It includes the reactive nature of British and American food aid, as well as the Indians who in turn gave food gifts to non-Natives. And it applies to the wartime men and women who ate unsavory fare of salt pork, boiled beef, cornmeal mush, and moldy bread far away from kitchens. The inclusion of alcohol in definitions of food diplomacy also poses challenges, given its separate historiography and the ramifications of alcohol use in Native communities.[26] This history deals with drink only when people connected alcohol disbursement to food or hunger.

Hunger brought people together, but it also divided them. The most belligerent form of food-related behavior was *victual* (pronounced "vittle") *warfare*. It often occurred when food diplomacy failed, though the two customs did sometimes take place at the same time. Victual warfare entailed stealing, withholding, or destroying grain or animals (or threatening to do so) with one of two outcomes in mind: to create hunger, instability, and chaos; or to prevent one's own hunger or the hunger of one's allies. Victual warfare has gone by various names: the feedfight, warfare against vegetables, scorched-earth campaigns, and total war.[27] But victual warfare is preferable to its precursors because the word victual can be used as a noun or a verb, so that the meaning includes the crops, animals, and salted meat that people destroyed, as well as attacks against forms of production and supply.

The last of these practices, *victual imperialism*, is an idea unique to this book. Victual imperialism could be collaborative or antagonistic, depending on the time and context. It was the use of hunger-prevention food policies—including the circumscription of hunting habits, institution of price-fixing food laws, and introduction of "civilization" programs—either to seize land or to disrupt and transform trade. Its land-related results thus refer to behaviors classed as formal imperialism, while its trade-related results fall under the remit of informal imperialism.[28] Victual imperialism was designed to preempt warfare and stop hunger; often, it had the effect of reducing food aid or negatively affecting another group's freedom to produce, market, or eat what and how they wished. Though this book does not suggest that historians should abandon settler colonialism as a concept of analysis, adding victual imperialism to this discussion reveals the more conscious choices that Indians made to cooperate with non-Native government officials as they chose from several less than ideal survival strategies.

These terms naturally raise questions about the value of imposing them on the historical narrative, when the people who practiced food diplomacy, victual warfare, and victual imperialism did not use them in the eighteenth century. I recognize the complications that such terms invite, while asserting that the historian's job is to make the past more comprehensible to present-day readers, using words that she has carefully considered. I am not suggesting that people in the eighteenth century used these terms, nor am I arguing that they would have recognized terms like food aid or food relief. I have applied these terms because they facilitate understanding of hunger's ever-changing contexts. In theorizing them, it is important to insist that they existed in practice if not in name before the late eighteenth century, that they changed before then, too, and that they are specific to period and place.

Some antecedent for each of these activities might be traced to different times and places in early modern British history, and in some cases even earlier; these examples are most relevant because this imperial power interacted the most with the groups discussed in this book. Food diplomacy changed before the revolutionary period and was not applicable to everyone in Britain or North America. English men and women of all classes gave edible gifts during the medieval period, though not all gifts served diplomatic purposes.[29] Food diplomacy with Native Americans before the Revolutionary War involved distributing food aid, sharing meals, hosting feasts at treaty gatherings, and providing rations to broker alliances with Native Americans. Powerful Indians expected non-Natives to learn and replicate these practices even when Indians did not need food. These conventions became crucial during the Revolutionary War because other types of diplomacy, such as trade diplomacy, became less effective. Revolutionary food diplomacy copied and then added to colonial customs. British and Patriot officials who needed the assistance of Creek, Cherokee, and Iroquois allies tried harder to accommodate Native tastes and etiquette. In rare cases, allies hungered together—sometimes deliberately, by destroying each other's food supplies—to strengthen military coalitions. Food diplomacy was not pertinent to enslaved people during the colonial period or the Revolutionary War. Between the 1780s and the 1790s, federal agents labored to reproduce these cooperative, revolutionary food customs during their work in U.S. Indian affairs, but confusion flourished because officials for the states sought an advantage over the federal government, and because federal and state officials had learned to associate Native hunger with outbreaks of violence. By the late 1790s, when the U.S. government's Indian food policy won out against the states' policies, its food diplomacy entailed reducing alcohol distributions and trying to cut food aid while limiting the use (and cost) of military campaigns against Indians.

In the early modern period it was Englishmen who were victual warriors, and the strategic aims of war determined the permissibility of destroying crops. Englishmen during sixteenth-century campaigns in Ireland targeted crops because they wanted the Irish to submit but not starve. By the mid-seventeenth century, crop eradication was designed to starve and annihilate Irish noncombatants, but by the end of the century civilian deaths again became unacceptable, even as attacks against crops continued. In the Americas, the English regularly waged scorched-earth campaigns against Native Americans (and, sometimes, other civilian populations). Indians also committed victual warfare: once they came to know how highly Europeans valued their domesticated animals, they aimed their violence at cows and pigs.[30] When Europeans convinced Indians to fight alongside them, Indians avoided the use of victual warfare against other Indians—even their enemies. Revolutionary victual warfare increased in scale in terms of the people who carried it out and the people who bore the brunt of it. American forces executed unprecedented, wide-reaching operations against the Iroquois and Cherokees, and Indians became likelier to attack other Indians' cattle and grain fields. Formerly enslaved peoples developed a striking relationship with victual warfare. During the war, Britons encouraged bondpeople to run away from rebel masters, fostering the rise of victual warriors who attacked former masters' systems of food production. After the Revolutionary War, the types of victual warfare did not change, but some of the practitioners did. Maroon communities of runaway slaves persisted in their raids on white plantations. Britons and Americans no longer attacked each other's crops and cattle. Soldiers continued to incinerate Native fields and gardens throughout the 1790s in some places, such as the Ohio Valley, but in the northern and southern regions non-Native civilians replaced military victual warriors and often engaged in unsanctioned violence against Indian foodstuffs because they wanted land that did not belong to them.

Of these three behaviors, victual imperialism represents the most significant change because it was only during the late eighteenth century that hunger-prevention initiatives and land seizures began occurring simultaneously. During the sixteenth through nineteenth centuries, governments in England and Scotland tried to restructure land use, which then altered crop-, dairy-, and meat-production methods and prompted price-fixing initiatives. Seventeenth-century Englishmen transplanted depictions of nonfarming barbarians to the New World so they could falsely claim that Native Americans misused their lands, which helped colonists to justify taking territory. Invaders enjoyed some success convincing Indians to raise domesticated animals—some cattle, but predominantly pigs—but they did not introduce these animals in concert with land seizures.[31] Native Americans did not take non-Native land, and when Indians took land from or ceded it on behalf of other Indians before the Revolutionary War—as in the case of the Iroquois-Delaware relationship—they did not interfere with food choices.[32]

During the war, British and American officials knew they had to try to avoid offending their Native allies. This knowledge had limited their victual imperialism. By contrast, in the new United States, Nova Scotia, and Sierra Leone, reformers tried to change land use *and* the agriculture and animal husbandry that yielded grains and meat. In the former American colonies, U.S. officials became the victual imperialists. Formerly enslaved people encountered victual imperialism in Nova Scotia, where white Loyalist refugees (American colonists who had sided with the British during the war) passed food laws that kept ex-bondpeople from making use of land. It was when self-liberated black men and women entered a wider Atlantic World in West Africa that they, too, realized how to become victual imperialists. They practiced victual imperialism by creating food laws that bore striking resemblance to the laws under which they had suffered in Nova Scotia. It was in Sierra Leone that victual imperialism transformed from land- to trade-related behavior. Free black colonists began passing food laws while trying to take African land, but over time the focus shifted to trying to change trade.

In the era of the American Revolution, food diplomacy, victual warfare, and victual imperialism explain how enslaved peoples and Native Americans waged and lost their fights against hunger, and thus how they won and lost power. Misunderstandings between Natives and non-Natives during the colonial period drove British efforts to adhere to Native negotiating rituals, including food diplomacy. No one enjoyed a clear advantage, and so the British did not try to distinguish between the many conflicting interpretations of Indian appetites, while Indians did not depend on non-Natives to prevent famine. During the Revolutionary War, American Patriots tried to gain an edge with protracted strikes of victual warfare against Britain's Indian allies, destroying their vegetables and prompting refugee crises. They miscalculated. Iroquois Indians won more authority by expanding food diplomacy to include the acts of fighting hunger, and creating and then coenduring it. Creeks and Cherokees, meanwhile, fostered confusion by destroying provisions and fed themselves by stealing domesticated animals. Blundering British and American officials who tried to control quantities of rations distributions instead found themselves apologizing for stinginess. Enslaved people, meanwhile, earned some power by allying with the British and fighting white hunger with stolen crops and animals, and to a limited extent by avoiding hunger through theft, migration, and labor. Mostly, they struggled, because they expected to endure dearth.

After the war, Native Americans continued to gain power during the 1780s and mid-1790s. As the nascent United States struggled to form a government and as a pan-Indian confederacy rose in the northwest, wrong-headed ideas about violent, famished Indians motivated American officials to generously distribute food at meetings and as aid because they feared the results of not doing so: victual warfare. Non-Native federal agents became better able to intervene in conversations about hunger deterrence because their diplomacy outdid that of state officials; they had studied Native appetites.

U.S. federal agents began to claim more knowledge about Native hunger during the mid-1790s, as Timothy Pickering did in his meeting with Cornplanter. This new authority, in concert with U.S. military victories and growing pressure from white settler colonists, motivated the federal government to bid for power by crafting a foreign policy that misrepresented Native agriculture and Native hunger. By the early 1810s, the federal government no longer cared about establishing whether or not Indians truly were hungry, and so it de-emphasized the customs of cooperation that addressed Native famine. Federal officials now conflated diplomacy with hunger prevention, which in turn allowed them to use food aid that fostered diseases, thus providing a cheap, destructive alternative to military campaigns. The U.S. Supreme Court may have declared Indians domestic and uncivilized in the 1820s and 1830s, but U.S. officials had started that precedent from the 1790s onward.[33] The government's food diplomacy had become victual imperialism.

Victual imperialism's relationship to power was slightly more ambiguous with respect to how formerly enslaved people encountered it. Black colonists in Nova Scotia suffered as white Loyalist refugees blocked their access to land while also curtailing their access to food. Hunger endurance rather than avoidance remained the norm. Former bondpeople finally gained power in Sierra Leone, after a series of negotiations with white officials granted them the right to enact their own food laws that forestalled hunger. These laws were temporarily successful, until they also targeted African peoples' trade in foodstuffs—particular that of the Susu and Temne. This victual imperialism was unsuccessful, because in the late 1790s Susu and Temne began to practice victual warfare against black colonists. White colonists grew unwilling to authorize black colonists' antihunger legislation, because they were reluctant to destabilize the Sierra Leone Colony's position of encouraging Africans' trade in legitimate commerce, and so they removed black colonists from power by deeming them rebellious in 1800. By portraying black colonists' food laws as illegal, white British officials elided history in much the same way as Timothy Pickering did in his conversation with Cornplanter. Memories of hunger-prevention initiatives were subject to all sorts of manipulation.

No Useless Mouth is structured around three overlapping periods of shifting power dynamics, because food diplomacy, victual warfare, and victual imperialism created systems of power relationships that everyone had a chance to work, with different degrees of power, in their interests. The book's first section describes the baseline notions of hunger that food diplomacy and victual warfare helped create during the colonial period. Then it explains how the bonds between Natives and non-Natives changed during the Revolutionary War as Iroquois Indians gained power using food diplomacy and Creeks and Cherokees practiced victual warfare with similar results. Power relationships fluctuate in the second section of the book. During the war, self-liberated slaves earned freedom and became victual warriors but felt almost as if they were re-enslaved after fleeing to Nova Scotia and encountering white victual imperialists. Cherokee, Creek, and Iroquois Indians continued to use food diplomacy and victual warfare to improve their bargaining positions with the United States during the 1780s and 1790s, but Delaware, Miami, and Shawnee Indians won and then lost control in a final campaign against a new U.S. army. In the final section of the book, Native Americans and black colonists struggle. Indians started to lose the battle against hunger when the new United States hijacked hunger prevention initiatives in the 1790s, 1800s, and 1810s. Black colonists won several victories in the fight against hunger in Sierra Leone, beginning in 1792, but they lost the war, which lasted less than a decade.

Historians cannot understand the American or British position in the American Revolution without reckoning with histories of enslaved peoples and Native Americans because those groups' power struggles were so entwined with British and American foreign affairs. From the 1770s to the 1810s, food diplomacy and victual warfare respectively granted Native and black revolutionaries the most leverage, but both groups suffered when white officials introduced victual imperialism. Native Americans held enormous influence over British and American officials before, during, and after the Revolutionary War, which in many respects was merely a blip in Indians' longer history of negotiating and fighting with non-Natives. Black colonists' efforts to win political and legal power were no less remarkable, not least because their situations changed so much in the space of a generation.

Any history of bondpeople and Native Americans must wrangle with the problem of sources: most documentation about enslaved people and Indians comes from Europeans. Accounts produced by Europeans observed Indians' actions but not their thoughts. This challenge offers readers at least three solutions: they can read those documents with skepticism and accept or reject assessments of Indians depending on the existence of corroborating evidence; they can claim that historians will never uncover the true story of what happened, but that these sources give us some sense of the time period under consideration; or they can use Indian sources to create an Indian-centered narrative. This book offers a fourth option: hunger-related actions become an additional base of information about people who left behind too few written records in comparison to their white contemporaries. By reading documents skeptically and cross-referencing assertions about Indian and black hunger with food-related actions, historians can try to discern the intentions of Native Americans and enslaved peoples through their responses to and preparations against hunger.[34]

In the pages that follow, readers will note the reliance on archival sources based mostly on twenty-one archives in eighteen towns and cities. I have focused on these sources despite the preponderance of edited document collections on the American Revolution. There is little reason to think that editors of these decades-old collections were concerned with food, enslaved people, or Indians, because only recently has it become commonplace to acknowledge that the War for Independence shaped, and was shaped by, the actions of these folks. Moreover it is only recently that it has become acceptable to write seriously about food and hunger. Military sources—letters of commanding officers, soldiers' diaries, papers relating to Indian affairs, and miscellaneous letterbooks—proved the most revealing in retelling the story of revolutionary hunger. The daily necessity of feeding thousands of mouths pushed the men in charge to write a lot about burning, butchering, farming, preserving, rationing, spoiling, and stealing. In this book I concentrate on the peoples for whom food seemed most important, and I confine its discussion primarily to land action, addressing the British Navy only when its movements affected those onshore—in large part because other authors have ably addressed this topic.[35]

No Useless Mouth considers a wide range of peoples: Indians, including the Six Nations Iroquois, Cherokee, Creek, and Western Confederacy (mostly Delaware, Miami, and Shawnee) peoples; free black colonists; enslaved Africans; rebel American Patriots; and Britons. At various points these groups separated into more factions, and it grows challenging to describe their identities. The Cherokees broke into blocs of neutral and Chickamauga Cherokees, and the Iroquois also divided. Hessians fought for the British, as did the Irish and Scottish who at times were considered British and at other times claimed more regional identities for themselves. Loyalties shifted, particularly for the self-liberated bondpeople who allied with Britons and Americans, and who fought more for freedom than they did for patriotism.

Historians have gone back and forth about proper terminology for indigenous peoples. In keeping with current accepted practices, this book uses *Indian, Native American, Native,* and *indigenous peoples,* but refers to specific tribes when the sources made it possible to identify them. *No Useless Mouth* uses *Iroquois* and *Six Nations* interchangeably because they were the most commonly utilized titles of the time, though these people would today refer to themselves as Haudenosaunee. In this book I employ the plural when talking about Indians: Creeks, rather than Creek, for example (and Creek, rather than Muskogee), because using the singular obscures the fact that tribes were often divided. Because Indians were so divided, I avoid using the word *Loyalist* to refer to them; many Indians offered military assistance not because they felt a sense of allegiance to non-Natives, but because doing so served their own interests. *British-allied* or *American-allied* are better phrases.[36]

The book's terminology follows similar conventions when discussing enslaved people. Although the term *enslaved* is preferable to the term *slave* because it grants enslaved peoples greater agency, switching between *enslaved Africans*, *bondpeople*, and *slaves* provides variability in the text. In this book I try to note when someone was free or not, and to provide a name when the documentary sources have revealed one. I do not use the word *Loyalist* to refer to self-liberated black people during the American Revolution, nor do I do so when discussing the time period when these former bondpeople lived in Nova Scotia. After the war, people became black Loyalists (which in this book is synonymous with *Nova Scotians*) as they emigrated out of Canada and forged new identities in Sierra Leone as British subjects.[37] This monograph does not use the term *African American* because the black Loyalists did not conceive of themselves as such; they tried to set themselves apart from Africans as well as from American colonists.

Before the American Revolution, people expected to encounter hunger; during the early modern period, crops failed, famine ensued, people died, and others survived. Black and Native American revolutionaries, by contrast, fought hunger, even if their successes were fleeting. The men and women whose actions are chronicled here were not hungry, useless mouths; they sometimes refused food, sometimes ignored hunger, sometimes created it, and sometimes defeated it. Their fights mattered because they were so different from those that preceded and followed them, and because U.S. and British officials misrepresented those battles. Those false histories created pernicious precedents. This book exposes them.

No Useless Mouth's baseline for understanding hunger starts with conflicting information. This story begins before the Revolutionary War, when a man named George Croghan was trying to teach British officials about Native appetites. Native Americans did not require support from non-Natives to survive, but colonists and British officials depended a great deal on Indians. Two centuries of food diplomacy and victual warfare had taught Englishmen precious little about Indian methods of dealing with hungriness, and so their perceptions were riddled with misunderstandings that require unraveling.

PART ONE

Power Rising

CHAPTER 1

Hunger, Accommodation, and Violence in Colonial America

After years of trading with Indians, traveling among them, and having sex with them, Irish fur trader and land speculator George Croghan could assert that hungry Native Americans resembled hungry Europeans. When asked, "Is the Appeal of the Indians for food, greater or less than the Europeans?" he answered, "I have Never observed thire appetites to be Greater than ours, unless after Liveing a Long Time very Scanty or without food . . . particklerly after a Debach of Drinking." He claimed that Indians ate no more than their European counterparts unless they had gone on a drinking binge—consuming alcohol that British officials had provided as a diplomatic gift, or that unscrupulous traders had supplied to con Indians out of skins or land. Croghan was responding to a set of queries presented by a man named Dr. William Robertson, of Edinburgh, who was writing a multivolume history of the Americas. Croghan had spent three decades interacting with Illinois and Ohio Valley Delawares, Miamis, Ottawas, Shawnees, and Wyandots as deputy superintendent of Indian Affairs, although he was retired from this position by the time he wrote to Robertson in 1773.[1]

Other English colonists described Indians whose appetites might have shocked Croghan, depicting them as pitiable, helpless, and hungry. Non-Natives lacked a consensus about Indian hunger because multiple discourses of Native hungriness existed: that of the hungry and useless civilian; that of the warrior using hunger as a metaphor before proving his military usefulness;

and that of the Native woman whose utility Europeans struggled to understand, because Native women shouldered the responsibility for producing crops and preventing hunger at a time when Europeans believed it inappropriate for women to farm. Between the 1500s and 1700s, two varying approaches toward dealing with food and hunger—accommodating and violent food-related acts—allowed inconsistent ideas about hunger to form, which in turn influenced how Natives and non-Natives exchanged food and destroyed it.[2]

Before the Revolution, Native Americans and Europeans enjoyed a relatively equal degree of power, but in the realm of hunger prevention, non-Native intervention failed to improve Europeans' bargaining position. Europeans and Indians gave and received edible items in ways that fit into their other diplomatic interactions. From the decades after the arrival of Columbus to the mideighteenth century, food functioned together with the alcohol, furs, trade goods, and wampum that Indians and Europeans imbued with practical and symbolic meanings. These cross-cultural dealings ensured the existence of a type of Native and non-Native diplomacy called forest diplomacy—and thus of peace. Food sharing, like other practices, could work within the framework of a commodity-exchange economy and a gift-exchange economy. The overlap between these two economies permitted creative misunderstandings and cooperation, while also fostering conflict.[3]

Cooperative food exchange was paralleled by battles over commodities, including the destruction of crops and attacks against domesticated animals. Europeans employed victual warfare against other Europeans during military conflicts of the seventeenth and eighteenth centuries; in North America, Indian warriors, soldiers, and colonial civilians practiced victual warfare. Whereas food diplomacy continued to change during the colonial period, the use of victual warfare remained relatively stable: it was a way for colonists and Indians to fight each other. The participants, however, did shift, because Europeans mostly stopped using victual warfare against each other while continuing to employ it against Indians. The absence of victual imperialism during this period underscores the relative evenness of power among colonists and Indians, and a significant power imbalance that favored enslavers over the enslaved. Mainland colonists did not practice victual warfare against enslaved Africans because they did not need to; they simply controlled access to food. Slaveholders ensured that bondpeople went hungry by restricting consumption and limiting their abilities to use land to grow garden produce.

Discourses of hunger buttressed contradictory ideas about usefulness. In the eighteenth century the Swiss-born military theorist Emer de Vattel described useless mouths when writing about sieges and civilian populations. If generals hoped to reduce "by famine a strong place of which it is very important to gain possession, the useless mouths are not permitted to come out," he explained.[4] His definition encompassed civilian women and children and was tied to intertwined ideas about war and famine. By the eve of the American Revolution, some of the men responsible for Indian affairs believed that Native children and women—and some Indian men—were hungry, useless mouths. Other British Indian agents, like George Croghan, assumed that Indian appetites were similar to those of Europeans, while also admitting the necessity of symbolically distributing large quantities of food at key moments to secure useful military assistance from Native allies. Without the knowledge to definitively assess and address Native hunger, and often lacking the know-how to conduct other diplomatic rituals, European negotiators depended on Indians to guide them, and Native power continued to grow.

To understand how this shifting baseline of hunger shaped and was shaped by food-related customs, it is necessary to examine the broader diplomatic efforts of the colonial period. Many English officials based their cooperative approaches on Iroquois protocols, and then copied them when meeting with other Indians. Iroquois practices stemmed from the ideas of Gayaneshagowa, on which the Iroquois League was founded, and Guswenta, which emerged after contact with Europeans. Deganawidah, the Iroquois prophet whose history is chronicled in several conflicting legends, created the Iroquois League on six principles expressed in three terms: peace, righteousness, and civil authority. Together, these comprised Gayaneshagowa, or the Great Law of Peace.[5]

During the seventeenth and eighteenth centuries, Gayaneshagowa allowed Indians to present a neutral face to the Dutch, French, and English while cultivating non-Native relationships, serving on military campaigns in ways that advanced Indian interests, limiting Iroquois deaths, and replacing dead kin with captives. Even when allied to competing European empires, Iroquois warriors agreed not to attack other Iroquois. Guswenta became an extension of Gayaneshagowa that applied to Europeans with whom the Iroquois wished to deal. Guswenta acknowledged that Natives and non-Natives could maintain friendship and peace by not interfering in each other's government, religion, or lives. It enabled the Iroquois to teach Europeans to use forest diplomacy to create recognizable but differently interpreted practices—mourning ceremonies, the smoking of peace pipes, the exchange of wampum, the use of metaphors, and the dispensation of alcohol, trade goods, and food goods.[6]

At least since 1645, those whom death left behind had performed a mourning ceremony that metaphorically covered graves, wiped tears from mourners' eyes, and (usually) prevented the proliferation of violent reprisals. When Europeans met Indians they took part in this condolence ceremony before moving on to the metaphorical brightening of the chain of friendship and a rehashing of past agreements. Only then did participants begin new business. Sometimes during such meetings, as in the region near the Mississippi River, people shared a calumet, or peace pipe. Southeastern Creeks and Cherokees occasionally attached the pipe to a white eagle-tail fan, or "white wing," which they held while delivering speeches. Speechmaking, and the figurative language and metaphors employed therein, featured prominently at these gatherings. Metaphors helped people communicate at the same time that they opened the door to misunderstandings when interpreted in different ways.[7] The Dutch, following Iroquois direction, called themselves "brothers" to the Iroquois in order to nurture kin relationships, while the French governor accepted the title of "Onontio" ("father"). Once the English defeated the Dutch in the Anglo Dutch Wars and took over New Netherland in the 1660s, they too assumed the role of brethren—albeit less convincingly—as they competed with the French for Iroquois trade. "We are all unanimously determined forever hereafter to hold fast the Covenant Chain, & live in peace & friendship with the English," said Cayugas at a 1770 meeting. The Iroquois famously described their relationship with the British as a silver chain (previously a chain of iron, with the Dutch) which became known as the Covenant Chain.[8]

Other Indian metaphors abounded. Creeks and Cherokees let Europeans know they had failed at diplomacy by portraying poor relations as crooked or red roads, and sent positive messages by describing amicable feelings as straight, white paths. Cherokees talked of their "nakedness" not because they lacked clothing, but because they sought trade goods to conspicuously consume. Speechmakers described taking up hatchets, passing them on to allies to encourage them to take sides—as the Delaware Captain White Eyes did at a 1776 meeting with the Iroquois—and burying them at the end of conflicts. Stockbridge Mahicans and Iroquois Onondagas talked about bad birds that spread rumors of discord. Edmond Atkin, who became superintendent of Indian Affairs in the southern district, described himself to Catawba Indians as "the King's Mouth" to indicate his ability to speak for colonists in the Carolinas, Georgia, and Virginia. Atkin positioned British officials as useful mouths who recited speeches to convey authority.[9]

Wampum made from seashells (which women and children gathered, men fashioned, and women strung) featured heavily during such oratories, from New England to the middle colonies to the southeast. The display of a new wampum belt or string accompanied each idea or section of a speech, and its appearance is often recorded in manuscript documents with the phrase "a string." Speakers used the amount of wampum to connote importance—large belts signified crucial messages—and the color to convey peaceful or violent sentiments; black wampum, for instance, suggested death or war. Returning a belt without proffering a new one rejected the speaker's proposal. In 1768 Sir William Johnson, superintendent of Indian Affairs in the northern region (and Edmond Atkin's counterpart), worried about the "verry dangerous tendency" of "Several Belts" circulating in Indian country.[10]

Of these many diplomatic practices, the exchange of trade goods was what Europeans struggled the hardest to learn. Trade goods may have served as mnemonic place markers that enabled better recall when memorizing long talks. An Indian's refusal of goods, like his rejection of wampum, also served a diplomatic purpose: Indians accepted medals as a gesture of allegiance, but returned them to suggest dissatisfaction or severed unions. In South Carolina, trade was so important that a trader marked the start of Cherokee country with the trade depot at Keowee, the first of the Cherokee Lower Towns. Between depots, traders and officials endeavored to protect goods from rain or snow—"a piece of Oil Cloth" sufficed—and drivers were supposed to carry extra "Horse Shoes, Nails, Hammer, and spare Ropes" in the event of accidents. There were many different types of goods, including guns, gunpowder, and assorted weaponry. A 1758 report from Pennsylvania listed Stroud mantles, stockings, knives, shirts, silver truck, wampum, gartering, and vermillion among the items given to Indian warriors as "presents" in return for their military service.[11]

As is clear from the fact that Indians received "presents" for military contributions, the trade diplomacy that was part of forest diplomacy could function in a gift-exchange economy or a commodity-exchange economy—which at times blurred together and created disagreements about Indians' usefulness. In a gift-exchange economy, participants are repeatedly allied, interdependent, and of similar rank. Gifts are passed down, and participants cannot reject a gift. Although something is expected in return, the exchange *symbolizes* "something for nothing." In a commodity-exchange economy, people are temporarily allied, independent, and of different rank. Goods are individually owned and kept. The giving of goods precedes the acquisition of material wealth: it is a "something-for-something" trade.[12]

Early European colonists viewed trade as commercial, and so disliked the Indian practice of using trade to seal alliances in a gift-exchange economy. British, Dutch, and French fur traders encouraged Indians' participation in a commodity-exchange economy by taking their furs in return for cash or goods. In this second system, trade goods became a type of payment.[13] When Indians came to William Johnson asking to be "pitied"—to be given goods to strengthen their alliance with the British without expecting reciprocity—Johnson distributed goods and then petitioned Natives for military aid; he insisted on a tradeoff. Sometimes officials withheld goods from southern Indians until after a military engagement, underscoring the use of goods as compensation. During the 1760s a group of Cherokees and Catawbas learned that they would receive "large Presents" only after a particular "Campaign as a Reward for your good Services, and a signal Mark" of King George III's friendship. Despite Europeans' efforts, Native Americans retained power in these relationships. Iroquois Indians used the market for furs to play Europeans off of each other, thus managing to procure premium trade goods. Sometimes, they even demanded bespoke items.[14]

Natives and non-Natives also acted as if trade diplomacy operated within gift-exchange economies. During the early colonial period Europeans found themselves obligated to reciprocate gifts that Natives offered because—as the seventeenth-century Indian leader Wahunsenacawh (also known as Powhatan) reminded colonist Captain John Smith—Indians maintained a strong hold on desirous commodities, from edible corn to valuable copper, and better control over potentially hostile indigenous populations. Trade-good exchanges allowed power to flow through goods, but more importantly through the kin networks and personal connections that gift exchange created. Upon receipt of some goods Native Americans forged relationships—redistributing gifts to other Indians as marks of esteem, prestige, and evidence of their own political authority. The Dutch grumbled but took part in a gift-exchange economy by giving trade goods as material necessities to maintain commerce; the French gave gifts with more enthusiasm because their regulated fur trade meant Indians received lower prices for their furs and needed additional incentives to sell to Frenchmen. In 1755, one man wrote to William Johnson and said that because "the frenchman had given a great gift to the Indians," he found himself "ashamed" and asked Johnson for "somewhat more presents." The English presented gifts to compete with the French. The overlap between these two economies resulted in balanced power dynamics.[15]

At the heart of these negotiations, misunderstood exchange economies, and diplomatic relationships was Sir William Johnson. Johnson, who was of Irish descent, moved to the colonies as a young man, and by 1756 had become superintendent of Indian Affairs for the northern colonies. Mohawk members of the Iroquois called him Warraghiyagey, or "he who does much business." He ate Indians' food, adopted Iroquois dress, lived with his Mohawk common-law wife, Molly Brant, and learned about Indian diplomacy. Johnson Hall (built in 1763), in New York's Mohawk Valley, sat between New York City and the Mohawks' territory. He entertained Indians there but also traveled often to conferences, where, working closely with Deputy Superintendent George Croghan, he habitually spent £1,000 on different types of gifts to establish and maintain alliances. His union with Brant and willingness to study and practice forest diplomacy allowed Johnson to strengthen kinship networks, thus forming and maintaining British alliances with Indians. His distributions of trade goods became crucial to British diplomatic efforts.[16]

Europeans, with Indian guidance, learned how to cooperate during the colonial era, but they remained ignorant in several respects. In 1758, one captain stationed in Pennsylvania described a cache of trade goods for the Indians as evidence of "the strongest Tye we can possibly have upon them."[17] The goods did not form the ties; the practices of distribution did. Non-Natives puzzled over the overlap between commodity- and gift-exchange economies, and they failed to grasp the full significance of trade-good etiquette. Indians proved their usefulness to Europeans who wished to ally with and employ them on military campaigns, but in a sense Europeans who were compelled to work within a gift-exchange economy did not have the clout to comment on Indians' utility. The officials who practiced diplomacy lacked the power to treat Indians as useless, because they needed them to fight their enemies.

Food and drink played a role in these practices, but it is challenging to analyze consumable items and their role in diplomacy for two reasons. First, because eighteenth-century Britons did not always recognize the significance of food exchange, sometimes even conflating trade goods and food goods. Second, because some of the foodstuffs that people exchanged were more valuable than others. In 1766 an observer assumed that Onondagas viewed "Rum, pipes and Tobacco as provisions" and had to "have them also." British records of Indian presents included butter, cattle, corn, flour, hams, Madeira, peas, pork, rice, rum, sheep, sugar, and tea—but they also included inedible blankets, gartering, knives, thread, and needles. Corn was central to Iroquois, Cherokee, and Creek diets and highly prized in religious rituals, but sometimes Indians wanted non-Native commodities they could not produce themselves—such as alcohol. Alcohol has an extensive, separate historiography; it destroyed Indian communities, but it also fit into Indian practices, such as dreaming. Other elevated foodstuffs included the dogs consumed in ceremonial feasts and the human flesh of Iroquois enemies. Game animals conferred prestige, but so too did the nuts and berries women gathered.[18] Food gifts also made for tricky prestige items because once consumed, they created the sort of "present" that no one wanted to reuse.

Attitudes toward meat—such as beef, pork, and mutton from domesticated animals—varied. By the mid-eighteenth century, some Creeks, Oneidas, and

Mohawks began raising cattle, hogs, and horses. To a smaller extent, Senecas also raised cattle, chickens, hogs, horses, and a few pigs. The fact that many Oneidas were Christian may have made them more amenable to cattle because Christian Indians lived in sedentary, agricultural settlements, where it was easier to store manure. It should, however, be acknowledged that much of non-Christian Native agriculture was also sedentary, and because farming in these communities required no plows, avoided soil disturbance, and preserved organic matter, it did not need manure for crops to thrive. Sometimes animals preceded colonists' imperial expansion (so Indians maimed them), sometimes they were status symbols for Indians interested in new forms of property ownership (so they accumulated them for redistribution), and only sometimes were they meat or manure sources.[19]

The starting point of European knowledge about what, how, and why Native Americans ate—and consequently, when they hungered—was informed by other diplomatic practices. People incorporated food diplomacy into forest diplomacy and the principles of Guswenta, and food diplomacy functioned within both a commodity- and gift-exchange economy. Sir William Johnson learned to distribute provisions at treaties, to visitors at Johnson Hall, at Indian feasts, to warriors going on expeditions, and as aid to villages when war caused disruption. Those familiar with Indian etiquette knew "that no public officer" could "avoid feeding them." As soon as a treaty was scheduled, people began writing to Johnson to inquire about "the Quantity of Provisions" he required. On the treaty's first day people made condolence speeches, performed greeting ceremonies, and smoked the calumet. Colonial negotiators distributed small glasses of wine or punch, and the Iroquois provided important Anglo-American newcomers with Indian names. Attendees then ate supper and went to bed, rather than beginning discussions. The next day the treaty began, and often lasted weeks; non-Native officials fed attendees for the duration. Afterwards, Indians got back on the road with "Provisions to carry them home."[20]

Building on other metaphors at treaties, Indians employed food language. When they called themselves "naked," they also said they were "starving." The "one dish and one spoon" (sometimes "eating out of one dish" or "eating out of the same dish") metaphor described alliances of fairly equal power from the Great Lakes to the Carolinas to New England. The common-dish trope changed upon contact with Europeans. Before 1701, the phrase signified war: enemies boiled each other in kettles. Afterward, the metaphor shifted to a peacetime one that symbolized the goal and foundation of cooperation. Eating out of one dish meant being bound together in a symbiotic relationship of usefulness that included kinship ties, wartime alliances, and willingness to share hunting territory. When the one dish was empty, everyone went hungry by mutual agreement.[21]

Metaphorical speechmaking helped to solidify treaty agreements, and treaties could end conflict or encourage Indians to join with British and French allies against their European enemies. In 1757 a captured French marine revealed that the French provided "as much feasting as the Indians please at going out, & on their Return," guns, clothing, and "as much provisions as they please, or can Eat." This generosity was significant; according to the Frenchman, their own provisions were "Scarce in general," bordering on the "very Scarce."[22] French readiness to provide for indispensable Native allies—even when the French themselves hungered—was part of the one-dish alliance. British officials, including Johnson, feared that these Indians' appetites would disrupt British military operations by pushing their allies toward the French.

Although there were similarities between food and trade diplomacy, there were also times when food diplomacy seemed different. Trade goods and furs tended to flow in one direction; Europeans gave goods to Indians, and Indians gave them to other Indians, but Natives rarely offered trade goods to Europeans. Furs likewise followed a one-way route from Indian towns to European markets. Natives and non-Natives both produced food, which again undermined accusations of Indians' uselessness. Permanent and intensive pre-Columbian indigenous cropping systems in North America created large crop yields. Natives received food, but their agricultural abilities also enabled them to grow and gather crops, such as the wild rice they distributed to Europeans—who were not good at growing it themselves. Indians could shoot game and supply themselves and non-Natives with venison, as Powhatans did in seventeenth-century Virginia, as Creeks did in mid-eighteenth-century Georgia, and as the Iroquois did when they came to stay in British forts.[23] Whereas they seldom offered trade goods, Native Americans could source food as payment and as a gift, thus decreasing the symbolic bargaining power of the comestibles that Europeans produced. Eminent Indians may have looked to the British for presents of food more than some of their brethren, but these presents indicated their status of strategic usefulness, not need.

As people exchanged, discussed, and learned about food goods, they defined the power relationships that underscored Native abilities to deal with hunger. Seventeenth-century Pilgrims, for example, shared their first harvest with Wampanoag Indians at the much-mythologized first Thanksgiving, but the Indian chief Massasoit's return gift of five freshly killed deer undermined Governor William Bradford's authority. Massasoit, by giving the venison to each of the colony's leading members, made it impossible for Bradford to distribute them himself, which reminded English colonists that they needed Indian allies to feed themselves. Indians remained self-sufficient during other times of real scarcity. After Jacques-René de Brisay, Marquis de Denonville's 1687 attack against the Iroquois, in which the French burned Seneca villages and claimed to have destroyed 1.2 million bushels of stored and standing corn, the Senecas dispersed. Warriors moved into the woods while civilian Mohawks went to live with Oneidas, and Senecas with Cayugas and Onondagas. During a significant famine in 1741 and 1742, Senecas skipped European meetings at Montreal and Pennsylvania, where food supplies would have been plentiful.[24] These dominant Indians did not need food goods from Europeans.

In the eighteenth century, Britons became better informed about giving food and food-related gifts but remained unable to gain the upper hand in power struggles, because Indians continued to feed themselves. "Women of the Six Nations . . . provide our Warriors with Provisions when they go abroad," even when warriors fought alongside Europeans, Johnson learned. Officials intermittently gave symbolic gifts of food to women, children, and significant chiefs. In 1774 one major reported feeding Native women and children near Detroit: "the Custom is to give them a Brick of Bread, and [a] Dram." Important Native leaders and their families received "a few Rations of Provisions." Nearby inhabitants thought it was "an exceeding good sign," to see the Indians "bring in Meat. & stay about the Fort in Winter," where they consumed some British offerings. Native Americans obtained meat for their stay, and women continued to produce crops for tribal consumption. Even Indian requests for British gift-giving were couched in the language of utility. A 1761 speech by a Six Nations Indian named Otchinneyawessahawe, delivered by the White Mingo, described Otchinneyawessahawe's loss of all his "powder & Lead," along "with a quantity of goods" when his "Cannoe split." He asked for "a little powder and Lead," without which he worried the Indians "must starve."[25] Otchinneyawessahawe asked not for more goods, but for ammunition to hunt game meat. His request suggests that Native petitioners sometimes had to remind non-Native officials of their ability to be useful to themselves.

Diplomatic food exchange nurtured the development of contrasting ideas about Native hunger and usefulness. Indians told Europeans they were hungry or starving even when they were not, because guests were supposed to exaggerate need so that hosts did not appear proud. Thus when Mohawks "complained much of the want of provisions," Johnson recorded providing them with powder, not foodstuffs, and when Oneidas and Tuscaroras came to see him "in a Starving Condition" because their crops had failed, he did not feed them immediately but gave them cash to purchase provisions. Yet British officials also had to ensure that provisions satisfied Native expectations.

Eighteenth-century officials concluded that at treaties, Indians could and did eat twice as much per day as colonists—and some men refused to make calculations because they said Indians "eat more than ten of our Men." Swiss-British official Colonel Henry Bouquet complained about the cost of provisions they distributed, at the same time calling Indians "Idle People."[26]

In 1765, after the British had defeated the French in the Seven Years' War, at great cost and with significant violence between Natives and non-Natives, Sir William Johnson described British abilities to address Native hunger. He complained, "all the Bull feasts ever given at Albany would not now draw down *Ten* Indians."[27] Johnson's statement could be read in three ways: he might have been suggesting that British offerings were too stingy; he may have thought that these Indians were not hungry; or he may have known how well these Indians could provision themselves. On the one hand, British officials, including Johnson, sometimes witnessed Indians' enormous appetites. On the other hand, sometimes even hungry Indians refused to do what the British wanted them to do—in this case, to come to William Johnson ready to fight for the British.

An examination of pre-Revolutionary food diplomacy, bound up in the policy of forest and trade diplomacy, thus reveals several conflicting baselines of Indian hunger: hungry, contributing Indians; self-sufficient, nonhungry ones; and Natives in need of food aid from other Indians after a European attack. These conflicting ideas stretched back at least to descriptions of Indians in the 1600s. Rather than offering a definitive assessment of pre-Revolutionary Indian hunger, it is more productive to conclude that before the 1770s there were two prevailing European perceptions of it. One strand of European thought found Indians not as hungry as they described themselves. The other strand of thought believed that Indian hunger was greater than European hunger, and that Indians possessed excessive appetites. At times people married the concept of nonhungry Indians with useful ones, and hungry Indians with useless mouths, but during other moments unpredictable ideas about usefulness emerged. These incompatible perceptions continued to exist in the mid-1770s, when men like George Croghan worked to convince their peers that the portrayal of self-sufficient, less ravenous Indians was the more accurate one. But how people used food to foster cooperation is only one half of the story of non-Natives' interactions with Indians.

Food-related behavior also resulted in conflict. Victual warfare was the counter to food diplomacy, and it originated in the so-called Old World, not the Americas. In Europe, armies burned villages and crops and withheld food—or prevented it from reaching other people—to cause hunger. Similar tactics characterized New World victual warfare when colonists arrived, but people also stole grain, introduced destructive domesticated animals, stole or maimed those animals, and in some cases even poisoned each other. In the New World, in contrast to the Old, not all practices related to victual warfare were designed to create hunger; sometimes they just helped aggressors to assert power.

Victual warfare was part of early modern European military tactics. During the mid-sixteenth-century English subjugation of the Irish in Munster, the English leveled charges of paganism and critiqued Irish customs, habits, and agricultural practices, which laid the groundwork to declare Ireland's people barbarians and their laws invalid. The Englishman Sir Humphrey Gilbert had his men kill noncombatants because their agricultural labor fed the Irish and kept them from famine. War in seventeenth-century Ireland was less consistent in its use of victual warfare; some campaigns included indiscriminate violence, and some were characterized by more commonly accepted laws of war. When Thomas Cromwell and his Parliamentarian troops arrived in Ireland in 1649, he adopted a twofold approach of denouncing the Irish while reassuring them that the army would behave; he discouraged pillaging by hanging disobedient soldiers, and he tried to make the army pay for the goods it took from local populations. At the siege of Drogheda, his soldiers killed civilian inhabitants. In 1651, Governor Colonel John Hewson encouraged the English to target the countryside, to destroy crops, and to kill livestock in the districts of Tipperary, Wicklow, and Wexford, because these actions kept the Irish enemy from obtaining supplies. They made famine conditions worse and encouraged the spread of disease, including the plague.[28]

In the New World, a hodgepodge of early modern writers influenced colonists' evolving understanding of war, but Hugo Grotius and Emer de Vattel stand out from the rest for the extent to which colonists read them. Dutchman Hugo Grotius's most famous work, *The Law of War and Peace*, was published in Latin in 1625 and translated into English in 1654. His evaluation of war as just or unjust was tied to *jus ad bello* (just cause, or why war is waged), and *jus in bellum* (just conduct, or how it is waged). Drawing on the laws of nature and nations, Grotius insisted that warfare abided by a set number of principles. A century later, Emer de Vattel's *The Law of Nations* appeared in French in 1758 and in English in 1760. Vattel challenged and elaborated on Grotius's understanding of property transfer and the treatment of noncombatants.[29]

The writings of Grotius and Vattel informed the ways that armies targeted foodstuffs, and such strategies shifted over time and space. In sixteenth-century England, people destroyed crops to control the countryside and undermine an enemy's ability to fight, but without intending to starve the local population. Grotius sanctioned destruction of noncombatants' property if such actions were necessary to sustain the troops.[30] By the 1640s, when the English garrisoned Dublin and cut off supplies to every town within a twelve-mile radius, a change had occurred: military strategy was designed not only to force submission and dependence but also to exterminate "savage" Irish noncombatants through starvation.[31] By the late seventeenth century, however, deliberate starvation of noncombatants fell out of practice in Western Europe.[32] Provisions, according to Vattel, belonged to the realm of peace (gunpowder and soldiers' clothing, by contrast, belonged to the realm of war). Even so, he declared it lawful for the army to take provisions from an unjust enemy, and to destroy what the army could not carry away, while at the same time calling for moderation "according to the exigency of the case."[33] Thus, at first, early Englishmen targeted crops to force submission but not starvation, then targeted crops to engender starvation and eradication of Irish noncombatants, and then continued to attack crops, but without intending to kill civilians.

Despite early modern efforts to regularize methods of waging war, strange contradictions emerged about fighting Native Americans. Part of the problem stemmed from the fact that although Hugo Grotius established separate rules for Christian warfare and non-Christian warfare, he nowhere explained which set of laws applied when a Christian nation fought a non-Christian one. Vattel condoned a "law of retaliation" against "a savage nation" that observed no rules and gave no quarter. He even suggested that because Native Americans hunted, they possessed no right to land, and, invoking John Locke, he concluded that another nation was morally obligated to take their land from them. Few people in the colonies cared that Indians actually did grow crops, offer quarter, and take captives, or that some Indians—Stockbridges, Moravian Delawares, Oneidas—were Christian. Europeans thought Indian torture was shocking and their treatment of dead bodies despicable. They asserted that Indians were a different type of enemy; by transposing concepts of savagery onto Native Americans, they justified attacks against them. Targeting Native noncombatants to starve them became an integral component of colonial strategies.[34]

Because many Europeans assumed that Indians were barbarous, military officials and colonists normalized victual warfare in North America. The French invaded Iroquoia on four separate occasions before 1700 to burn homes, crops, and food stores. Five English expeditions out of Jamestown, Virginia, in 1610 resulted in burned villages, pilfered crops, and dead Algonquians—including the children of a Paspahegh werowance, whom the English shot. During the Pequot War, Englishmen accomplished huge destructions of Native corn.[35]

These methods of violence eventually became linked with results so effective that both Natives and non-Natives began to use them. Colonists and Indians alike targeted crops and animals during King Philip's War in the 1670s. The Cherokee War of 1759–1761 pitted Carolinians against Cherokees. A 1761 attack destroyed fifteen towns and approximately fourteen hundred acres of corn. In Virginia, Governor Lord Dunmore led a 1774 expedition against the Shawnees of the upper Muskingum River, burning cabins and cornfields along the way.[36] Crop destruction and animal theft practiced for the explicit purpose of attacking noncombatant populations, engendering hunger, and asserting dominance had long characterized strategies of violence by the 1770s.

Domesticated animals also became potent food-related targets of violence. Animals, or "creatures of empire," came to symbolize colonists' incursions onto Indians' lands at the same time that they became desirable commodities to own, and sometimes eat. Indians from the Chesapeake to the Mohawk Valley thus ate cattle, pigs, sheep, and sometimes horses, but they also stole, maimed, or destroyed them. During periods of war it became common for Indians to target a farm, capture as many people and animals as possible, kill the rest, and set fire to crops and farm buildings before moving on to the next farm. During times of peace, British military officials complained that Shawnees in Pennsylvania stole horses. In the 1720s, Delawares in the mid-Atlantic criticized the Germans whose cattle destroyed Native cornfields. They may even have retaliated; during the Seven Years' War, Dutch and German farmers charged Indian warriors with killing their livestock. Indian farmers reported British soldiers who let army cattle wander through their fields. Alabama Creeks killed cattle.[37]

This range of activities suggests that official warfare and unpredictable outbreaks of violence sometimes blurred together, especially by the mid-eighteenth century, when North America witnessed a rise in Indian-hating. Colonists' warfare consisted of three different approaches: they practiced extirpative war making, created specialized units to fight Native Americans, and rewarded scalp taking to motivate private expeditions.[38] Colonial soldiers as well as Indian warriors could and did disobey orders. They sometimes went too far in their destruction of crops, maiming of animals, and execution of noncombatants. The impermanence of colonial military entities, along with colonists' land hunger, meant that former soldiers could transition easily into hunting Indians and taking their scalps for profit. Victual warfare allowed British and American soldiers to attack colonial farms and fields to appropriate grain and moveable meat supplies. It condoned the behavior of Indians employed by Americans and Britons for the same reasons. For decades, victual warfare also justified the actions of colonists who lived beyond the control of military authority, and the activities of Native warriors who sometimes ignored the political and peacemaking arms of Native governments.

Years of victual warfare prompted changes in Indian husbandry. Although women tended to take responsibility for growing crops, after the Seven Years' War even some Native men, such as the Oneidas, could be found working on their farms. Some women ceased planting corn, beans, and squash in small mounds, while men took up plowing. Mohawks, surrounded on all sides of their territory by colonists, started fencing cornfields to prevent damage from cattle. Violence between Indians and colonists interfered with Indians' hunting and planting. Native men would not go out to hunt when they feared attacks on their villages. Indian raids against colonists' towns resulted in similar effects: colonists grew wary when planting, and protective of the domesticated animals that belonged to them. Iroquois Indians in the 1760s broke into gardens and threatened to take everything that had been planted until they were paid for the land on which the garden had been built.[39] Conflicts over crops existed before the Revolution, but the increasing value that Indians placed on diminishing farmland made the situation more volatile.

In 1761, during the Cherokee War, future lieutenant-governor of Florida John Moultrie described burning houses and "destroying fine fields gardens [and] orchards" belonging to Cherokee Indians. He also, in the same breath, confessed to "making free" with a "Cherokee Squawh," raising questions about an unnamed Native woman's lack of consent during this invasion.[40] Crop and animal destruction became more than mere military actions; they became institutionalized forms of violence that created hunger, readjusted power dynamics, and granted future politicians the license to abuse authority. These behaviors were not yet victual imperialism, which was largely absent from colonial North America. Colonial governments and the individuals living in those colonies encroached on Native land, but during this period non-Natives failed to consistently interfere with Native food sovereignty.

And what of accommodation and violence with respect to enslaved peoples? People of African descent, like Native Americans, also produced and consumed food, but during the colonial period on the North American mainland, enslaved peoples' labor to produce foodstuffs did not grant them much power. In addition to growing cash crops such as tobacco, enslaved Africans plowed fields, grew rice, cooked their masters' dinners, and hawked food. The marketplace was a venue where whites sold black bodies, but it was also a place where black men and women sold produce. When possible, enslaved people grew such produce on their private *pelicula*, then sold it at market to whites and free blacks. Bondpeople planted vegetable gardens, raised chickens for meat and eggs, and supplemented their diets with hunting and fishing. Although differences in foodways existed between the Lowcountry and the Chesapeake—Lowcountry slaves ate less maize and meat from domesticated animals, grew more vegetables, foraged more frequently, and were likelier to incorporate African influences—enslaved labor in both of these regions produced some of the food that made it to masters' tables. Lowcountry slaves' fishing activities cornered the market. In many instances southern slave hucksters' prices for dairy, meat, and perishable goods rose higher than those set by whites because slaves had more customers.[41]

Despite these contributions to the food system, food diplomacy was not applicable to enslaved and free black colonists, who lacked sufficient leverage in their interactions with slaveholders. Although bondpeople claimed power by stealing food and refusing to eat, the entrenched nature of slavery made it all too easy for enslavers to enact greater violence by controlling black mouths, which they did by force-feeding people and withholding food.[42] Slaveholders did curtail enslaved peoples' access to food, but there was little land, save for enslaved garden plots, to take away from them—which made victual imperialism similarly irrelevant. The fact that mainland slaveholders did not need to practice victual warfare, the fact that enslaved peoples in North America were not yet victual warriors themselves, and the fact that victual imperialism was not yet effective—none of these conditions should undermine the utility of these analytical terms. To the contrary, the emergence of these practices among black migrants in the late eighteenth century becomes all the more striking as commentary on the ways that hunger creation and prevention changed during the Revolutionary War. Before the late eighteenth century, enslaved people suffered from hunger—but they also embraced and ignored it.[43]

Before the War for Independence, food diplomacy does not stand out for its notable successes, but confusion over the best way to practice it within the constraints of forest diplomacy—which resulted from differences between commodity- and gift-exchange economies—exposed several strands of European perceptions of Indian hunger. Europeans described starving Indians, they wrote about hungry Native allies, and they talked of those with insignificant appetites. According to Englishmen, starving Indians required provisions when victual warfare and crop failures interfered with Indians' food supply—but those Englishmen also called Indians starving when they hosted them at treaties, because that is how Indians described their own needs. The non-Native observers who said Indians had normal or insignificant appetites depicted Indians who, during times of famine, avoided dependency on Europeans and ignored their own hunger, who were unexcited by promises of feasts, and who seemed likelier to refuse food. At least in the 1750s, 1760s, and 1770s, these last ideas about hunger seemed to prevail among those who worked most closely with Native Americans.

George Croghan's own observations about Indians emphasized that Indians remained self-sufficient—they were useful to themselves while appearing useful *and* useless to Europeans. Even before Croghan's 1773 claim about Native Americans' reasonable appetites, he witnessed Indians repeatedly prove that they did not feel compelled to accept British provisions for survival. In times of very extreme weather, many Indians chose to stay in their villages rather than make the journey to British forts for presents. "The Expence of Indians this Winter has been but trifling," Croghan wrote to Henry Bouquet in 1762. "It will be so every Winter as they will be a hunting." Bouquet probably welcomed the news that he could avoid giving more provisions to Indians. In 1765 Croghan likewise informed William Johnson that he had not found himself saddled with the task of feeding Indians at Fort Pitt because the harsh weather had curtailed Indians' mobility. As a result of "So Sevair a Winter and Spring att this plese Since I have been aquainted with this Country," he said, "butt fewe Indians" had arrived. During the summer they became more demanding, he conceded, but only because they had little else to do "but travel about." When Indians did not "go to Warr" they went "Visiting their friends," and while on their move they arrived at English forts with "Expectations."[44]

The knowledgeable Croghan suggested that food exchange did not form the crux of British policy in North America. Yet it is telling that he failed to convince his Edinburgh correspondent, Dr. Robertson, of his claims about Native appetites. Robertson accepted Croghan's assessment only partially in his history, writing, "The strength and vigour of savages are at some seasons impaired by what they suffer from a scarcity of food; at others they are afflicted with disorders arising from indigestion and a superfluity of gross aliment."[45] At times the doctor thought Indians' health deteriorated due to a lack of food, and at other times he critiqued them for overeating. Robertson, like other observers, remained ambivalent in his assessment of Native hunger. These conflicting British, Indian, and American notions of hunger, and thus of food diplomacy and victual warfare, would transform in the coming decades as the war got underway.

CHAPTER 2

Iroquois Food Diplomacy in the Revolutionary North

"The number of Indians victualled at Niagara is prodigious, and if not by some means reduced, must terminate very disagreably." So wrote General Frederick Haldimand, governor of the British Province of Quebec, in September 1780. "No useless Mouth, which can possibly be sent away" could be allowed to "remain for the Winter," he concluded, before asking for "a Minute Return of every Person upon the Ground, exclusive of the Troops, for whom Provision is drawn."[1] A year before Haldimand wrote this letter, during the summer of 1779 (and in the middle of the Revolutionary War), the rebel American army mounted a devastating victual-warfare campaign, known today as the Sullivan Campaign, against Britain's Iroquois allies. By autumn of that year, Iroquois refugees had moved from burned villages into British forts, where they expected their military partners to feed them. Haldimand's alarm deviated from George Croghan's assessment of Native appetites less than a decade previously. Haldimand, like some of his predecessors writing during the 1750s and 1760s, imagined noncontributing, ravenous Indian civilians whose useless hunger took food out of the mouths of indispensable British soldiers.

What is striking about Haldimand's complaints is how ineffective they ultimately were. Rather than losing power, Iroquois Indians gained it in the wake of the Sullivan expedition, and they did so partly by promoting their own interpretation of Native hunger. Shifting British perceptions of Indian hungriness changed food diplomacy and reworked the related military idea of the useless mouth. Iroquois guidance on British hunger-prevention efforts consequently increased British food aid to Indians. Here, too, however, were rumblings of a nascent American hunger policy, born out of the ashes of the 1779 campaign. Under future president George Washington, that policy aimed to cause Native hunger for the explicit purpose of legitimizing food-aid distributions to conquered enemies.

Diplomacy itself—with all its fluid, improvisational qualities—had started to collapse in the two decades before the start of the war. Signs appeared in fur scarcities, land battles, divisions among officials in North America and between them and their superiors in England, and conflicts over trade goods after the Seven Years' War. Goods became scarce in the 1760s and early 1770s, but after shots rang out at Lexington and Concord in 1775, Britons and Americans had to move fast to secure allegiances with Indians.[2] Because trade diplomacy was becoming less effective, they needed additional means to secure strategic connections. Food diplomacy provided the answer, but it, too, required adjusting in light of new wartime power relationships.

Early in the war, food diplomacy did not change much; Americans and Britons replicated the practices that Natives and non-Natives had created together during the colonial period. British officials relied on symbolic gifts of food at strategic moments to maintain the loyalties of important Iroquois Indians (also known as Six Nations). The Americans deployed food metaphors while asking for Iroquois neutrality before haphazardly distributing different types and quantities of provisions. Neither Britons nor Americans regularly gave the Six Nations large amounts of food. After 1779 these strategies proved untenable, and Frederick Haldimand became unable to avoid feeding those whom he called "useless mouths." American campaigns had forced the Iroquois from their homes, resulting in a situation that allowed Indians to create a new form of food diplomacy that drew on revised notions of hunger.

The 1779 campaign was more effective than previous instances of victual warfare in North America in its ability to create significant, enduring famine. Two major related changes occurred after the expedition. First, British descriptions of Iroquois hunger by the 1780s allowed most officials to envision Indians as useful mouths who could overlook hunger while also requiring more provisions. British Indian agents ignored Haldimand's contention that the Six Nations needed to be removed from British strongholds and instead bowed to Indians' insistence that war was a time to stay together to share experiences of dearth in forts and on campaigns.

This altered perception of Iroquois hunger created a second change: a reworking of Iroquoian food diplomacy into something more violent than its previous iterations. Indians started to deprive their allies—rather than their enemies—of food when it suited them. People had destroyed enemy food-stuffs since the colonial period but did not often target their military allies. Iroquoian food diplomacy in the American Revolution was thus constituted, in part, by mutual fasting—a policy the Indians sometimes had to enforce through the use of aggression. This diplomacy took Indian requests for certain types of provisions into account, obliging non-Natives to go out of their way to accommodate Native tastes. By the time the northern military campaign came to a close, these behaviors were apparent among other Indian nations, who also used them in their interactions with the British.

The American Revolution ravaged Indian communities, including Iroquois ones, but, during the war, changing British perceptions of hungry Indians allowed the Iroquois to challenge the state of power relations at a time when contemporaries assumed they were powerless in the face of crop destruction and land losses.[3] Iroquois abilities to ignore and endure hunger made it impossible for their British allies to think of them as useless mouths; those who did not hunger could not eat uselessly. It is impossible to say what prompted Indians to alter their approach to hunger endurance, but non-Native misunderstandings of Indian hunger were crucial to British and Indian food diplomacy. Indians used hunger to fight back.

Iroquois strength had fluctuated during the colonial period. In the 1650s the Iroquois had waged a series of wars that resulted in their alliance with the Dutch, the defeat of the Hurons—their major competitor in the fur trade—and a cycle of captive-taking and violence that rearranged the Native populations of North America. After these conflicts, which are known as the Mourning Wars, many Indian refugees went to live with the Iroquois, or in entirely new villages. Up until 1680 or 1690, the Iroquois claimed dominance over tribes such as the Delawares, Shawnees, and Susquehannocks. These tribes gained a respite from Iroquois interference in 1681, when the colony of New York split from Pennsylvania, and Pennsylvanians, under the influence of Quaker William Penn, offered them protection from the Six Nations. Two peace treaties in 1701, between the Iroquois and the English, and the Iroquois and the French, helped to consolidate the strength of the Six Nations. By 1736 William Penn had died, and Pennsylvania also recognized the Six Nations' right to cede the land of other tribes. Although there is some disagreement over whether these Iroquois actions constitute those of a formal empire, it is clear that victual imperialism was not a factor in these power struggles.[4] The Iroquois may have taken land from other Indians, but they did not try to change those Indians' food choices.

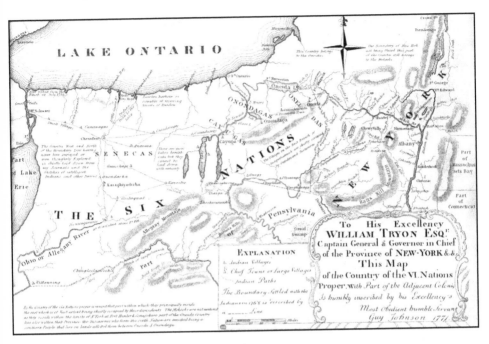

Guy Johnson, "Map of the Six Nations," 1771, *The Documentary History of the State of New-York*, ed. E. B. O'Callaghan (Albany, NY: Weed, Parsons & Co., 1851), vol. IV, 1090. The Mohawks and Tuscaroras are not pictured; the Tuscaroras lived between and below the Onondagas and Oneidas, and the Mohawks east of the Oneidas. Courtesy of the Institute of Historical Research, London.

By the 1760s, between sixty-four hundred and ten thousand Iroquois claimed the region south of Lake Ontario (it is difficult to estimate population numbers of Native towns because officials frequently omitted women and children in their surveys). The Mohawks occupied the villages of Canajoharie and Tiononderoge in the Mohawk Valley, and the Oneidas and Tuscaroras shared the Susquehanna Valley region and the area around Oneida Lake. Further west, the Cayugas and Onondagas dwelled by the Finger Lakes, while the Senecas, the most numerous members of the Iroquois, lived in the Genesee and Allegheny River valleys and around the Seneca and Canandaigua Lakes.[5]

The Seven Years' War (1754–1763) and the subsequent conflict known as Pontiac's War (1763–1766) prompted changes in Indian affairs because of declining French influence, Indians' inabilities to play imperial powers off of each other, and new British trade policies. Thereafter, clashing empires, imperial agents fighting with ill-informed English politicians, declining trade, and land hunger undermined many diplomatic rituals. The Seven Years' War in North America stretched from Nova Scotia to the interior of the Ohio Valley, with other conflicts reverberating around the globe. By the war's end the British claimed land around the Great Lakes, the Ohio Valley, and present-day Canada. Throughout the conflict French and British officials fought over Native alliances. The British increased their diplomatic efforts because the Iroquois controlled the waterways over which the British needed to move their cannons. French officials' inabilities to cooperate with each other, combined with austerity measures passed down from Versailles, ensured a British upper hand. By 1757 most Natives refused to assist the French in future campaigns at the same time that the French became more cautious about employing them. By 1758 most Indians agreed to a truce at Easton, Pennsylvania. Crucially, by the time the English defeated the French, the Iroquois expected not only symbolic gifts of trade goods, but also larger amounts of goods as evidence of English officials' sincerity.[6]

Although the British maintained Indian alliances, their ability to use trade goods to do so decreased in the 1750s and 1760s. At the same moment, the fur trade began to suffer too. It is uncertain which game animals died out fastest; some beaver, deer, and otter populations dropped as early as 1670. It is hard to count seventeenth-century beaver numbers because of Indians' tendencies to use metaphors to exaggerate their poverty. Skins of smaller animals—"raccoons," "otter[s]," "Musquashes" (muskrats), and "Cats"—do appear for sale in William Johnson's correspondence, but Johnson also continued to record sales of beaver pelts and deerskins. Seneca hunting transitioned from beaver to white-tailed deer before 1750. In 1762 Mohawks further east reported that deer were scarce.[7]

What *is* clear, even if precise numbers for animals remain elusive, is that the *trade* changed. In the 1750s, a growing French presence in the Ohio Valley threatened to keep English traders from the fur market. Furs, which in the first half of the century had constituted more than 25 percent of all New York's exports to England, plummeted to 2 percent of exports by 1775. Transforming deer-hunting practices disrupted gender divisions in Native communities; in Creek and Iroquois country, power shifted from the sachems in charge of hunting and the women who prepared skins to younger male warriors. The Iroquois continued to overhunt game, but the scarce nature of pelts challenged Natives' abilities to control the value of the furs they exchanged and, consequently, the prices of the trade goods they bought.[8]

Trade goods remained similarly elusive, and trade diplomacy became unworkable for non-Natives. In some regions, like the *Pays d'en Haut*, trade goods had been scarce as early as 1745. Britons' destruction of French shipping inhibited French abilities to transport and distribute goods. French influence further inland in turn prevented British goods from reaching Indians. In 1758 Colonel Henry Bouquet told a group of Delawares that because "we are at

War with the French," the British "can't send Traders amongst you as we formerly did, to be robbed and plunder'd by the Enemy." He promised future trade goods but provided none at the time. By 1761 Sir William Johnson relayed Indians' complaints about "the dearness of goods, & extortion of the Traders."[9] He knew something had to be done.

In response to Indians' complaints, Johnson, with Commander-in-Chief Jeffery Amherst's approval, issued regulations to reform trade to Native Americans' benefit. He limited commerce to British posts, appointed commissaries, and fixed prices for skins at various strongholds from Pennsylvania to present-day Ohio in an attempt to standardize exchanges of furs for trade goods.[10] Word of his changes spread from official to official at Detroit, Niagara, and Oswego, and the atmosphere seemed to improve. In the main, however, British efforts to maintain forest diplomacy did not go well because Jeffery Amherst took Johnson's trade regulations too far—thus provoking Pontiac's War. In August 1761, Amherst, in addition to encouraging Johnson's directives, wrote to Johnson and instructed him "to avoid all presents in future," demanding that officials abolish the practice of gift giving to cut costs. Amherst, like others before him, did not recognize the overlap between the commodity- and gift-exchange economies of Indian diplomacy. William Pitt's military policies had increased Britain's debt. Although Johnson agreed with the idea of restricting gift giving, he worried about any abrupt changes to Indian Affairs. When he objected, Amherst overruled him.[11]

Amherst's actions accelerated the conflict that came to be known as Pontiac's War. Although the war bears his name, the Ottawa chief Pontiac espoused the teachings of Neolin, a Delaware Indian hundreds of miles away, who preached that Native Americans needed to distance themselves from European influences. During a time when Native Americans, affected by the First Great Awakening, sought new modes of spirituality, Neolin advocated for renewed attention to Indian rituals, a rejection of British trade, and the gradual abandonment of European-made goods. He also promoted venison consumption over pork and beef, and abstinence from alcohol. This boycott was significant because it demonstrated Indians' attention to what non-Native commodities they consumed and how they did so.[12]

Neolin's followers severed alliances. A group of Cherokees fought against their former British allies from the late 1750s until 1761. In April 1763 Pontiac convinced Potawatomis, Ojibwas, and Ottawas to strike British forts throughout the Ohio and Illinois country. Although most of the Iroquois avoided the conflict, the Senecas participated. Other non-Iroquois Indians—Delawares, Hurons, Kickapoos, Mascoutens, Miamis, Mingoes, Ojibwas, Ottawas, Piankashaws, Potawatomis, Shawnees, Weas, and Wyandots—readily "took up the hatchet," as they might have described it. Indians seized every British post west of the Appalachians with the exception of Detroit, Niagara, and Fort Pitt. The war stretched until 1764, when most of the Indians made peace.[13]

In the aftermath, forest diplomacy momentarily recovered. British Indian Affairs officials, led by William Johnson, articulated the need for a four-pronged policy that enforced land boundaries, regulated trade, resolved disputes, and assigned Indian agents who could make decisions without needing approval from London. At the Treaty of Augusta in 1763, Scottish agent John Stuart managed to distribute gifts, discuss trading arrangements, and confirm peace with Catawba, Cherokee, Creek, Chickasaw, and Choctaw Indians. Further north, William Johnson set about redistributing gifts with a generous touch. By 1764 the London Board of Trade had accepted many of Johnson's initial recommendations, and imperial agents on the ground in North America enforced them at the key posts that had been rebuilt following Pontiac's War. And in the early years of the 1770s, Amherst's hated policies drifted into disuse.[14]

This calm was not to last. Whereas in 1764 Whitehall seemed amenable to Johnson's recommendations for trade, by 1768 the ministry formally rejected them. Reverberating debt from the Seven Years' War siphoned money from Indian Affairs. Johnson retained his position as superintendent, and thus official management of Indian diplomacy, but the ministry allowed each individual colony to become responsible for regulating trade.[15]

Colonial governors proved more interested in acquiring Indian land than in protecting Indians from land-grabbers. The King's Proclamation of October 7, 1763, was designed to stymie white encroachment beyond the Appalachians, and the 1768 Treaty of Fort Stanwix, which Johnson helped to negotiate, was supposed to reassert this demarcation line. In theory the Fort Stanwix treaty created a "line of property" that protected Native American land interests in the northwest, separated Indians from colonists, and opened present-day West Virginia and Kentucky to white farmers. Further to the south, Natives and non-Natives set a similar dividing line between the Cherokees and North and South Carolinians by 1768. In reality, colonists continued to ignore established boundaries, and squatters from Virginia and Pennsylvania flooded into the Ohio area. Large portions of these lands, which the Iroquois sold despite Shawnee and Cherokee claims to them, became contested in Dunmore's War, a 1774 attempt by Virginians to seize territory by provoking the Shawnees to violence.[16]

It was during a council at Johnson Hall on July 11, 1774, in the midst of trying to convince Iroquois leaders to limit violence in Dunmore's War, when William Johnson collapsed. Two hours later, he died. Johnson's death threw the British Indian Department into an uproar. His son, John Johnson, was offered the position of superintendent of Indian Affairs, but he refused it. Although Guy Johnson, William Johnson's cousin and son-in-law, smoothed things over by agreeing to take over the job, no one would ever be able to reach the diplomatic heights that Sir William had previously attained.[17] It is impossible to say whether Johnson's death, problems stemming from unclear land boundaries, and divided policies between North America and London would eventually have proved surmountable had war between Britain and the mainland colonies not broken out—but it did. It represented little change at first to Native Americans, who had been fighting colonists and each other since the 1750s.

William Johnson may have had a sense of the impending conflict and its ramifications for Indian relations, but others were less prepared. Non-Native fighting began at the Battles of Lexington and Concord in 1775, and in July 1776 the Continental Congress voted for independence. Before 1775, rebel American officials may have considered violence against Indians, but few had trained themselves to think about Native American diplomacy. American negotiators who wished to ally with Indians would find that their own nonimportation policies, combined with the Continental Congress's lack of funds, made it difficult to obtain requisite gorgets, glass beads, medals, vermillion, and clothing for gifts.[18] Once military campaigns against the Americans began, British ships sank or, on occasion, fell into the hands of the colonists—which in turn curtailed British gift-giving abilities. Land problems did not disappear. When goods once again became less obtainable, diplomacy disintegrated almost beyond repair.

As officials struggled to practice diplomacy, food became a more useful commodity in alliance building. Many practices resembled colonial ones and granted Native Americans leverage. British military leaders knew to provide some rations to warriors, and officials sent foodstuffs into individual villages, as they had in previous years. But in contrast to earlier decades, military forts at all times of year housed huge quantities of nonwarriors, who stayed for longer periods and appeared to consume more provisions. Their presence prompted renewed discussions about the usefulness of Native allies. American rebels, lacking significant stores of food to distribute and insufficient experience to broker allegiances, practiced a less nuanced food diplomacy that used metaphors to connote ideas of cooperation.

Diplomacy constituted part of broader efforts to partner with Indians, who held their own meetings and made decisions too. As early as September 1774, the British considered asking Natives to aid them; they implemented that plan in 1777 under the direction of the new imperial secretary of state, Lord George Germain. Part of cementing this union involved giving the Iroquois massive gifts of cattle, flour, and rum. The Americans also made plans. In July 1775, Congress delegated liaisons with the Six Nations and their allies to the Northern Department, with the Cherokees, Creeks, Choctaws, and Chickasaws to the Southern Department, and with all other tribes to the Middle Department. Eventually most Oneida and half of the Tuscarora members of the Iroquois sided with the Americans, and most Cayugas, Mohawks, Onondagas, and Senecas supported the British. Iroquois warriors and clan mothers—including Mohawk Molly Brant, William Johnson's widow—took part in this decision-making process.[19]

Americans (and, to a lesser extent, Britons) struggled to administer diplomacy with limited funds and foodstuffs. Congress established the Continental Army in June 1775, but disagreements between the army, state troops, and militia meant that it became difficult for Americans to regulate food supply and distribution. There was more than one account of bread that contained "some villainous drug . . . that took all the skin off" men's mouths. Bad, frequently "impassable" roads blocked provisions convoys. Heavy snow, driving rain, destructive pests, and stifling summers interfered with storage. In 1778 the Hessian fly devoured Virginia and Maryland wheat before buzzing north to New York. Violent storms compounded the problem by destroying Virginian mills, which made it difficult to process surviving grain into flour.[20]

The British Army struggled for different reasons. During the Seven Years' War the military had procured grain and animals from the colonial countryside, but the army had trouble getting rebel enemies to produce provisions for them. The British believed they could not plant crops near Indians' towns without violating the 1768 Treaty of Stanwix, and thus British-Indian alliances. In this instance, the British probably misunderstood Iroquois ideas about hospitality, which allowed allies and tenants to grow food on Indian lands. This misunderstanding contributed to food-production problems, which worsened in 1781, when the army's northern food caches were "devoured by Caterpillars" and "Hay, Corn & Vegitables . . . suffered in common."[21]

On the supply end of things, whereas roads bothered the Americans, tacticians in Britain disagreed about how many provisions to ship from England, which commodities to send, and how frequently to send them. Initial shipments of flour were actually "American Flour," probably sent from the colonies before British-American relations soured. The flour was already quite old when British contractors shipped it back to North America for their soldiers. Sometimes it "got wet on the Wharfs" and was then "sold & bought again by the Commissaries and served out to the Troops." Even when the navy sent vessels through Cork, Ireland, bread continued to spoil. The opening of the southern campaign in 1780 invited the prospect of purchasing provisions from Jamaica, but West Indian colonists who had lost access to mainland grain and meat remained reluctant to export foodstuffs because they feared food shortages, hunger, and thus, potentially, slave revolts.[22]

Additional inconsistencies in British food diplomacy occurred because the British Indian Department functioned in tandem with, but officially separate from, the British military. Although General Burgoyne had curtailed his use of Indians on the battlefield after his defeat at Saratoga, the autumn of 1777 and spring of 1778 witnessed an increase in the Indian Department's use of British-allied Iroquois in raids and guerrilla warfare. Letters from Daniel Claus, who mediated with the Six Nations, and Major John Butler, who worked frequently with Mohawk Joseph Brant (Molly Brant's brother), revealed that these Indians consumed poorer provisions compared to British troops.[23] Butler worried that the Indians tasted "very little" fresh meat, except "the heads, Offals, & feet" of cattle flesh "too poor to be issued to the Garrison." Fresh meat marked for the Indian department instead went to the garrison at Niagara. Joseph Brant, who operated a group of Indians and Loyalists known as "Brant's Volunteers," suffered the disdain of British officers because his unit was unpaid and had to scavenge at Niagara for their rations. Initially such inequalities did not cause Indians problems, because Iroquois women continued to produce enough corn, squash, and beans to sustain their people. Iroquois Indians produced large crop yields in comparison to their Anglo-American contemporaries.[24]

By 1778, however, effective British policy also meant providing food aid to individual towns. That spring British officials reported that "almost all the Indian Villages" stood "in a distressed condition for want of Victuals." Younger warriors had "neglected" their spring hunting season, which meant that Iroquois Indians had been eating stored corn instead of venison. Even though the Indians were not starving, British aid increased: twenty-seven hundred Native women and children came to Detroit, where they ate "all the Beef . . . in six or seven days." After he fed them, one lieutenant colonel reflected that he had felt obligated to do so. If he had refused, "this Garrison must have been distressed or the Savages offended," and "cou'd have joined the Rebels," he explained.[25] Whereas before the war officials had sporadically distributed food relief to individual villages, now officials expected to supply Natives at British forts whenever they showed up, and excessive consumption became more common. Britons who misjudged Native appetites risked losing their military partners, so it was better to be generous.

As the British struggled to balance strategic sustenance with high provisions costs, the Americans also tried to maneuver with the Six Nations, employing Indian metaphors to describe their hopes for peace with Britain. Representatives of twelve of the colonies met Oneida, Tuscarora, and some Mohawk members of the Iroquois in 1775 (on the Indian side of things some Stockbridges also attended, and on the American side Georgia was missing). Officials Philip Schuyler, Oliver Wolcott, Turbutt Francis, and Volkert Douw led the delegation, though they required the assistance and translation of Samuel Kirkland and James Dean. Speaking through translators, the Americans said, "If our people labour in the fields, they will not know who shall enjoy the crop. If they hunt in the Woods, it will be uncertain who shall taste the meat or have the skins." Implying that Britons had made it hard for colonists to farm and hunt, they used the possible absence of flesh and grain to explain their rebellion. Colonists, they concluded, "cannot be sure whether they shall be permitted to eat drink and wear the fruits of their own labour and industry."[26] Officials expressed their hope that in the future their relationship with Britain would mend so that they would be able to "eat and drink in peace" with them. By gesturing to the Indian metaphor of a common dish, the rebels signaled their desires to end conflict with the British at the same time that they maintained their claim to British-controlled land.

Indians' responses at this meeting indicate that these metaphors proved unconvincing. Abraham, a sachem of the Lower Mohawk Castle, complained of decreased trade opportunities. "The shops are every where empty," he said, and Indians "cant get any Cloathe or necessaries which we want." The Americans reminded him that wartime was different. "You Brothers in Time of war do not hunt so much as in Time of peace," they responded. Colonial officials' description of the conflict in terms of game scarcity justified their reasons for rebellion, but cognizant of the weakness of their metaphor, they did not request assistance from the Six Nations. Instead, they asked the Indians "to remain at home and not join on either side." It proved difficult for them to obtain even this promise, because they did not possess sufficient financial backing or organization.[27]

By January 1776 rebel American colonists distributed actual foodstuffs to the Natives to remain competitive with British diplomacy. One American Indian commissioner recorded providing Mohawks with victuals enough for thirty people, "11 Cayugoes and 1 Onnondaga" with three meals each, and 120 unnamed Indians with 36 pounds of bacon, "2 Fat Swine," and "70 Loaves of Bread." Perhaps he supplied the Mohawks because he hoped to undermine British negotiations, or perhaps he did not know enough to identify the likeliest allies. Americans became more efficient in their distributions by March 1778, when "3 or 400 of the Warriors of the six Nations" joined the continental service, and Albany commissioners resolved "to furnish" them with "provisions from Time to Time." At first these were slapdash allocations—meals here, a pig there—because in early 1776 a state of war was not yet official. During the war, however, lists of contemporary provisions indicate that Indians received rum, beef, and bread in ration-like quantities after returning from Washington's camp.[28] This decision, like the Britons' decision to provision Iroquois women and children, was likely a symbolic gesture rather than a full supply of food on which Indians depended.

At the start of the war independent Iroquois retained power as they had done for centuries: by drawing on Gayaneshagowa and Guswenta. Iroquoian food diplomacy remained consistent with earlier eighteenth-century practices. The Six Nations used metaphors to communicate; they requested edible goods; and they supplied British and American troops with provisions, which at times allowed them to influence the actions of the soldiers who depended on them. The Iroquois, in contrast to Americans and Britons, used food to communicate with enemies as well as allies because Iroquois neutrality remained paramount. At a 1778 meeting between American-allied Oneidas and American commissioners, Oneidas reflected that although "It is probable that there are some . . . who are inimical to us and who would wish to give Information" to British Major John Butler, they would willingly "cause them to be supplied with provisions" and rum for "the Journey to Niagara." The Oneidas worried that other Iroquois might report details of their meeting, but they still planned to supply them with food and drink for the trip. Before the Revolution and at least since the late seventeenth century, the Iroquois had limited Iroquois-on-Iroquois violence, refusing to fight against their brethren when France and England warred.[29] After conflict began between Great Britain and the American colonies, Oneidas treated food and drink as necessary components of this nonaggression pact, which suggests the continuing importance of Gayaneshagowa.

Iroquois Indians also continued to accept food as payment for services rendered to non-Natives. By requesting consumables, Natives reminded military officials that they needed to purchase Indians' allegiance. In September 1778, a group of British-allied Onondagas desired "provision to carry on the Service." The Onondagas wanted food and ammunition sent to "Irondaquat Bay in Lake Ontario" because it was "nearest to the Seneca & 6 Nations Country." They stated their willingness to fight and then asked for the sustenance to do so. They even stipulated a location for British distribution. That August, Onondagas had told *American* commissioners of their intention "to remain in the strictest friendship with the United States," despite the influence of the "great many evil Birds among us."[30] That these events occurred within a month of each other underlines both the factious nature of relations within tribes and the Indians' inclinations to say what they needed to say to obtain supplies. British and Patriot officials had been right to worry that refusing provisions to Indians might result in a shift in allegiance—not because Natives required food but because diplomatic protocols mattered to them. It is also possible that non-Native officials were too ill-informed to identify factions within the Iroquois and thus confused divided groups with the act of switching sides.

Native Americans also supplied food to Americans and Britons, which non-Natives sometimes accepted as gifts and sometimes purchased from Indians to cultivate alliances. Although Iroquois women's control of provisions had decreased before the revolution (in part because of William Johnson's efforts to become the main distributor), women still acted as key producers. Iroquois oral histories today tell the story of Oneida Polly Cooper, who went with other Iroquois to feed the Continental Army at Valley Forge in 1777–1778. Cooper supposedly showed the Americans how to prepare corn for soup, and later received a bonnet, hat, and shawl from Martha Washington as thanks. The British also required supplies that winter, particularly at Niagara. One officer reported that he had felt "obliged to buy up all the cattle the Indians had to spare," doing "everything in [his] power to keep the Savages in good Temper."[31] His use of the word *obliged* likely indicates that he purchased cattle from Indians to broker good relations by overpaying *and* overfeeding them.

Occasionally, Britons encountered difficulties obtaining something to eat from British-allied Indians, even when out on joint expeditions. One man's 1778 journal lamented that while on the march with "about 300 Indians of different tribes, chiefly Senecas and Delawares . . . we many a time had very hungry times." Repeatedly, he went "into a wigwam and waited for the Hommany Kettle with the greatest impatience to get a trifle and was as often disappointed," he complained.[32] Sometimes Natives charged what the British considered to be exorbitant prices, and sometimes Indians did not feed them at all. Native women doubtless wondered why useless British mouths could not be fed by non-Native women. Where food was concerned, Indians could supply food and accept it, and the records provide evidence that some Britons depended on Indians rather than the other way around.

If food diplomacy granted the Iroquois the most power and the rebels the least power, then victual warfare also continued to test power relationships. Americans used victual warfare by attacking Indians' towns and villages—as they had during the colonial period—and sometimes by stealing Natives' animals. In 1777, Molly Brant was "insulted & robbed of every thing she had in the world by the Rebels & their Indians" for the role she played at the Battle of Oriskany in August of that year. She had warned the British of American movements, and her information ratcheted up the number of American and American-allied Iroquois deaths. Legal depositions from 1778 reveal the extensiveness of New Yorkers' punitive thefts of crops and animals from the Mohawk Upper Castle at Canajoharie during the fall of 1777. Peter Deygart, chairman of the Tryon County Committee of Safety, spent three days "Riding Indian Corn & Potatoes from the Canajohary Indian fields." Someone else saw "Old Christian young, pulling up and Distroying Potatoes, Turnips, Cabbage, and other Gardian Stuff." They dug barrels of flour up from the ground, and took those too. The New Yorkers also stole sheep and hogs.[33]

Non-Natives persisted in using victual warfare against Indians because they characterized them as a savage enemy. They also, however, convinced Indians to act as proxy victual warriors in their attacks against other non-Natives because it exonerated them from blame. Americans used their Iroquois allies to target British supply wagons. In April 1779, Joseph Brant relayed a warning that some "of the ill disposed Trib[es] of the Six Nations" planned "to cut off or interrupt" a British "convoy of Provisions and Store."[34] Brant used his knowledge of British supply networks to prevent the other Iroquois from carrying out the action as well as to demonstrate the Mohawks' value to the British.

To fill their own stomachs, the British encouraged Native allies to pilfer cattle, horses, and grain from American farms and supply wagons. During a July 1778 expedition near Wyoming, Pennsylvania, rangers and Indians "killed and drove off about 1000 head of horned Cattle, and sheep and swine in great numbers." By destroying and stealing the animals that pulled plows and yielded meat, John Butler speculated, "we can prevent the Enemy from getting in their grain," and "their Grand Army (who are already much distress'd) must disperse and their Country of course become an easy prey to the King."[35] The British hoped that causing hunger in the American countryside would limit supplies to the American army. This strategy echoed English attacks against the Irish in Dublin over a century earlier, but now Britons used Indians to attack civilian food caches in order to make the rebels starve and to feed British soldiers.

Not everyone was comfortable with this decision. In 1778 Daniel Claus implored Frederick Haldimand to make sure that only Indians participated "in the glory of such petite guerrers as burning and destroying," and he claimed it "would look much better in the eye of the public" if such actions came "rather from Savages than whites." Men fighting in the combined unit of Natives and non-Natives known as Butler's Rangers asked that the phrase "To Serve with the Indians" be struck from the terms of their commissions because they worried about the consequences of being linked with such tactics if the Americans captured them.[36] Both Britons and Americans seemed to have a sense that victual warfare was unacceptable when used by non-Natives against non-Natives, but they got around this dilemma by urging Indians to practice it.

Their encouragement led to Indians practicing victual warfare against other Iroquois. Oneida Indians also took part in the retaliatory attack against Molly Brant in 1777. Led by Oneida chief Hanyery, or Tehawenkaragwen, Oriska Oneidas joined the rebels in plundering the Mohawk castle at Canajoharie. The Oneidas' orders stated that if in the past they had "lost, one Cow, Ox, horse Hogg Sheep . . . that we should take two in liu thereof." Oneidas reacted against the actions of Mohawks by participating in animal theft, stealing twice as many animals as the Mohawks had taken from them. Escalations of this kind threatened to do more than send a symbolic message; they may actually have hurt Mohawk meat supplies. Whereas in some contemporary instances of inter-Indian food diplomacy the Oneidas expressed their willingness to feed enemy Indians, here they received instructions to steal as many animals from the Mohawks as they could. This event was unusual.[37] Even in this instance, the Oneidas waited until the Mohawks left Canajoharie; they attacked crops but not people.

By 1779, all parties knew that the destruction of crops and thefts of domesticated animals made for an effective method of causing chaos. Joseph Plumb Martin, the white private who had described problems with adulterated bread, even named the absence of grain and meat: he called it "the monster Hunger."[38] Yet hunger had thus far been a manageable foe for the Indians and Britons who fought it. British food diplomacy had involved giving Indians symbolic gifts of food that did not make up the majority of their diets, even if British officials felt obliged to offer such gifts frequently because they knew they had to continually reaffirm Six Nations' fidelity. Indians used food to talk to each other, whether that meant diplomatically promising food supplies to traveling enemies or stealing animals as signs of victual warfare when other Indians' actions violated the standards of acceptable behavior. They had proved capable of disrupting supply, demanding food when they felt justified in doing so, and stealing it when necessary. But 1779 was a year with all the right conditions for a food crisis.

In 1779 Americans' summer incursions into Iroquoia ushered in food shortages that coincided with a harsh winter and sparked an Indian refugee diaspora. Thereafter, ideas about hunger and the protocols of food diplomacy both changed. These civilian refugees arrived at British forts ready to consume larger quantities of provisions because Americans' victual warfare had increased to such an extent that it became effective at causing Native famine; Iroquois Indians began to die. In a paradoxical twist, this hunger made British-allied Iroquois more capable of enforcing a new version of food diplomacy, which came to mean the use of or forced abstention from grain, meat, and alcohol to forge or maintain connections between allies. Natives chose to alter how British troops and officers fought alongside them by curtailing Britons' access to food. Rather than voicing their need for and dependence on British food supplies, Indians refused provisions, destroyed stored grain, crops in fields, and cattle, and welcomed starvation, thus challenging British ideas about Native hunger and military service.

In July British strategists found that they could not drive "off Cattle from the Enemy's Frontiers," as they had during earlier years, because the rebels had protected those cattle with "a Chain of Forts," which made raiding for animals dangerous. The "considerable Quantity" roaming through "Indian Country" the previous fall, John Butler observed, had "been chiefly consumed by the Indians themselves." Bark from elm and basswood trees, birds, boiled bones, dogs, eels, mussels, muskrats, and even rotten meat were more conventional famine foods, but sources such as Butler's imply that at least some Iroquois ate beef during times of hunger. Now this option had disappeared. To add to these issues, the Indians had not planted "the usual Quantity" of "Corn, Pulse, and things of that Kind" because a combination of military service and colonial attacks had prevented Native men from being able to protect their towns as women planted corn.[39] Scattered settlement patterns had given the Iroquois many years to stockpile emergency caches, but an American attack could still prove problematic.

And attack they did. The 1779 campaign was a crusade of devastating victual warfare against British-allied Seneca and Cayuga Six Nations' towns and villages that signaled Americans' growing interest in causing hunger and strategizing about its consequences. George Washington instructed Major General John Sullivan that the campaign's "immediate objects are the total destruction & devastation of" noncombatant "Settlements." He anticipated that the men and women Sullivan assaulted would "in their distress" welcome "supplies of Provisions." Washington hoped to create hunger and then distribute food aid, but he also warned Sullivan against offering either provisions or peace before Sullivan's men had accomplished "the total ruin" of their villages. Later, when it seemed such aid would not convince the Iroquois to break with their British allies, he would charge Sullivan with the task of "throwing [the Indians] wholly on the British Enemy."[40]

In April, Colonel Goose Van Schaick moved west from Fort Schuyler to begin the intrusion into Iroquoia, striking the main Onondaga village, where he and his troops killed a dozen people and took another thirty-three noncombatants prisoner—some of whom the Onondagas accused soldiers of raping and then killing. During the summer three armies under direction from Congress and led by Sullivan, Brigadier General James Clinton, and Colonel Daniel Brodhead raced across New York. Sullivan destroyed at least seventeen Seneca settlements between Chemung and Genesee Castle, and Brodhead's men razed eleven settlements on the Allegheny River. This operation hearkened back to the sixteenth century in its design to force submission of the Indians, their dependence on the British, and their extermination, when possible.[41]

American rebels spent the summer burning the evidence of Iroquois women's labor—their letters committed their actions to history.[42] They torched "very fine and extensive" cornfields. Soldiers wrote letters and diary entries about making "large fires with parts of houses and other woods" and "piling the corn on the fire" to ensure total destruction. On August 13 at Chemung they lit "a glorious bonfire of upwards of 30 buildings at once" before cutting down "about 40 acres" of the fields. In another town "called Kanegsae or Yucksea," they burned corn for four hours on September 13. It must have been a sleepless night; they rose at six the next morning to spend eight hours burning twenty thousand bushels at the Genesee Flats. At Chemung and Oswego they "destroyed all their crops," and near Canadasago they "girdled the fruit trees" (so they would not produce fruit in future years) "and destroyed the corn."[43] Some soldiers found the task of mutilating fruit trees too extreme and asked Sullivan to excuse them, likely because Emer de Vattel singled this act out (along with tearing down vines) as one of savage barbarity. Sullivan forced them to do it anyway.[44] Finally, after burning "the Genesee Village and destroy[ing] the Corn," the Americans retreated. By September the expedition had consumed Iroquois villages. To add to the distress of these physical attacks, Natives also suffered the mental anguish of knowing they would be unable to return home: by October, white American reavers had moved into the abandoned dwellings in the Lower Mohawk Castle, finding serenity in the "great plenty of Grain; several Horses, cows and waggons" that the American army had left in place for the non-Native invaders.[45]

Sullivan claimed his men destroyed at least 160,000 bushels of corn, other vegetables, and animals. His men did not distinguish between the destruction of stored and standing corn, so it seems possible that the campaign scorched large portions of grain reserves. Each Iroquois person ate approximately 6 bushels of corn per year.[46] Even if one takes the lower pre-Revolution population estimate of sixty-four hundred people, the Iroquois required 38,400 bushels of corn per year—and Sullivan probably destroyed four times that quantity. The campaign resulted in abrupt losses of food and life and altered future diplomatic relations. In the immediate wake of the attacks, Indian communities fought and reexamined their various loyalties. Americans had asserted their dominance but also possibly frightened the colonial-allied Oneidas and Tuscaroras—who perhaps never imagined how completely the colonists would destroy the towns of their brethren. British-allied Indians, of course, possessed better reasons to reassess their position, given the severe consequences of supporting His Majesty's troops.

As a result of the campaign, the Americans achieved their goals of evicting the Six Nations from their villages, pushing them toward the British, fostering famine, and, consequently, killing Indians. Hundreds would die of starvation and related diseases that winter. On his return to Niagara, John Butler sent word that "all the Indians with their Families are moving in, as their Villages & Corn are Destroyed." More than five thousand Iroquois Indians arrived at Fort Niagara alone.[47] General Haldimand noted that this phenomenon was not confined to the Mohawk, Onondaga, and Cayuga Indians at Niagara; "old men, women and children . . . of the Shawanese & Delawar Nations" faced "the Same Predicament at Detroit," further to the southwest. These migrations affected other Native peoples; as refugees reached Detroit, Grand River, Niagara, Pensacola, Saint Augustine, Saint Louis, and Schenectady, others headed west beyond the Mississippi, requesting Spanish permission to resettle. Such population shifts had a domino effect as these migrants then encroached on the land of Apaches, Comanches, Osages, and Pawnees in the Native-Spanish borderlands of the southwest.[48]

Reports of British-allied Iroquois sentiments from this period are contradictory. John Butler was "happy to acquaint" Frederick Haldimand that the Indians appeared "Still unshaken in their Attachment to His Majestys Cause." "As Soon as they have placed their Women & Children in Security," he reported, they planned to "go and take Revenge of the Enemy." Butler's missive belied conditions on the ground, as evidenced by the fact that when Guy and John Johnson arrived at Niagara, the Iroquois chiefs at first refused to conduct the diplomatic welcoming ceremony that always attended the start of a meeting.[49] Some Iroquois had questioned the strength of their British allies and signaled that diplomatic customs required reform.

The Sullivan expedition likewise prompted the British to reexamine their relationship with their homeless Native supporters. Haldimand proposed provisioning Indians less frequently. He was probably motivated by animal scarcities, crop failures near Detroit and Niagara, and qualms about the economic and military costs of feeding Indians. The "quantity consumed by the Savages is enormous," he complained. He asked John Butler to remind the Indians "that all our distress . . . proceeds from the amazing quantity of provisions they consume" at the same time that he decided against supplying Butler's Rangers with more rations. By September he was asking that the Indians "make demands for Provisions as seldom, and as moderate as their wants will admit of."[50]

Haldimand objected to feeding Indians because his definition of usefulness turned on military assistance, and he thought that food diplomacy interfered with other military operations. He argued that the cost of supplying the Indians "far Exceeds all ordinary and Extraordinary Expences in this Province, including [the] army, navy, Enginieer & all Departments." To have the troops be "obliged to abandon the Purpose of their Enterprize for want of Provisions," he wrote, "would be followed by much more fatal Consequences than if they had never undertaken it."[51]

Whereas before the war Britons noted excessive consumption predominantly at treaty meetings, now some military leaders viewed any Indian as an enormous eater who threatened their whole enterprise. The presence of Indian warriors and noncombatants collected at Niagara and Detroit placed Haldimand reluctantly under "the Necessity of Feeding" them to keep the warriors from changing their allegiance. In the fall of 1780 Haldimand penned the lines that titled this book, in which he demanded "that no useless Mouth" would remain at Niagara for the winter.[52] Seeking to avoid a repeat of the previous year, Haldimand sought to decrease the number of Indians he would need to feed. He now conceived of useless mouths as not only too hungry and costly but also easy to resettle.

Haldimand failed in this quest to evict Iroquois allies and promote his definition of uselessness, because Indians' attitudes toward hunger and service also changed. Their actions implied that they were useful partners to the British; they portrayed hunger for strategic reasons and could teach their allies to better deal with it. The aftermath of the 1779 campaign was similar to *and* different from the colonial period. It was similar because the British officials who tried to curtail Indian hunger did not succeed. Natives reminded Britons of the one-dish metaphor, and they accepted food as a gift without reciprocating with military service. By September 1779 one official related that John Butler had encountered "difficulties" obtaining food and thus in "assembling the Indians."[53] Indians continued to eat in ways that deviated from British expectations of reciprocity—but British perceptions also changed.

The months after 1779 were therefore different from the colonial period for two reasons: First, because of the increase in British provisions to Indian warriors in addition to noncombatants' provisions during previous decades. Second, because the campaign had transformed Indian and British attitudes about Native hunger. Whereas in previous years Britons assumed that they would feed Iroquois women and children symbolic gifts while men hunted game and women grew crops and managed war provisions, during and after the winter of 1779–1780 the British expected to feed nearly all Indians. In February 1781, Indians around Niagara would arrive "upon us sooner than could be wished" because of their lack of success "on their hunting grounds" and "the severity of the last winter."[54] Natives now arrived at military forts in time for winter, and Britons planned to host them for its duration.

The first real signs of this uptick in Iroquois power came during the 1779 campaign, when one lieutenant colonel reported that someone at Niagara had "endeavoured to persuade the Indians . . . that they were paid too small a price for their Cattle," Indians chose to charge more for the few cattle they possessed, and British purchasers chose to pay those prices. Other reports indicated Indians' growing discontent with Haldimand's vision for British food diplomacy; British unwillingness to supply them looked too much like bad faith. British-allied Indians resented all the worry over food, warned that "they could no longer fight the King's Battles," and voiced annoyance that the British "talked of nothing but Provisions." Britons, concluded their Indian allies, "could have no excuse for not assisting them," because they possessed a quantity of extra food at Quebec.[55] At this point in the war the Six Nations charged the British more for the beef they supplied to them and manipulated the British for more provisions when they could. Once British unwillingness to feed Indians became actual inability, the situation gave the Iroquois the upper hand.

Six Nations Indians implied that allies should share the experience of hunger when food was not available for everyone. At the same time that they accepted more British foodstuffs, Natives also proclaimed themselves less hungry, more willing to undergo scarcity, and more insistent that the British should abstain alongside them. By making it impossible for the British to feed them, the Iroquois challenged power relations. It is difficult to say what prompted this change. Certainly the shift followed the 1779 expedition. Perhaps warriors accustomed to fasting before attacks sought to extend that behavior to British engagements.[56] Perhaps in 1779 the metaphor of sharing a common dish meant going hungry when the dish was empty. Perhaps the Iroquois knew that their allegiance was so valuable that they could dictate the terms of their military service. Or perhaps they simply sought to prepare themselves for starvation. Whatever their motivations, this new form of food diplomacy, which included mutual abstention from provisions, altered contemporary ideas about hospitality as well as British food policies.

In response to the campaign and the growing refugee crisis, officials first attempted to remove Indians from their forts to save money. At an October meeting Guy Johnson and John Butler tried to convince the Iroquois at Niagara to go to Carleton Island and other parts of present-day Canada because the lateness of the season meant trouble shipping "a sufficient Quantity of Provisions across the Lake." Daniel Claus proposed sending warriors' families to Montreal. After citing transportation costs, officials tried to tell the Six Nations that leaving Niagara was their best chance for receiving comestibles. In November Guy Johnson finally "prevailed on" some fifty Indians to depart for Carleton Island and several hundred others to go out hunting.[57]

For the most part, the British did not succeed in removing the Indians because the Iroquois privileged their proximity to each other. Indians declared that they would simply withstand hunger. Those remaining stated their lack of interest in provisioning problems. The Cayuga Twethorechte told British officials, "We of the Six Nations have been much cast down by the great Loss we have sustained in the Destruction of several of our Villages and Corn-Fields." He appreciated "what has been said on the Score of Provisions," but said that the Indians "cannot think of separating." If the Indians had "to suffer for Provisions we cannot help it." They felt "determined to persevere in the Cause," and would "endeavour in some Measure to help [them]selves by Hunting." Although Johnson worried that the Indians seemed "already to complain that your Allowance of Provisions is small," most of the Indians made plans to stay put.[58] Indians ignored British worries about costs and set an example of weathered soldiers willing to experience hardship. Crucially, the Iroquois stopped emphasizing their hunger and made it impossible for the British to feed them at the precise moment when starvation became a reality. Twethorechte's words indicated that Indians may have been motivated by concerns other than food.

At this point in time, Iroquois Indians' military service changed. Indians were the counterpart to white soldiers who rioted over absent rations, but they did so much more effectively because they were better at convincing observers that monstrous hunger did not scare them, and because they were not subject to penalties for disobedience and desertion.[59] By the end of 1779 Iroquois Indians were going beyond voicing doubts about British food diplomacy and trying to obtain more provisions from British officials; they were making their British allies hungry by damaging pilfered food supplies in the field and leaving joint expeditions too early. In August 1779 John Butler reported on an action with Mohawk Joseph Brant and a number of Delawares and Senecas. After failing to persuade the Indians to retreat, Butler lamented having "Scarcely time to dress a few Ears of Corn" before attacking. Once the action failed, "many of the Indians made no halt, but proceeded immediately to their respective villages."[60] In this instance, the Delawares and Senecas dictated where and how they would stand against the enemy; they ate only a tiny snack before they fought; and upon retreat they privileged their return to their villages over an orderly retreat with the British, no doubt to see whether the rebels had succeeded in destroying their villages' food stores, as they had in so many other Indian towns.

Indians' behavior forced their British allies to experience deprivation. In 1781 a combined party of Indians and rangers met at Oswego, and the Seneca Indian headmen "held a council . . . without advising" the British of their plans. They informed two British officers that they would go to Monbackers (in present-day Rochester, New York) and "to no other place," because they were "in a starving condition" and because it was "a verry rich country." One officer even remembered that he felt obliged to go with them, "altho contrary to my Instructions." Here the threat of hungry Native allies seemed to loom large, but given what happened next it is not clear whether the Senecas were really starving or whether their starvation was metaphorical.[61]

Once the action commenced, the Indians at first pursued only one aspect of victual warfare: ruining food supplies, rather than stealing or eating them. The party destroyed "thirty large storehouses," grain, and animals. In encountering a fort defended by the Americans, the attackers chose to burn the party of rebels, with the "large quantities of grain" inside of it, rather than giving quarter to the troops. The officer retelling the story tried to save face by reporting that *he* had suggested the destruction of grain houses because he did not have enough men to take the forts. In reality he had lost control of the situation: a few days later, after the Indians had stolen some cattle, the officers were horrified "to see the Indians kill and take the greatest part of the cattle that were captured by the Rangers," leaving the rank and file in "a starving situation."[62] The men in charge could do nothing to stop them. Even during moments when Indian hunger seemed paramount, Indians themselves avoided eating and then stopped their allies from doing the same. The British officer was less interested in the fact that the Senecas had stolen some cattle; what mattered to him was the fact that the Indians violently caused British starvation.

Over time this conduct manifested among Indians who were not Iroquois. In June 1780 a group of Shawnees and Great Lakes Indians arrived at the American-held Fort Liberty with Britons Henry Bird and Alexander McKee. Before they entered the fort, the Indians agreed to let the British take "the Cattle for Food for our People, and the Prisoners." While McKee and Bird were inside the fort finalizing plans for the following day, however, the Indians "rushed in," killed several of the civilians, and slaughtered "every one of the Cattle, leaving the whole to stink." The Natives' obliteration of all of the food stores ensured that the British could not appropriate any of them. They repeated these actions at the next fort, where "not one pound of Meat" survived. Bird recorded that they "had brought no Pork" and were "reduced to great distress." The prisoners stood "in danger of being starved."[63] Although food stores were scarce in the wake of the 1779 campaign, Indians in the archival record persist in destroying allies' access to meat and grain. The most persuasive explanation is that Native Americans throughout the northern theater of war had come to associate hunger with times of combat, and that these Indians did not view beef cattle as acceptable sources of meat.

Some British officers missed the connection. Frederick Haldimand was infuriated by the Indians' behavior. He had conceived of the Shawnee operation as a way "to cheque the Encroachments of the Enemy, so loudly complained of by the Indians." Instead, he concluded, that by "killing and destroying the Cattle," the Indians "not only prevented Captain Bird from pursuing his Success, but reduced him to the last Extremity for want of Provision." Haldimand did not consider the fact that his military purposes might have differed from the Indians' goals. By killing the Americans' cattle, Indians were, in fact, revenging themselves for this encroachment, much the same way as Native Americans in the earlier colonial period acted out their anger against similar "creatures of empire."[64] Haldimand also misunderstood why the Indians had worked to deprive his men of ready, mobile food supplies. These useful mouths went where they wanted, and they continued to teach Britons how to hunger—sometimes violently.

By the 1780s British food diplomacy had turned away from Haldimand's attempts to reduce supplies. In spite of Haldimand's complaints, commands, and entreaties to officers working in Indian Affairs, the British kept making plans to feed Indians. Haldimand was even shocked to find that Iroquois Indians who were "Intermarried, with those of Canada" had received provisions twice— once as Indians belonging to the Seven Nations of Canada, and again as Indians belonging to the Six Nations. Increasingly, Britons sought to discover and accommodate noncombatant Natives' food preferences. Officials expanded food distribution. Each month the superintendent of Indian Affairs assessed how much food villages required by sending men to obtain a headcount; Indians then received tickets from the commissary, which they could redeem for provisions.[65]

The British also tried hard to accommodate Native tastes. Haldimand's correspondence reveals a summary of Indian preferences: corn was best, "as the Indians would rather have it than flour." If there was no corn, Six Nations preferred baked bread to flour supplies. Commissaries tended to issue more pork than beef, suggesting another opinion about taste. Natives voiced their desire for salt provisions or fresh provisions when it suited them. Indians did not like "the Effect of living entirely upon Salt Meat," because they found themselves "getting sickly." As early as 1778 the Mohawks had convinced one official to give them half fresh and half salt provisions after receiving only salt provisions for half of the year. By 1780, however, Indians around Montreal were requesting five days of fresh provisions out of each week—more than twice what they had received in previous years. These Natives complained that a salty diet threatened their health, and, by inference, their manpower. In spite of the logistical problems involved in preserving and transporting fresh meat, Haldimand granted their request less than a week later. British expenditures on supplies to Niagara increased from £500 New York currency at the start of the war to £100,000 in 1781.[66]

Native Americans would also, to an extent, refuse to grow food themselves. In May 1781, the British distributed hoes and corn for the use of the Six Nations, the Delawares, and the Shawnees to encourage them to plant crops at their home at Buffalo Creek. In December of that year, however, these Indians again appeared at Fort Niagara, claiming, "The Trifling quantity of Indian Corn Issued" was their "reason for coming in to be Supply'd with provisions."[67] In effect, Indians suggested that the amount of seed the British gave them in the spring was too paltry to produce an abundant crop or to sustain them with the strength to carry out the task of planting rows of corn.

It is also possible that the British supplied them with the wrong kind of hoes. There were many different types of hoes—for tobacco, rice, and sugar production—and Native American hoes were different from West African hoes, which were, in turn, distinct from European-produced utensils; not all hoes were designed for corn production. British officials discovered as much in 1784, when someone observed that axes and hoes produced near Montreal were much smaller than those that came from Europe, and Indians would not use European tools until they had been reforged.[68]

These were some of Indians' reasons for not growing corn, which allowed them to claim British support over the winter. Two years later they offered additional justification: Guy Johnson wrote that "the rememberance of their late losses . . . were too recent for their entering with alacrity on planting." He was talking about the Sullivan expedition; he explained that even those Indian "Towns that escaped the Rebel invasion" now required British aid, because other refugees had turned to them for supplies.[69] In sum, Indians refused to plant corn when they could receive provisions from the British. They were not lazy, hungry, or dependent; they were traumatized communities who expected the rightful terms of their partnership.

Meanwhile, Americans continued to make clumsy use of victual warfare and food diplomacy. They used the 1779 campaign to remind their Six Nations allies of the consequences of hunger. "For their Breach of the Covenant Chain," commissioners told the Oneidas and Tuscaroras, British-allied members of the Six Nations found themselves "without Food or Shelter," "driven from their Country," and forced to "wander in the wilderness. This," they concluded, "is the constant Reward of Treachery!"[70] The Americans revised history to suggest that the Covenant Chain had been forged between the Iroquois and the Americans, rather than between the Iroquois and the English or the Iroquois and the Dutch, and implied that those who "became" traitors by switching sides would suffer scorched-earth campaigns. Knowing as they did that opposing factions of the Iroquois continued to communicate with each other, they probably hoped that the Oneidas and Tuscaroras would pass along the message. As long as the Americans were doing well in the war, they could afford to hold the threat of burned ground over the heads of supporters and enemies.

Americans' continued use of food metaphors that drew on the shared experience of scarcity may eventually have worked to their advantage. At a meeting between commissioners and American-allied Oneidas, Tuscaroras, and Caghnawagas in 1781, the non-Native officials described how the "long War has impoverished us." But what differentiated American from British food diplomacy was rebels' willingness to undergo deprivation with their Native allies. Of course, the former colonists possessed little choice in the matter of hunger, because the war was fought in their towns and throughout their farmlands. But this position ironically gave them a better chance of using food diplomacy, because Indian allies might have empathized. Although the Americans promised "that your way hereafter [would] be better supplied with provision and necessaries," they also guaranteed that when "hardships are inevitable," the Indians should "be of good comfort: We suffer with you."[71] The Americans evinced their willingness to eat when there was food, and to go hungry when there was none. Yet this meeting also demonstrated Indians' abilities to alter American food diplomacy. No longer could U.S. officials rely on metaphors to maintain Natives' allegiance; they also promised a future delivery of provisions.

Six months before the Seneca named Cornplanter listened to Timothy Pickering's misuse of history in 1791, he sent George Washington his own history of Iroquois relations with the United States. Unlike Pickering, Cornplanter was more interested in recent events. "When your army entered the country of the Six nations, we called you the town-destroyer; and to this day when that name is heard, our women look behind them and turn pale, and our children cling close to the neck of their mothers." Cornplanter knew his people's history of the 1779 campaign, how harrowing it had been for the civilian members of the Six Nations. He also knew Washington's Iroquois name: "Conotocarious," meaning "town destroyer" or "devourer of villages." Washington's choices had consumed Iroquois territory. Timothy Pickering knew all these things too, because the reason historians have a copy of Cornplanter's message is that it was enclosed in a letter to Pickering.[72]

Notions of history were expansive in the eighteenth century, when oral history, storytelling, and personal knowledge mattered just as much as if not more than what got written down. William Johnson's death was so disruptive immediately before the Revolutionary War because no one else possessed his depth of knowledge about Iroquois protocols. In the 1760s, when Johnson watched as power relationships fluctuated and diplomatic customs faltered, he probably knew what to do—but he died before teaching others how to copy him. Food diplomacy offered a workable alternative to colonial practices, but it required a revision of colonial precedents. The Iroquois stepped in to engineer those changes, and the power they gained from doing so helped them survive the Sullivan campaign.

After John Sullivan's 1779 burnt-corn expedition, the Iroquois fought against hunger, they fought to create it, and they fought for a role in making hunger-prevention policies. They altered their food diplomacy to dictate the terms of their military service, to make demands about food supply, and to make the British starve when it suited them. They succeeded in enacting these reforms because non-Native ideas about Indian hunger and usefulness had shifted. Two previously separate strands of European perceptions had fused together. Britons began to think of Indians as enormous eaters at the same time that they described Indians as capable of withstanding hunger. Indians did not, however, become dependent on British foodstuffs. Iroquois decisions to refuse food and endure hunger at key moments forced the British to recognize that Indians were still useful to them. As a result, officials went out of their way to accommodate Indian demands about eating specific foods. In 1783, when the Iroquois claimed that they could not plant because the memory of their losses—the newest chapter in the tribe's history—was still too upsetting, the British distributed food aid.

The American Revolution was not merely a war fought between Americans and Britons, but also one that embroiled some 150,000 Native Americans living east of the Mississippi, with ramifications for Indians further west.[73] Changing discourses of hunger underscore the degree to which the Iroquois retained their power in a disastrous situation. By 1781 people increasingly practiced food diplomacy according to Indian notions rather than British or

American ones—they paid attention to Native tastes, and they hungered together whether they wanted to or not. During the war itself everyone had the potential to grow, eat, and destroy food, and thus it became harder to tell who was dependent and who was independent.

Indians were useful mouths who portrayed their hunger in specific ways, ignored it, *and* tried to avoid starvation. Although Iroquoian food diplomacy allowed Indians to maintain power in their alliances with Britons and Americans, the physical act of eating was not important everywhere. And in some cases, even food diplomacy proved less important. In the southern colonies, hunger—and non-Natives' perceptions of it—continued to matter, but food diplomacy rapidly became ineffective. For this reason, Creek and Cherokee Indians defaulted to an almost constant state of victual warfare, and violent episodes predominated.

CHAPTER 3

Cherokee and Creek Victual Warfare in the Revolutionary South

In August 1775 rumors abounded among South Carolinian colonists that the British were working to secure Cherokee interests. Some Indians seemed unwilling to ally with Britons, but others, like the Overhill Cherokees, were "preparing to Fight for the King." "In short," wrote Minister William Tennent to Henry Laurens—the recently elected president of the South Carolina Council of Safety—the British and their Native supporters were "preparing a great Dish of Blood for you." Tennent had been trying to ascertain potential threats in the event of war between the colonies and England, and his letter encapsulated the state of southern Indian relations. It revealed that Indians remained divided over the question of what to do. The letter, probably without meaning to, evoked the one-dish metaphor that Natives and non-Natives used to suggest military alliance and respect for land boundaries. Tennent's message also transformed the metaphor. This was no shared meal; the bloody dish represented the connectedness among power struggles, confusion over who was in charge of Indian Affairs, violence, and hunger in the southern theater of war.[1]

In Georgia, North and South Carolina, Virginia, and West and East Florida, food diplomacy failed almost entirely, in spite of various attempts to practice it. It was not for a lack of trying that food diplomacy proved unfeasible. Officials and Indians championed continuity in diplomatic practices, and rebels and Britons kept up some distributions of food goods and gifts. By the 1780s some officials even invoked the metaphor of shared hunger and sent food to meetings because they knew they needed to host attendees. In a few instances, southern Indians even destroyed the foodstuffs of their allies so that everyone suffered together. At the same time, infighting among both the British and the rebels grew frequent, resulting in diplomatic blunders. Non-Native officials, after considering these multiple obstacles to good relations, tried to block each other's food diplomacy rather than practicing it themselves. When this tactic did not succeed, Britons and Americans turned to victual warfare—against each other, and against Indians whom they considered disloyal. Whereas Iroquoian food diplomacy won out in the north, a bloody dish of victual warfare prevailed in the southern colonies and then states.

Victual warfare—the burning of grain, the destruction, maiming, or theft of domesticated animals, and the deployment of threats to engage in these actions—broke out when food diplomacy faltered, and helped Native Americans claim power more effectively than non-Natives. Food diplomacy's shortcomings did not *cause* victual warfare, and sometimes interactions related to violence and peacemaking occurred alongside each other. Non-Natives who could not practice food diplomacy with their Indian allies recognized the strategic value of creating hunger among their Native American enemies. They hoped that by destroying Indians' corn—and thus inducing famine—they could force southern Natives into compliance. In a few instances, they also hoped to appear benevolent by distributing food aid to enemy Indians after such attacks. They miscalculated, because victual warfare had an unpredictable relationship with hunger. In the south, Britons and Patriots discovered that although they practiced victual warfare primarily to create hunger, Indians practiced victual warfare to create *and* fight hunger.

Three periods of bad food diplomacy, victual warfare, or a combination of the two methods of communication—during 1775–1778, 1779, and 1780–1782—illustrate how confused policy, hunger, and violence became intertwined. The first time span reveals inadequate food diplomacy and changes in victual warfare. Indians' behavior shifted from killing and maiming animals to stealing, butchering, and eating them. During the second period previous changes, in combination with the death of John Stuart—the southern agent for British Indian Affairs and a key official among the Creeks—disrupted Anglo-Indian alliances. This year was characterized by extreme confusion caused by shoddy British food diplomacy, and by increased American attempts to create Native hunger, which they did by intensifying their victual warfare and circumscribing food-aid distributions. From 1780 to 1782 power relations were hard to predict. As British military leaders deprioritized Indian diplomacy, American states grew more likely to use the threat of victual warfare to try to create hunger and control people. At the same time, the states' Indian policies became inconsistent. Unsuccessful food diplomacy had three results: it created confusion, it made white Americans reluctant to distribute food aid, and it forced people to associate victual warfare with famine creation, famine prevention, and violence.

The prewar land problems and changes in trade that had affected the Iroquois also destabilized southern Indian affairs. Edmond Atkin—William Johnson's counterpart as southern superintendent of Indian Affairs—made efforts to reform trade, just as Johnson had. In the late 1750s Atkin recommended implementing additional controls on traders, building permanent forts and outposts, destroying French forts, and creating a southern Indian confederacy that would mirror the diplomatic might of the Iroquois.[2] It was a tall order.

The fourteen thousand Creeks and the twelve to fourteen thousand Cherokees living in North America by the 1770s enjoyed less room to maneuver than the Iroquois. The Creek confederacy was young, having emerged during the early eighteenth century. The 1763 Peace of Paris that ended the Seven Years' War impeded the Creeks' practice of triple-nation diplomacy: their abilities to play British agents off of French and Spanish ones. Creek attacks against colonists in December 1773 and January 1774 prompted the British to embargo the trade of the Creeks who lived in present-day Alabama, Florida, and Georgia.[3] Relations with the Cherokees had been fraught since campaigns against them in 1760 and 1761. The causes of these conflicts seem clear. Virginian and South Carolinian colonists, who privileged their landgrabs over Indian sovereignty, embarked upon scorched-earth campaigns that perpetuated a cycle of retaliatory violence between them and Overhill and Lower Cherokees. By 1775 a Cherokee population gutted by warfare and disease had dropped from twenty-two thousand earlier in the century. The Creeks ceded land in 1773, and the Cherokees sold away most of Kentucky and Middle Tennessee in 1775. Georgia's white population quadrupled between 1745 and 1760, and by 1775 eighteen thousand colonists stood primed to invade Creek lands.[4]

When war broke out, British and rebel American officials scrambled to gain control of an already chaotic situation. Congress had made plans to divide Indian Affairs into three departments in 1775, allotting ten thousand dollars to the southern portion and placing the Irish-born trade agent and go-between George Galphin in charge. Only in August 1776 did South Carolina learn about this plan. John Stuart, a Scots immigrant to South Carolina, had taken over for Atkin in his role as superintendent for the southern tribes in 1761; he remained employed for the British. He would eventually command a company

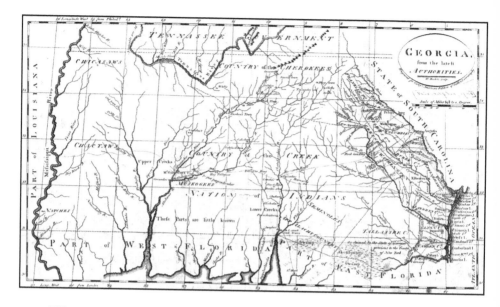

William Barker and Mathew Carey, "Georgia, from the latest authorities" (Philadelphia: Mathew Carey, 1795). Courtesy of the Library of Congress.

of Loyalists "Wholly Annexed and Attached" to the Indian department; they fought alongside Indians.[5] Galphin and Stuart found that the American Congress and ministers in England, respectively, sent instructions that were often at odds with conditions on the ground.

To a small extent, food diplomacy continued to matter in the southern region. In October 1776, for example, John Stuart decided to redirect Creek efforts away from war with Cherokees and Choctaws, and toward assisting the British against the rebels. He set about trying to supply himself with "necessaries, for engaging the Indians firmly in his Majesty's interest," including "a supply of provisions." Although in 1778 he criticized the Creeks for wavering loyalties, he still felt that he could not afford to refuse to feed them. Indeed, Stuart wrote that "Many of the Creeks remain here the whole Winter for the sake of Provision." They were joined by "about five hundred Cherokees," causing "a very great Expence of Presents and Provisions." In 1779 Alexander Cameron, Indian agent to the Cherokees, procured corn from Cherokee towns that he described as "Neutral" to redistribute to other Cherokees, while at the same time proclaiming the "Neutral" Cherokees' inclination "to serve me as ever."[6] The British distributed rations to Native warriors to gain alliances and to maintain them, and they fed the Native civilians who arrived at British strongholds during pauses in the war. They also sometimes overestimated their influence with their Indian allies.

Rebel government officials also made diplomatic overtures; they substituted domesticated animals and alcohol for trade goods and gunpowder, promised to regulate trade irregularities and colonists' land encroachments, and used food metaphors. In July 1776 members of the Georgia Council of Safety observed that Indians would "expect to be well paid, even for neutrality." Georgians knew that Natives would prefer "Ammunition & Cloathing" but also acknowledged their inability to provide those articles. Their solution came in the form of "Cattle as a substitute." In September 1777, when word arrived in North Carolina that nearly three dozen Middle, Overhill, and Valley Cherokees planned "to wait on the General Assembly," the governor's office agreed "to appoint a Commissary to furnish the said Indians with provisions." At a 1783 meeting with the Cherokees, Georgia governor Lyman Hall used as many metaphors as possible. He offered goods to the Cherokees so that Cherokees and Georgians could "embrace each other as Friends . . . Eat out of the same Dish and drink out of the same Cup," and "have a plain open Path to you and you to us."[7]

Indians also attempted to employ food diplomacy during the war. They used food to delineate the terms of their military contributions, used the one-dish metaphor, and requested and distributed goods and foodstuffs. In the winter of 1776, when John Stuart sought the aid of the Creeks, "their Answer was 'That they were willing to assist us but it must be in their own Way . . . with White Men who would furnish them with Provisions.'" The Creeks also warned that "any great Number of Red Men could not subsist in a Body together." In the same letter Stuart wrote that another group of Indians would only agree to attack "Georgia, as soon as a sufficient Quantity of Corn could be got to support them upon the Expedition."[8] Indians demanded additional fighting men and rations, refused to commit to extended terms of service, waited to fight until they could be sure of their supplies, and stated their expectations that non-Native military commanders would accept the fact that Indians fought differently.

Southern Indians also continued to use food metaphors. During a 1782 meeting with Georgians, an Upper Creek named the Tallassee King expressed a desire for "a white and straight" path before proclaiming, "that it was ordained that our Children should eat out of one Dish that is one with a Red Hand and the other with white." Indians who asked for trade goods, like their northern counterparts, called themselves "naked" or "hungry" to underscore the generosity of those who provided gifts. British and rebel officials, however, likely remained confused about whether these Indians were hungry or not.[9]

These practices make clear some of the similarities between the northern theatre of war and the southern colonies, but food diplomacy in the Revolutionary south was different because its efficacy in maintaining peace proved short-lived. It is unclear whether, in 1779, when Alexander Cameron sent corn to Cherokees, they really were willing "to serve" him, given Indian attitudes toward military service. Georgian Lyman Hall did well to use mutually comprehensible food metaphors, but because Hall and his associates gestured to future rules for regulating trade, rather than setting them there and then, readers must be skeptical of Georgians' negotiating efforts because Indians likely were too.[10] The shared experience of hunger, which was so crucial to northern Indian relations, did not seem to matter as much during the moments when people in the south used food diplomacy. Officials could not escape the fact that their food gifts made poor substitutes for the guns and ammunition that southern Indians preferred. Whereas an Iroquoian form of food diplomacy dominated the New York region by 1780, southern inhabitants by that time had not institutionalized comparable practices, and divisions between rebels, British officials, and Indians contributed to outbreaks of violence in the form of victual warfare.

Between the beginning of the Revolutionary War and the end of 1778, failed food diplomacy and an expedition of victual warfare against the Cherokees prompted some changes and revealed other continuities. Rebel colonial leaders tried to block British diplomacy rather than replicate colonial practices, and then further undermined their negotiations with a Virginian, North Carolinian, and South Carolinian scorched-earth campaign against the Cherokees in 1776. These factors created a split between the Cherokees, which represented not only a joining of Cherokees with Britons and British-allied Creeks, but also an event that deprived rebel-allied Cherokees of provisions. Victual warfare in this region differed from its northern counterpart. The 1776 campaign illuminates mostly preemptive (rather than retaliatory) attacks on edible supplies. Whereas the Americans struck Iroquoia to punish Indians for their alliance with the British, they targeted Cherokee towns even earlier to create fear and hunger, and because southern colonists had a longer history of attacking southern Indians. The motivations behind Indians' victual warfare also changed: during the late 1770s, Creeks and Cherokees shifted from killing cattle to stealing them, which stopped their own hunger and presaged famine-prevention efforts later in the war.

In July 1775 South Carolinians seized British Indian Superintendent John Stuart's estate as "a security for the behaviour of the Indians in the Southern Department." Then they attempted to pressure him into providing "copies of all my correspondence on Indian affairs," which, citing his "duty to the King," he refused to do. Colonists correctly suspected that Stuart was trying to secure the southern tribes to the British interest (he denied that he was also attempting to arm slaves and Indians). One of the confiscated letters revealed that Stuart hoped to gather the Creeks and Cherokees together in St. Augustine, East Florida, where he would use "all possible means . . . for engaging the Indians firmly in his Majesty's interest." He feared that he would "find difficulty in getting a supply of provisions," because he knew that he would need food to solidify alliances.[11] Stuart wanted to court the southern tribes; colonists did, too, which is why they tried to limit his contact with Indians.

Southern rebel colonists also tried to stem the flow of diplomatic trade goods. In July 1775 colonists' schooners intercepted two British ships bound for Georgia bearing "Arms, Ammunition and Indian Trading Goods." This letter did not describe the goods seized, but contemporary letters suggest that "goods" often included food supplies—so it is possible that this event involved the confiscation of provisions as well as trade presents. Creeks needed gunpowder to hunt deer for the venison they ate and for the deerskins they sold to non-Natives. The following year, when the Georgia Council of Safety contemplated substituting cattle for trade goods, they imagined that the swap would be most successful "if the communication" between the Creeks "& our Enemies were cut off."[12] It was easier for South Carolinians to interfere with the diplomacy of other imperial officials rather than try to maneuver with Indians, and easier for Georgians to improve the appeal of their presents by limiting British-Creek contact.

Soon southern American colonists proved uninterested in pursuing an accommodating Indian policy. The Cherokee Dragging Canoe had raised a war standard at Chota and raided the Holston, Clinch, and Powell Valleys in May 1776. In the summer of 1776 fears that Indians would mount a more extensive assault resulted in a concentrated strike against Cherokee towns. The aims of Americans' campaign mirrored the 1779 expedition into Iroquoia: "a Corps of at least fifteen hundred men" sought "the destruction of the Crops of the lower Nation" and to provoke "necessary terror." Henry Laurens described the burning of towns, crops, and stored grain as "the only possible way of reducing the Barbarians."[13] In this instance, as in earlier English campaigns, aggressors justified their military decisions by portraying Indians as savages.

Three separate groups of soldiers proceeded into the Cherokee towns. A Virginia and North Carolina force under Colonel William Christian headed toward the Overhill villages, while North Carolinians under General Griffith Rutherford moved against the Middle and Valley towns, and a South Carolina army led by Major Andrew Williamson struck out for the Lower towns. None of the American columns met with serious resistance (Andrew Williamson's suffered some casualties in two ambushes). In general, most Cherokees dispersed and refused to come to close quarters with the rebel militia. In

September and October 1776, forces destroyed more than thirty-six Cherokee towns.[14]

Americans might have portrayed this campaign as a revengeful one. No
such claim could be made the following year, when the rebels fell once more
"upon the poor distressed Cherokees," destroying "their Villages and Crops."
Rebel officials would only deign to make peace in 1777, South Carolinians and
Georgians at the Treaty of DeWitt's Corner, and Virginians and North Carolinians at the Treaty of Holston. The Cherokees who signed these treaties officially split from the Cherokee Dragging Canoe, who formed a British-allied
polity of Cherokees, Creeks, and self-liberated bondpeople often called the
Chickamauga Cherokees.[15] John Stuart, who described these distressed Cherokees, argued that the rebels had attacked British-allied Indians overaggres-
sively. His tone implied that the Americans may already have succeeded in
subduing their enemy by the time they attacked again in 1777; he denigrated
preemptive American war tactics. No one could deny their terrible efficacy.

This more violent victual warfare initiated conversations about the Indian
hunger such campaigns were designed to cause. Rebel soldiers' destruction of
Cherokee crops and villages tested even Chickamaugas' loyalty to the British.
Dragging Canoe sent word that "they cou'd not be of any Service" to the King,
and that, further, "if they shou'd not raise Bread this Year the white People
nor no one else wou'd have occasion to kill them for they wou'd all die with
Hunger." Dragging Canoe's message lacked the metaphorical tropes that In-
dians used to request provisions. These Native families were not "naked," nor
were they "starving"; some of the Indians had already felt "obliged to eat
Horses & Dogs & any Thing they can get," and some were "dead already."[16]
These were famine conditions. Dragging Canoe's information about dying
Cherokees evokes similar worries of Iroquois men in 1779; in that instance,
too, Natives questioned their trust in British allies. The Iroquois had critiqued
Britons' obsession with provisions, expressed their willingness to withstand
future hunger, and destroyed allies' foodstuffs to strengthen alliances. Chickamauga Cherokees questioned their support for the British by emphasizing
deaths by starvation. In both instances, hunger tested alliances.

Despite Dragging Canoe's doubts, he and the rest of the Chickamaugas ultimately chose to assist the British. He was joined by his brother, Little Owl,
along with Bloody Fellow, Hanging Maw, Young Tassel (John Watts), Kitegiska,
and Outacite. Older Cherokees opposed this move, as did many Cherokee
women. This division also resulted in blocked food aid: British officials provisioned the five hundred hungry Chickamaugas but prevented these supplies
from reaching other Cherokees.[17]

Indians had to explore new ways to fight hunger, which is why the late 1770s witnessed increased domesticated-animal use, particularly cattle ownership, among them. Native Americans were about a century late to the beef craze; in England, long-distance cattle trade from the Scottish Highlands and Lowlands to London's Smithfield Market increased significantly after the 1707 Act of Union, and in North America, by the end of the seventeenth century, beef consumption had risen from 14 to 58 percent of meat consumed in the Chesapeake. In some towns Creeks were acquiring horses (but probably few cattle) by the 1760s, and a "New Order" of cattle ranching and slaveholding made animals more important during and after the American Revolution. Some Cherokees had encountered horses, because Dragging Canoe mentioned people eating them. It was likely as a result of the Treaty of DeWitt's Corner that additional horses and cattle entered rebel-allied Cherokee towns. One article of the treaty stipulated that Cherokees could keep the cattle, horses, and goods belonging to any unlicensed trader in Cherokee country after they turned such traders in at Fort Rutledge. The treaty also demanded a *return* of horses and slaves stolen from South Carolina, Georgia, North Carolina, and Virginia, indicating that an increase in animal thefts preceded the treaty.[18]

Given the fluctuating symbolic and practical meanings of domesticated animals in the mid-eighteenth century, it is unlikely that Creeks and Cherokees always viewed cattle as food sources. Some animals functioned more as status symbols; they signified the ability to accumulate property. Natives also used cattle in ways that differed from colonists' practices. When Scots-Creek leader Alexander McGillivray tried to bequeath his cattle and horses to his sons, the matriarchs in his mother's clan ended up with the animals. Yet it would have been possible for cattle to take on symbolic meanings as property without losing practical value as meat sources. Creeks expected provisions while traveling through lands they had ceded to the British—a practice they recognized as part of hospitality, but which non-Native inhabitants viewed as hostility. In a 1763 talk an Upper Creek called the Mortar explained that Creeks killed "the Cattle they meet in these lands" because "their Buffalo, Deer and Bear" were "being drove off the Land and killed." "They fill their Bellies when they are hungry having nothing else to do with it," he concluded.[19] Indians, when denied hospitality, might have preferred game meat, but due to declining game populations they hunted cattle instead. During a time of game scarcity it is clear that some beef made its way into Indian cooking kettles.

Obviously, some Indians did acquire cattle and eat beef before the Revolution, as the Mortar's talk implies. This tendency is also confirmed by the fact that in 1769 Georgians considered a bill to prevent "the Stealing and driving away [of] Horses and Cattle." For the most part, in the decades prior to the Revolutionary War, Indians killed cattle. A 1733 law stated that when traders chaperoned Indians on visits to Georgia, the trader would be expected to "make good all Damages done to any of the inhabitants by such Indians . . . by killing of Cattle or otherwise." Stolen animals did not pose a significant enough problem to merit explicit mention. By 1750 Creeks, acting in concert with Yuchis, were spotted "plundering" cornfields but still killing colonists' cattle. A 1771 talk by George Galphin to the Lower Creeks criticized the Indians for stealing horses but destroying cattle and corn.[20]

The proliferation of cattle thefts during the war is consequently arresting, and reveals how British-allied Indians obtained these animals. "The Creek Indians have broke with Us," wrote one Georgian correspondent to Henry Laurens in October 1778. These Indians "killed & cruelly butcher'd upwards of thirty of our Inhabitants," drove "off large Gangs of our Horses & Cattle," and shot down what they could not "conveniently carry away." This strategy combined the tactics of animal mutilation and destruction that had characterized previous decades with newer thefts of animals—either to prevent other people from taking them or to restock Indian herds. Often, Indians acted in concert with British allies; a South Carolina report explained how a combined force "carried off a considerable number of Negroes and not less than two thousand head of cattle."[21] Whereas Iroquois Indians used violence to make their allies hunger in a way that highlighted Native indispensability, Creeks and Cherokees used violence to obtain animals from their enemies, which in turn prevented their allies from calling them useless.

The British had more success than the Americans at managing alliances with powerful southern Indians during this first phase of the war, but even British approaches to working in Indian Affairs required adjusting between 1776 and 1779, as two letters to Superintendent John Stuart demonstrate. In May 1776 General William Howe wrote to Stuart to say that because Howe was working from "such a distance" in the northern military theater, he trusted Stuart to make decisions about Indian negotiations "without expecting particular directions from me." In 1779, by contrast, Lord George Germain complained to Stuart from Whitehall, London, that "the Expence of your Department has increased so prodigiously that it is become a matter of public and parliamentary observation." As new alliances formed, as the Americans mounted preemptive campaigns of victual warfare, and as Indian violence grew more pronounced, the British position changed. When British spending on co-campaigns increased, high-ranking officials demanded more oversight. British-Indian attacks from St. Augustine into Georgia continued throughout the 1770s and early 1780s.[22] This uncertainty made crucial the presence of officials like Stuart who remained capable of working with their Indian allies—at the same time that it made London ministers nervous. Germain had good reason to worry, because John Stuart never read his letter; he was dead before it arrived.

In 1779 the death of Superintendent John Stuart created immense confusion in British Indian Affairs, which reduced the effectiveness of British food diplomacy and moved rebel food diplomacy further along toward the violent end of the accommodation-violence spectrum of behavior. Reports of famine among the Creeks beginning in the summer of 1778 necessitated generosity during 1779, the precise moment when British officials, because of administrative mix-ups, could not secure funds for food gifts.[23] Stuart's work with Creeks, Cherokees, Chickasaws, and Choctaws had lent stability to British relationships with southern Indians, but his successors struggled to transition into their roles as intermediaries. British food diplomacy never fully recovered after Stuart's death, and officials, in desperation, fell back on the practice of trying to block rebel diplomacy. The Americans seized on the confusion in the British Indian department to again set fire to extensive stretches of Cherokee cornfields, and then to offer a new, less compromising form of food diplomacy to force Creeks and Cherokees back into a state of neutrality. By this point in the war the food diplomacy of the rebel southern states did not include distributions of actual foodstuffs; the Americans instead tried to portray their "generosity" as restraint from victual warfare. Because Creeks and Cherokees possessed new, aggressive ways to avoid hunger, results proved disastrous.

In March 1779 British brigadier general John Campbell reported the death of John Stuart. The whole Indian department stood "in the greatest Confusion." It is difficult to say how Indians reacted to the news, but the fact that Stuart had intermarried into the Cherokee Long Hair Clan and been adopted by them suggests that his demise was likely troubling. In their reorganization of the department, the British split it in two. In October Alexander Cameron, who had until Stuart's death acted as superintendent for the Cherokees, became superintendent of the Choctaws and Chickasaws; Colonel Thomas Brown was appointed to the Catawba, Creek, and Cherokee Indians. They each received a salary and could employ deputies and interpreters. Brown got £1,000 as "allowance for presents, Rum, Provisions, Carriage and all other contingencies." Cameron feared that such changes would hinder British-Native alliances. He received a sum of £1,450, which he found "barely sufficient to defray the Sallaries of Officers," let alone satisfy "Visiting parties of those Nations under my management."[24]

For one thing, British leaders had been critiquing John Stuart's overspending for several years; £1,450 was not likely to go far for Cameron or Brown.

For another, Indians tended to engage with the diplomacy practiced by the men whom Native women had married; Mohawks had been tied to Sir William Johnson, Creek loyalties had been tied to Stuart, and Alexander Cameron had been responsible for the Cherokees. Now Johnson and Stuart were dead. By moving Cameron from his position among the Cherokees, the British weakened this node of patronage and ignored the fact that it would take Cameron time to cultivate ties with the Choctaws and Chickasaws. "The Cherokees will all return to the Rebels," wrote Cameron, as "soon as they are informed that I am deprived of the Management of their Affairs." Cameron worried that his departure would push Cherokees to reestablish alliances with another imperial power, so he delayed acting on his orders. By September the Indian department was again "in Confusion" because Cameron had not yet left the Cherokee nation.[25]

Even if Indian loyalties *were* secure, Britons would soon find that they did not possess the means to maintain them, in part because they could not procure food. In September 1779 a ship "laden with 300 Barrels of Provisions And a considerable Quantity of Rum . . . ha[d] unquestionably fallen into the Enemy's Hands," and the Indians could not be employed "for want of Provisions" on the Mississippi. Spain declared war on Great Britain in 1779, and Bernando de Gálvez, Spanish governor of Louisiana, decided to launch preemptive attacks against the British at Manchac, Baton Rouge, and Natchez to protect the valuable port of New Orleans. The Indians in this report may have been Chickasaws, and the enemy Spanish rather than American, but the overall sentiment was the same: theft resulted in British inabilities to secure Indians' assistance. And this letter was the same letter that reported on the confusion that resulted from Cameron's dithering. When supplies made it through, distribution problems occurred. Stuart had died in debt. In February 1780 five hundred barrels of pork destined for the Indian department had been sent to Stuart's attention instead; this slip in address meant that the pork was "seized upon" by Stuart's executor and "will probably be sold by him as private Property." "This Pork would be of the utmost advantage" at an upcoming "Congress with the Indians," complained another official—but the pork was unrecoverable.[26]

To add to the chaos, right before this bureaucratic change in the British Indian department, Virginians had mounted a scorched-earth campaign, which they followed with offers of curtailed food diplomacy. They attacked neutral Indians and British-allied Chickamaugas with equal vigor. In April 1779, Virginians attacked "Chicgamaga a New Settlement," where they "surprised the Women & Children," killed five people, destroyed "Their Homes & Corn," and "carried off" all the Indians' "Horses & Cattle." According to Alexander Cameron, this action reduced the Cherokees "to the utmost distress."[27]

When Cameron arrived at the Chickamauga towns at the end of May, he "found matters in very great Confusion." He discovered that "a Commissary appointed by the Stadtholders of Virginia to Superintend the Cherokee" was laboring, "Through the Mediation" of the Cherokee warrior Oconostota, to convince the Indians to take him up on his offer "to Support them with Provisions and all the Necessaries of Life providing they would return to their Old Towns and live Neutral." Luckily for the British, Cameron's arrival precipitated the American agent's departure: "not Chusing to risque his Safety in my Neighbourhood," the man "returned to Virginia" when Cameron appeared. Cameron convinced the Cherokees not to agree to peace and provisions, but to wait for their own corn to ripen, when "we should then march to Carolina or Georgia and take Revenge."[28] According to Cameron these homeless Cherokees had no corn, no horses, and no cattle. The disarray of the Indian department meant that Cameron could not offer to provision the Cherokees in exchange for their service. In this case, however, he invoked Cherokee cycles of planting and warfare to get them to agree to the timing of this expedition.

What happened next was not to Cameron's favor. The rebels had heard of this future attack and sent South Carolinian general Andrew Williamson and his cavalry to march toward the Chickamauga Cherokee settlement.[29] Upon arrival Williamson promised the Cherokees "that he did not mean to hurt them or their Effects, providing they would lay neutral" and allow him "to take or destroy" Cameron and his men (Cameron discovered that the Indians had received these talks after the fact, when it was too late).[30] Cameron prepared for a fight between the Americans and his company of approximately three hundred Indians and forty Loyalists, only to encounter "the Enemy . . . in Three divisions, and Five Hundred horsemen in each Division."[31] They were outnumbered.

At first the Cherokees seemed to privilege the prevention of their own hunger over their promise to fight with Cameron. It seemed that these Cherokees *did* still have some corn, because they called a council and decided to send two of their own "to treat for Peace and save their Corn." Williamson told them that if they would deliver Cameron "into his Hands," he would agree not to burn their crops. But then the Cherokees told Williamson "that if he would not treat upon any other Terms, he might burn their Towns as soon as he pleased." Williamson accordingly "Burned Six of their Towns and destroyed their Corn . . . after which he offered them every assistance and Protection they could wish for Providing they would return to their Old Towns and live in peace."[32] Cameron escaped.

The disorder in the British Indian department made it difficult for the British to try to remedy the situation with food aid. Cameron explained that he had hoped to gather the Indians together "and revenge the loss of their Corn." In October he finally managed to purchase three hundred bushels for the Chickamaugas from the other Cherokees—"those Indians who lie neuter and listen to the Virginia Folks." If the Chickamauga population consisted of five hundred families, each family would have received two thirds of a bushel of corn. It is difficult to estimate the weight of a bushel of corn, especially with such a brief description. Britons and Americans measure bushels differently today, and Cameron was a Scot working for the British in North America, so it is hard to say which measurement he might have used. Measurements for American bushels range between 56 pounds per bushel of shelled corn and from 35 to 70 pounds for corn in the ear. This would mean that each family received between 33.6 pounds if Cameron obtained shelled corn, and between 21 pounds and 42 pounds if the corn was unshucked. Given that each Iroquois person (not family) consumed six bushels per year, and that a future attack against the Cherokees destroyed fifty thousand bushels at once, three hundred bushels does not seem like a significant quantity of food relief.[33]

In any case, Cameron's plans to provide additional foodstuffs and to lead a retaliatory attack were foiled by his receiving word that he was no longer in charge of superintending the Cherokees. The funds he possessed could not be spent on more corn or anything else for the Cherokees. Cameron professed himself "much afraid that few of the Indians of this District will join or give Assistance to His Majesty's Troops this Season." In October he reported that the Chickamaugas were "living in the Woods upon Nuts and whatever they can get besides."[34] Their corn supplies from the neutral Cherokees had dwindled. Failures in British supplies could have offered Andrew Williamson an opportunity, but he chose to assert power through destruction.

The attack against the Chickamaugas provides evidence of alterations in violence and peacemaking, and continued misunderstandings of Native hunger. Southern rebels' policy regarding Natives consisted of engaging in aggressive, preemptive victual warfare, reneging on promises made, and, once a campaign successfully ended, offering terms of peace. Americans now offered postattack "assistance" to enemy Indians, but, in a move that anticipated George Washington's instructions to John Sullivan, they did so only once they were confident of Indians' defeat and future neutrality. The British, represented by Cameron, struggled to provide provisions. Cameron had to encourage Cherokees to plant their own crops. Cherokees, in contrast to Britons and Americans, and like the Six Nations, continued to use food diplomacy somewhat effectively and may have continued to overstate their hunger to non-Native observers. The fact that the Chickamaugas possessed some corn for Williamson to destroy, and the fact that Cameron obtained corn from neutral

Cherokees to give to their Chickamauga brethren, testifies to the existence of corn and the importance of grain in retaining bonds between factions of southern Natives. Given the uncertain conditions of crop production, however—no one could say whether the corn would be allowed to ripen without suffering another scorched-earth attack, whether the weather would turn too soon, or whether the harvest would fail—hungry neutral Cherokees may not have had much to spare.

The absence of provisions, incompetent distribution of what little foodstuffs the British obtained, and infighting prolonged the confusion. In December 1779 Alexander Cameron complained that a group of Creeks had visited him and requested food, which he could not deliver because he was not their superintendent. Desperate, he wrote to Governor Peter Chester at British-held Pensacola and recommended that Chester "Order at least provisions and Ammunition to be Issued to those Indians" as a matter of "Interest and Safety of your Province." Cameron warned that without provisions, the colony at Pensacola would "become a prey to" the Creeks, who would retaliate with violence that interfered with "Communication betwixt this place and Savannah through the Creek Nation."[35] Governor Chester ignored this warning from an Indian agent, and not for the first or last time.

Chester had refused to provide ammunition and provisions to a group of Creeks in 1774. Part of his stubbornness can be explained by a general lack of funds; when, in the late 1770s, Chester requested troops from British secretary George Germain, Germain said no because he assumed that previous supplies to Indians would suffice to convince Native warriors to help Chester. But Chester also made his own mistakes. In 1780 he went as far as to refuse to receive the Creek Indians who came to visit him. By 1780 one official successfully convinced Chester "to incur a small expence to keep our red allies in a good temper," but it seems that those efforts did not content the Indians.[36]

After Chester gave in and used part of his annual allowance of £1,000 to furnish "them with a little Provision," the Creeks, "being disatisfyed with their Reception . . . began to kill the Cattle about Town." They had also "sold most of their provisions for Rum," and "when drunk" became "very insolent and Riotous." This destruction of cattle is striking in its resemblance to Iroquois and Shawnee cattle destruction at almost the exact same moment. It is possible that Creek motivations were different. Perhaps they remained ambivalent about cattle ownership. But it is also possible that these Creeks, like the Iroquois and Shawnees, destroyed foodstuffs provided by their allies because symbolic violence and hunger endurance were as important as hunger prevention. The subsequent decision to privilege rum purchases over provisions suggests a continuing disinterest in eating and the increasing temptation of alcohol. By

February 1780 Chester had started to seize Creek lands and distribute them to "his Favorets and Dependents." That month Creeks were spotted "Plundering the English Inhabitants of this Province."[37] These actions might have symbolized retaliation—which is how some Britons understood them—but they might also have represented Creeks taking animals as the expected gifts of non-Native hospitality, or destroying them to ensure a shared experience of hunger. The year 1779 gave rise to a host of contradictions, which had not resolved themselves by the Battle of Yorktown.

On the day in 1781 that the American siege of Yorktown ended in British surrender, a man named St. George Tucker wrote a poem. Tucker, a Bermuda-born Virginia lawyer who had recently been wounded in the nose by an exploding shell, appeared rather glum, despite the American victory.[38] He wrote:

> See Terror stalking through the' affrighted Land!
> Grim Rage and fell Revenge his Steps pursue,
> Rapine, and harpy—Famine join the Band,
> And Murder, leading on his hellish Crew:
>> The wretched Victim's dying Groans,
>> The widow'd Matron's tender Moans,
>> The Virgins plaints, the orphans cries,
>> Ascend in Concert to the Skies:
> There hollow want in anguish pines,
> No more relieve'd from plenty's chearing Hoard;
> There pale Disease the parting Breath resigns,
> And Desolation waves around her flaming Sword![39]

Even as the Americans triumphed against the British, Tucker's iambs personified the characters of murder, rage, rapine, revenge, terror, and famine—always famine. His verse concluded with additional references to want and the absence of relief. The twelve months of 1779 had been characterized by incompetent diplomacy on almost all fronts, and although Yorktown marked a turning point, the war was still not over. Now, Indians' victual warfare had resulted in an unintended consequence: it encouraged fears of murderous, terrifying, and powerful Indians.

During the early 1780s, people in the revolutionary south proved incapable of practicing food diplomacy. Britons, who suffered a major defeat at Yorktown in 1781, fell back on trying to undermine rebel negotiations with Indians. Southern American states struggled because of individual states' failures to cooperate, which resulted in mixed messages of peaceful overtures, self-congratulations for withholding victual warfare, and intermittent attacks. Rebel-allied Indians used peaceful food metaphors that British-allied Natives contradicted by committing victual warfare. Non-Natives, consequently, became unable and unwilling to distinguish between the Indians responsible for mediation and those responsible for war. British and American representatives complained about Indians who seemed peaceable one month and then, confusingly—sometimes "treacherously"—switched their allegiance and destroyed crops and animals. The Americans usually erred in favor of attacking rather than attempting to figure out which Native Americans wanted peace. During these later years of the conflict, non-Natives' fears of Indian violence became interwoven with their anxieties about hungry Indians.[40]

Life was chaotic in the early 1780s. After Cornwallis's defeat at Yorktown the military conflict was effectively over for the southern British troops, but other sorts of hostility continued; 1780 to 1782 was the most violent part of the conflict. During the last part of the war Britons continued to interfere in rebels' negotiations with Native Americans. In September 1782, more than two hundred Creeks from Cusseta, Okfuskee, and Tallassee met Americans in Augusta, Georgia. They agreed to return stolen animals and enslaved people, but before the parties formalized the arrangement, the British distracted them. They "Sent up an Indian" who told them "to come and gett goods" from the British, who knew "they ware in great want of goods." Many of the Creeks who seemed friendly to the Americans now decided to head to St. Augustine to meet the British. Those who remained on their way to Augusta expected "that they will gett goods boath as presents and for them to have a treat, or they say it will be impossible for them to give the satisfaction Required."[41] British promises of additional goods divided the party of Creeks.

The Indians who still seemed willing to meet the Americans traveled with increased expectations that trade goods would function as payment and presents. Americans would be unlikely to supply them, and without trade goods they possessed few additional options but violence. Alexander Cameron died on December 27, 1781, eliminating yet another person capable of brokering British diplomacy with Indians. George Galphin died in 1782, which prompted a similar situation for the Americans.[42] Spanish involvement, noticeable since the late 1770s, became more prominent after Yorktown, which hurt not only the British but also the southern states because it offered Creeks more leverage in their negotiations with imperial powers. Peace seemed elusive indeed.

Divisions between American states contributed to a lack of cooperation, which led to inconsistencies in food diplomacy and Indian policy. In the early 1780s North Carolinians and Georgians both sought to make peace with various Cherokee factions, with minimal success. In July 1781 one North Carolina official reported the arrival of "Some of the principal Head-men of the Cherokees" to Holstein River for a treaty. He worried, "The Commissioners are exceedingly embarrassed for want of money" because the Virginia treasurer was "refusing to pay." During Indian treaties, he remarked, "not only the Ambassadours, but their Wives, and their Train &c; has to be fed by the European negociator." He pointed out the strategic necessity of "amusing and keeping two numerous Indian Tribes still, or in suspense, during this critical Campaign"—likely referring to American efforts up and down the coast that would culminate in the siege at Yorktown—but worried that this goal would prove impossible to achieve without food supplies.[43]

The following year it was North Carolinians who disappointed Georgians by failing to appear at a meeting between Georgia and the Cherokees. A Georgia man described not getting "the Busnes Compleated as was Expected upon the account of the faithless North Carolina Men not Meeting agreeable to their Repeated Promises." He feared that "the scarcety of Provisions"—which may also have impeded the treaty's success—coupled with an absence of ammunition placed Georgians in a "totering situation" along "our fronteers."[44] In both cases one state's inability to cooperate with another state combined with a food shortage to undercut the stability of Indian affairs.

By 1782 some southern officials' food diplomacy consisted of telling Indians they should be grateful for an absence of victual warfare. This policy lumped Indian allies together with antagonists. Andrew Pickens, a future federal Indian commissioner, spent part of 1782 touring Cherokee country, sometimes delivering talks to Indians himself and sometimes sending them with other messengers. In one talk sent to the Middle and Valley Cherokees, Pickens's representative referred to a previous expedition where the man in charge "did not hurt any of the Red People nor suffer his men to pull an ear of their Corn." The Americans claimed that "by that means we thought to convince your nation that we did not wish to hurt you," and only push "the Rogues & bad White Men . . . out of your Country." Soon after that, complained the speaker, Cherokees attacked, intending "to burn & destroy the whole Country," though they were prevented when Americans fired upon them. These Indians "run home" after "burning a few Houses & Stealing Some Negroes."[45]

This was a telling exchange. Pickens, speaking via this go-between, congratulated the Americans for refraining from violence and the destruction of Middle and Valley Cherokee crops—during a campaign whose history he may have modified to downplay rebel atrocities—and after differentiating some Cherokees from Cherokee "Rogues" and white traders working for the British, he then criticized all Cherokees for the attack. Pickens assumed that he knew the Indians' intentions, when in fact their actions suggested plans for a small raid rather than a larger, more damaging strike. He refused to distinguish between peaceful American-allied Cherokees and the Chickamaugas and Creeks who moved against American towns, and he was unwilling to allow them to retain the cattle they stole to feed themselves. Pickens later demanded that the Indians show good faith by returning domesticated animals stolen during the war.[46]

Interactions with the Creeks in Georgia proved even clumsier. Like Pickens, Governor John Martin blamed one faction of Indians for the actions of another. In a July talk to the Creek headman the Tallassee King, he blamed the British-allied "Treacherous" Emistesigo, who, "for the sake of a few trifling presents . . . Did wantonly fall on our Warriors in the Night." Although Martin admitted that Emistesigo, whatever his motivations, acted without consulting the Tallassee King, Martin blamed the Tallassee King for the damage. He also demanded compensation for the victual warfare of other Creeks. Once the Tallassee King agreed to "deliver up . . . all our Negroes, horses & Cattle that are among you," Martin looked forward to "Burying the Hatchet, Brightening the Good old Chain of Friendship, & mak[ing] the path streight, Fair and open, so that we shall live like friends & Brothers, living upon the same land and Eating out of the Same Dish."[47] It is possible that Martin held the Tallassee King responsible because Okfuskee Creeks also possessed horses and cattle and enslaved people as their property. It is also likely, however, that Martin could not be troubled to differentiate between Creeks. Like his contemporaries, Martin used many metaphors, some of which relied upon the one-dish trope to portray shared territory.

Martin may have been echoing the Tallassee King, who had made overtures of friendship to Georgians only a week after news of a Creek and Chickamauga Cherokee attack in Georgia that May. The Tallassee King warned Martin of a new attack by a combined party of Creeks and Cherokees. At the meeting—which both Upper and Lower Creeks attended—the Tallassee King used the one-dish metaphor to convey his hopes for peace. The "ordained" nature of children eating "out of one Dish" with a combination of a white and "a Red Hand" reminded listeners that some of the Upper Creeks remained loyal to Georgia—though the Tallassee King did not attempt to apply the statement to all Creeks. The Tallassee King's maneuvering illustrates the two growing factions of Creeks after the Americans took Savannah. The problem was that even in light of this talk, Georgian motives remained questionable. When the Tallassee King and several other Creeks arrived in Augusta around October, the Georgians had no goods to distribute.[48] This dish cried out for blood.

Georgians also emphasized their attacks against the Cherokees as a threat to the Creeks, and admitted that they currently had few provisions to distribute. "See what the Cherokees are now reduced to, by their folly and pride," said Governor Martin to the Tallassee King and several warriors and headmen of the Upper and Lower Creeks in 1782. "They are almost brought to nothing." He prefaced this warning with a reminder that the Georgians had already demanded their "horses, Cattle and Negroes." He could provide no food— "We have just been able to raise provisions for our present support," he said— but soon Georgians would "raise plenty of Rice," and "Ships from all nations will flow in upon us, and we shall be able to supply you with goods of all kinds, and take your Skins in return." Martin's portrayal of a free-trade United States emphasized the link between food and trade goods while mentioning his government's current inability to mete out either. He even went as far as to try to limit the number of men who intended to accompany the Tallassee King on a visit to see Martin in Savannah. Martin noted that "we have neither provisions, nor presents to give them." Martin died shortly thereafter. By January, when the Tallassee King's arrival was finally imminent, and the Tallassee and Fat King had complied with Georgian peoples' requests and "chearfully gave up" slaves, provisions remained in short supply. All attempts to purchase corn from "the Publick" had "been in vain."[49] The procurer in charge doubted his ability to find even enough grain for the Tallassee King alone.

Such blundering not only helped to provoke victual warfare but also ensured a continuous cycle of it, in which non-Native attacks destroyed Indian foodstuffs, and Indians then committed victual warfare to steal grain and cattle that would prevent hunger—which, in turn, prompted retaliatory campaigns against them. In 1780, North Carolinians sent five hundred men against the Chickamauga towns; in 1781 Virginia and North Carolina also attacked, targeting houses and provisions specifically. Men led by John Sevier pursued the Cherokees into present-day middle Tennessee and Northern Alabama, burning towns and killing noncombatants. In the spring of 1782 Indians responded. Chickamauga Cherokees and Creeks attacked Georgia. They burned houses, stole "two & a half Waggon loads of Corn," destroyed a "Potator house & turned in a number of hogs to Distroy what Remaind." They also killed two people, wounded three, and took four prisoners.[50] These Indians destroyed *and* stole foodstuffs because they found victual warfare useful for the dual purposes of hunger creation (among the Americans) and hunger prevention (among themselves).

Suppose that St. George Tucker was a more prolific poet, and had composed lines to precede and follow his Yorktown ode: what might they look like? Perhaps he would have penned some sorrowful words on the state of his nose.[51] If the muses had inspired him to write about Indian affairs up until 1779, he might have introduced readers to the monsters Failure, Thievery, and Confusion. From 1775 to the end of 1778, British and rebel failures to practice food diplomacy occurred alongside increased instances of victual warfare in which Americans preemptively attacked Creeks and Cherokees, and Indians stole cattle. A reexamination of this period suggests that Indians practiced some aspects of victual warfare to prevent their own hunger, which allowed them to gain power even during times of reported famine. It is difficult to say whether bad diplomacy *caused* victual warfare. What readers *can* conclude is that failed diplomacy and increases in victual warfare occurred in close connection to each other, and they both destabilized power relationships.

The following years were characterized by worse violence that was birthed from the confusion after John Stuart's death. His absence made diplomatic solutions nearly unobtainable at the exact moment when the British most needed them. Although Stuart had understood the stakes of feeding Indians, his successors were fairly useless at employing food to negotiate. Meanwhile, American food diplomacy became more closely bound to aggressive crop destruction; it came to mean restraint in scorched-earth campaigns, and sending limited food aid to the enemy villages that had suffered the brunt of those attacks. The last phase of the war can be linked to the erasure of Indian factions from contemporary historical records. Beginning in the late 1770s both British and southern state officials struggled to distinguish allies from enemies; they became incapable of identifying the people who practiced victual warfare. Times of confusion were difficult times to preserve accurate records of the past.

St. George Tucker's final poem would have needed to reveal a final monster: the Master who enslaved other people.[52] Numerous Patriot officials observed that in addition to Creek and Cherokee tactics of sharing grain with enemy Indians and stealing cattle, Indians worked together with formerly enslaved people to attack the Americans. White American slaveholders sometimes portrayed these acts as "stealing" slaves, and sometimes as encouraging enslaved people to run away. These black men, women, and children constitute the last group of people whose relationships with hunger and usefulness during the War for Independence merit readers' attention—but in contrast to Native Americans, people of African descent enjoyed less power during the war itself.

PART TWO

Power in Flux

CHAPTER 4

Black Victual Warriors and Hunger Creation

Food is omnipresent in Revolutionary-era stories about bondpeople and free black men and women. In 1781 a cook named Dinah supposedly made such a delicious, slowly served fried chicken breakfast for British officer Banastre Tarleton and his men that it gave a messenger time to ride to the rebels and warn them of the arrival of the British troops. A different Dinah was said to have protected her master's home in Poughkeepsie, New York, "by 'softening' British hearts with her freshly baked bread." In another tale, George Washington visited Fraunces Tavern in New York City, where someone—sometimes Samuel Fraunces, the free black tavern owner, and sometimes a girl named Phoebe, said to be his daughter—"thwarted an assassination attempt against Washington by throwing a plate of poisoned peas out the window to the chickens."[1] None of the heroes in these apocryphal stories are depicted eating bread, peas, or chicken themselves. These myths resemble real occurrences during the Revolutionary War when enslaved peoples and self-liberated men and women used food to shape the war in ways that failed to address their own hunger. People of African descent gained only a marginal amount of power during the war itself; they proved themselves to military entities by saving soldiers from deaths by starvation and related diseases, but they often did so while ignoring their own appetites.

Enslaved people could make themselves useful to the British Army because it was the British who first granted them a chance at freedom. In November 1775, before the colonies declared independence, Virginia governor Lord Dunmore issued a proclamation that offered freedom to slaves of rebel masters, setting the stage for an exodus of thousands of self-liberated men and women from colonists' homes and plantations to British lines. Dunmore's Proclamation was also responsible for changing white colonists' and British officers' ideas about hunger prevention and just war. Because southern masters conflated the loss of slaves with the loss of other "property," like domesticated animals, it became easy for colonists to equate "stealing" slaves—or encouraging them to run away—with other acts that decreased their access to foodstuffs and fostered hunger. Rebel Americans, in turn, changed British ideas about victual warfare between members of the same nation. When their slaves ran to British ships, colonists stopped provisioning the British sailors aboard. The British then described the decision to withhold food and the refusal to sell it at a fair price as acts of war. Once these matters were settled, the British had to try to create a coherent military strategy that united former slaves, Loyalists, and Indians against American Patriots.[2]

Dunmore's Proclamation affected white colonists and Britons less than it did free black folks, enslaved people, and former bondpeople. People of African descent played various roles in the conflict, though not all documents indicate whether someone was enslaved or free, or whether that person served as a soldier allowed to bear arms, or as a waggoneer, cook, waiter, or camp follower. Dunmore's offer turned some men into victual warriors capable of creating and preventing white hunger. When food ran short, commanders sent soldiers out of camp on foraging expeditions for the army, which offered the additional strategic benefit of allowing soldiers to feed themselves by pilfering grain and domesticated animals. In the south, black victual raiders often set out first because those men knew where on the plantations of former masters they could find movable, edible goods.

This pillaging approach, which ameliorated British hunger with stolen foodstuffs while simultaneously creating hunger among the American rebels, engendered two results. First, it put free blacks and escaped slaves at great risk of suffering the wrath of white colonists, who now had to deal with a large gap in southern provisioning. Second, it made black men more mobile. Husbands left wives and children to undertake dangerous missions, or took up butchering or marketing work that necessitated living apart from their families. Their responsibilities as thieves, cooks, and waiters forced them to range farther from military forts but also made them privy to meetings of higher-ranking officers when they remained in or returned to camp. By procuring provisions, these ex-bondmen improved their skills in acquiring and sharing information.

Black people's involvement in the war transformed these men and women from relatively powerless actors in one food system into active creators of a new food system that they were somewhat more capable of using to their advantage. As slaves, bondpeople had labored against white hunger by producing and selling garden produce and by growing cash crops that whites sold for provisions. Their newer hunger-prevention efforts were extralegal; former slaves achieved them through labor, migration, and theft, but not yet by law. Throughout the war, self-liberated men and women did not enjoy the luxury of worrying overmuch about their own appetites—and sometimes, hunger seemed immaterial. But their experiences created the knowledge that would later become necessary to institutionalize a food system that granted black colonists the political authority to fight hunger.

While London ministers weighed the costs and benefits of invading the colonies, British colonial governors considered making appeals to slaves—just as they had to Native Americans—to shore up support in case the British Army arrived. In April 1775 the governor of Virginia, John Murray, third Earl of Dunmore, infuriated colonists with his decision to remove gunpowder from the Williamsburg powder magazine. He claimed that he had moved it to protect white Virginians in the event of a slave rebellion. Skeptical colonial leaders argued that the absence of powder would instead encourage revolt, which southern colonists constantly feared. "Some wicked and designing persons have instilled the most diabolical notions in the minds of our slaves," they observed that month in the *Virginia Gazette* newspaper. By May Dunmore was admitting privately that he intended to encourage rebellion. He had claimed, "with a Supply of Arms and Ammunition [he] should be able to collect from amongst Negroes Indians and other persons a force sufficient if not to subdue Rebellion at least to defend Government."[3]

He put this plan into action in his November 1775 proclamation. He invited "every person capable of bearing arms to resort to his Majesty's STANDARD," including "all indented servants, Negroes, or others (appertaining to rebels) free, that are able and willing to bear arms."[4] By specifying that he would welcome only slaves belonging to rebels, Dunmore may have hoped to maintain good relationships with Loyalists. Determined enslaved people ran from loyal, neutral, and rebel masters alike. Slaveholders possessed good reasons to be nervous, because Dunmore's Proclamation produced palpable results—though they were more visible in the long term. At first the proclamation offered self-liberated men only the freedom to die; in December 1775 the "Ethiopian regiment," as Dunmore called it, had suffered staggering losses at American hands.[5]

By his Excellency the Right Honourable JOHN Earl of DUNMORE, his Majesty's Lieutenant and Governour-General of the Colony and Dominion of Virginia, and Vice-Admiral of the same:

A PROCLAMATION.

AS I have ever entertained Hopes that an Accommodation might have taken Place between *Great Britain* and this Colony, without being compelled, by my Duty, to this most disagreeable, but now absolutely necessary Step, rendered so by a Body of armed Men, unlawfully assembled, firing on his Majesty's Tenders, and the Formation of an Army, and that Army now on their March to attack his Majesty's Troops, and destroy the well-disposed Subjects of this Colony: To defeat such treasonable Purposes, and that all such Traitors, and their Abetters, may be brought to Justice, and that the Peace and good Order of this Colony may be again restored, which the ordinary Course of the civil Law is unable to effect, I have thought fit to issue this my Proclamation, hereby declaring, that until the aforesaid good Purposes can be obtained, I do, in Virtue of the Power and Authority to me given, by his Majesty, determine to execute martial Law, and cause the same to be executed throughout this Colony; and to the End that Peace and good Order may the sooner be restored, I do require every Person capable of bearing Arms to resort to his Majesty's S T A N-DARD, or be looked upon as Traitors to his Majesty's Crown and Government, and thereby become liable to the Penalty the Law inflicts upon such Offences, such as Forfeiture of Life, Confiscation of Lands, &c. &c. And I do hereby farther declare all indented Servants, Negroes, or others (appertaining to Rebels) free, that are able and willing to bear Arms, they joining his Majesty's Troops, as soon as may be, for the more speedily reducing this Colony to a proper Sense of their Duty, to his Majesty's Crown and Dignity. I do farther order, and require, all his Majesty's liege Subjects to retain their Quitrents, or any other Taxes due, or that may become due, in their own Custody, till such Time as Peace may be again restored to this at present most unhappy Country, or demanded of them for their former salutary Purposes, by Officers properly authorised to receive the same.

GIVEN under my Hand, on Board the Ship William, *off* Norfolk, *the* 7th *Day of* November, *in the* 16th *Year of his Majesty's Reign.*

D U N M O R E.

G O D   SAVE   THE   K I N G.

"By his Excellency the Right Honourable John Earl of Dunmore, his Majesty's Lieutenant and Governour-General of the Colony and Dominion of Virginia, and Vice-admiral of the same. A proclamation," 7 November 1775. Courtesy of *American Memory*, the Library of Congress.

Following additional efforts to recruit them, enslaved people ran to the British in unprecedented numbers, and they ran farther and farther afield. By 1777 Virginia planter Robert Carter estimated that fifteen hundred bondpeople had "availed themselves" of Dunmore's offer. In April 1778 the British in Boston contemplated raising a regiment to welcome runaways. At the Siege of Savannah in 1779, armed slaves "did wonders in the working way and in the fighting." Henry Clinton's 1779 Philipsburg Proclamation promised "full Security" and "any Occupation which he shall think proper" to "every Negroe who shall desert the Rebel Standard." Not all of these efforts worked to Britain's advantage; Clinton's decision in particular pushed otherwise loyal white inhabitants into supporting the rebels. Estimates of the number of former slaves who ultimately joined the British cause range from fifteen thousand to twenty thousand. Almost a fourth of the pre-Revolutionary slave population migrated out of South Carolina and Georgia. Men and women also ran from Maryland, North Carolina, and Virginia.[6]

Dunmore's Proclamation damaged good relations with colonists, but the announcement also altered how Britons and southern colonists thought about food and hunger in two significant ways. Slaves ran, and took refuge onboard British ships. Only after British naval officers ignored colonists' protests about runaways and continued to harbor escapees did colonists stop supplying provisions, thus curtailing the ease with which British ships and sailors traveled along rivers and coasts. First, therefore, the proclamation led to colonial leaders' refusal to victual British ships, which in turn prompted British naval leaders to interpret withholding food and setting high prices as acts of war. Second, Dunmore's Proclamation underscored the crucial role slaves played in the southern food system. White rebel colonists, who were relatively useless at producing food without enslaved labor, conflated voluntary flight with "thefts" of their animals and stored provisions because these episodes threatened food security.

Word of Dunmore's Proclamation travelled quickly. In December 1775 the South Carolina Council of Safety resolved that if British leaders "continue[d] to receive and detain slaves," they would order that the supplies of provisions for the British navy "be discontinued." Mid-December, Henry Laurens, acting as president of the council, revealed to the captain of the British ship the *Tamar* that South Carolinians saw "less reason . . . for supplying provisions at this time" because of the "robberies and depredations committed" by "white and black armed men, from on board some of the ships under your command." The decision to shelter runaways encouraged former slaves to plunder southern colonists' plantations. Colonists were outraged. The Council of Safety resolved that because the British persisted in sheltering runaway slaves, the colony was justified in its decision "to cut off all communication" with the British. In January 1776 the *Cherokee* joined the *Tamar*, the *Raven*, the *Syren*, and an unnamed vessel called a sandwich packet, and the ships sailed from South Carolina to Georgia in search of foodstuffs. "Since the practice of harbouring & protecting our Negroes on board the Cherokee," wrote Henry Laurens, "we have refused to Supply them." He expected that the British were bound for Georgia "to obtain provisions of Bread."[7] It was a victory of mixed emotions for South Carolina rebels. They had forced the British to move elsewhere—but also facilitated former slaves' passage on the departing ships.

By the end of the month the British were interpreting the provisioning issue as an act of revolt. Andrew Barclay, the commodore of those ships, decreed that inhabitants who refused "to Supply provisions or attempt an hostile defence" would "be deemed & treated as Rebels." He equated fighting with not provisioning his men; the choice to withhold food had in this context become a declaration of war. Barclay warned Governor Wright of Savannah "That if they coud not be Supplyd with provisions" they would "if in their power attack" Savannah and "destroy it." Wright was probably willing to allow the British into Savannah; he remained loyal to Great Britain, and in March he would attack the port with Barclay's assistance. In January, however, Georgian inhabitants had forced Wright to flee the colony, so even had he wished to do so, Wright could not stop inhabitants from controlling the food supply. In February it became clear that colonists had begun to rethink their responsibility to prevent imperial officials' hunger during a time of tension between colony and metropole. That month Barclay wrote to Wright and angrily complained that anyone residing in "his Majesty's Dominions" should be able to obtain provisions at "the Market Price."[8]

At first it was unclear whether the colonists' refusal to provision British ships or sell food at lower prices actually constituted rebellion. In times of peace some governments may have let civilians decide local prices, but during previous periods of war and famine governments had intervened to fix prices to prevent hunger. During the Revolutionary War, the rebel government struggled to regulate civilian food prices. June 1777 witnessed "a considerable number" of North Carolina merchants making "it their business To deny up all the necessaries of life in order to fix what price they please." "If we were as virtuous as we ought to be," commented Henry Laurens's son, John, in 1778, "those who are enriching themselves by Commerce, Privateering and Farming" would instead want to supply the army "with every necessary and convenience at a moderate rate." His father received a letter that begged him "to put a Stop to the practices of those miscreants the Monopolizers of Food."[9]

Even during the war, when the rebels could not regulate their own prices, they did not accuse these monopolists of rebelling against them.

The question of military purveyance further complicated matters. By the late medieval period, English subjects came to accept that the crown had the right to seize goods and services without paying for them immediately; legislation existed to regulate this practice, but it existed to discourage corruption and ensure timely compensation, not to clarify when seizures were allowable. Military theorist Emer de Vattel said that a nation in want of provisions could compel its neighbors to provide them at a fair price, or that it could take them by force. Neutral nations were not supposed to deprive one nation something provided to another nation. Vattel also wrote that a nation had "no obligation to furnish an ally" with provisions when the first nation required them for its own purposes, and he argued that the nation that was asked for corn could refuse to supply it if so doing would exacerbate its own food shortages.[10] When British ships began welcoming escaped slaves aboard in late 1775 and early 1776, the colonies had not yet declared war on Britain, so it was unclear whether ship captains had the authority to demand certain prices, and unclear whether the law of nations required colonists to provision British ships. Americans who still identified as British subjects could point to their own provisions scarcities to avoid feeding the British navy, or they could imply that Britain was a hostile foreign power whom they were not obligated to supply.

In 1776, the Model Treaty, which John Adams helped to draft, stated that if one party was at war and another party was neutral, the neutral party could trade with the enemies of the party at war, as long as the items traded were noncontraband items (food stores were characterized as noncontraband items; enslaved peoples themselves *would* be deemed contraband, but not until the Civil War in the mid-nineteenth century). Noncontraband items on neutral vessels could not be seized, but such items on vessels belonging to nations at war *could* be.[11] This rationalization adjusted expectations again, making it justifiable for both British and American sailors to seize foodstuffs from each other's ships. Ultimately, rebel politicians chose to suggest that because British officials did not run the colonial government, the Patriots had little motivation to set prices fair enough to prevent British hunger—thereby redefining who was responsible for dealing with it.

As British officials in North America continued to welcome former bondpeople into their ranks, rebel colonists took violent steps to try to stop them, warning that slaves who ran would suffer whipping, transportation out of the colonies, or execution. In July 1775 North Carolinians moved to appoint patrollers to search for people away "from their masters Lands without a pass," and gave these patrollers the power to administer "thirty nine lashes or less if they think proper." An enslaved person "found with any fier arms or aminition in his or her possession," and who did not "willingly surrender their arms," was liable to be shot.[12] Some of these regulations merely continued longstanding practices from the colonial period—but after Dunmore's Proclamation, bondpeople with guns, colonists reasoned, could have received them from the British.

In December 1775 the Virginia Committee of Safety decreed that any slave found "in arms against this colony, or in the possession of an enemy, through their own choice" would suffer transportation "to any of the foreign *West India* islands." Later that month, an act of the General Assembly proclaimed "that all Negro or other slaves, conspiring to rebel or make insurrection, shall suffer death, and be excluded all benefit of clergy."[13] As time went on, Virginians, Carolinians, and other southern colonists instituted more and more strident punishments to deter those eyeing the chance at freedom with the British. These punishments reveal a number of fears: that enslaved people would obtain guns, commit violence, or flee.

As it became clear that assaults on slave labor threatened food production, Britons and colonists started to have trouble separating thefts of slaves from other forms of victual warfare, such as thefts of cattle and horses. Bondpeople who fled forced southern slaveholders to wait on themselves, to grow their own crops, and to cook their own meals. Some slaveholders would have been more helpless than others; Lowcountry slavers did not regulate labor beyond allocating the daily tasks of black men's and women's work and thus may have possessed little knowledge about day-to-day rice production. Chesapeake masters worked more closely with enslaved farm laborers and may have been able to manage on their own.[14]

In October 1777 Georgians' "Domestics" ran to the British while "Their Scouts & Indians . . . carry off our Stock." When South Carolinian and future governor Arnoldus Vanderhorst reported his damages in the wake of a British attack, he recorded "Stock of Cattle sheep Hogs Horses" and "30 Negroes 2/3 grown." He valued the animals at £2,000 and the enslaved children and adults at £1,200. Vanderhorst's claim reveals that some adults fled alongside children and teenagers; these may have been families on the run. Resident Paul Trapier also lost "10 young Negroe men." Immediately after listing these runaways, he described losing "Almost the whole produce of . . . Rice, Corn, Oates &ca" as well as "Cattle & sheep" and other "Cattle, Hogs & Goats."[15] Slaveholders' claims listed various horses, cattle, and bondpeople missing, in addition to bushels of corn burned, liquor stolen, and buildings destroyed. "Thefts" of slaves resulted in further losses of crops, because no enslaved people remained to grow them, and in losses of animals, because no one remained to guard them.

Documents relating to Indian affairs make clear that British-allied Creeks and Cherokees were heavily involved in "stealing" enslaved people (as the Americans might have called it) or encouraging them to run away (as the British likely understood it). These associations between Indians and formerly enslaved peoples worried American rebels who had spent much of the eighteenth century trying to foster antipathy between Natives and slaves—often by employing Indians to catch runaway bondpeople and using enslaved people to defend against Indian attacks. In 1776, for example, the South Carolina Council of Safety asked Catawba Indians to scout for runaways in the parishes of St. George, Dorchester, St. Paul, and St. Bartholomew. In March, South Carolinian Stephen Bull opined that runaway slaves "had better be shot by the Creek Indians, as it . . . will establish a hatred or Aversion between the Indians and Negroes." Self-liberated men and women defied colonists' attempts to encourage hostility and banded together with Indians during the Revolutionary War. In August 1776 British and unidentified British-allied southern Natives made "alarming incursions into Georgia, carr[ying] off a considerable number of Negroes and not less than two thousand head of cattle."[16] Many of these bondpeople likely *chose* to ally with the Indians.

British-allied Indians, by facilitating escapes for people whom rebels considered their property, attacked colonists' day-to-day existence while adding to their own possessions of enslaved people and domesticated animals. Bondpeople likely ran not only because a chance at freedom was more attractive than slavery, but also because there is evidence indicating that Indian slavery offered more autonomy than being a bondperson in a white British colony. David George, a man who eventually made his way to the British lines, was first enslaved during the colonial period before he ran away to Creek country. He was a captive among the Creeks, where he labored as if he were a Creek woman. "I made fences, dug the ground, planted corn, and worked hard," he recalled, "but the people were kind to me." When his white master's son came to reenslave him, George ran. A 1790s account related that in Creek villages on the Flint River, black Creek men owned cattle—sometimes as many as one hundred—and made butter and cheese from cows. Enslaved people in Creek country paid only a small portion of their crops to Indian masters and kept the rest as property to eat or sell. In helping Indians by farming and stealing animals, bondpeople made themselves useful, creating a space for themselves in Native communities. Other black men and women who ran to the Creek nation won freedom for their children, who became property holders of significant stock as well as dairy producers.[17]

As the war continued, and runaway slaves threatened the food system with their physical absence, southerners took steps to protect their access to foodstuffs. North Carolina placed an embargo on "all Beef Pork Bacon & Common salt" leaving the state in April 1778, excepting supplies sent to the Continental Army or North Carolinian troops. South Carolina placed an embargo on provisions, including rice, in June 1778, extended it in October, and continued it until January 1779. In 1780 a broadside in Thomas Jefferson's name informed Albemarle, Virginia, residents of a "specific tax" that obliged them to provide "a supply of provisions, and other necessaries for the use of the army." Jefferson, channeling Vattel, reminded people of the "compulsions of the law" requiring them to provide salted meat and other items, though he also tried to be persuasive by mentioning that "the prices offered are generous." But Jefferson was in for disappointment; Horatio Gates wrote to him, wishing he "could say the Supplies from Virginia" had arrived, but in fact both Virginia and North Carolina were guilty of "unpardonable Neglect." They had sent nothing, and Gates urged that "Flour, Rum, and Droves of Bullocks, should without Delay be forwarded to this Army or the Southern Department will soon want one to defend it."[18] To be sure, some southern colonists likely managed well during the war, and their failure to send provisions to the army suggests that perhaps their hunger was overexaggerated. Some rebels who refused to provision the Continental Army were keeping some of their produce for themselves—but others were reckoning with food shortages.

It is clear that rebel Americans feared the flight of enslaved peoples from their plantations, even trying to bribe bondpeople to convince them not to run. Before the Revolution, enslaved peoples' diets were unhealthy and unchanging. Most men and women received a pound of salted fish, preserved beef, or preserved pork, and a pint of cornmeal or rice per day. Sometimes, however, men and women chose to remain in bondage when they could readily obtain meagre sustenance and good treatment. Samuel Massey, a literate man enslaved by Henry Laurens, wrote to Laurens to tell him that his slaves at one plantation "can hardly be purswaided to Stay." At another plantation called Mepkin, however, people were "all for Staying at home as Both your field and thear oan are in a flurishing way." Bondpeople sometimes lingered where their gardens and fields yielded produce, but they were motivated by more complicated desires as well. When Henry Laurens's informers described the connection between hunger prevention and enslaved peoples' willingness to stay put, they also revealed the other factors at play. Samuel Massey admitted that although the slaves at one plantation enjoyed plentiful crops, "the negroes does not want to Stay with mr camel."[19] Slaves who disliked a particular overseer may have wanted to run, even if their supplies of provisions seemed secure. Hunger prevention, in other words, was not always the top priority for bondpeople.

In other instances slaveholders tried to retain bondpeople merely by prom-ising them future sustenance. In July 1776, after a British ship appeared on the Potomac River, Robert Carter went to his Cole's Point plantation and called a meeting. First, he warned the enslaved people there that Dunmore was un-trustworthy and planned to reenslave and sell those who ran. He likely pres-sured them into admitting, "We do not wish to enter into Ld D's Service . . . but we all fully intend to serve you our master." After hearing such pleasing declarations of allegiance, Carter told them that if any of Dunmore's men landed on Cole's Point, the men should take their "wives, Children, male & female Acquaintances, beding & tools, removing all into private places . . . and send a person off to Nomony Hall . . . to advise me at wt Place ye are gotten too." If they served him well in this regard, he would "give Directions, tend-ing for [their] imediate relief."[20] Carter urged these men and women to hide and to secure valuable farm tools, and in return he promised to send them enough to survive.

None of them deserted him, for the moment. Carter attempted to use sup-plies (which must have included food) as a bargaining tool. Only if his slaves apprised him of their whereabouts would he send them "relief." Robert Car-ter's promise, however, belied his weak position. If people ran, they would of course take food with them. And depart they did: thirty-two men and women in total when the British came close enough to Carter's plantation. Landon Carter, Robert's father, was similarly unlucky; eight bondpeople liberated themselves from his plantation, a fact that Landon chronicled in his diary with no small degree of venom.[21]

Some of the enslaved chose to remain on plantations, not because masters fed them well but rather because the location offered opportunities. Some who stayed stole food from absentee or distracted masters. Obviously, historians know more about what happened to those whom authorities caught. One Sa-vannah slave named March was detected stealing rice. The "desperate fel-low," according to Henry Laurens's friend, John Lewis Gervais, "Cut off his left hand above the Thumb" before threatening an overseer with a knife. It is difficult to say why March maimed himself. Perhaps he hoped to avoid being sold, or maybe by "punishing" himself he sought to preclude further reprisals from whites. The *Virginia Gazette* reported that one slave, who was "tried and found guilty of sheep-stealing," was "sentenced to be burnt in the hand." Branding a slave in the hand was permissible in lieu of execution if the per-son accused could recite a Bible verse, thus claiming benefit of clergy.[22] Per-haps March preferred a quick self-amputation to the prolonged burn of branding. Thus, at times, enslaved peoples lingered on plantations and stole to prevent hunger, and at other times adequate food supplies were not enough to compete with the powerful lure of freedom among the British.

In the face of mounting runaways, American rebels acknowledged the strategic value of adding enslaved peoples to their own military units. African American veterans, in their postwar pension records, recalled serving with the Patriots most frequently in the Battles of Monmouth, Stony Point, and Yorktown. Typical black soldiers served with the infantry as privates, and sometimes without arms. About 250 slaves bet their lives on the chance for freedom and joined Rhode Island's black battalion. Connecticut, too, formed an all-black company, the Second Company of the Fourth Regiment. Massachusetts and New Hampshire also sent slaves to war. For the most part, slaves serving in the American military worked in mixed regiments throughout the northern states, and sometimes in tandem with Indians, as they did in Rhode Island and Connecticut.[23]

The inclusion of black regiments rose and fell with the tides of war. Immediately after Lexington and Concord, the Americans began to accept slaves into military units, but by early 1776 state militias passed acts that excluded blacks, mulattoes, and Indians. By the end of that year, however, Dunmore's Proclamation had forced Americans to reconsider. By early 1777, even the southern states were partially amenable: Virginians recruited free blacks, and many enslaved people passed themselves off as free in order to join. In 1778 John Laurens proposed taking some of his father's "able bodied slaves" to form a group he conceived of romantically as "defenders of liberty." Henry Laurens, himself a prominent slaveholder, initially refused his request, but John Lewis Gervais proposed a similar slave regiment. John Mathews, governor of South Carolina, followed suit with a similar plan in 1782; at least a few white men took the notion seriously.[24]

The forward-thinking enthusiasm of slaveholders in the southern states should not be overstated. Laurens made public his son's proposal, but the Continental Congress rejected the plan in 1779. Rather than recruit black men, South Carolina considered bribing potential white enlistees with the promise of giving them one enslaved person (who would be enslaved for life) for each year of the white man's service, and offering a bondperson to anyone who could "procure Twenty Five Recruits to Inlist."[25] Americans' adoption of slaves as soldiers occurred piecemeal when it happened at all. British numbers were higher because Dunmore acted sooner.

Dunmore's Proclamation created a world of people on the move. George Galphin, who had taught the Patriots how best to cultivate Creek interests and was labelled "an Antiloyalist" for his efforts, fled his Silver Bluff Plantation when the British approached Savannah. David George, whom Galphin had en-

slaved, chose that moment to strike out for British lines.[26] Dunmore's offer of
freedom was important because it encouraged behavior that bestowed power.
American rebels failed to separate thefts of and by slaves from thefts of animals and grain. Their anger pushed them to withhold food from British ships,
which prompted the British to include American food deprivation and price
fixing in their concept of acts of war—which in turn expands this book's definition of eighteenth-century victual warfare.

By early 1776, victual warfare included not merely the destruction or theft
of foodstuffs but also the refusal of purveyance, even to a military entity not
yet officially at war with the colonies. The proclamation made colonists more
aware of their own hunger when slaves ran, both because of a decline in food
production and as a result of increased acts of black victual warfare. It also
probably increased Americans' animosity toward Native Americans. These
changes, which paralleled the inclusion of slaves into the British and American militaries, foreshadowed further transformations in the southern food
system.

Before the Revolutionary War, enslaved people prepared meals for their own
families and for white masters. During the colonial period bondpeople were
part of a food system in which they enjoyed little say in their access to provisions. Their responsibilities for stealing food during the war gave them the leverage to help *shape* a food system of hunger creation and prevention. Before
the conflict many slaves traveled from big-house kitchens to southern colonists' tables to markets and to the open-air religious meetings where black
bondpeople worshipped. They could share news over several hundred miles
in a week or two.[27] During the war these travel networks expanded because
commanders expected the black soldiers in their militaries to absent themselves
for longer periods when obtaining provisions for troops. After Dunmore's
Proclamation, self-liberated slaves and free black people became victual warriors who traveled from forts to plantations to raid for food and create white
hunger among American rebels. Thereafter they also moved from camp to
camp to transport provisions and feed soldiers. Ex-bondpeople leveraged their
relationship with provisioning networks to become the butchers who wan-
dered along roads and to and from markets, the waggoneers with easy access
to extra flour, and the cooks and waiters who overheard valuable information.
As they transformed the food system, former bondpeople maintained an unpredictable relationship with their own hunger—alternately ignoring, dealing
with, and preventing it.

Once rebels and Britons incorporated black soldiers into their armies, they
needed to decide how to feed them. On the one hand, it could be said that

with the exception of some black soldiers' rations (such as those of the Black Pioneers—the escapees who formed small groups or companies, were assigned to British and provincial regiments, and then eventually relocated to Nova Scotia and Sierra Leone), provisions were inferior to those that white soldiers received. Dunmore reported possessing "four Ovens and pretty good Barracks for our Ethiopian Corps" in 1776. In 1778 when John Lewis Gervais proposed a black Patriot regiment, he suggested that the men could survive on one pound of meat and a quart of rice per day. In 1780 Henry Clinton decreed that "those Negroes who belong to Rebels . . . are to work in the Departments with adequate Pay, Provision, and Cloathing."[28]

As evidenced by this relatively late assertion from Clinton, people in charge rarely articulated a coherent strategy for feeding these men in the same way that they did for white soldiers (and eventually for Native Americans). Sometimes they continued to refer to black men as property (note Clinton's use of the term *belong*). Sometimes they figured out how to procure bread but not meat, and when they apportioned rations the meat component was sometimes the same as that provided to white soldiers, but the rations contained no bread, no flour, no alcohol, and less starch than a white soldier's ration. Black refugees serving in the army found their own food and built their own shelters. Charles Cornwallis's orderly book shows that freed bondpeople in the southern campaign received peas instead of flour, which, like rice, proved harder to cook without camp kettles; two such kettle shortages occurred in 1779. Although the writing in Cornwallis's orderly book is at times disorderly, readers can see, scrawled between general orders, an admission that "Grat abusses" were observed "in vitling the Nigroas."[29]

On the other hand, it could also be said that black participants' rations improved over time, *and* that in some instances the men in charge went out of their way to feed black soldiers. British observers might have perceived former slaves as useless mouths—similar to the way they characterized Indians—when in fact the former slaves' relationships with food and hunger underscored ineffable power dynamics. The Black Pioneers from South Carolina and Georgia received weekly rations and were entitled to shares of plunder taken from rebels, even during the campaigns when they were not paid or provided with provisions. White Loyalists found these rights difficult to accept. In 1779 British brigadier general Augustine Prévost in Savannah felt "obliged to victual almost all of the Loyal Inhabitants and many Negroes," even though the cost "bore hard upon our Provisions," given the fact that food stores for the troops stood in a state of "urgent distress."[30] This report appeared during the same time that Indian affairs were in confusion, in the south because of John Stuart's death, and in the north because of the Iroquois refugee crisis—so it is worth pausing to emphasize the significance of British provisioning in this instance.

Former slaves were responsible for obtaining food for the army. Early in the war, bands of Dunmore's followers—called "Dunmore's banditti"—descended on the plantations of former masters, carrying off livestock and crops. News of these raids broke about a month before Henry Laurens made the decision to stop supplying British ships with provisions, so Americans likely associated provisions shortages with black soldiers' raids. Many of the raiders' names are unrecorded, but some are known. Titus, who was enslaved by a man named John Corlies, ran to Dunmore in 1775, and though he died before the end of the war, in 1778 he became known as Colonel Tye, leading other victual warriors in New Jersey as they searched for food and other necessaries. Augustine Prévost, in his 1779 proposal for the Black Pioneers' responsibilities, made contradictory comments about the usefulness of these men. He wrote that during the Siege of Savannah they had been armed and "very usefull" in "the working way and in the fighting." He also described them as "an useless burthen upon us or plundering the country."[31] He characterized black soldiers as useful during the siege when they were working *and* when they were fighting, but after this event he associated only their violent labor with utility.

Perhaps some Britons, in their decision to harbor and provision former slaves, were driven by an early form of humanitarianism. Maybe some thought them uniformly useless. It seems clear that some observers alternated between perceptions of escaped slaves as useless and views of them as useful to the army's strategy, particularly when their raiding proved tactically valuable for the psychological and physical challenges it posed to the Patriots.

Black men and women also appear in the records procuring and preparing foodstuffs through nonviolent means. Women worked as cooks, laundresses, and maids, and men cooked, foraged for food, and waited on officers in army camps. Shadrack Furman offered provisions to the British. William Allen, aged twenty-three, a "Stout Man" bound for Halifax in 1783, cooked for them on board the *Nancy*. After David George made his way to Savannah, he and his wife Phillis took turns supporting their family. Phillis George took in washing for General Henry Clinton, and "out of the little she got maintained" them. Together they raised corn with their compatriot, George Liele, who traveled between the Piedmont and the Lowcountry. After the siege of Savannah, when David George caught smallpox and told his wife to leave him to die, she listened.[32]

He recovered, they reunited, and using money from the sale of a steer that his wife's part-Indian brother had gifted them, he began buying and butchering meat for the British. He was able to move again after borrowing money "from some of the Black people to buy hogs," which he killed and sold to the British to broker safe passage for the family to Charleston. David and Phillis George, like the unnamed families on Robert Carter's plantation and in Arnoldus Vanderhorst's claim, separated, worked together, and drew on larger networks with Native Americans to ensure their family's survival during the war.[33]

British-allied men were not the only ones to obtain provisions. Boyrereau Brinch (sometimes called Jeffrey Brace or Jeffrey Stiles) detailed his kidnapping in Mali in the 1750s, his enslavement in America, and his Revolutionary War service to the Patriots. He remembered "plundering" a British store before the evacuation of New York and coming away with "seven loads of excellent Provisions." He also managed to steal a Tory farmer's hog. Johnson Green, who served the Americans in the northern campaign, recalled stealing butter, cheese, and chocolate near West Point, New York, in 1781. Charles Grandison cooked for the Americans, and Levi Burns and James Coopers waited on American officers and served them food. Scipio Handley sold fish in Charlestown.[34]

Throughout the conflict, escaped slaves did what they could to fill their bellies. By late 1775 there were approximately five hundred black runaways living on Sullivan's Island, South Carolina, where they supplied themselves with crops and stolen cattle. In December Colonel William Moultrie planned "a Secret Expedition" against the island with a detachment of 150 men. Moultrie instructed the major in command to seize everyone, set fire to their buildings, and drive off or destroy all the livestock. The expedition took place later in December. Afterward, Henry Laurens reported "such a check . . . as will serve to humble our negroes in general." Soldiers "burnt the house in which the banditti were often lodged, brought off four negroes, killed three or four, and also . . . destroyed many things which had been useful to the wretches in the house." Despite the obvious risks, runaways created temporary communities where they could gather together and supply themselves.[35]

Black soldiers also found ways to keep themselves from going hungry while serving in the British army. Some of these men in Virginia and North Carolina were responsible for loading wagons and shelling corn. In 1781 British commissaries observed that "by the Carelessness and little Pilferings of Conductors, Waggoners, &c," "about 600 gallons of Spirits and 7000 Pounds Weight of Flour were lost at different Times."[36] Although they made the connection between the fact that black men loaded wagons and the fact that foodstuffs loaded onto wagons were likely to disappear, there seems to have been little effort to punish these laborers for stealing. In a world where soldiers lived a few delayed provisions shipments from starving, it seems reasonable to assume that black soldiers took advantage of lapses in surveillance to help themselves to extra provisions, just as white soldiers did during their service.

The rebel army seemed less tolerant of black thievery, whether undertaken to avoid hunger or for other reasons. When Johnson Green stole, he explained, "I only was detected . . . and punished by receiving one hundred stripes." Green was eventually executed in 1786 after embarking on a post-Revolutionary bender during which he reported taking no less than "near a bushel of meal," "three or four dozen herrings," "two cheeses," "thirty weight of salt pork" (and another twenty or thirty pounds in two other instances), "a quarter of mutton," and "one case-bottle of rum."[37] It is unclear whether Green became such an avid thief because he was hungry, or because he enjoyed the subversiveness of stealing so much.

Quests for food, illicit or otherwise, enabled former bondpeople and free black men and women to pick up key bits of intelligence. British-allied Mohawks captured Charles Grandison near Montreal in September 1779. Grandison stated that he was free and had lived with an American rebel named Colonel Warner as his cook. Although "every thing was kept a secret from the Men" in camp, Grandison related that "he heard the Officers talk over at Table" and was thus privy to their plans. By explaining that he was a cook who also waited tables, Grandison could reasonably claim to possess privileged knowledge. Loyalists in the mid-Hudson Valley in 1777 knew enough about black information networks to warn fellow Loyalists that they should hold their tongues while around "Blacks in the Kitchen."[38]

Perhaps the men to whom Grandison spoke remembered previous meals, during which they too had blabbed while waiters brought food to the table. Whereas middling white soldiers ate their meals crouched outside of tents and around campfires, Charles Grandison ventured into officers' tents and overheard their mealtime conversations. Black cooks and table waiters could use their invisibility to consume and then circulate news. Grandison's information garnered credibility because the British were already aware of American John Sullivan's punitive 1779 campaign against the Iroquois. His report on Sullivan's expedition "against the Indians" established his credibility, which made believable his warning about "an Expedition intended this Winter against Canada." Daniel Claus, the British Indian agent who examined him, concluded that he was "most Intelligent."[39] The word conveyed a double meaning in this instance: Grandison was smart, but he also used his wits to convey actual intelligence to those who mattered. Given the hunger that the 1779 campaign created in Iroquoia, the British would likely have welcomed advance warning—or confirmation—of any additional attack. Black allies' mobility as waiters, conveyors of food to the troops, and buskers at various markets allowed them to travel through friendly and enemy territory with ears and eyes usefully open.

After the War for Independence some escapees remained unaffiliated victual warriors. In 1787 South Carolinians and Georgians found themselves inundated by attacks from a group of escaped slaves—or "the daring banditti," as one brigadier general called them—who ensconced themselves on an island on the Savannah River. The raiders had been known to "carry off whole stacks of rice at a time" from Georgia and South Carolina. Southerners worried about "The free booty they reap" as well as the fact that "their numbers" were "daily increasing." This was an extralegal community of hunger preventers, perhaps even extant since the war. Because the possibility of such a lawless body was too terrifying for any southerner to imagine, Georgia and South Carolina acted quickly to stamp out the black settlement once they learned about it. An early May expedition comprised of whites and Catawba Indians "left six of their head men, dead on the ground." The expedition wounded several others and removed all "Their baggage & provisions."[40] For self-liberated men and women—as for Native Americans—the War for Independence continued beyond its formal conclusion in 1783. The journey from bondpeople to formerly enslaved men and women to hunger-preventing and hunger-creating victual warriors had taken nearly a decade.

When Dunmore's 1775 proclamation enticed enslaved peoples away from plantations, colonists interpreted British actions as a two-pronged assault on the established colonial food system: one strike that deprived colonists of producers, and another that made those formerly enslaved producers into food destroyers. Both aspects created white rebel hunger while offering strategies for the British to better supply themselves. Ultimately, it was this attack on American slavery that prompted the colonists to withhold food from British ships and that helped tip the balance toward war. Rebels refused to supply the British with provisions after Dunmore's proclamation not simply because they were angry but also because the proclamation was something they viewed as an act of victual warfare. The British, in turn, examined the Americans' decisions to charge high prices for food and then withhold it, and called these choices acts of war, perhaps because contemporary theorists such as Vattel could not help observers clarify the foreign-policy relationship between colonists and Britons.

Black soldiers who survived on irregular rations, butchers who needed to obtain hogs, waggoneers who transported provisions, and black waiters in camp tents shared something: they were real people with families whose presence in the archival record shows them traveling between and beyond liminal spaces. During the American Revolution useful black food networks encouraged the growth of parallel information networks. Former bondpeople depended on black and Native communities to obtain food and information, and pursued roles that retained and strengthened those connections. They received provisions in return for their service, but so too did they obtain, produce, prepare, and do without various types of foodstuffs.

Black soldiers, like Iroquois, Cherokee, and Creek Indians, attacked white farms and plantations and stole food for the British. Unlike Indians, however, black men and women may not have had to use hunger for protest because during much of the war they could provision themselves. Sometimes former slaves benefitted when Britons went out of their way to feed them, and sometimes they ate poorer provisions than white combatants. Useful black mouths helped hungry British soldiers to stave off starvation. Although Americans may have watched for escaped slaves so that they could capture them, black victual warriors became adept at obtaining provisions while avoiding reenslavement.

There is also evidence suggesting that black hunger, like Indian hunger, was different from white soldiers' hunger—at times black hunger did not matter. When South Carolina–born Boston King heard of a "dreadful rumour" from New York stating "that all the slaves, in number 2000, were to be delivered up to their masters" in light of the peace between Britain and the United States in 1783, he could not have eaten even had he wanted to. "We lost our appetite for food," he remembered, "and sleep departed from our eyes."[41] Black soldiers avoided hunger through labor, theft, or migration, but they also at times placed hunger prevention much lower on their scale of human requirements. They were not yet capable of fighting for a coherent, formal, legal food system to prevent hunger; that would come later, at the end of the Revolution, when the vicissitudes of war took them far away from the original thirteen colonies.

In April 1783 Frederick Haldimand wrote that the United States and Great Britain had agreed to the terms of peace that would cause Boston King so much distress. Haldimand was also worried, because of the rumor that the Indians "are not considered in the treaty." Ex-slaves, it turned out, *would* be considered, but for the moment the British worried more about their Native American allies. One brigadier general understood the implications almost instantly. When he wrote to Haldimand after seeing the peace terms, he predicted, "the Indians will be outrageous." Officials in the new United States assumed that they had won a transfer of all lands stretching to the Mississippi River—lands occupied and claimed by British-allied Natives who were unlikely to recognize such a cession.[42] Such land transfers were complicated. The transfer of food diplomacy from the British to the Americans occurred only haphazardly, when it happened at all. In the 1780s and 1790s, Americans would have to negotiate with Indians. They had their work cut out for them as they set about trying to prevent useful mouths from becoming hungry, vengeful enemies.

CHAPTER 5

Fighting Hunger, Fearing Violence
after the Revolutionary War

In 1792 James Seagrove, a U.S. commissioner of Indian Affairs, described conditions in Creek country: "The great drought which hath been all this Summer with the Creek nation & also the upper part of this Country, makes a famine much dreaded. I find I shall be obliged to give those Indians Corn to carry home with them to prevent their families from starving." Seagrove warned that "unless assistance is given by the United States in this way . . . many of the unfortunate people of the Creek nation must perish as their crops of Corn are nearly destroyed." He wondered "whether it would not be policy as well as great humanity in our Government to send a supply of Corn from the Northward. . . . It cannot be had in Georgia at any price." Seagrove was writing to the secretary of war, and he stressed the immediate relevance of potential armed conflict. "Should a change of affairs make it necessary to assemble a force on this frontier (at this time) they must be fed from some other country than Georgia."[1]

Seagrove was paranoid and perhaps uninformed. He said that drought had demolished Creek corn, and the separate "country" of Georgia was unable or unwilling to assist with a delivery of food aid. Seagrove slipped from discussing food relief into anticipating a frontier campaign, suggesting that he associated unfed Indians with violence. He described a drought, but he warned about a future famine rather than a current one. He made no mention of Indian food reserves, such as the Creek houses containing whole rooms for storing corn, potatoes, and other vegetables, in addition to nuts, dried grapes, and persimmons.[2] Creeks might have been on the brink of famine, but they might also have been metaphorically describing their hungriness to Seagrove. In any case, it is evident that Seagrove's *fears* of Indian starvation informed his assessment of Indian relations, which in turn influenced his opinions about best practices for federal policy. After the Revolutionary War, Native Americans increased their authority by working with the U.S. government to circumvent hunger. The federal government failed to win power because it cost so much to distribute food aid, and the government was not yet powerful enough to refuse to do so.

Postwar Indian country was a place of simultaneous resilience and desolation; although burned villages and scattered tribes provide plentiful evidence of disruption, there were numerous sites where Indian power waxed, at least until the mid-1790s.[3] Approaches to Indian affairs, which included food policy, varied from state to state and evolved in three separate regions in the 1780s and 1790s: the southern states of Georgia, North Carolina, South Carolina, and Virginia, the mid-Atlantic states of New York and Pennsylvania, and the old northwest region of the Ohio Valley. Food negotiations reveal similarities between federal and state approaches, but also demonstrate that it was the competition between the states and the federal government that by 1795 left Native Americans more willing to accommodate U.S. officials in a joint cooperative fight against hunger.

In the southern region, from the Battle of Yorktown until 1785, much remained the same: officials built their food diplomacy on promises of food and food metaphors, rather than the physical article, and continued to point to scorched Cherokee villages as threats when dealing with the Creeks. Southern Natives persisted in stealing animals and attacking state inhabitants. During the war American and British officials prevented each other from practicing diplomacy; after it, southern states interfered with each other instead. When, in 1785, the United States appointed its own Indian commissioners, southern officials and U.S. officials began to compete with each other for Native loyalties—often by trying to block each other's access to Indians.

Further north and northwest, the British undermined American negotiations with Indians—a tactic that did not last. By the 1790s, U.S. Indian agents had conducted enough research about protocol to know that feeding Indians depended on more than merely satisfying hunger. They used this new knowledge to replicate British diplomacy, and also tried and largely failed to curtail Native consumption and its costs. In the Ohio Valley region American food diplomacy failed among Western Confederacy Indians, though more as a result of British interference than because of American inepti-

Robert Sayer and John Bennett (Firm), "The United States of America with the British possessions of Canada, Nova Scotia, New Brunswick and Newfoundland divided with the French, also the Spanish territories of Louisiana and Florida, according to the preliminary articles of peace signed at Versailles the 20th of Jany. 1783" (London: Printed for Robert Sayer, 1783). Courtesy of the Library of Congress.

tude. Western Confederacy Natives' victual warfare evolved from a defensive strategy that involved the destruction of their own foodstuffs to an offensive strategy built on attacking American soldiers' food convoys. Non-Native officials learned the costs of waging a losing war against Indian enemies and the continuing effectiveness of scorched-earth campaigns. They discovered how to transition from generous distributions of foodstuffs at treaties to stinginess. They also began to take seriously the Native women—particularly Creek and Iroquois women—who appear in the archival records during these decades.

The overarching theme for the 1780s and 1790s is that of the unexpected: Native Americans refused or ruined provisions when non-Natives thought they needed them, and ate too much when officials tried to reduce food aid. These unanticipated reactions to hunger underscore the need to reassess contemporary claims about hungry Indians so that power relations can be described more accurately. Negotiations in the north show that supplying the Iroquois with food went beyond preventing starvation; diplomats had to practice proper etiquette and overfeed Indians too. Western Confederacy Indians destroyed rather than stole food, which emphasized their continuing ability to go without it. To some extent they could wreck American foodstuffs because they received provisions from the British, but it is crucial to note that the Indians who welcomed British beef, pork, and corn did not always welcome British advice. British food aid failed to give the British the degree of influence over Indians that they might have liked. Non-Native southerners' attempts to invoke white hunger to obtain Creek and Cherokee lands provoked a set of Indian responses that ranged from outbreaks of animal theft to accepting state officials' treaty hospitality while ignoring their demands for land.

The transfer of power from Britain to the United States was not smooth in the north. In 1783 British-allied Iroquois lived in three clusters: at Loyal Village, south of Fort Niagara, at Buffalo Creek, close to where Lake Erie met the Niagara River, and at Cattaraugus, near the bottom of the southeast tip of Lake Erie. Migrations were underway. The American-allied Oneidas who remained to the south of Oneida Lake gradually lost territory to land-hungry white inhabitants. Senecas remained in the Genesee Valley. In 1784 the British purchased 2,842,480 acres of land from Mississauga Indians. This territory ran "about Six Miles on each Side of the Grand River called Oswego." Mohawk Molly Brant's brother, Joseph Brant, tried to convince the Iroquois to unify at this waterway, but when he deferred to the clan matrons, they chose instead to split the Six Nations—Brant's Mohawk faction would reside on the British side of the Niagara boundary line, near Grand River, and the other half would live on the American side. The Treaty of Stanwix between some Iroquois and the United States, also in 1784, further divided the Six Nations by pleasing the Oneidas and angering Buffalo Creek Iroquois because it dispossessed them of their villages at Cattaraugus.[4]

The British, in violation of 1783 peace terms between Britain and the United States, maintained their forts in Upper Canada because Indians threatened bloodshed if the British surrendered them. British officials continued to cultivate Indian goodwill by providing meat, grain, and alcohol to satisfy commodity- and gift-exchange expectations. In July 1783 Frederick Haldimand, who had tried to reduce Iroquois eating after the Sullivan Campaign, received requests from his men for flour, pork, and butter supplies at Niagara, Carleton Island, and Detroit. These provisioners assumed they would "Continue to Victuall the Same Number of Troops and Indians we have done." At Niagara, some three thousand Indians collected rations each day in August. The Mohawks in Montreal received fresh meat (which they likely preferred) rather than salted because of "a Scarcity of Salt," and their "small Allowance of Rum" continued "as usual."[5]

Upon moving into Grand River in 1784, Brant asked the British to "assist them with a reasonable Quantity of Provisions." That same year Frederick Haldimand asked Brant to find out what American "Commissioners from Congress" were saying, and to "report the same to him." Brant provided the information in exchange for provisions, but he also procured food for his people by other means: by encouraging non-Natives—mostly Loyalists—to settle and farm at Grand River, where they paid Mohawks rent with the produce they raised.[6] Many Iroquois men and women in the 1780s thus prevented the tribe's hunger—as they had before the Revolutionary War—with rent paid to them in crops and garden produce, which they supplemented with British rations.

Britons frustrated would-be American diplomats by thwarting their attempts to negotiate with Indians. In August 1783, U.S. commissioners tried to reach the Iroquois, bringing boats "Loaded with Rum to trade at the Upper Posts" and documents granting passage from New York officials. British brigadier general Allan Maclean refused to grant them passage through Niagara and was pleased to report that one of "Our Indian friends," mistaking an Englishmen for one of the American commissioners, drunkenly asked him, "You damn Yankee what brought you here."[7] The rum was important in this instance because it might have been used to open meetings at the welcoming ceremonies that forest diplomacy required. Gifts of food and drink had long featured at such negotiations, but they nearly always *began* with a symbolic drink. Blocking American rum prevented the meeting from starting and made future encounters more difficult. Officers happily related instances when Indians critiqued Americans—even if they mistakenly identified their nationalities.

At the federal level U.S. Indian policy was one of conquest. At the 1784 Treaty of Stanwix—which bore little resemblance to its 1768 namesake—the Americans made it clear that they expected fealty, obedience, and land from the Iroquois. They confirmed Haldimand's worries about the 1783 peace treaty between Britain and the United States, observing that in that agreement, "no mention [was] made by the King of Great Britain of any Indian nation or tribe whatsoever."[8] "You are a subdued people," the Americans crowed. "You have been overcome in a war which you entered into with us, not only without provocation but in violation of the most sacred obligations." American commissioners at Fort McIntosh in 1785, similarly, told Chippewas, Delawares, Ottawas, and Wyandots, "we claim the Country by conquest, and are to *give* not to *receive.*"[9] These were rhetorical tricks. Because they had not considered themselves subjects of Great Britain, Indians disagreed that they shared the same fate of the country the Americans had defeated.

Fortunately for Native Americans, the early U.S. government lacked the organization to enforce this cant of conquest under the Articles of Confederation, which were ineffective in the realms of foreign and domestic policy. Congress did not establish a Department of Foreign Affairs until 1781, when it consisted of a secretary and four employees; the secretary could attend Congressional sessions but was barred from asking questions and proposing actions. The short-lived post gave way to the secretary of state, whose role expanded at a much slower pace than roles in other departments. The Articles made it tough for the federal government to levy domestic taxes, which left little in the way of funds for the presents and provisions of foreign treaties with Indians, and still less to pay soldiers to go to war against Native Americans. U.S. officials who wanted an advantage over individual states thought about both of these options, which remained important to agents like James Seagrove even after the Constitution replaced the Articles. The Articles prevailed until 1789 (1788 in New York). Without sufficient financial and military capabilities, the federal government had to backpedal on this position of transferred sovereignty by the mid-1780s.[10]

When politicians realized that they did not possess the leverage to make unequivocal demands, they tried to improve relations with Indians while the Articles of Confederation stood. In March 1785 Congress passed an act appointing United States Indian commissioners.[11] Federal politicians knew that they needed to prevent settler colonial and state landgrabs, and to counter the overtures from other imperial powers—the British among the Iroquois, and the Spanish and British among the Creeks and Cherokees.[12] The problem, however, was that state commissioners were bound to butt heads with U.S. agents as they competed for Indians' attention.

Under the Articles of Confederation, Congress's power to manage Indian relations covered only Indians who were not "members" of the thirteen extant states. State officials, who could expand their state's geography during boundary disputes with other states, stood to benefit. Native Americans would have laughed at the idea of belonging to a state—it would have been more accurate to say that states belonged in Indian country—but the states nevertheless asserted authority over the federal government in their dealings with

Indians because they assumed that direct dealings with Indians would yield more favorable land cessions. Some made more effective efforts than others to establish good relations. New York governor George Clinton studied the treaty diplomacy of opening ceremonies, speeches, wampum use, private conferences, and presents to ingratiate his state with the Iroquois. New York's congressmen claimed the Six Nations as their own and tried to interfere with treaty negotiations from Stanwix onward. In 1785, the Seneca Cornplanter moved his faction away from Buffalo Creek to two villages near the western portion of the New York-Pennsylvania border. When the national capital moved to Philadelphia in late 1790, Cornplanter's followers enjoyed better access to federal Indian officials.[13]

State and federal policies evolved against a backdrop of environmental changes. Crops failed in Connecticut, Massachusetts, New Hampshire, New York, Pennsylvania, Vermont, and the area in present-day Canada from Niagara to Quebec and into the Maritimes in 1782, 1784, 1787, 1788, and 1789. Drought and crop failures in 1785, 1789, 1791, 1792, and 1794 also pervade the sources on Cherokees and Creeks. At times Iroquois clan mothers pressured other Indians into ceding land because they wanted "peace and food relief, which hinged upon the state's goodwill," as they did in 1785 at Fort Herkimer. The 1789 crop failures resulted from the return of the Hessian fly in 1788, which destroyed the wheat harvest. Shortages became evident after a cold 1789 spring and worsened after rumors sparked a surge in grain prices. Native Americans had delayed their planting that year because relations with non-Natives were so bad that they feared a repeat of the 1779 campaign.[14]

Yet previous Iroquois actions—such as destroying British foodstuffs or refusing British provisions—suggest that Indians' eating habits were more complicated than mere dependency on food aid to address hunger. The Iroquois may have treated with New Yorkers because New Yorkers provided food aid, but they might also have treated with New Yorkers because New Yorkers were good at practicing other types of diplomacy. Stored corn reserves should also be considered in assessing the extent of Indian hunger, because the Hessian fly eats wheat, barley, and rye, but not corn.[15]

The diplomacy of federal officials suggests that distributing provisions at the proper time and place was just as important as providing a lot of food; these were not uniformly starving Indians gorging on provisions. Six Nations housed at Buffalo Creek and led at various points by Captain Pollard, Cornplanter, Farmer's Brother, Red Jacket, and Young King spent time teaching food protocols to federal agents, implying their willingness to work with those agents, first, in addition to state ones, and eventually, instead of them.[16] In the 1790s these federal officials replicated previous British and Indian practices. The

Iroquois did not destroy foodstuffs or demand that Americans hunger along-side them, but as they did during the Revolutionary War, they shaped the diplomacy that non-Natives practiced to address Indian hunger.

When he began work as a federal Indian commissioner, future secretary of war Timothy Pickering required instruction from Natives. He began his education before a meeting to cover the graves of two murdered Seneca men. Pennsylvania footed the bill for the condolence presents, but the U.S. government assumed the more expensive cost of hosting the council. As he prepared to meet Senecas in November 1790, Pickering received a message from Indian runners. Little Billy informed him of the impending arrival of a large number of Senecas. He asked Pickering to have "provisions prepared for them" at two locations called the Painted Post and Newtown Point. Little Billy depicted this act of "hang[ing] some kettles" as one of "Antiant customs." In addition, he requested "a little Staff" or "walking staff." The kettles symbolized food—sometimes grain, sometimes meat, sometimes cooked, sometimes not—and the staff was watered-down alcohol.[17]

The British would already have known to anticipate these customs of providing for Indians as they journeyed to and from meetings. Pickering cautiously stepped into a similar negotiator's role. He promised to "have ready plenty of beef, flour & corn . . . and Some rum," but warned that "the provisions furnished at those two places can be no more than what will be absolutely necessary to enable them to come on to this place."[18] Like Jeffery Amherst and Frederick Haldimand, Timothy Pickering tried to limit Indians' consumption. Soon he too would learn the error of attempting to do so.

After sending this message Pickering panicked because he worried that dissatisfied Senecas would commit victual warfare. New York resident Bezaleel Seely told Pickering that Indians dealing with a "lack of Provisions" could be found "killing & pilfering" the "property" belonging to the town's inhabitants. Seely did not appear to know that Indians took foodstuffs because they expected them as part of hospitality, but he was sure that thefts of animals and vegetables would provoke retaliation. Rumors "that the Indians were coming on in good humour" made Pickering anxious to keep them that way, "and apprehensive that the restricted provision . . . would be insufficient," he dispatched someone "to procure all necessary additional Supplies" to contend with the Senecas' "voracious eating."[19] Even during this period of relative calm, Pickering, like James Seagrove, feared the violent result of ignoring Native hunger.

Once everyone arrived and observed the condolence ceremony together, Farmer's Brother put Pickering in an awkward situation. After Pickering had welcomed the Seneca men, Farmer's Brother observed, "Our women expect you will Show them equal attention . . . you may See one who may please you." Although Indian agents frequently enjoyed the sexual company of Native women, Pickering declined the offer. The invitation evoked "a general laugh" from those present, though records do not indicate how the Seneca women reacted. They would have attended and influenced the outcome of such meetings before the Revolutionary War, but since the 1760s men like Sir William Johnson had tried to silence the women who participated. Pickering's response was crucial. He dealt with the situation not by accepting sexual gifts but by offering consumable items. "I invite you to my quarters, where we may eat & drink together in friendship," Pickering recorded telling the women. And walking around and shaking hands "with every woman present," Pickering said, "I now take you by the hand as my sisters."[20] He showed respect to the Senecas by inviting them to dine. By calling them his sisters he evoked a kinship metaphor that negated sexual overtures and acknowledged the bargaining position of Native women.

It is possible that Pickering assumed he had won control of the situation while the Indians assumed that Pickering was a generous host. Ultimately he had to study "to please" the Indians "in every thing," provisioning 220 people at a cost of £150.[21] During this moment, six years after American commissioners told the Iroquois that they had defeated them, federal agents scrambled to build relationships with Senecas. The balance of power remained uncertain.

Americans continued to try to improve their behavior at future meetings, and this research on diplomatic practices yielded additional opinions on Native tastes, diet, and hungriness. American-allied Natives such as Captain Hendrick Aupaumut, a Stockbridge Mahican, assessed the sorts of provisions non-Natives could supply. His observation that Indians preferred pork to beef confirmed earlier British claims. Benjamin Rush, the renowned American doctor, sent Timothy Pickering questions about Indians, including queries about diet. Pickering described Indians' alimentary (and sometimes excretory) habits, relating that those who had eaten "often, & a great deal" experienced "excretions by Stools . . . more frequent than those of the white people." He explained that Indians handled food shortages by "tying their belts closer & closer" and eating "Spikenard root, which allays hunger." In preparation for such periods, Indians ate "two or three pounds of beef a man per day, besides bread and vegetables" when they could get them.[22]

Observers were struck by the fact that, compared to white soldiers, Indians could eat two to three times the quantity of meat. When Henry Knox received a letter about Native appetites, his correspondent underlined the fact that each person "expects double rations."[23] These post-Revolutionary studies reveal two non-Native perceptions of Indian hunger: first, that Indian appetites were at times greater than those of non-Natives, and second, that

Indians could deal with hunger but could not stop it from happening. Such details drove government decisions to spend a lot of time and money on Indian affairs.

During most meetings Indians held the advantage. In the summer of 1791 Pickering was supposed to meet the Senecas again, this time in the company of a number of other Iroquois Indians on the Tioga River. It was at this event that Pickering delivered his false history of early English industry and Native American starvation. Once more, before the gathering Seneca messengers asked Pickering "to hang on the kettles & furnish them with a walking Staff" at a certain location. Pickering responded that it would "be exceedingly difficult" to fulfill their request because "the lowness of the water of the Tioga river" made "the goods and provisions" impossible to transport without getting horses and oxen to drag canoes behind them. In what he thought was a compromise Pickering proposed to hang the kettles fifteen miles closer, where the Indians would find "beef & corn in plenty . . . a quantity of potatoes," and a "walking Staff." When the Indians arrived, the Oneida named Good Peter chided Pickering, supposing "that the business of holding treaties with Indians was novel to me, or I should have hung on the kittles for their refreshment."[24]

Good Peter implied that although Pickering had provided the walking staff, he needed to study up on food distributions, and he guilted Pickering by saying that he had been "obliged to ask for provisions at Canadasago." Chastised, Pickering paid Good Peter for the food the Indians had purchased. He also had to listen to the Seneca Red Jacket's assessment of his history lesson. Red Jacket criticized Pickering for a "discourse . . . intermixed with friendship and trouble." "In ancient times," Red Jacket remembered, "We did not repeat misfortunes, when brightening the chain" of friendship.[25] Red Jacket did not explicitly call Pickering a liar, but he disagreed with Pickering's approach to recalling the past when practicing diplomacy. This meeting included 1,050 Iroquois. At its end Pickering sent them home with "one barrel of rum for a walking Staff" and a promise of "hanging on the kettles for them at Sundry places." Despite the fact that "the great expences of the treaty mortif[ied]" him, Pickering salvaged the situation.[26]

Additional exchanges of food continued throughout the 1790s. In 1790 a small number of Senecas—Cornplanter, Half-Town, Great Tree, Guyasuta, and two others—went to Philadelphia for a visit that lasted from October to March while they met with federal and state officials. In 1791 Timothy Pickering again invited "four, five or Six . . . of their most able & prudent chiefs" to Philadelphia. A larger group of Cayuga, Oneida, Onondaga, Seneca, and

Tuscarora Iroquois met federal officials in Philadelphia in 1792, staying for over a month.[27] In sum, large numbers of Indians proved willing to meet with American officials because those officials seemed amenable to learning Indian diplomacy, which in turn familiarized non-Natives with Native abilities to withstand hunger—but not stop its occurrence.

Southern officials also scrutinized and sometimes misunderstood Indian appetites. Cherokees and Creeks requested provisions from state and federal officials, who proved quick to compete with each other in their quests for Native land. Almost immediately after the appointment of federal commissioners, states began trying to outdo federal negotiators. In June 1785 one Georgia assemblyman learned that Creeks led by the Tallassee King and the Fat King were headed toward Beard's Bluff, "with a request that we would have provisions ready for them." The meeting was intended to settle a "boundary line" between Georgia and Creek territory. Georgians said that the meeting was "of the first Consequence to the state . . . as the Commissioners from Congress will shortly be on the same errand." "If we get through with this before they Commence," Georgians speculated, "it may be a capital point gained."[28] These records reveal that Creeks, like the Iroquois, expected people to provide food on their way to a meeting, that some non-Natives knew about these protocols, and that state officials were animated by a spirit of competition against the federal government. State representatives needed to negotiate separately with the Creeks—and wanted provisions as part of this process—because their delimitation of land boundaries differed from the U.S. government's. Small wonder that James Seagrove thought of Georgia as a separate country a few years later.

Other state politicians also championed their own interests. Before a 1789 meeting with Creeks and Cherokees, William Blount, North Carolina state senator, argued that because the Cherokees were "the only Indians that are troublesome to here," state commissioner John Steele needed to speak to them first because "such as are first treated with fare best as to Provisions and Presents." If Steele prioritized this meeting, North Carolina could potentially sign "a better Treaty" with them. Blount separated provisions from presents but acknowledged that hospitality and treaty gifts were both necessary to lead to an outcome beneficial to the state. The U.S. Congress, however, had anticipated North Carolina's actions, and had "absolutely forbidden" state commissioners from demanding land.[29] This order meant that even if North Carolinians succeeded in reaching the Cherokees before U.S. officials did, there was little for the state to gain.

In contrast to the northern states, southern state inhabitants seemed to expect more violence between Natives and non-Natives. "We shall make their Towns Smoak with fire, and their Streets run with blood—the whole will be consumed in one general conflagation [*sic*]," promised Georgia governor George Handley in 1788. State campaigns continued to focus on burning Native villages, and white inhabitants' domesticated animals destroyed the crops untouched by soldiers' firebrands. By 1790 it had grown difficult for southern state agents to maintain the fiction that they cared about Indians' interests. That year, the Intercourse Act prohibited land sales between Indians and individuals and between Indians and the states, supposedly establishing the federal government as the sole entity capable of signing treaties with Indians.[30]

As in the north, federal officials in the south nurtured Indian alliances because they feared Indian hunger and because they worried about the growing influence of the states. By spring of 1786 reports of Indians stealing horses appeared in North Carolina. Accounts from 1787 depicted Chickamauga Cherokees and Creeks cutting down crops, stealing horses, killing hogs and cattle, and murdering white inhabitants. Additional intelligence circulated into the 1790s. It is not coincidental that reports of crop failure and Indian starvation were both prevalent during this time. In 1792 U.S. commissioner James Seagrove suggested to Secretary of War Henry Knox that the United States needed to supply corn to Creeks to prevent famine. By 1794 other officials worried about starving Cherokees. In August 1792 Knox had Seagrove relocate to Creek country to counteract dissension with "Goods, Corn, and Money."[31]

Although the expense of feeding Indians increased, and although federal agents remained worried about Indian violence and interference from the states, they remained unable to reduce the amounts of provisions they provided. After a 1786 meeting with Cherokees, Andrew Pickens, Benjamin Hawkins, and Josiah Martin said that to prevent them from "starving, through indolence," they would work with the Cherokees' interpreter and four chiefs to facilitate their "procuring provisions" on their way home. They had also "supplied them with provisions on the road" to the meeting.[32] These men supplied food even to the Indians they characterized as lazy.

Seagrove attempted to regulate food distribution in 1791. When the U.S. government agreed to send corn from Philadelphia for Creek consumption, Seagrove informed them that in order to obtain the corn, the Creeks would have to come to him. Once met, they would "make arrangements for distributing the provision . . . Which your people can receive at any time afterwards." Seagrove, unlike his British counterparts, did not envision a food-aid system in which officials visited villages to distribute provisions. He tried to prevent the appearance of the women and children who usually accompanied men to meetings—and thus the additional cost of hosting them. "No greater number than what I have mentioned may attend at our meeting," he wrote, "as a croud of people only prevent business being done."[33]

Nine months later, given the "Critical situation at this juncture," Seagrove explained that he had "been obliged" to accommodate Creeks' "craving dispositions" because he "thought it would be bad policy to fall out with those people, and let them go home discontented." No one "who is not an Eyewitness to the enormous eating of Indians can have an Idea of it," he wrote. At one point Seagrove tried to limit Creeks to the equivalent of military meat rations: "a pound of Beef [per] Man each day, but found it would not do." The Indians "got out of all tempter with that mode, and threatened to leave me, if I would not give them their *belly's full*." "There is no middle road with these people," he warned. "So soon as the United States decline purchasing their friendship as above; I would recommend by all means that they have a force ready to oppose them in the field."[34] Here again, Seagrove associated empty bellies with the need for violence. His anxiety helps explain why men like Hawkins and Pickens were so ready to provision Native Americans.

One of the definitive battles over the future of southern Indian relations occurred not between Native Americans and federal officials, but between federal and Georgian agents. Readers may be familiar with the fight over federal versus state power in the 1820s, which preceded Cherokee removal in the 1830s. Conflict between the states and the federal government was also evident decades earlier, at the 1796 Treaty of Colerain between U.S. commissioners, Georgia commissioners, and Creek Indians. Although discussions at the treaty involved land, it was also a food fight in which Georgians invoked their own hunger in a gambit for Creek territory.

In 1796, in an effort to broker peace in the midst of Georgians' unscrupulous dealings in the Yazoo Land Fraud—in which former governor George Mathews and other Georgian politicians sold territory in present-day Alabama and Mississippi to their friends at low prices—the United States and Georgia acted together. They invited the Creeks to a treaty at Colerain, on the St. Mary's River. In April, James Seagrove, by now the superintendent of Indian Affairs in the Creek nation, sent a talk to the Upper Creeks, Lower Creeks, and Seminoles that requested their attendance. George Clymer, Benjamin Hawkins, and Andrew Pickens joined him as U.S. agents—they were from Pennsylvania, North Carolina, and South Carolina, respectively. James Hendricks, James Jackson, and James Simms acted for Georgia. Seagrove remained invested in cutting costs: "Plenty of every thing that is good will be provided," he promised Creeks before the meeting, but only for "The principal men of every Town." The season was "a time of the year when you seldom go a hunting," he argued, so the men could "leave your Women and young people to make your Corn."³⁵ Seagrove anticipated Indians' excuses for not coming to the treaty and preempted them, and he also tried to limit attendance.

The Georgia commissioners, meanwhile, planned to outdo federal agents, sending periodic reports to the governor, Jared Irwin. Georgia's commissioners expected 7,000 Indians and were ready to host them. State agents examined "various accounts of the quantity of Beef an Indian would devour." After learning "that from five to seven pounds were daily given them," they figured that each Indian probably ate three rations and "wasted or jerked" the remainder "for the Nation." The state's figures for Indian meat consumption were higher than those for the Iroquois and higher than Seagrove and Pickering had previously reported. Georgia's contractor had to make additional trips for extra provisions once state agents made their estimates. Georgians at Colerain were prepared to be generous even though they were paying for half the costs of treaty provisions. Luckily for Southern budgets, the Indians' numbers came closer to 430 than 7,000, including 31 women and 29 children.³⁶ Creeks ignored U.S. commissioners' instructions to leave their women and children at home, temporarily giving Georgia the advantage of appearing more welcoming.

U.S. commissioners, like the British around Niagara, tried to control other officials' access to Indians. On May 31 Georgians denounced the orders that Hawkins and Clymer posted on the garrison gates: U.S. agents had decided that no man could speak to the Creeks without a permit issued by one of them. Other regulations forbade people from selling or gifting alcohol, or engaging in "any Commercial Traffic" with Indians. The Georgians countered that the treaty grounds stood in Georgia, "under the actual jurisdiction of the State." Benjamin Hawkins replied that Georgian authority was subservient to federal authority.³⁷ U.S. commissioners, by asserting federal power in trade negotiations with Indians and standing between the Georgians and the Creeks, circumscribed Georgians' maneuvering through forest diplomacy.

Although the Georgians arrived at Colerain ready to feed the Creeks, they came to the treaty unprepared to present an acceptable talk: they intended to demand serious concessions from the Indians while misusing a hunger metaphor. In a calculated move, U.S. commissioners "helped" by reading and approving the offensive speech before the Georgians delivered it. Georgians later claimed that Seagrove had undermined state authority by holding a private meeting with the Creeks at his residence at Muscogee, "where the Commissioners of Georgia, owing to the regulations before protested against, had no access."³⁸

Notes from the actual recitation of the speech do not exist in the state commissioners' papers, so one must read the draft talk while imagining Native
reactions to it. Before the treaty began, the state commissioners had collected
lists of the slaves, cattle, hogs, and horses taken in acts of revolutionary victual warfare from all the counties in Georgia. They began their message with
a demand that Indians return bondpeople and animals, and then continued:

> The Nation which has fewest people & most land, ought to part with a
> little of it, to the other nation at a reasonable price . . . we have not land
> enough, to raise corn for all our people. . . . No Red man would refuse
> a white man something to eat, if he came hungry to his Cabin, and yet
> a refusal of this land, will be like a denial of bread to many hungry fam-
> ilies, who want to raise corn on it, to feed themselves . . . your hunts
> we are told are not very profitable on this land . . . it is fit for the pur-
> pose we want it . . . to raise corn for our hungry people. . . . We have
> brought you a large parcel of goods . . . if we can agree about the
> land. . . . They will comfort your Wives & Children, & will be of more
> value to you, than the profits of many years hunts, on the lands we wish
> to get from you.[39]

The speech blended American and Native ideas. The Georgians suggested that
the Creeks should cede land to be hospitable and because they could sympa-
thize with non-Native hunger. The talk relied on figurative language ("like a
denial of bread"), which, though not a precise one-dish simile, would probably have been recognizable. But the Georgians erred by suggesting that Creeks
only hunted and non-Natives only farmed, by privileging Georgian hunger
over Creek hunger, and by asking for a reversal of victual warfare in the return of domesticated animals and ex-bondpeople.

Given the ineffectiveness of metaphorical food diplomacy, the maneuvering of U.S. officials, and the long history of violence in Georgia, the odds were
stacked against the state commissioners, despite the extensive and generous
provisioning plans they had made for the treaty. Georgian officials' ability to
keep treaty attendees from going hungry would not make them capable of
making everyone happy.

On June 18, 1796, the Creeks gathered in the treaty square (or *tcoko-thlako*)
appointed by the U.S. commissioners to hear what the Georgians would say.
Later the Georgians related that during their oration, Creek women appeared,
joined by the wives of George Clymer and James Seagrove. State commissioners observed that "not one of them were present" when federal agents spoke
the previous day. Creeks and U.S. officials would have known that women

could not enter the square ground while men were still deliberating, and thus their presence indicated the end of negotiations.[40] The Creek women who came to the Treaty of Colerain implicitly supported the efforts of the U.S. commissioners and undermined the Georgians' efforts by occupying a traditionally male space. The Georgians obliviously proceeded to deliver their talk and then retired to await the Creeks' response.

Benjamin Hawkins, who anticipated the impending clash, waited four days to tell Georgia's commissioners "what the Indians had done." The Creeks had produced a reply unfit for Georgians' ears. They renounced previous treaties at which they had not been united—among them the treaties of Augusta (1783), Galphinton (1785), and Shoulderbone (1786). They had repudiated these treaties at the Treaty of New York in 1790, which transferred jurisdiction to federal officials. They seemed to think Georgia needed to be reminded of these repudiations. The Creeks cited their return of some bondpeople and said they would return others. Most importantly, they argued that at the Treaty of New York, Creeks had been "assured by the President of the United States and his Congress that no more demands should be made for Indians lands." The Creeks' answer, mediated through the American commissioners, and all the more shocking for their refusal to deliver it aloud, denied Georgians the cession they requested. Although Hendricks, Jackson, and Simms objected, Hawkins informed them, "no other answer might be eafected but thro the Commissers. of the United States."[41]

Then the Creeks took the Georgians' hunger metaphors and threw them back at them. They claimed that "both sides" stole and maimed hogs and cattle, and that it was unfair for only Creeks to return war spoils. The Indians detailed their land-use and hunger-prevention efforts: "the very streams of water are found valuable for Mills to grind the wheat & Corn that is made on those lands." Dead pine trees yielded tar. Furthermore, the goods the Georgians gave them on previous occasions had turned "rotten & gone to nothing."[42] The Creeks reminded Hendricks, Jackson, and Simms that they did farm, and emphasized their production of non-Native wheat as well as Indian maize. They needed their land for crop production. Their statement that the Georgians gave them useless goods symbolized their lack of faith in the state at this treaty and at future meetings. The huge quantities of food that Georgia had supplied for the treaty had done nothing to obtain what the state commissioners might have considered a good deal.

Hendricks, Jackson, and Simms decided that their only recourse was to refuse the written talk and to ask for an oral response from the Creeks, who received them the following day. During this interaction, the state commissioners protested that it was not their fault that the goods were rotten, especially because the Creeks neglected to say so at the time they received them and "sold us the land for them." The state representatives considered that contract binding and pressed once more for a cession: "We told you of the goods we brought . . . they amount to 20,000 Dollars at least. . . . This will more than pay you for the loss of skins and meat" the Indians garnered "from that land." "It will do you good and make us all friends," they concluded optimistically. After this exchange the Creeks remained silent, and on the following day Hendricks, Jackson, and Simms once again demanded a reply. "We do not know what the people of Georgia wish to Learn," complained a man called the Bird Tail King. "Do they think we have not given a determined answer?"[43]

In the fight between American commissioners and Georgian ones, the U.S. agents had emerged triumphant. U.S. officials successfully blocked Georgians' access to Indians, undermined talks crafted by the state agents, and cultivated the federal government's relationship with the Creeks. Creek Indians reminded everybody that they needed land for their own agriculture. By the end of the treaty it became clear that Georgians could not succeed against the U.S. agents. The battle between U.S. Indian agents and Creeks was still to come. In the meantime, the federal government had more pressing concerns.

In addition to interfering with states' diplomacy with Creeks, Cherokees, and the Iroquois, the federal government turned its attention to the Ohio Valley, where the Western Confederacy gathered strength. Diplomacy and warfare in the north and south retained familiar forms but passed from British to state to federal agents. In the Ohio Valley, by contrast, the British retained the upper hand in negotiations until 1795. A conflict called the Western Confederacy War (sometimes the Northwest Indian War) raged on past the War for Independence, consuming five-sixths of the federal budget between 1790 and 1795.[44] Victual warfare was different in this region. Natives burned their own crops, nearly always destroyed rather than stole American soldiers' provisions, and accepted British meat and grain while ignoring British counseling. Their actions lend further specificity to evolving eighteenth-century ideas about hunger and suggest Indians' abilities to retain power when short on food.

The Western Confederacy consisted of a number of Indian tribes— Chickamauga Cherokees, Chippewas, Conoys, Creeks, Delawares, Hurons, Iroquois, Miamis, Mingoes, Mahicans, Munsees, Ottawas, Potawatomis, Reynards, Sacs, Shawnees, and Wyandots—many of whom had been forging alliances since before the Revolution. Shawnees introduced Miamis to the British in the late 1740s. Delawares and Creeks possessed ties to the Shawnees. The Chickamauga Cherokees and Shawnees created an alliance after 1776. When the Shawnees sent the Chickamaugas a war hatchet in 1784, the Cherokees agreed to take hold of it. Americans' massacre of pacifist Delawares at Gnaden-hütten in 1782 brought Shawnees and Delawares closer together in desires for war. These tribes continued to develop support networks with the British. Around 1785, Huron and Ottawa (Wyandot) First Nations granted a tract of land at the mouth of the Detroit River to British Indian department officials Henry Bird, Matthew Elliott, Alexander McKee, and Simon Girty. By July 1787, while the Constitutional Convention met in Philadelphia to address the Articles of Confederation and the country's inability to raise an army, "authentic information" circulated about "a confederation" of Indians "on the North West side of the Ohio [River]." A triumvirate led by Buckongahelas of the Delawares, Little Turtle of the Miamis, and Blue Jacket of the Shawnees bound the Indians together.[45] They possessed many grievances against the new United States.

During treaties at Fort McIntosh in 1785, Fort Finney in 1786, and Fort Harmar in 1789, U.S. officials demanded land while threatening to raze Western Confederacy villages. At Fort McIntosh Americans demanded territory from Delawares, Ojibwas, Ottawas, and Wyandots. At Fort Finney Americans pressured 230 Shawnee men and women into ceding land, and despite other Shawnees' repudiation of the treaty, Americans recognized cessions made without tribal consensus. At Fort Harmar the Americans met the Delawares, Potawatomis, Ojibwas, Ottawas, Senecas, Sauks, and Wyandots. Officials warned that Indians who refused to engage with the Americans (and, by implication, to cede land to them) could "rest assured that the United States will take speedy and effectual measures to . . . reduce you to such terms, as may cause you to regret the loss of so advantageous a peace." Between 1774 and 1794, Shawnee settlements suffered eight different assaults. One village called Chillicothe was attacked four times even though the Shawnees kept rebuilding it in different locations.[46] The Western Confederacy War became a conflict of ongoing attacks and retaliations.

Indians' defensive tactics left them well positioned to undermine the Americans. In September 1790 the Miamis burned their own town rather than allow advancing American troops to do so. This preemptive destruction meant that American soldiers could take no corn; the Indians, on the other hand, could find game in the woods and shelter and stored grain in neighboring villages. Warriors divided into smaller self-sufficient groups of approximately twenty men, who fed themselves by hunting. Twelve hundred warriors could kill approximately two hundred deer and two hundred turkeys per day, making them less reliant on grain. Indians also continued to expect British assistance.[47]

The Western Confederacy gathered power. In 1790 the Indians overcame American General Josiah Harmar and his men, and their 1791 face-off against

Arthur St. Clair yielded another victory. Afterward, reports circulated of vindictive Indians stuffing dead soldiers' mouths with soil in a symbolic act against those who hungered too deeply for Natives' lands. The Confederacy worked to build alliances with southern Indians. In September 1792 Governor William Blount of Georgia wrote, "the Five lower towns of the Cherokees have declared War against the United States." By October their numbers had been augmented by Upper Creeks. A 1792 meeting at the Glaize (the area in present-day Ohio where the Auglaize and Maumee Rivers meet) drew together Cherokees, Chippewas, Conoys, Creeks, Delawares, Hurons, Miamis, Mingoes, Mahicans, Munsees, Ottawas, Potawatomis, Reynards, Sacs, and Shawnees.[48]

By this time the federal government was working to build up its military, and finally had a stronger apparatus to raise money for soldiers' pay. Harmar's campaign had consisted of militia and federal troops who lacked training; Arthur St. Clair's men were similarly motley. When, in 1792, General "Mad" Anthony Wayne accepted command of the new American Legion, he did so with a vision of order. He drew on support from the new U.S. War Department (founded in 1789) and spent a year putting together supplies and men, whom he trained in guerrilla warfare.[49]

In 1793 Wayne went on the defensive to protect his food supplies. "I am here under the order of the Commander in Chief, with a Strong Detachment of the Legion . . . to protect your beef Catle," one general proclaimed to suppliers in November 1793. Wayne knew that he had to protect his supply line, which stretched over one hundred miles and proved difficult to maintain and defend. He stockpiled rations at Greenville and stored smaller caches at other forts. The War Department's agreement with the contractors who provisioned the western posts contained stipulations that guards would escort food convoys and cattle, as well as agreements on financial compensation for "losses sustained by the depredations of the enemy."[50] It was necessary to appoint cattle guards to fill soldiers' stomachs in a timely manner.

As the Confederacy gained strength, their tactics shifted from the defensive to the offensive. Most information about their strategy came from William Wells, who was raised among the Miamis but turned spy for the Americans after 1793. Indians intended to target Americans' "plenty of Cattle & Corn," to attack Wayne's provisions convoys, "to kill the pack horses" responsible for transporting said provisions, and "to harrass the Army by firing frequently upon them in the Night," Wells warned. He was right; the Indians set fire to hay, making it hard for soldiers to feed horses, transport supplies, or reconnoiter the area, and they attacked and abandoned wagons loaded with corn. The Americans puzzled over the fact that Indians who struck at their convoys left edible goods behind, but Indians possessed little cause to steal food when

they could hunt and when British officials such as Alexander McKee promised to keep them well fed. Many Americans may not have known about British support, so it is possible that the war further mythologized Native abilities
to withstand food deprivation. Wayne's assertion that "The Savages . . . can't
continue long embodied for want of provisions" was bluster.[51] The Confederacy forsook supplies and interfered with Wayne's operations.

While the Confederacy was fighting Wayne's Legion, the United States also
considered diplomatic mediations with those Indians. The British hoped to
quash such efforts. A 1793 meeting at Sandusky, near Lake Erie, was U.S. officials' last chance to try to agree on a boundary line with an increasingly capable enemy. Commissioners Benjamin Lincoln, Timothy Pickering, and
Beverly Randolph possessed no way of knowing that the council would never
take place. In February the War Department prepared to transport Madeira,
port, rum, and sherry; beef, bread, butter, cheese, ham, and pickled pork; and
chocolate, coffee, sugar, and tea.[52]

The British set about blocking American food diplomacy and practicing it
themselves. Since 1792 British governor John Graves Simcoe had lent military
support to the Western Indians to protect British interests in the Ohio Valley.
In 1793 Simcoe, possibly under influence from Joseph Brant, prohibited the
United States officials from feeding Indians. If they received "their dinners from
the party with whom they were treating," Simcoe contended, Natives could
not "treat on independent grounds." The Indians "objected to . . . being supplied by the United States," he concluded, ignoring half a century in which
Britons had supplied dinner to Indians with whom they had negotiated. While
Lincoln, Pickering, and Randolph stayed with Simcoe, and then at British Indian commissioner Matthew Elliott's house on the Detroit River, the Western
Confederacy gathered at Alexander McKee's storehouse at the bottom of the
Maumee rapids.[53] The Confederacy never met the U.S. commissioners; instead,
the two parties passed messages through British and Indian intermediaries.

In June 1793 the commissioners sent Mahican Hendrick Aupaumut to try
to open negotiations by asking whether the Confederacy would cede the Ohio
River as a boundary line between Indians and the United States; the Confederacy's previous reluctance to do so had helped cause the war. The United
States was offering "a large annual Rent" and permission to "hunt on the same
lands as long as you can find any game." Although the Western Confederacy
split into two camps, a response came only from the Shawnees. Their answer
was that they could "retreat no farther; because the Country behind, hardly
affords food for its present inhabitants." Money was "of no value" to them,
and "no consideration whatever" would convince them "to Sell the Lands on
which we get Sustenance for our women and children." These Indians cited

their hunting needs, and argued that the lands west of the Ohio would not support their additional numbers. The Shawnees sarcastically suggested taking the money the commissioners had proposed giving to the Indians and offering it instead to poor non-Native inhabitants to fund their relocation out of the Ohio Valley. The commissioners interpreted this response as representative of the whole Confederacy, making future conflict unavoidable.[54]

British food diplomacy, meanwhile, continued uninterrupted. In 1791 Hendrick Aupaumut reported that the British were encouraging the Shawnees' and Miamis' desire for war by promising "three years provision." An interpreter reported that after Harmar's defeat, Simon Girty supplied the Indians with "great quantities of provisions" and ammunition. Matthew Elliott even possessed a boat named "Indian Feeder" (before he changed the name to the "Shawanoe," a clear nod to the Shawnees). While the Western Confederacy awaited word from the American commissioners at Niagara, they received live cattle, bags of corn, and barrels of flour, peas, and pork given out at Alexander McKee's storehouse.[55]

These were items to please everyone: cattle for those invested in acquiring non-Native domesticates as property; ready-to-eat pork to cater to Indian meat preferences; and corn, always corn, to replace what the Indians had burned. Gifts of food gave British officials the confidence to counsel the Indians against treating with the Americans. McKee persuaded them not to go to meet the commissioners on June 1, the date initially fixed by the Americans. Later missives indicated that Simcoe "had positively said, *That there would be no peace*," and that McKee had promised them food supplies "in case they went to war."[56]

After receiving the Confederacy's negative response, the American commissioners gave up. Alexander McKee "ordered three Beeves to be killed in order to make a War feast." A translator reported a Shawnee chief observing that now they would be ready for war, given the fact that McKee "sais we shall not want for Amunition Clothing or Provisions." Alexander McKee provided both a present and future testament of British goodwill; he offered meat in preparation for war, as well as the promise of food to come. On August 23, 1793, Lincoln, Pickering, and Randolph wrote to General Anthony Wayne and informed him that the meeting had failed. In September Henry Knox wrote to Wayne in hopes that his Legion would "be adequate to make those audacious savages feel our superiority in Arms."[57]

Wayne continued to focus on protecting his supply line, but he also tried to create divisions between Indians by fomenting accusations about poison; perhaps he hoped to reduce the number of enemies he would face in the field. In January 1794 a Seneca war chief named Captain Big Tree "put a period to his own existance" by committing suicide. Wayne tried to drive a wedge between the Iroquois (who had not yet declared for either side) and the Western Confederacy, which he did by implying that the Delawares had poisoned Captain Big Tree. In a talk sent to the Iroquois he observed that Captain Big Tree had engaged in "some Angry talk with the Delawares." Whether he "eat or drank with them . . . or whether they gave him something, that put him out of his reason," Wayne could not say.[58]

Next, Wayne cast suspicions on the Miamis. He recalled hearing that the previous summer, many of the Six Nations died, "in consequence of Something that you had eat when at the Council with the Hostile Indians at the rapids of the Miami." "This mode of Making war," Wayne continued, "is Cowardly & base." Wayne's concept of victual warfare, then, approved of food spoilage but classified alleged poisoning as a dishonorable step too far. In spite of Wayne's efforts, he worried that the loyalties of the Senecas remained "cool & backward." Joseph Brant asked the Americans for more time before his Iroquois faction decided whether to support Britons or Americans. "In such very weighty business" it grew impossible to deliberate quickly, Brant claimed. By spring of 1794 Joseph Brant's group had once more declared for war against the Americans. This unwillingness to betray the British may suggest the ineffectiveness of Wayne's accusation. Wayne found the uncertainty exhausting. Writing to Henry Knox, he confessed, "it is a very unpleasant kind of Warfare . . . with famine & *faction* . . . altho' I have hitherto sustained & halted all the attacks of this Hydra, yet I feel both body & mind fatigued by the Contest."[59]

The Western Confederacy's numbers, meanwhile, had dwindled. Dragging Canoe's death in 1792 dampened Chickamauga Cherokees' resistance. In November of that year Chickamaugas, Creeks, and Shawnees struck Buchanan's Station in Georgia, suffering defeat and significant casualties. In June 1794 the Confederacy mounted an attack against Fort Recovery that resulted in the shattering of their union. Testimony from a Potawatomi woman captured during the attack described 1,454 Chessaw, Delaware, Eel River, Miami, Ottawa, Potawatomi, Shawnee, Six Nations, and Wyandot warriors who had gathered outside the fort's walls on June 30.[60] What the Shawnee Blue Jacket had envisioned as an ambush against a party of dragoons turned into a frontal assault led by the Ottawas. Indians attacked a convoy, stole the horses, and drove off the cattle. After failing to penetrate the fort, the Indians retreated beyond the line of fire, where they "killed & eat several Cattle & Packhorses" in sight of the garrison. They were preparing for a long journey, and thus a period of dearth. In late June the Ottawas headed home. The Ojibwas and Potawatomis followed them. By the time that Anthony Wayne built Fort Defiance at the junction of the Maumee and Auglaize Rivers—the former home of the Indians' confederacy—Little Turtle had also relinquished his hopes of defeating the Americans. By August 1794, Blue Jacket presided over a heavily diminished force of only three hundred Delawares, one hundred Miamis, two hundred Shawnees, and one hundred other Indians of various tribal affiliations.[61]

The last military action of the war, the Battle of Fallen Timbers—so named because the ground was "cover'd with old fallen timber probably occasioned by a tornado"—commenced around 10 a.m. on the morning of August 20. Wayne's Legion of three thousand soldiers fought for just over an hour before defeating the Confederacy. "It is with infinite pleasure that I now announce to you the brilliant success of the Federal Army under my Command," bragged Wayne to Henry Knox, before devastating the surrounding countryside to ensure Natives' total compliance. The engagement itself was less important in ensuring a lasting victory than Wayne's postbattle vegetable warfare. Soldiers pulled up bean vines, cut pumpkins "to pieces," and "destroyed all the Vegitables they could find." For three days Americans wrecked houses and cornfields around the British-held Fort Miamis on the banks of the Maumee River. They laid "waste the villages & Corn fields for about Fifty miles on each side of the Miamis" and then headed toward the Auglaize River for more destruction.[62]

The aftermath of Fallen Timbers was similar to revolutionary campaigns against the Cherokees and the Iroquois because in this instance British food diplomacy also became ineffective, but it was different because Indians did not try to alter diplomacy to maintain the alliance. Wayne urged his men to such devastation to "produce a conviction to the minds of the Savages, that the British have neither the power or inclination to afford them that protection which they had been taught to expect." In some accounts Indians' faith in the British broke during the battle, when British officials refused to fight or to shelter retreating Indians inside Fort Miamis after their defeat. In other interpretations the British refused to provide aid at all. In fact, Indians continued to accept provisions from British negotiators for months after the battle.[63] What *did* change was Natives' behavior after receiving provisions—and this change was in keeping with changes in Iroquois, Creek, and Cherokee country.

Although British food diplomacy continued after the Battle of Fallen Timbers, Indians behaved as if it was less powerful than it had been in the past. In October 1794 Governor Simcoe sent for Joseph Brant, Blue Jacket, Buckongahelas, Little Turtle, and Captain Johnny to ensure that they remained "well & regularly Supplied with provision." Throughout the fall, winter, and following spring, British officials kept feeding them beef, butter, flour, peas, pork, and rice sent from Detroit via the Maumee River. When the Americans fixed on a time and date for a treaty with the Indians in June 1795, McKee and

Elliott held "large Feasts, and Drunken parties daily in order to keep the Indians back from the treaty if possible." These were the same practices that Britons used during the Revolution; they gave food to important leaders, they offered food to individuals, and they let the rum flow at key moments. And yet they failed to poison the Indians against the Americans; the Indians went to seek peace terms anyway.[64] Britons continued to provide provisions, but they lost the ability to offer advice that Indians would heed. Whereas in 1779 scorched Indian villages and a *lack* of British food aid maintained Indian alliances, in 1794 burned villages and generous British food aid lost them.

The following eighteen months witnessed the transfer of most non-Native political power from British to American hands in the northwest, and from Spanish to American hands in the southeast. In November 1794 John Jay's treaty of friendship with Great Britain ensured Britons' departure from the frontier. The United States would sign the Treaty of San Lorenzo, otherwise known as Pinckney's Treaty, the following year—meaning that Creeks lost some Spanish support. In the interim the Western Confederacy sought terms. In April 1795 the Potawatomis delivered up prisoners in a demonstration of goodwill and asked for "something to eat, & not a little Keg, but a big one." In May the Delawares appeared at Fort Defiance "almost Starved" and requested not only beef and corn but "a little Corn to plant," or "seed Corn." And Blue Jacket appeared to relinquish his British stipend to earn the Americans' trust, and to promise to "Bring his Nation to Make a Village" near the Americans if they would "Supply them with Corn to plant."[65] These appeals signified more than physical alimentary need—Delawares and Shawnees implied that they expected provisions but would also supplement American food aid with their own, useful agriculture. This compromise played into developing American ideas about Indians' lack of "civility," which would feature heavily in the 1790s and 1800s.

In the summer of 1795 over a thousand Indians assembled at Greenville, an imposing fort in present-day Ohio surrounded by beautiful meadows. On July 30 the Indians relinquished their claim to the Ohio River boundary line.[66] As Indians arrived they made it clear that they anticipated welcoming hospitality. Anthony Wayne, acting as treaty host, promised early arrivals "a little drink to wash the dust out of our throats . . . without however, passing the bounds of temperance and sobriety." Perhaps worried that Wayne would stop with the welcoming drink, Le Gris, a Miami leader, told Wayne, "We expect to be treated as warriors." "You have told us we should share your provisions whilst we stayed with you." The Indians, he asserted, "would like some Mutton & pork."[67] In depicting himself and his fellow men as soldiers, Le Gris set himself on a level with Wayne and demanded a fair share of meat. He asked for the non-Native protein Indians most preferred but also seemed willing to try other alternatives.

The Indians implied that failure to comply with their requests would result in a failed treaty. The Sun, a Potawatomi chief, complained, "we get but a small Allowance." "We eat it in the morning and are hungry at night," he said, indicating that Wayne was not showing enough generosity. "We become weary & wish for home," he concluded. The Sun suggested that the Americans were willing to provide only the minimum of diplomatic concessions, but Indians expected the liberality of Americans' British predecessors.[68]

Wayne handled the situation by bending on issues of etiquette, making it clear that he remained in charge, and trying to foster dissension between Indians. He singled out the Sun by noting that he "alone complains of scarcity." He asked those assembled "to consult generally," and to let him know if they "really [did] not receive enough." Pork, he responded, was unobtainable, so the Indians could have none of it. Mutton, he said, "are for the Comfort of our Sick," and, on occasion, for the officers. Wayne acquiesced that sick Indians "shall most chearfully share" the sheep, and he would also "with pleasure" share a meal of mutton "with your Chiefs." When Blue Jacket and his cohort arrived, Wayne warned them, "my plate and my table are not very large," but he hoped "to see all your Chiefs in season and in due rotation."[69] Wayne, by relegating sheep to officers and sick men, depriving the Indians of pork, and deciding when and how he would sup with the Indian chiefs, set the tone for future food diplomacy and thus for future U.S. Indian food policy.

The fact that the Indians agreed to Wayne's terms suggests that to some degree even this newer, restrictive posture was successful. There is little evidence in the treaty record that other Native Americans complained about meals, provisions, or alcohol, and although treaty records are problematic, often incomplete documents, it seems odd that observers would have recorded one complaint but not others. Most of the Indians did not go on record to challenge the boundary line Wayne proposed. When Little Turtle said the cession the Americans claimed would "confine the hunting of our young men within limits too contracted," Wayne ignored him. Indians nevertheless exhibited their disapproval in other ways—in fact, using one of the methods Wayne had earlier accused them of. Sixty Potawatomis died after the council, and although the Indians accused the Americans of poisoning their leaders, the British suspected that it was Native opponents of the treaty who had murdered those who had acceded to its terms.[70]

After the overthrow of the Western Confederacy, the Americans sought to force peace with all remaining hostile tribes. The Southwestern Territorial militia struck a major blow against the Chickamauga Cherokee towns of

Nickajack and Running Water in 1794. Wayne enjoyed success with the Cherokees in August 1795 after sending them a message that he had "signed and exchanged, Articles of a permanent peace" with the Western Confederacy. By September Wayne anticipated "the pleasing prospect of eating my Christmas dinner at Waynesborough," in Pennsylvania; his job was done, but other work continued.[71]

U.S. commissioner Benjamin Hawkins, who would play a significant role revising Indian food policy, had begun to study Native Americans' grievances. In a letter to George Washington he explained that after "the close of the war," Americans deliberately forgot "the rights of the Indians . . . we seized on their lands, and made division of the same." Land policy, he argued, was "the source of their hostility," but he also observed that non-Native diplomats had promised and then failed to furnish the Indians with "such comforts as they had been accustomed to receive" from Britain.[72] Hawkins was writing in 1792, not 1794 or 1795. He was describing the history of Indian affairs after the American Revolution, but the government's quest for Native American land had not ceased by the end of the Western Confederacy War either. Hawkins seemed skeptical that U.S. land policy could ever favor Indians, but he hoped that some wrongs could be righted by reviving British forest diplomacy. That diplomacy included attempts to assuage Native hunger.

Yet there were numerous instances in the 1780s and 1790s when food appeared not to matter to Indians. Creeks at Colerain were unimpressed by Georgians' claims that they were hungry. Shawnees and Miamis left Wayne's provisions supplies lying in the road. The Iroquois chewed a root that allowed them to ignore hunger but also ate a lot at treaties. Attendees at Greenville complained about stinginess and then stopped complaining even in the face of reduced treaty hospitality. Non-Native observers largely sidestepped these moments to hone in on one organizing idea: the conviction that hungry Indians were violent people. Federal agents were paranoid about the consequences of Indian hunger, even when they misunderstood it. That fear was crucial to shaping an Indian policy that sought to prevent Indian hunger as it appeared to non-Natives, and this willingness made the federal government seem likelier to protect Indians' interests at the expense of states' rights. As had Creeks, Cherokees, and Iroquois before them, Western Confederacy Indians chose a combination of hunger and federal U.S. food aid by 1795.

Looking at these events reveals an additional battlefront: the tensions between Native and non-Native accounts of history. During the 1780s and 1790s, when power relations remained in flux, white negotiators experimented with using Native American approaches to interpreting the past. Federal officials rolled back some of the earlier British attempts to erase Native women's presence at diplomatic meetings, acknowledged women's history of shaping tribal decisions, and recorded interacting with them more frequently. Hawkins tried to learn where the United States had made mistakes. Georgian officials, despite their failure to get what they wanted at Colerain, still knew enough about Creek history to recognize that an oral speech could carry more legitimacy than a written one. When officials slipped up, non-Native leaders attacked their versions of history—as Red Jacket did when speaking to Timothy Pickering in 1791.

Native Americans were already staunch defenders of their own history and well on their way to winning battles against hunger when they wanted to wage them. British and American officials continued to consider Native American interests, but they worried less about the people of African descent who had fought for them during the war. Formerly enslaved people had gained a little power by fleeing from rebel American masters and turning into hunger creators and preventers. Next, they had to make it out of the former American colonies and to Nova Scotia. There, they experienced hunger that they would fail to master. Their fight against hunger had just begun—but luckily for historians they kept careful records of those struggles.

CHAPTER 6

Learning from Food Laws in Nova Scotia

On the first Thursday of October, 1781, St. George Tucker, who would go on to write a few lines about hunger personified, reported almost four hundred dead horses floating in and sprawled along the shore of the York River in Virginia. The corpses indicated that Lord Charles Cornwallis had ordered the animals killed to save on forage and had "no Intention of pushing a march" from his besieged position at Yorktown. Cornwallis was close to surrendering to the American rebels. His men, who had been short on provisions even before reaching Yorktown, now battled an outbreak of smallpox.[1] Throughout the Revolutionary War, ex-bondpeople had prevented British hunger. But when the tides of the war shifted, the military had little use for black victual warriors, for the provisioners like David George and Boston King who had supplied soldiers, or for their families.

Formerly enslaved men, women, and children struggled to obtain British help after Yorktown. Cornwallis ousted the runaways from a hospital at Gloucester to save on rations, while dogs ate the amputated limbs left behind. It was during this chaos that Boston King heard rumors that the British were planning to return escapees to former masters, and it was also during this period that he recalled his loss of appetite. Yet people like Boston King, and like David George, who had used provisioning roles to ensure their mobility from one colony to another, also managed to leave the former American colonies and go to Nova Scotia. David George would dictate his history to the editor of *The Baptist Annual Register*. Boston King would take care to indicate that his memoir was self-authored, though he likely received some assistance writing it.[2]

The food system that these men and women encountered and described in maritime British Canada in the 1780s emerged from a state of uncertain power relationships that resembled Native and non-Native affairs in the United States. In contrast to Indians, however, black and white colonists in Nova Scotia were relatively powerless in 1783, when they arrived. These migrants sought power in Nova Scotia in different ways; black colonists won temporary and informal economic power, and white colonists won lasting legal rights. During black colonists' first year in Nova Scotia, disorganization and lack of structure gave them temporary freedom to produce garden vegetables, to fish, and to buy and sell what they wanted in various marketplaces, but they rapidly lost that mobility and ability. Only white Loyalists—the colonists who had also sided with the British during the War for Independence—would gain the legal right to fight hunger, but even they struggled to convince Great Britain of their authority during the colony's founding months.

When white Loyalists fled the mainland American colonies, they transported ideas about hunger prevention with them. As refugee colonists, they advocated for food aid based on their knowledge of previous colonization efforts. In Nova Scotia they blocked black colonists' access to land while taking more of it for themselves, and they enacted food laws to avoid famine. Their actions became a way to fight white hunger while ignoring—and sometimes creating—black hunger. Because white Loyalists interfered with black people's food choices while keeping them from obtaining land, their actions in Nova Scotia can be characterized as victual imperialism. These food laws were so consequential because they stopped black colonists from producing and obtaining edible commodities using the methods that had previously worked in land-scarce environments. Black hunger was a product of several factors: inadequate planning prior to migrants' arrival in the province, land dearth, distance from food-aid distribution centers, unfavorable weather, and, finally, the introduction of laws controlling bread production, fish harvesting, and marketing practices.

Accounts of black hunger in Nova Scotia varied. During the Revolutionary War, black runaways had provisioned themselves and could thus at times seem to ignore hunger. In Canada observers began to talk more about famine, and to link its presence to a state of slavery—even though many of the black colonists had obtained freedom. At the same time, however, black colonists did not advocate for the immediate eradication of hunger, nor did they agitate for the right to prevent it themselves. Instead, they drew upon established ideas about aid, charity, and usefulness to make a case to Britain's abolitionists that they should be granted the ability to migrate. These families once again sought to move—using food and information networks—and to escape, one last time, to Sierra Leone.

First, self-liberated men and women needed to get out of the United States to avoid reenslavement by vengeful masters. When General George Washington met with Sir Guy Carleton in May 1783 to finalize peace terms, the two men disagreed about how to define an American slave. Earlier, in 1782, when they decided upon the provisional articles of British surrender, the seventh of those articles stated that the British would withdraw all troops without transporting Americans' bondpeople out of the former colonies. Carleton delayed negotiations in 1783, when he modified his stance and argued that people who had run away to British lines after proclamations such as Dunmore's of 1775 and Clinton's of 1779 had earned their freedom. By his reasoning the seventh article did not apply to these men and women, so the British could not be accused of carrying them away. Some British records state that "such Negroes as were taken *after the day of Treaty*, or that came within the Lines, were given up" to the Americans, but the absence of a date in these records makes it difficult to say whether the "Treaty" mentioned referred to the provisional articles or the 1783 peace agreement.[3] In any case, despite Washington's protestations that the provisional article forbade the removal of any black people, Carleton had already allowed some fugitives to leave the country. Others would follow in large numbers.

At the end of the Revolution, over sixty thousand white Loyalists departed the American colonies. This diaspora took them to places like Great Britain, Canada (the Maritimes, Ontario, and Quebec), the Caribbean (Jamaica and the Bahamas), Florida, and France, and even further afield to Australia and India. They transported fifteen thousand enslaved people with them. Nearly forty thousand Loyalists established themselves in the Maritimes—about half of them in Nova Scotia. Slavery continued to exist; some of these white refugees were southern planters, and their removal from the United States did nothing to free the two thousand bondpeople who traveled with them.[4]

Nova Scotia was not uninhabited before the Loyalists arrived. Early on it was Mi'kmaq territory, invaded by French colonists throughout the seventeenth century. The French had ceded Nova Scotia to the English after the War of the Spanish Succession (1702–1713), and although Mi'kmaq peoples continued to live alongside English inhabitants, many of them had died. Natives, French, and English continued to fight over boundaries before, during, and after the War for Independence. In 1779 British officials reported, "The

Indians of Nova Scotia consist[ed] of about Five hundred familys, all Roman Catholicks, containing near three thousand persons." Prior to the beginning of the Seven Years' War, some fifteen thousand non-Natives had lived in the borderlands between British Nova Scotia and French Acadia (present-day New Brunswick); the victorious British expelled these Acadians. After they left, Nova Scotia's population stood at about fourteen thousand people.[5]

In addition to the white Loyalists who traveled to Nova Scotia by choice, a separate group of formerly enslaved people—including three thousand of the men and women over whom Carleton and Washington had quarreled—moved to Nova Scotia as freedpersons. In the last half of April 1783, Carleton's commissioners in New York began counting; they recorded 328 men, 230 women, and 48 children headed to Nova Scotia. They listed their names, ages, and physical descriptions in a long document now known as the "book of negroes." Boston King, the man without an appetite, and his wife, Violet, arrived in August. Their ship, *L'Abondance* (translated as "Abundance"), was an ironically named testament to their wartime past and refugee future. King would become a Methodist minister during his time in the colony.[6]

More people continued to migrate; another 165 free blacks were registered when the first two vessels docked in Nova Scotia in June. From April to November, ships continuously transported people from New York to the Maritimes. By November, 2,714 formerly enslaved colonists had gone to Nova Scotia, with another 286 slated to depart. Of these, 1,336 were men, 914 were women, and 750 were children. Two-thirds hailed from Virginia, South Carolina, Georgia, and North Carolina. The rest came from New York, New Jersey, and Pennsylvania.[7]

British organizers made some preparations that would hypothetically allow the colony to thrive. Land surveys constituted part of this project, as did hunger-prevention efforts. In a January 1783 meeting, the Port Roseway Associates—the name the white Loyalists in New York gave to themselves—learned that they had "chosen the best Situation in the province for Trade, Fishery, and Farming." The surveyor general described "the Lands back of Port Roseway, Jordan River, and towards the An[n]apolis to the good," but cautioned colonists to "expect some indifferent land in every part of the Province." They would find that "Strawberry's are in great perfection," as well as "Currants, Rasberrys, Cherrys, Gooseberrys, Plumbs, Apples, & Pears and almost every other New England fruit but peaches at Port Roseway." They could grow "Oats, Barley, Rye, and the best of Flax," and during the previous year inhabitants had raised "Siberian Wheat in perfection."[8] In this early evaluation, most of the land was marked for farmland, and orchards and fish would provide additional sustenance. The double use of the word *perfection* in the summary of this report suggests that land assessors worked hard to portray the territory as a paradise. The American colonies may have fallen, but refugees could build a new Eden to the north.

The British government also organized supplemental provisions for the Loyalists' first months in Nova Scotia. This decision was a standard one; officials had made similar arrangements for the colony at Liverpool, Nova Scotia, about two decades prior to the Loyalist diaspora. The Port Roseway Associates anticipated receiving food aid for white emigrants and for the enslaved people they brought with them—whom the Associates referred to as "servants." These bondpeople would receive rations as long as their masters traveled in government vessels. Colonists who sailed on their own ships would not collect provisions. It is possible that officials imposed this rule in order to keep track of the number of people entering the province, and to prevent refugees from claiming more compensation than that to which they were entitled. Once on the ground, all white and enslaved people over the age of ten were to draw an allowance of six months' full provisions, while children would get six months' half allowance. Accordingly, on March 8, 1783, members of the Port Roseway Associates in New York passed a motion that proposed, "that each member do immediately give . . . a correct list of their names and families, with the age of every person in the family, describing their sexes, and that the same may be attended to with respect to their Servants."[9] The Associates made some efforts to count the number of people embarking, to make sure they would receive food, and to effect this process quickly.

Even before embarkation, white Loyalists tended to challenge the hunger-prevention efforts they deemed insufficient, while at the same time ignoring the free black population migrating alongside them. White colonists complained when they learned that the Nova Scotian government had revised some of the provisioning plans. By the start of 1783 Governor John Parr decreed from Halifax that although men and boys over thirteen years of age would get six months of full provisions, half provisions would suffice for women, and children under thirteen would receive one-fourth of the full amount.[10]

At the end of March, Rhode Island–born Captain Joseph Durfee, one of the key Port Roseway leaders, reported that after hearing about these arrangements, some Loyalists "were much affect'd and discouraged." He said that they had "indulged the Idea . . . they were to have the same allowance, as those Loyalists, who went to Nova Scotia" during the previous autumn of 1782. Durfee noted that some of them "were so much dismayed that I believed many of the number would not go." The Associates drew on past precedent to claim their right to comparable aid, but there is no evidence in the archival record that they advocated for similar assistance for free black refugees. When the first of these black colonists arrived in Canada in 1782–1783, there were no provisions waiting for them—though they may have witnessed white Loyalists' preparations for themselves.[11]

British officials did not concern themselves overmuch with complaints about provisioning—or the lack thereof—because they did not believe white Loyalists' threats to remain in the United States. Guy Carleton responded to Durfee even though Carleton would not take charge as governor-in-chief of Upper Canada until 1786; technically, Frederick Haldimand still performed that role. Carleton also drew on past precedent—and its absence—to explain the government's stance on food aid. His response to Durfee was "to say that Six Months Provision was ordered, [and] that all Males and Females upwards of ten years of Age would draw full allowance, which was never done before." Carleton reminded them that the Loyalists who had relocated the preceding fall had been "obliged to live the whole winter on their Provision, and our Associates would (if they arrive there early) have equal benefit." He reassured them that the Government would not "set a number of people down there, 'And say, *We will do nothing more for you*; You may *starve*. There is no doubt but if they are in want they will be supplied.'" Carleton then switched from this amicable tone to one that conveyed his annoyance with the Loyalists' wavering. "Government did not Chuse to make a bargain with the Association," he chided, "and if any were dissatisfied they had better *Not Go*, if they could do better for themselves."[12] Carleton offered encouragement, restored full provisions to women, and agreed to feed more children by pushing the age limit for full provisions back to ten instead of thirteen years of age. But he also explained that the government's food policy would be largely reactive, not preventative. The government would supply some provisions, but thereafter, *if* people were starving, *then* they would receive assistance. There was no mention, yet, of food laws to manage famine in a more coherent way. Ordinary people could question these decisions but not revise them.

And so, the colonists sailed. One group of Loyalists arrived on May 4, 1783, and established themselves about 130 miles southwest of Halifax, in Port Roseway, which they renamed Shelburne. Free black colonists lived in predominantly white communities such as Shelburne or Preston, and they also lived in mostly black towns. Ex-bondpeople constituted the majority of the population at Birchtown, Brindley Town, and Little Tracadie. Birchtown is on the Shelburne harbor, four and a half miles away from Shelburne itself; Brindley Town is now called Jordantown, and is about a hundred miles away on the opposite, northwestern side of the peninsula; Little Tracadie is the farthest away from Shelburne, over two hundred miles, on the northeast portion of

Nova Scotia. One 1784 Birchtown muster stated that Birchtown officially housed a large portion of these black refugees—1,521 of them—but the black population in all of Shelburne County was more likely at least double that number.[13]

Many of the black colonists, particularly the Black Pioneers, who had fought for the British during the war, came with the skills necessary to provide food for themselves and their families. Robert Roberts was twenty-four when he arrived in Birchtown; his wife, Jenny, was twenty-three. Record keepers listed Roberts as a farmer in the Shelburne muster book. Other farmers included Richard Laurence and Charles Wilkinson of Captain Nicholson's Company; Anthony Cooper, Henry Darling, Thomas Freeman, Pompey Donaldson, Jacob Williams, and Richard Jarrat of Captain Scott Murray's Company; and Anthony Davis, William Fortune, and Peter Daniel of Captain Jacob With's Company.[14]

Many of the other occupations recorded suggest abilities to gather, process, or prepare foodstuffs. David George was described as a farmer, but his narrative makes clear that his wartime activities also included butchering; once in the colony, he would become a Baptist preacher. Anthony Post, aged thirty, was a miller; Thomas Kane, thirty-one, was a fisherman; Marsh Jones, forty, was a gardener; Isaac Taylor, forty-three, was a butcher; John Charles Glass, forty, and John Brown, forty-seven, were both cooks; and men named Fortune Rivers and Norfolk Virginia were a cook and a baker, respectively. Women were less likely to have their occupations recorded, but readers might speculate about the ways that female travelers aided with or took charge of food preparation. Phillis George, David George's wife, had taken in washing and might have continued to do so. John Thomas was a baker, but he died either en route or upon arrival. Perhaps his wife, Elizabeth, took over his work in order to feed their daughter, Christiana, who was nine years old.[15]

For a very brief period of time, the government's disorganization was an advantage to black colonists. And the government *was* disorganized in most regions of diasporic Canada. Loyalists arrived in Quebec, for example, to find that new towns had no names, only numbers. Birchtown's black colonists thrived in this environment, experiencing a degree of control over local markets that mimicked but also improved upon their previous lives as victual warriors. Some people accumulated enough wealth to become an influential buying force: when a large number of black colonists left the Preston-Dartmouth region for Sierra Leone in 1792, their imminent departure caused the price of potatoes to drop from three dollars and one shilling to two and a half dollars per bushel, meaning that white potato farmers earned less for their produce.[16]

During the early 1780s, Nova Scotia did not possess a central marketplace. In this regard, it lagged behind food systems in many areas that belonged to, or would become part of, the United States. In the eighteenth-century Mississippi Valley, colonial officials had wavered between allowing slaves to openly market their goods and produce and requiring them to carry written permits from their owners. As early as 1763, Savannah's market had moved to Ellis Square, where planters policed the goods that enslaved people could sell. In 1784, New Orleans officials had established a fixed marketplace, where they required sellers to do business in rented stalls, and made it difficult for bondpeople to obtain stall permits and licenses.[17]

In Nova Scotia, by contrast, a number of locations, either in the center of urban areas or along the roads of the hinterland, served as venues where free black inhabitants could buy and sell produce with relatively little oversight. There were "Several markets in Halifax," and the "Butchers and Fishmongers" who "for want of a public market" set up "shops and stands in different places about the Town." These men "hawk[ed] their meat and poultry through the Streets." People in Preston sold seasonally caught fish—dogfish, eel, flounder, haddock, herring, salmon, shad, skate, and sturgeon—to whites in various local markets. Remembering the black colonists after they left, Sir John Wentworth, lieutenant governor of Nova Scotia, reflected that they "contributed very materially to . . . supplying this Market with Vegetables and Poultry." Even as late as 1797, when a central market existed, some of those who remained in British North America enjoyed the fact that their produce garnered a "great profit" in Halifax.[18] The absence of food regulations benefitted black colonists.

For the most part, the profits and self-sufficiency that former bondpeople enjoyed did not last. Land problems quickly became apparent in September 1783, when surveyor Benjamin Marston discovered that another surveyor had encroached on lands reserved for black colonists by reserving those lots for white emigrants instead. Only 184 of the 649 Birchtown residents obtained land, and those lots averaged 34 acres, compared to white allotments, which averaged 74. By 1785 in Annapolis County, seventy-six free black people had received land grants of 1 acre each, all in Digby, whereas white occupants each had received between 100 and 400 acres. Here, as well as in Annapolis, black refugees spent months waiting for lands that took a long time to be given out. In Clements in 1789, 148 out of 184 acres went to ex-bondpeople. Each person was supposed to receive 50 acres, but the transactions on these grants were rarely confirmed—these families did not get the land promised to them either. At Tracadie, Preston, and Hammond's Plains, the land was notably barren. By 1788 most of the refugees in all of Nova Scotia had received their lands, but these lots averaged 40 acres—a significantly smaller allotment than those given to most white colonists. Southern slaveholders in the United States restricted slaves' free time but not their access or ability to grow produce on garden plots. British officers during the Revolutionary War left black victual warriors to their own devices so that they could feed themselves by stealing. In Nova Scotia, black colonists possessed time but no economy of land.[19]

In addition to preventing black colonists from receiving land, white colonists also began to seek out better foodstuffs for themselves while controlling formerly enslaved peoples' access to provisions—thus creating black hunger. An anonymous writer of a 1787 depiction of Shelburne observed, "Never were known greater mixtures of privy & meanness than many of the families here exhibit." Some people, most likely whites, "seem passionately fond of all kinds of delicious food & drink." These people reminded the writer of what St. Paul said "in the Characters of the Cretians 'Whose God is their Belly & who glory in their shame.'" In Halifax, white Loyalists received provisions of codfish, molasses, and hard biscuit, with a very occasional supply of meat; black colonists, by contrast, subsisted on cornmeal and molasses.[20] Although provisions for white people could hardly be called luxurious—contrary to the Shelburne writer's claims—these foodstuffs became more prestigious because some people could not have them.

In other instances, white colonists denied black people food altogether. In Shelburne, all Loyalists were hypothetically entitled to pork and flour, but black "servants" who left the white families with whom they had migrated—either through emancipation or by running away—lost their rights to government-issued rations. Often, white employers continued to draw those provisions in their absence. When they provided food aid to former bondpeople, distributors doled out provisions in Shelburne, meaning that the former slaves who lived in Birchtown faced a three- to six-mile trek through frozen woods to collect the same weekly subsistence to which white residents were also entitled. By December 1,784 black people in Digby had received 12,098 pounds of flour and 9,352 pounds of pork. This distribution amounted to eighty full days of rations for 160 adults and 26 children, total—the only rations they would ever receive in Nova Scotia.[21] Despite the preparations of the Port Roseway Associates, the skills of black colonists, and their momentary influence in Nova Scotian marketplaces, the process of obtaining food grew more and more difficult.

The state of usefulness that free black colonists had enjoyed in Nova Scotia's various marketplaces declined beginning in the mid-1780s as a result of new food laws—but they were new only in Canada, because similar regulations had existed elsewhere for centuries.

Governments had passed food laws to fight famine in the medieval and early modern periods in Europe, and such practices had traveled to the North American colonies. These laws have come to be known as the "moral economy," or a model in which, during times of scarcity, common folk stop accepting inequalities of power and wealth to pressure wealthy men into fulfilling their end of the social contract by guaranteeing access to food at a just price.[22] People did not expect to legislate against hunger themselves, but they did expect the government to do it for them.

During the medieval period English leaders played their role in the moral economy by fixing the price of bread and allowing the size of the loaf to change; by the early modern period local governments periodically changed both the price of the loaf and its size. Price-fixing of other foodstuffs—codified between 1580 and 1630 and published as the *Book of Orders* under Charles I— became common in England during the reign of the Tudors in reaction to population growth and enclosure. Such practices for regulating grain distribution also existed in places like France, where officials controlled the conduct of farmers, officials, millers, and bakers. People asserted their right to be protected against dearth, and governments passed laws to fight hunger, particularly during wartime, and often in reaction to riotous subjects. In the colonies, Revolutionary northern state governments, in response to food rioters, supply struggles, and the behavior of self-interested colonists during the war, began to experiment with price-fixing and embargoes.[23] In all of these instances, people pressured the government to fix prices but did not suggest that this right should be allocated directly to the people.

During the late eighteenth century much of Canada's government oversight had occurred at the local level. In Nova Scotia the county court system was the primary body responsible for adjudicating questions of government and legality (and thus questions about the moral economy) until the 1830s. At the start of 1784 the Shelburne Courts set about passing food-related laws. Joseph Durfee, who had worked with Guy Carleton over the issue of white Loyalists' provisions, assumed the judgeship over the Court of Common Pleas, and a Court of Sessions was established to handle matters of everyday governance.[24]

The structure of land allotments meant that these laws, and the patterns of marketplace hunger prevention that they codified, affected black residents of Shelburne and Birchtown. In February 1785 the Shelburne court ordered that bread sold by bakers "shall be a six-penny loaf, to Weigh one pound, thirteen ounces. . . . And that all such Bread shall be made of good, sound inspected Wheaten flour." In June of the same year the court further stipulated that people who sold bread needed to shape it into "single, or double Loaves," the pricing of which would "from time to time be regulated."[25] Bread laws may have meant that free black bakers, like Norfolk Virginia, who practiced baking as a side occupation and who baked with cheaper cornmeal—a slave staple—or rye flour, would find it difficult to conform to government-decreed standards of weight and appearance. The surveyor who reported to the Port Roseway Associates had established that rye flour could be grown, but there is little evidence of black colonists raising either corn or rye. Even if they had, it is easy to shape a loaf of bread made with wheat flour because the gluten gives the dough structure; dough made from cornmeal and buttermilk, by contrast, does not hold its shape well unless placed in a pan or skillet, where it will form a denser cake. It would have been challenging to bake such bread into loaves.

More significantly, the courts also modified the meaning of the marketplace itself, making it harder for freedpersons to hawk edible goods. In May 1785 the court forbade meat, fish, vegetables, "or other articles of provisions" from being sold "in any street, lane, or on the strand, or shore of this town, other than in the market, or places established by order of Sessions," such as "Markets in King street, and at the Cove." Not everyone adhered to these laws, as evidenced by the fact that even as late as 1800, members of the Shelburne Grand Jury observed "That the want of some place as a Market for the reception of a Number of small articles of the Provision kind, brought by the Country People" caused "a Number of Inconveniences, & indeed, Impositions." "In many Instances" these foodstuffs were "bought up, and sold again at a shameful advance."[26] The court complained that "country people"—likely black inhabitants who lived in the country precisely because of unequal land distributions—were taking advantage of the lack of a central marketplace to purchase and resell goods for profit. People still managed to sell provisions in odd places and at high prices, but the passing of such regulations began to limit participation in the market economy. For the most part, free black people could no longer sell their goods where they wished, which meant that *if* they could obtain permission to sell out of a market stall, they would then need to adhere to market prices that delayed profits.

Another set of rules and regulations passed on April 10, 1786, limited fishing activities—one of the main ways in which people without lands supplemented their diet and income. Boston King later observed that upon first arriving in Nova Scotia, white colonists were too focused on "building large houses, and striving to excel one another in this piece of vanity." Only "when their money was almost expended" did these inhabitants begin "to build small fishing vessels"; they realized that they, too, would require additional food sources. Once white colonists began to catch, eat, and sell fish, fishing laws began to appear. Whites prohibited fishing nets and seines from reaching more than a third of the way into a river; fishing was banned from Saturday to Monday; and erecting a dam on the river was not allowed "under any pretence whatever" as a means to "obstruct the Passage of the Fish."[27]

This practice of restricting land use near riverfronts deviated from earlier practices. In mid-eighteenth-century Liverpool, for example, all single men owned a share in the fish lots laid out along the shores of rivers and harbors. This egalitarian lot-sharing seems to have fallen out of practice (if it ever existed in Shelburne) by the mid-1780s. These rules also tended to give preference to white fishermen: people who owned advantageous land by the river got the first choice of net placement. Later remembrances indicated that black colonists did not receive riverine land, and subsequent court decisions indicate that white Loyalists did in fact restrict black people's access to the water, thus making it impossible for these fishermen to fish in the same way as white Loyalists.[28] If a man had to work on a white man's farm during the week, he could not fish on the weekend; and if he was lucky enough to live on the river but far away, the law prevented him from damming it to trap fish. These regulations allowed whites to gain control of the fish trade. Although it is difficult to prove that whites enacted such laws with the intention to circumscribe black access to food, the laws nevertheless threatened black food security specifically.

Land problems and changes in the legal system were challenging enough, but hunger became a real problem as a result of adverse weather. During the late 1780s extreme cold weather led to short planting seasons, which in turn resulted in sparse crops. Nova Scotian food supplies suffered from the same agricultural challenges that plagued upstate New York and the southern states during this time period, but there had been far less time to build up grain reserves. Most white Loyalists possessed the means to leave, and the fact that many of them moved closer to Liverpool, Tusket, and Yarmouth underscores the reality of these food shortages. Some freed blacks followed them, but those without the funds to do so stayed behind. By the late 1780s, Shelburne was turning into a ghost town. In 1785 a nameless slave was hanged in Halifax for the crime of stealing a bag of potatoes. The cold winters did not help the situation: some of the Nova Scotians spent them living in shoddy shelters that were really holes in the ground with flimsy roofs.[29]

Poor harvests should have compelled government officials to issue more food provisions, as Sir Guy Carleton had said they would, but instead, in 1787, the British government ignored its moral economic responsibilities and stopped sending provisions. The central government had a history of ceasing provisions supplies a couple of years into a colony's development; it halted the arrival of foodstuffs two years after colonization of Liverpool. Even white colonists worried about this change; some of them noted that officials still had not distributed land, and "future subsistance by Agriculture has been denied." They complained, "It is now above six weeks since the Salt Provisions provided for the use of the Loyalists have been expended, and now there remains no provisions of any kind in his Majesties Stores." They speculated that the absence of land combined with the lack of provisions meant that "the horrors of Famine must ensue."[30] It is not difficult to understand why the black colonists, denied land with even greater frequency than whites and struggling under the burden of new legislation, likely found this situation even more troublesome.

Whereas in Liverpool earlier in the century, where the British government had assisted the poor even when general provisioning ceased, in Shelburne the local people tried to exile its poor, mostly black population. In 1789 a body called "the overseers of the poor" sent a petition to the magistrates of Shelburne. They noted, "there are a great number of Black people, both in this Town & in Birchtown, who are in the most distressing Circumstances." Because "the number of white People, whom we have constantly to supply, are very considerable," they explained, "it is not in our power to afford the Blacks that assistance" they required. The petitioners pleaded with the magistrates to "free this Infant Settlement from a Burden which it is by no Means in a Capacity to bear."[31] Absent from the records are black colonists' reactions to this petition to push them out of the province.

By the eighteenth century, overseers of the poor had become common to deal with growing numbers of unemployed people and vagrants, so the office was not unique to the institution of slavery. It is difficult to tell what formerly enslaved black colonists made of the fact that the men in charge of providing them with aid were known as "overseers," or what they thought about being described as a burden when white Loyalists' land interests and legislative changes had taken away their abilities to make themselves useful. The overseers clearly hoped that Shelburne magistrates would lean on the British government to begin the process of relocating black colonists. Between 1789 and 1791 Nova Scotia earned the nickname "Nova Scarcity," and former slaves began to reconsider whether they wanted to call such a place their home.[32] The combination of land issues, scanty or nonexistent provisions, and restrictive food laws made Nova Scotia a colony where victual imperialism ensured the continuation of black hunger while at the same time giving displaced white Loyalists an advantage over black refugees.

While the British failed to apportion land in Nova Scotia, a group of British abolitionists in England confronted the institution of British slavery and their options for ending it. They had hoped to create an antislavery colony in Africa that stood as an example that would convince other countries to eradicate the slave trade, but thus far they had been unsuccessful. Several schemes on the upper Guinea coast had failed: the province of Senegambia, the colony of Bulama, and the first Granville Town colony of London's Black Poor. In 1791 Thomas Clarkson, his younger brother John, Granville Sharp, Henry Thornton, and William Wilberforce formed the Sierra Leone Company to supervise a new antislavery venture in Africa. On August 19, 1791, John Clarkson sailed on the *Ark* from Gravesend to Halifax, arrived on October 7, and began making preparations for departure to Africa. In Nova Scotia he witnessed the effects of hunger on the colony's black population.[33]

John Clarkson associated land dearth with hunger, and thus with bondage and powerlessness. When he arrived in Halifax, he observed that because black refugees had "never had Lands," they had been "obliged to live upon Whitemens property . . . and for cultivating it they receive half the produce so that they are in Short in a state of Slavery." He interviewed various people in late 1791, linking land and food absences. "Jacob Coffee" had "served in the army last war," but "never rec[eive]d either Lands or Provisions." He made the same annotations about a man named Samuel Jones.[34] Men and women without land, who had previously provided useful military assistance, now earned provisions instead of wages. According to Clarkson, people without land felt forced into remaining in Canada because they depended on whites with farmland to give them the labor that allowed them to earn their bread.

David George and Boston King also described the efforts they made to obtain provisions through usefulness—George, after receiving government and charitable aid, and King, by traveling widely to find work. David George, who separated briefly from his wife and children so that he could work as a preacher in Shelburne, returned to find that the new governor, Governor Parr, had arranged six months of provisions for the Georges as well as a quarter acre of land. The family still struggled to establish themselves with a comfortable subsistence, despite George's efforts to convert people to the Baptist faith. During a later, difficult period, a white Baptist colonist named Ann Taylor gave him money "to buy a bushel of potatoes," from which George produced "thirty-five bushels."[35] In his narrative he made sure to explain that this Christian charity—which came from one person, rather than from the government—prompted him to make better plans to become self-sufficient by planting part of her gift to him.

Boston King survived by moving and attributed his deliverance to his faith in God. In 1787, a year of "dreadful famine," he left Birchtown because he "could get no employment" and so "travelled from place to place, to procure the necessaries of life" to support him and his wife. He described his resignation "to the divine will" and began to pray more. He saved his family by making a chest that a white captain paid for in maize, which gave him "a reprieve from the dreadful anguish of perishing by famine." "Oh what a wonderful deliverance did GOD work for me that day!" he wrote. He also built fishing boats in exchange for corn. King favorably compared his ability to work for food to the situation of his "black brethren, who were obliged to sell themselves to the merchants, some for two or three years; and others for five or six years." Thereafter he resolved "to live by faith, and to put my trust in him, more than I ever had done before."[36]

Even though David George and Boston King were only two men, their writings offer several readings of what it meant to be hungry and different strategies to avoid want. During the 1787 famine that King described as "dreadful," people perished. He wrote that they "fell down dead in the streets, thro' hunger," while those fortunate enough to survive did so by killing and eating "their dogs and cats." He himself was "pinched with hunger and cold," and while he searched for work he remembered falling "down several times, thro' weakness," expecting "to die upon the spot."[37] His hunger was a test from God, and his remembrance clarifies the comments that Clarkson had made in his observations about black colonists receiving no wages from white landowners. King seemed pleased to earn food instead of wages, indicating that payment in foodstuffs was not necessarily a bad thing as long as it seemed that God had willed it. Black colonists may also have believed that this sort of compensation was tolerable as long as they retained a say in limiting the length of their employment. Boston King thought himself useful, but he also believed that God made him fortunately so; it was not his fellow colonists' uselessness but unluckiness and perhaps lack of faith that forced them to sell themselves into a state of indenture that resembled slavery.

David George's portrayal of eating, by contrast, offered black men and women a great deal more power. One Christian's charity allowed him to plant potatoes and thrive in subsequent months as a Baptist preacher. He told the story of a moment at St. John's, where he went to baptize other black colonists. George wrote that when he disembarked from his ship, the people "were so full of joy that they ran out from waiting at table on their masters, with the knives and forks in their hands, to meet me at the water side."[38] In this vivid image, black people abandoned their roles as food preparers and servers, taking with them the cutlery that allowed people to serve food in a civilized way. If these white masters wished to remain satiated, George implied, they would need to eat with their fingers.

Black experiences with hunger were tied to ideas about charity, freedom, and usefulness. In John Clarkson's estimation, it was difficult to distinguish between freedom from hunger and freedom from slavery. David George's account provided readers with one of the few possible examples in the early years of British colonization of Nova Scotia in which black people created white hunger—or at least delayed white Loyalists from eating. His focus on formerly enslaved people running away from tables to be baptized at water's edge, furthermore, prioritized addressing spiritual hunger over physical want. Boston King conceptualized hunger as something that made people physically weak, and sometimes killed them. It was also something that people could avoid, given the right combination of providence and hard work. He had been ambivalent about migrating to Sierra Leone but changed his mind when he heard that colonists would receive "provisions till we could clear a sufficient portion of land necessary for our subsistence."[39] The absence of a time limit on provisions distributions, compared to those years in Nova Scotia when government aid disappeared, gave him confidence to think that black colonists could attain a state of usefulness—to themselves, to their fellow colonists, and perhaps even to the British Crown—in Africa.

Sierra Leone Company officials envisioned Nova Scotia's formerly enslaved population as potential migrants, and Clarkson sailed to Halifax to resettle them because of the actions of a man named Thomas Peters. Peters, a Yoruba man who had labored on a sugarcane plantation in French Louisiana, had run away from slavery in North Carolina, joined the Revolution on the British side, and earned a position as a private in the Black Pioneers. In November 1790, at the age of fifty-three, he sailed to England to petition for the black colonists' removal from Nova Scotia to a more advantageous place. Peters heard about the plan for a colony in Sierra Leone after another, unnamed black man, who was waiting on a party of people eating dinner, overheard them talking about the scheme; he passed the news on to others. Here again, colonists' relationships with food service was important—in this case, not because it offered freedom from hunger, but because it offered freedom of mobility. When Thomas Peters arrived in London, General Sir Henry Clinton procured a meeting for him with Sharp, Wilberforce, and the Clarkson brothers. Peters confirmed that these men were indeed envisioning a new colony "on the River Sierra Leona" and viewed this plan as a resettlement opportunity. In a bold petition to them, he argued that Sierra Leone would be "an Asylum much better suited to their Constitutions than Nova Scotia and New Brunswick," and suggested that he and the black colonists be allowed to migrate.[40]

The various groups of black colonists reacted to the idea of the new colony in different ways. By the time Clarkson arrived in 1791, Shelburne was divided between four free black factions, led by a free-born Barbadian mulatto, Colonel Stephen Blucke; Methodist Boston King; another Methodist preacher called Moses Wilkinson; and David George, who led a Baptist congregation. In Halifax Clarkson met David George and Stephen Blucke. George expressed enthusiastic interest in the Sierra Leone project, whereas Blucke denounced it as a foolish death mission. Blucke might already have heard rumors about the unhealthy and dangerous environment in Sierra Leone and judged Nova Scotia preferable. Stephen Skinner, Blucke's former militia commander, bribed others into staying with promises of two years of free food rations. When another group chose to remain behind, they felt justified in asking Governor John Parr for funds for "a Cow & two Sheep," because the expense "is by no means adequate to the vast expence of transporting so many of our fellow Subjects to Africa."[41] By demonstrating that they required less funding and posed less inconvenience to government, they also used their knowledge of food aid to loyal subjects. Wilkinson's and King's congregations, like George's, prepared to depart.

Clarkson did what he could to promote the new colonization scheme. After witnessing the starving conditions of landless black colonists, he even made land-related promises on behalf of the Sierra Leone Company that he was unauthorized to offer.[42] Little by little, prospective colonists and their families trickled in from various points to Halifax; by the beginning of December over a thousand people had gathered to wait for officials to sort out provisions and shipping matters.

At the very end of December, Clarkson received a joint petition from Thomas Peters and a man named David Edmonds on behalf of the people bound for Africa. Anticipating that this year would be "the larst Christmas day that we ever shall see" in America, they asked him "to grant us one days alowance of frish Beef for a Christmas diner."[43] The men knew that the Nova Scotian government had failed to prevent black hunger, but they nevertheless appealed to the established notion that organizers of new colonial projects would provide them with food aid during times of celebration. Yet this beef was not meant to sustain them in the long term; it was a symbolic request that asked Clarkson and the other gentlemen to make a gesture of good faith. This was the colonists' last request for food aid in Nova Scotia. It, along with Thomas Peters's, was also one of their first petitions. They set sail for Sierra Leone in January 1792.

Decades later, during the mid-nineteenth century, English reformers would argue that only hunger could teach the poor the morality they needed to want to labor virtuously.[44] Authors like Boston King, who contended that hunger could be avoided through a combination of hard work and God's grace, were already articulating the morality and work ethic that anticipated these English Poor Law reforms by almost half a century. When Thomas Peters and David Edmonds requested beef for a Christmas dinner in light of provisioning failures in Nova Scotia, they were appealing to British imperial agents' sense of moral obligation, but they did so while planning to be useful in Sierra Leone—both men would seek political office there.

The colonists who sailed were entering a fluid, expanding Atlantic World. That world had connected people, plants, and animals at least since Europeans had invaded North America, but the black refugees who sailed were some of the first to cross back across this oceanic network to Africa. In the sixteenth and seventeenth centuries, it was possible to imagine lines that forcibly connected enslaved Africans to the Caribbean and the Caribbean to North America. In the eighteenth century, imperial officials and ordinary folks imagined new connections between the former American colonies and Nova Scotia, and between Nova Scotia and Sierra Leone.

Black colonists used food and information networks to leave the former American colonies, but most of those networks froze up in Nova Scotia. After food laws went into effect, Boston King and David George did not try to address their hunger by procuring, producing, or preparing food, even though they possessed those skills. They had to prove their usefulness in other ways because white Loyalist lawmaking had inhibited the abilities of black colonists to participate in the Nova Scotian food system. Even the black colonists associated with food preparation in Canada—the men and women who may have been servants or may have been enslaved—tended to ignore their food-related responsibilities when given the opportunity, casting their forks and knives aside.

The black colonists' time in Nova Scotia taught them new strategies about old practices. It showed them how conventional food laws could be used to control the lives of other people, and it also illustrated the potential of failure when hunger prevention was left jointly in the hands of local courts and distant government. When Clarkson made his offer of migration, a third of the population decided to take their chances in Sierra Leone. Imperial officials like Clarkson and the other members of the Sierra Leone Company had learned to look further abroad to help the British Empire expand. They also drew lines between North America and India as it became clear that the empire's interests lay further east to make up for its lost North American colonies.[45]

Timothy Pickering knew about this imperial expansion, and he wanted Native Americans to know about it in ways that served the interests of the

United States. So when he met Cornplanter in 1791 to deliver his history lecture, Pickering also offered a lesson in demography. "Brothers, on the other side of the Great Water, far beyond the nations of white people," he told the Iroquois, "there are many nations of Indians who have dark skins, black hair & black eyes, like you. But these Indians are farmers, carpenters, Smiths, Spinners and weavers, like the white people." The existence of these Indians mattered to Pickering, but it was not his main point; "above all tea is brought from those countries, and from those countries alone," he explained.[46] Historians could say a lot about this comparison: about the importance Pickering placed on tea, which after all had mattered so much to the colonists who rebelled against Great Britain; about his conflation of Native Americans with Indians from India and evolving notions of race in the eighteenth century; and about whether Pickering spoke out of malice or ignorance.[47]

For our purposes, the moment is significant because Pickering was trying to use this information to convince Cornplanter that by becoming farmers and weavers, the Six Nations could also grow and enjoy the tea they drank at treaties. The federal government was making plans for its own food policy and thus its own hunger-prevention initiatives, ushering in a new era of American victual imperialism.

PART THREE

Power Waning

CHAPTER 7

Victual Imperialism and U.S. Indian Policy

In 1791, Timothy Pickering, U.S. Indian agent, recited to the Seneca named Cornplanter a false history of European self-sufficiency and Native hunger in early America, in which Indians hungered because they hunted and non-Natives flourished by eating the abundant yields of their farms. Pickering hoped that his interpretation of the past would persuade Cornplanter and other Indians to change their methods of food production and conform to the U.S. government's new policy, known then as the "Plan of Civilization." The time had come, Pickering argued, for Indians to "adopt some of the ways of the white people. Instead of depending on hunting," he urged, "let your children be instructed in farming, raising of cattle, Sheep and hogs." Federal officials created this strategy to alter Native cattle-raising, agriculture, pricing, and eating habits in order to legitimize the government's landgrabs.[1] Their choices signaled a transition from a food policy of diplomatic exchange and aid distributions to one that succeeded in changing Native food systems, and a transition from a weak federal Indian policy to one that sought greater power in the country's Native American foreign affairs. The 1790s witnessed the rise of American victual imperialism.

The U.S. government could not take large amounts of Native land until Indians lost the power to fight hunger themselves. During the 1780s and 1790s, U.S. Indian commissioners had copied generous British diplomacy because they feared Native hunger. As the federal government gained an advantage over the states, U.S. officials tried to decrease the cost of such practices by telling Native Americans about alternative ways to prevent hunger: by producing crops, meat, and dairy. The Plan of Civilization relied upon the idea that Indians who adopted American notions of proper husbandry could become usefully independent, and could use less land to do so.[2]

A few problems delayed the plan's implementation. First, non-Native officials misunderstood Indian appetites and remained uncertain about the extent to which starvation was truly a problem. Second, Indians already grew crops; Americans' destruction of corn bushels during the Revolutionary and Western Confederacy Wars provided evidence of extensive Native farming. Although it was hard for U.S. officials to accept Indian agricultural methods, it was equally difficult to convince Indians to farm when Native women already did so. Finally, several groups—Western Confederacy Indians, some Creeks, and some Iroquois—refused American officials' offers to implement the plan in their villages. Ultimately, the federal government managed to push the policy through because some factions of Creeks, Buffalo Creek Senecas, Genesee Oneidas, Onondagas, and Senecas proved willing to collaborate with U.S. officials.[3] Once officials had changed the ways that Indians prevented hunger, the government could step in to convince Indians that it could prevent Native hunger more efficiently than Indians.

By the mid-1810s the Plan of Civilization's promoters had succeeded in decreasing food aid and distributing provisions that physically sickened Native Americans. The scheme, rather than preventing Indian hunger by transforming Indians into husbandmen, instead ate up Indians' territory while killing Indians. The Plan of Civilization was a federal land *and* food policy that pervaded interactions between Indians and federal Indian agents, and it shows how ideas about hunger prevention served as both a diplomatic tool and a weapon from the 1780s to the 1810s.

Victual imperialism in the new United States was slightly different from the victual imperialism that free black colonists encountered in Nova Scotia, underscoring the necessity of insisting on precise definitions for the term across time and space.[4] In Nova Scotia the local courts were effective, and centralized government was not. White Loyalists exercised what little power they had by stopping black colonists from getting land rather than by taking it from them. They emphasized concomitant laws that created controls on black people's food access. Diplomacy between white and black colonists did not exist because diplomacy requires some balance of power, and in Canada white colonists claimed the majority of power. In the United States, by contrast, victual imperialism consisted of the institutionalization of a centralized, federal food policy—built on the introduction of plowing, cattle ranching, and then price-fixing food laws—that facilitated sales and seizures of Native American territory.

American victual imperialism worked alongside the Native and non-Native diplomacy that continued into the 1810s. Victual imperialism and food diplomacy both mischaracterized Native hunger while encouraging select groups of Indians to collaborate with non-Native officials to implement and enforce changes in the food system. Once this process was underway, victual imperialism replaced food diplomacy, and Native Americans lost this particular battle.

Although various eighteenth-century authors had written about attempts to "civilize" Indians throughout the colonial and postwar period, it was only in the late 1780s and early 1790s that various men connected this project to the prevention of Native hunger. They suggested making changes to crop production, hunting customs, and education; their ideas formed the basis for the federal government's Plan of Civilization. Samuel Kirkland, a white Christian missionary, had lived with and preached to Iroquois and Stockbridge Indians in various villages since the 1760s. He received funding from the Society in Scotland for Propagating Christian Knowledge, and direction from its board in Boston.[5]

Descriptions of Iroquois hunger permeate the journal entries that Kirkland penned in the late 1780s. In early April 1789, Oneidas and Tuscaroras had been fasting and praying "on account of the scarcity of provisions." Later that month others told him that they were considering dispersing for the year so that shared foodstuffs stretched further. That May, he recorded a meeting with "an aged Indian" who worried that "God is angry with us Indians. We are reduced to extremity. Never was such a time with us Indians. We are very hungry and almost starved. . . . My family have not tasted any bread, or meat, for many days; nothing but herbs and sometimes small fish. I am so weak I can't hoe my corn."[6] The year 1789 *had* been a year of hunger and near famine, but mentions of hunger had long featured in Natives' interactions with non-Natives. The Iroquois were dealing with this period of scarcity in familiar, useful ways: by overstating their hunger and refusing to hoe corn in order to receive more food aid, by imbuing fasts with religious meaning, by dispersing to avoid overstressing grain reserves, and by turning to fishing and gathering.

A reform of Indian behavior would address these problems of hunger, Kirkland thought, and so he eagerly reported instances when Native Americans asked for or approved of his changes. In December 1789 he spoke to Seneca chief Big Tree (Karontowanen, sometimes called Great Tree—possibly the same man whose suicide Anthony Wayne later tried to exploit) and Captain Isaac (Tolaghdowane). Kirkland intended to gradually remove "Your wandering manner of life, your strong attachments to the customs of the Fathers, & your prejudices against the white people in general." He believed that Indians could become good Christians by embracing his ideas about civility and permanent settlement in a fixed location. Like other critics, Kirkland wanted Indians to become more sedentary, which would in turn promote the sort of productive farming he envisioned while also reducing conflict between Natives and non-Natives. That year he described Buffalo Creek and Genesee Oneidas, Onondagas, and Senecas asking him "to make provision for the education of some of their youths." These Indians had asked Kirkland to adopt Native children "into [his] family" and teach them "the english language, to read & write the same." He noted that "The other kind of schooling" needed to take place "in their respective Villages."[7]

That other schooling—instruction in non-Native agricultural methods—soon became clear. In 1791 Kirkland wrote down his ideas and requested funding from Scotland. He envisioned a school "in the vicinity of Oneida" near a non-Native village. He hoped to admit two Seneca children, one or two Oneidas, and one Onondaga and Cayuga. White children would matriculate alongside Indians. They would all learn history, law, government, arithmetic, and to read and write English and Indian languages. The curriculum also included instruction in "the art of husbandry" but failed to distinguish this husbandry from extant Native agriculture. The editor of Kirkland's journals observes that Kirkland intended children to cultivate plots near the school, and that each Indian village would also gain a resident farmer. Once Indians established agriculture suitable to non-Native standards in their villages, women would go to workhouses to learn to read and write and then would take courses in domestic economy, spinning, and weaving.[8] Kirkland's plan rested on the school's proximity to non-Natives, on teaching academic knowledge alongside practical skills, on changing Native gender roles, and on removing Indian children from villages.

There are reasons to be skeptical of Kirkland's assessment of Native hunger and his ideas about ameliorating it. For one thing, he seemed ignorant of the fact that Native Americans already knew history, and had their own methods of recording the past. For another, he was not self-sufficient, so he was the wrong person to change Indian agriculture by example. His itinerant preaching contradicted his model of a more settled life, and at various points in his diaries he admitted depending on Indians for food. In January 1785 he lived "almost intirely on strawberries, with now & then a little fish" while preaching to Stockbridge Indians. His Christian spirit flagged "for want of sustenance." Stockbridge Indians shared food with him, but it was not enough; the Indians consequently "consented to release me till the latter part of the summer, by which time they expected the fruits of the Earth would enable them to afford me some little subsistence." Four years later, in 1789, he confessed the pressing necessity of making "some improvements in husbandry & cultivation so as to raise my own provisions in the vicinity of Oneida, or I shall remain under embarrassed circumstances during my whole life."[9] Kirkland's "embarrass[ment]" may have been a simple description of his financial situation, but his inability to grow the crops he urged other men to plant probably made him into an awkward figure of uselessness. It is also possible that Kirkland's hunger—which he was less capable than Indians of enduring—made the Iroquois and Stockbridges doubt his ability to prevent theirs.

This was victual imperialism in action; it was a plan to reform Indian husbandry while taking Indian land. The preacher not only passed messages between and translated for the Iroquois and the U.S. government; he also funded his school from the donations of land speculators. After the Revolution Kirkland's missionary zeal gave way to his own financial concerns—not least of which involved acquiring a tract of Oneida land, which he subsequently expanded by aiding other speculators and Massachusetts and New York state officials (who also sought cessions). Ultimately, Kirkland's school succeeded, but not in the form intended. New York governor George Clinton authorized the school's charter in January 1793. The schoolhouse burned down, and though another one was rebuilt around 1794, the Society in Scotland refused to fund it. The repaired school became Hamilton College, which educated white pupils, not Indian ones.[10] Kirkland's attempts at reforming Native crop production and education, consequently, did not enjoy widespread success.

Other men were ready with alternative suggestions for changing Indian husbandry while eyeing Indian land. Timothy Pickering also penned ideas for "the means of introducing the art of husbandry, and civilization, among our Indian neighbours" in 1791. Samuel Kirkland had corresponded with Pickering about his idea for a school, and they agreed on some points but not others. Both men thought that proper male husbandmen should cease hunting and ranging and farm in one place, while women should no longer farm. Like other American officials both Pickering and Kirkland planned to stop women's agricultural labor by encouraging them to become spinners and weavers. Pickering believed that Kirkland's approach could succeed in teaching "Indian youths" to farm, but unlike Kirkland he worried about what would happen when those men returned "to their own country" and, in his words, reverted into "mere Savages."[11]

"The remedy Seemed obvious" to Pickering. He proposed leaving children in their villages, educating them with just a little "reading, writing and arithmetic," and allowing them to "*practically* learn the art of husbandry" through instruction by non-Native teachers who would reside among them. He pro-posed, as further encouragement, sending "a cow, a yoke of oxen, a plough, a cart, and the other proper instruments of husbandry" to three separate Iro-quois locations. Pickering even drew up a budget for the U.S. government to consider.[12] His approach preempted backsliding, did not require removing children from villages, and defined non-Native husbandry through a detailed discussion of domesticated animals, meat and dairy production, and plow ag-riculture.

This focus on cattle and plows revealed some of the contradictions of pro-posals for this initiative. People voiced conflicting ideas about corn, wheat, and beef during this time period. In Virginia, planters shifted their focus from to-bacco to wheat production, which in turn demanded the plow, but further south the loamy soils were so poor that until the mid-nineteenth century even Anglo-American farmers eschewed plows. Some people simply became un-interested in owning land altogether, particularly in certain regions of Ken-tucky, Maryland, and Tennessee. Indians may have preferred to grow and eat corn, and indeed some non-Native writers (from Benjamin Franklin to doc-tor Benjamin Rush to poet Joel Barlow) championed it. Other Americans, however, would come to believe that wheat was a cheaper, more elevated, and nutritious grain than maize.[13]

Plow and wheat agriculture required more farmland—not less, as Picker-ing claimed—than the hoe and corn agriculture on which Indians had previ-ously relied. Iroquois hoe use produced crop yields that surpassed non-Native ones, and it kept soils healthier for longer. Cattle presented another problem: American breeders remained insecure about their cattle, which seemed wilder and bonier than well-bred British cattle.[14] Pickering, who assumed that enthu-siasm for the plan would spread from village to village, ignored the practical considerations necessary to ensure successful implementation.

And then there was the problem of Pickering's perception of Native hun-ger. By summer of 1791 he was arguing that his version of the plan was a good one because he mistakenly assumed that Indians' requests for provisions stemmed from useless, insatiable appetites rather than adherence to established diplomatic practices. When pitching his plan to Indians, he emphasized the potential abundance of Indian food production. In a conversation with Corn-planter, Pickering championed the superiority of American husbandry, describ-ing a society in which each man played a specialized role. Farmers farmed, but they were the endpoint of a long system that enabled them to do so. Smiths forged "plough-irons, hoes, axes, scythes, and all other iron tools" that made it easier (he thought) to plow fields. Carpenters built "houses and barns" for storing food, in addition to "ploughs, carts, and other things . . . for the use of the farmers." With these types of aid farmers raised "abundance of cattle and corn, wheat and other grain," which in turn let them feed "thousands of families" as well as their own. If they adopted this system, Pickering implied, Indians would not need to ask the Americans for rations because they would raise their own surplus. Even at a time when Pickering was heavily involved in conducting Indian diplomacy, he did not understand that Indians asked for food because they expected rather than needed it. The people to whom Pickering reported trusted his assessment of the situation; Secretary of War Henry Knox, who approved of Pickering's scheme, convinced George Washington to follow Pickering's recommendations.[15]

Some Iroquois did seem amenable to receiving the animals and undertaking the farming reforms that were integral to the Plan of Civilization—probably because they already farmed and owned domesticated animals. Seneca leaders Big Tree and Captain Isaac, who in 1789 heard Kirkland's description of his school, said that they would "submit wholly" to Kirkland in the matter of its location. In 1791 Big Tree and some other Senecas (Half Town and Cornplanter) asked at a meeting if federal officials would "teach us to plough and to Grind Corn," and offered "to Send nine Seneka boys to be under your care for education." Part of this request was posture; Indians already ground corn (though it is unclear whether Big Tree was referring specifically to men, in which case they might indeed have needed to learn to grind corn). Plow agriculture would have been less widespread. George Washington agreed conditionally to the application. He delegated Secretary of War Henry Knox to say that the U.S. preferred to keep Indian children in Native villages, and would send "one or two Sober men to reside in your Nation, with proper implements of husbandry." In March 1792 the U.S. Senate agreed to devote $1,500 for "clothing, domestic animals and implements of husbandry, and for encouraging useful artificers to reside" in the villages of the Six Nations. By 1796 that annuity had grown to $4,500.[16]

Efforts further south mirrored those in New York and Pennsylvania; officials described the Plan of Civilization, and some Indians voiced assent (though perhaps not enthusiasm). The 1790 federal Treaty of New York with Creeks led by Scots-Creek Alexander McGillivray offered the opportunity to promote the idealized version of non-Native husbandry to the Creeks under McGillivray's influence. This treaty—which confirmed a land cession Creeks had made at the 1783 Treaty of Augusta, returned land ceded in 1785 at Galphinton, and transferred what remained of Creek territory from Georgia to federal jurisdiction—offered U.S. officials the leverage to promote a shift in Indian food-production methods. In return for good behavior the U.S. proposed to adjudicate future land sales (as they did at Colerain) and to "furnish gratuitously . . .

useful domestic animals, and implements of husbandry." This gift would ensure that "the Creek nation may be led to a greater degree of civilization, and
to become herdsmen and cultivators." Timothy Pickering phrased it differently in a letter to George Washington, in which he suggested that these presents would change Creeks "from hunters to husbandmen."[17]

Some Creeks—such as the "New Order" Creeks who already owned
cattle—would have appreciated such valuable domesticated animals. Calves
and cows cost approximately ten dollars, and beef steers sold at two and a half
dollars per year for every year the animal had lived. Bacon sold for around
thirty cents per pound.[18] Here too, however, U.S. officials directed their "civi-
lizing" hunger-prevention efforts at Creeks who *already* raised cattle, perhaps
having stolen them during the Revolutionary War.

By portraying the farm implements and animals as presents, treaty negotiators could claim to be stopping Native hunger, practicing diplomacy, *and*
pursuing their civilization agenda. The Treaty of New York stated, "No citizen or inhabitant of the United States shall attempt to hunt or destroy the
game on the Creek lands." The government, by restating its interest in stopping non-Native incursions, committed to record federal recognition and protection of Creek-owned land. Although this stipulation had appeared on
other treaties, it had proved difficult to enforce; back in the 1750s Creeks had
complained about non-Natives who deliberately overhunted deer in and near
Creek territory, which kept Creeks from profiting from deerskins.[19] In 1790,
U.S. officials connected drought to crop failure, attacks and murders against
white invaders, victual warfare against the horses and cattle that accompanied
them, and famine—sometimes more imagined than real. Their efforts to secure animals for Indians must be read as preemption against imagined Indian
hunger and its violent consequences.

Cherokees also encouraged Americans' hopes that Indians would "become"
husbandmen, and it was not coincidental that observers connected Native willingness with Native want. In January 1792 a group of Chickamauga Cherokees "surprized" Henry Knox "with a vizit."[20] They reminded him of the terms
of the 1791 Treaty of Holston and said they had come to claim "the annual
allowance of Goods." The Cherokees also requested "some ploughs and
othe[r] implements of husbandry, as mentioned in the treaty." In 1794 a group
of Cherokees comprising "three old Fellows and a Squaw" approached a fort
and begged for food. Observers said they were "almost starv'd with hunger"
and fed them. The Chickamaugas' 1792 visit may have startled Knox, given
their previous British loyalties—but Dragging Canoe's death had changed the
face of affairs. The 1794 travelers may have been starving, or they may have

been using a hunger metaphor that non-Native observers misinterpreted. By reaffirming treaties, asking for plows, and playing on American perceptions of Native hunger, Cherokees managed to get Americans to distribute trade goods, farm implements, and food aid. In 1796 George Washington sent a talk to the Cherokees that made clear the additional—and by then standard—expectation that Native women would become spinners and weavers if they wanted to receive such distributions.[21]

Not all Indians rushed to implement the U.S. Plan of Civilization; it met with resistance from Indians who had a stable relationship with the federal government and from hostile groups too. The Seneca named Cornplanter was one of the first to point out the inconsistencies in the Americans' policy. Cornplanter had fought for the British in the American Revolution but had been working with the Americans since then. In the same speech that reminded listeners of George Washington's reputation as a "town-destroyer," Cornplanter described the current state of Indian villages. "The Game which the Great Spirit Sent into our country for us to eat, is going from among us," he observed in a December 1790 message to Washington. Although he claimed that the Senecas believed that the Great Spirit "intended, that we Should till the ground with the plough," Cornplanter wondered whether the Americans "mean to leave us and our children any land to till."[22]

In his reply to Cornplanter, Washington promised "that all the lands Secured to you by the [1784] treaty of Fort Stanwix . . . are yours . . . only your own acts can convey them away." He liked Cornplanter's focus "on the Subject of tilling the ground" and pledged that "the United States will be happy to afford you every assistance."[23] At least at this point, Washington's Indian policy assumed that Indians could and should deal with hunger themselves but needed new strategies to do so.

At this moment, however, Native Americans remained skeptical of the federal government's stance on land cessions. During the same meeting where Cornplanter said that Senecas were invested in plow agriculture, he also asked for a return of land that the Six Nations had ceded to the United States at the 1784 Treaty of Fort Stanwix (the Six Nations had refused to ratify the cession once they returned home, but the government acted as if the cession were valid). Washington refused Cornplanter's request. Other members of the Six Nations showed even less enthusiasm for plows and domesticated animals. Samuel Kirkland sighed at Oneidas' and Tuscaroras' "cool reception to the benevolence & generosity of Congress." They "cared nothing for *oxen*, or *plows*." By contrast, even though Cornplanter had expressed concern, his "attachment and fidelity . . . could be relied upon," both in 1791 and 1792. From his seat on the New York-Pennsylvania border, Cornplanter continued to listen to the Americans because Iroquois factionalism made him less willing to ally with Mohawk Joseph Brant and the Seneca Red Jacket.[24]

Joseph Brant continued to distrust the U.S. government, and he mocked the Plan of Civilization; he was familiar with the longer history of American barbarities like the Sullivan Campaign. From Grand River he monitored goings-on in the United States while continuing to influence the British under the lieutenant governorship of John Graves Simcoe in Upper Canada. Although Brant assured Americans that he would negotiate with them, in his interactions with other Indians he made it clear that he would not. In 1792 he ridiculed George Washington's invitation to Philadelphia, "particularly" the part related "to planting & Sowing." This offer "was not important" to Brant, "for he already knew how to plough & to Sow." Brant also refused to travel to Philadelphia for fear that "the hostile Indians . . . would See and blame him." His influence over the Western Confederacy Indians had waned before this time because of Western Indians' longstanding suspicions of the Iroquois. Many Americans did not place much faith in Brant's ability to negotiate with the Western Indians: Anthony Wayne said that Brant was "too late, to render us any service with the hostile Indians."[25] It is uncertain what the Americans made of Brant's critique of the government's Indian food policy.

To say that the Western Confederacy offered a lukewarm reaction to U.S. proposals would be putting it generously. In March 1791 George Washington sent a talk to the Miami and Wabash tribes, indicating the Americans' desire to make the Indians "understand the cultivation of the earth" and to teach them "how much better it is . . . to have comfortable houses, and to have plenty to eat and drink . . . than to be exposed to all the calamities belonging to a Savage life." In this assessment Indians lived in a catastrophic state of impermanence and want. Secretary of War Henry Knox sent a speech the following year to Chippewas, Delawares, Miamis, Ottawas, Potawatomis, Wyandots, "and all Other tribes residing to the Southward of the lakes east of the Mississipi, and to the Northward of the River Ohio." The Americans invited them to Philadelphia, where the United States sought "the opportunity of imparting to you, all the blessings of civilized life." Such largesse included the chance "to cultivate the earth, and raise corn . . . oxen, sheep and other domestic animals, to build comfortable houses, and to educate your children, so as ever to dwell upon the land." Washington's message conveyed a threat in case the Indians refused his invitation: if they chose to reject the way of life he offered, he warned, "your doom must be Sealed forever."[26] The United States issued threats even when it was incapable of making good on them; the Western Indians would defeat Arthur St. Clair later in 1791.

The Western Confederacy rejected the plan. "The great spirit" gave them "land and fill[ed] it with abundance of wild creatures," the Wyandots, Ottawas, Chippewas, Delawares, and Munsees said.[27] They did not want to become husbandmen because the Great Spirit had provided them with animals that ensured not only a subsistence but an abundance. They also continued to enjoy eating British provisions, which helped support them through the Western Confederacy War. Later, in 1793, the Shawnees would refuse on behalf of the confederacy to negotiate a new boundary with the Americans at Sandusky. Anthony Wayne met those Indians in battle one last time at Fallen Timbers in 1794—and his victory and the subsequent Treaty of Greenville in 1795 changed the face of affairs.

The Treaty of Greenville, in combination with mid-1790s treaties between the United States and Great Britain and the United States and Spain, enabled the government to adopt a less compromising Indian food policy from a position of greater strength.[28] During the 1790s and early 1800s, Creek, Cherokee, and Iroquois collaborators helped U.S. Indian agents turn the ploughshares of agriculture into the sword of victual imperialism. Officials, in response to Indian claims about hunger, expanded their victual imperialism to include the introduction of fixed prices for foodstuffs. Because Native Americans approved of this price-fixing, the U.S. government was also able to standardize methods of distributing provisions, and to begin thinking about ways to cut down on the quantities of food they dispensed. By the 1810s these changes had reduced Indian land holdings, circumscribed the amount of food aid given to Indians (who were portrayed as increasingly hungry), and turned such food aid into a weapon that destroyed Native bodies.

U.S. officials could not promote the Plan of Civilization without help from Native collaborators, who advised them on everything from land cessions to Indian tastes—sometimes to the detriment of other Indians. Hendrick Aupaumut aided the Americans in 1793 by telling them about Native food preferences, but his efforts were likelier more useful to Americans than they were to Native Americans. It was Aupaumut who suggested that the Americans save money by substituting flour instead of corn "every fourth day" of provisions distributions to the Iroquois. There is some evidence that increased wheat consumption was tied to increased risk of anemia—though, of course, late-eighteenth-century eaters would not have put it in quite those terms.[29]

Other Indians facilitated land sales. The U.S. government arranged the Treaty of New York through the cooperation of Alexander McGillivray. It was because of McGillivray that Creeks received "a Number of Ploughs & other implements of husbandry" from James Seagrove. For his part McGillivray secured a spot as a brigadier general in the United States army, as well as the right to import tax-free goods through Pensacola, Florida. Although the practice of making side deals persisted, the men making them fall into and out of the records. Alexander McGillivray died in 1793. By that point in time, Cornplanter had fallen from power, and Dragging Canoe was also dead.[30] New partnerships would form as a result of Benjamin Hawkins's work with southern Indians.

In *A Sketch of the Creek Country in the Years 1798 and 1799*, first published in 1848 by the Georgia Historical Society, U.S. Indian agent Benjamin Hawkins described his approach to the Plan of Civilization and his method of forging collaborative ties with Native Americans. Hawkins's travels to Indian towns to provide instruction in plow use resembled Samuel Kirkland's methods earlier in the decade. Like Pickering, he did not want to send Indian children to faraway schools, and he expanded on both Pickering's and Kirkland's ideas by constructing a model farm. He also distributed provisions. One striking difference between the southern arm of the Plan of Civilization and its northern counterpart was the order in which Hawkins hoped to "convert" Indians: he focused on women first and men second. He theorized that if he could convince women to spin they would grow independent of their husbands, thus forcing Native men to farm to reestablish their wives' dependence on them. Hawkins needed to balance Indian practices, government wishes to reduce the cost of gifted trade goods and provisions, and the maintenance of peace between non-Natives and Natives. Hawkins occupied an ambivalent position from his post in Indian country: he was an elite white American, but he also understood Creek customs better than other officials because of his commitment to living with Indians.[31]

A "well cultivated and planted" fruit and vegetable garden; an orchard of peach trees; plans to fence his fields; residence among the Lower Creeks on his own farm; his distributions of provisions when he deemed it suitable: these were the actions and possessions that Benjamin Hawkins used to bolster his authority. He wanted to use his farm "to introduce a regular husbandry to serve as a model and stimulus, for the neighboring towns who crowd the public shops here."[32] Hawkins set up his farm in a location where he believed the Creeks seemed most likely to seek trade goods and gifts of food in lieu of growing provisions for themselves. He hoped that his garden's bounty would champion farming to the Indians he perceived as idle. His efforts had a better chance of succeeding than Kirkland's in part because Hawkins could, by growing his own food, also play the role of a generous host.

It is almost certain that Hawkins, like so many before him, labored under the mistaken belief that hungry Indians depended on him. These convictions existed in tension with Hawkins's realization that the Creeks were good at feeding themselves. He had gained experience in Indian diplomacy at the Treaty of Colerain, where he became familiar with contemporary assessments of Indians' appetites. Creeks made an exception in allowing Hawkins to become self-sufficient. Usually when they allotted garden plots to the non-Natives who lived among them, Creeks controlled the amount of food residents could grow because they expected men to purchase most of their produce from Creek women.[33] It is possible Hawkins did not know about this limitation.

Sometime in 1798 or 1799, it became clear that the plan to farm by example was not winning many followers. Writing in the third person, Hawkins stated his doubts "of succeeding here in establishing a regular husbandry." If his approach did not gain adherents, Hawkins decided that he would move his farm away from the town, "and aid the villages where success seems to be infallible."[34] Previous experience had taught him not to hope for immediate victory in altering Indian farming, but he also wrote a backup strategy that would fudge the number of converts by providing aid only to the villages that already seemed amenable to Hawkins's methods. His tactics also borrowed from Pickering's ideas, which provided for the presence of American Indian agents in Native villages as a stopgap against young men relapsing back into hunting habits and, more significantly, as a preventative against famine.

There was no need to implement his backup plan because he found Indians who were willing to work with him. He related varying success in the thirty-seven Creek towns he charted on the Coosa and Tallapoosa Rivers, as well as among the Cherokees. He bestowed the most praise on Natives who used plows, raised cattle, and enslaved Africans. The Creek called the Bird Tail King, who had mocked the Georgians at Colerain, lived at Hitchetee, where he resided on a plantation "well fenced, and cultivated with the plough." Hawkins spent a day with the Bird Tail King in the spring of 1799, bringing "a plough completely fixed" and showing him "how to use it." Hawkins reported that the Bird Tail King preferred the plow "over the slow and laborious hand hoe." His description of a Creek man's opinion about hoe efficacy transferred responsibility for agriculture into male hands. Hawkins seemed happy to see that the Bird Tail King's family had "more than doubled their crop of corn and potatoes." They "begin to know how to turn their corn to account, by giving it to their hogs," he wrote. Hawkins also reported that some of the Cherokees "old and young appear to be happy" about the growth of their farms, "vegetables to be had in plenty . . . bacon, colewarts, and turnips, at several houses," and an increase in "their stock of hogs and cattle."[35]

Not only did Hawkins demonstrate his eagerness to live among the Indians and serve as a visual example of how to farm; he also traveled to various villages and made sure that Indians used American plows properly, produced corn to feed their animals rather than themselves, and grew abundant provisions that Hawkins deemed suitable for Natives. It is interesting to note that some of these crops could not be eaten. Hawkins reported offering Creeks "cotton and flax seed" to plant in 1797.[36] His reforms reveal the conflicting ideas that undergirded U.S. victual imperialism: assumptions that Indians would grow edible crops, and expectations that Indians would produce cash crops instead of grains.

It must be remembered that there was little reason for Indians to worry about what Americans thought of their food production, and so there were limits to the extent to which Native Americans proved willing to collaborate. Creeks and Cherokees continued raising domesticated animals in ways that suited them. One Creek chief, Toolk-au-bat-che Haujo, owned five hundred cattle, but "although apparently very indigent," observed Hawkins, "he never sells any." Instead, Toolk-au-bat-che Haujo offered "proofs of unbounded hospitality; he seldom kills less than two large beeves a fortnight, for his friends and acquaintances" despite the fact that "The town is on the decline . . . badly fenced . . . [and] the land is much exhausted with continued culture." Although the town's soils suffered from depletion, Toolk-au-bat-che Haujo refused to sell cattle for cash, as Hawkins and others encouraged him to do, and Hawkins made no mention of manure fertilization. Toolk-au-bat-che Haujo slaughtered domesticated animals as prestige gifts to obtain and maintain the loyalty of other Indians. In other towns Hawkins critiqued Indian animal usage for different reasons. In describing a village below "Coo-sau-dee," Hawkins lamented the fact that the Indians kept no cattle and only owned "a few hogs and horses." Their pig raising did not meet with his approval either; they used to possess "the largest and best breed of hogs in the nation, but have lost them by carelessness or inattention," he wrote.[37]

While some southern Indians annoyed U.S. officials by raising livestock in irregular ways, others worried observers by refusing to plant crops as regularly as their non-Native counterparts. Hawkins described the Cussetas, by then the largest village of the Lower Creeks, who "associate, more than any other Indians, with their white neighbors." These Indians, according to Hawkins, "know not the season for planting, or if they do, they never avail themselves of what they know, as they always plant a month too late." They became "fond of visiting" the whites nearby, and their young Indians "are more rude, more inclined to be tricky, and more difficult to govern, than those who do not associate with them." Other Indians continued to ask for provisions. Creek women came to Hawkins to ask for corn and salt. They also crept onto Hawkins's fields to steal vegetables such as cabbage.[38] Even Lower Creeks, who had in the past enjoyed peaceful relationships with U.S. agents and the country's inhabitants, proved reluctant to adopt the Plan of Civilization in its entirety. Creeks who lived near whites seemed disinclined to farm, and such nearness, according to Hawkins, bred rudeness, unruliness, and discontent.

In addition to trying to "reform" Indian agriculture and animal use, Hawkins made two other significant changes. First, he began to fix prices for food and regulate its sale in response to the Indians who asked him to do so. By 1799 he had set the costs of Indian-produced bacon, beef, butter, capons, cheese, corn, eggs, field peas, fowls, ground peas, hickory nut oil, pork, potatoes, and pumpkins. Whereas before his residency "there was no market for provisions," and "The wants of the traders were few," he had established "a regular market" and instituted a system of "weights and measures."[39] In 1807, he prohibited white traders living in town from trading livestock, because their prices interfered with Indians' profits. Hawkins observed that Indians themselves had little regard for conventional pricing. He complained that Creeks priced cattle high because they had been "accustomed to sell fowls, bacon, and beef at Pensacola, at an extravagant price" and now expected "the same" at home, "making no allowance for the expense of carriage or between the war and peace price of provisions." Creeks charged lower prices for pork and corn than merchants in Baltimore, Boston, Charleston, New York, and Philadelphia around the same time period, and they charged more than the market price for summer butter.[40]

On the one hand, Hawkins's price-fixing initiatives were more indicative of early modern and colonial moral economies—and thus of continuity—than of a major transformation in Indian country. When prices favored Creeks, Native women who grew, raised, and prepared most of these foodstuffs, and who competed with the garden produce sold by enslaved Creeks, likely appreciated the fact that Hawkins made it easier for them to sell their food.[41] On the other hand, there was change here too in Indians' desires to be able to intervene more decisively in price-fixing choices. When prices seemed unusual, the autonomous act of deciding costs probably mattered more to Indians than profits.

The second major change that Hawkins introduced in the south was a continuation of Anthony Wayne's reform of U.S. food diplomacy at Greenville, which had set a precedent for limiting food aid. Hawkins subsequently reduced alcohol distributions at treaties, cut gifts of trade goods, and insisted upon the use of rations as payment for services rendered. Indian advisors had urged U.S. officials to regulate alcohol use at treaties. In 1793, for instance, Hendrick Aupaumut claimed that "a dram after each council" would suffice, because if attendees reached the point of demanding rum by the cask it would not do to refuse them—but the consequences would be dangerous. At a 1797 meeting with unidentified southern Indians (probably Cherokees), Hawkins described receiving an application from the Indians that he "indulge them with a little whiskey." Hawkins "answered no, not one drop till the business they convened on was completely adjusted." He reported that "after some hesitation, the chiefs agreed that this decision was just" on account of the injuries "done them when in a state of drunkenness."[42]

Anthony Wayne had acted similarly at the Treaty of Greenville, and Little Turtle would echo this sentiment in 1802, when he asked President Thomas Jefferson to prohibit the sale of liquor not only in Indian camps at treaties but also in their towns. Hawkins gave flaxseed and cotton to the Creeks in lieu of giving away presents. He observed that Indians seemed skeptical about the decrease in gift giving. In 1801 he bragged that the Creeks, who used to be "the most numerous, proud, haughty and ill behaved Indians in the agency South of Ohio," changed their ways when he limited them to one thousand rations a year. These he apportioned "only to use on public business and at the request of the agent." Although "This regulation" of distributing rations as payment "was disliked at first," by 1801 a Creek chief "going to the frontiers will come 20 or 30 miles to me to know if I have any commands which he can execute to get an order for provisions."[43]

Changes to pricing and diplomacy helped to create a paradoxical food policy that characterized Indians as simultaneously self-sufficient, needy, and violent. These Indians could agree with Hawkins that drinking alcohol was a mistake, which theoretically paved the way to greater independence from the United States. They also, however, continued to steal "hogs, beef and horses" after being denied presents.[44] But whereas during the 1780s and 1790s the U.S. government had responded to such contradictions by practicing generous diplomacy, its stance on Indian affairs shifted between the late 1790s and early 1810s.

These efforts constituted an entering wedge that, in the late 1790s, the U.S. government used to reduce their food aid to Indians. In 1796 the Americans moved into Niagara, announcing as they did so that they would stop feeding the Indians who traveled there. This move to reduce provisions distributions affected Indians from Creek country to Iroquois territory. In 1796 Timothy Pickering wrote to his successor as secretary of war—James McHenry—and suggested that American generosity had to end. "While the Indian war continued at the westward, and a British war was apprehended," he explained, "the Government was unceasing in its endeavours to Secure the friendship of the Six Nations." Treaties "were held and liberal Supplies furnished." "Now," however, "circumstances are so changed as to render a restriction of Such Supplies both proper and practicable." Pickering encouraged McHenry to confine his budget to the annuity advanced to the Indians. From these funds, blacksmiths would receive money to forge plows and shoe horses, and officials would pay schoolmasters to teach and enforce the art of American-style husbandry. "Provisions and cloathing," Pickering cautioned, should be "issued very Sparingly." Although he admitted that no one would be able to enact these changes immediately, the Americans could "curtail" the supplies "more and more, until the expenditures come *nearly* to the fixed annuity."[45]

These trends conformed to broader developments in U.S. policy. Correspondence in the late 1790s reveals the War Department critiquing military commanders for holding talks with Indians (which resulted in "great and unnecessary expenditures of the public provisions"). In May 1800 the U.S. government moved to standardize the distribution of foodstuffs to Indians. A representative from the Ways and Means Committee observed to the House of Representatives that the prices for rations had risen in previous years. Budget makers struggled to track these costs. Different military posts recorded their distributions of provisions for Indians inside the accounts with "the usual supply of army provisions"; no separate account of Indian rations existed. The committee suggested the need for separate accounts so the government would "know how much money is expended in this manner."[46] Rations for Indians were to come from military budgets, but they were to be kept distinct from budgets for soldiers—and they were to be distributed by nonmilitary men. This was the triumph of a commodity-exchange economy. The Americans succeeded where Jeffery Amherst and Frederick Haldimand had failed. The feasts, the gifts of animals, the providing of food on the way to treaties, and even the military rations distributed in larger quantities to Indians than they were to non-Natives became subservient to rations as payment. This was the endgame of Indians' fight against hunger on their own terms.

The first two decades of the 1800s witnessed pan-Indian movements led by the Shawnees Tecumseh and Tenskwatawa, further fractures in Creek country that led to the Red Stick war, and the War of 1812, which revived U.S.-British antagonism. Indian portrayals of their hunger varied widely during this period. During the early 1800s, Indians whom Benjamin Hawkins had convinced to farm began selling their surplus produce at the prices he had fixed, rather than depositing it for communal crop storage. In July 1805, a Creek called Hopoie Mico blamed Hawkins for the death of two Native girls. "You know this enemy called hunger," he said, and chastised Hawkins for his inability "to save many of our little ones from being murdered" by it.[47] Hawkins was not yet himself an opponent of the Creeks, but the Creeks *were* fighting a proxy war against the personified adversary that Hawkins's policies had helped to create.

Creeks *were* hungry—some were even dying of starvation—but they also continued to ignore and embrace hunger in symbolic acts. In 1811 Tecumseh had appeared in Creek towns to rally Indians to war against the Americans. In August 1812—one month after the beginning of the War of 1812—unidentified Indians (likely Red Sticks) committed victual warfare. They "Murdered a young man[,] . . . Burnt Several Cabins," and began "Collecting their Cattle . . . to drive to the Nation." It was no mistake that Tenskwatawa called for a total eschewal of non-Native foodstuffs among Iroquois, Chickamauga, Creek, Delaware, Miami, and Shawnee followers. Alcohol, bread, and the meat of domesticated animals became anathema, as did tools forged in the American style, such as plows. Tenskwatawa, like the Delaware prophet Neolin before him, wanted Indians to return to a diet of beans, corn, maple sugar, and deer meat—the diet of a semisedentary, hunting people.[48]

These calls did not stop Creeks from eating cattle, but they ate them only when necessary. In addition to stealing cattle, the Red Sticks also started "to destroy the cattle, hogs, fowls, implements of husbandry" and to throw "hoes and axes into the rivers."[49] Indians sometimes wrecked non-Native foodstuffs, sometimes stole them, and sometimes made it difficult to continue producing them. Supposedly hungry Creeks killed and ate non-Native sources of meat and broke the non-Native tools used to produce crops and prevent hunger. By the 1810s Red Stick Creeks implied that Indians should share hunger with each other in victual warfare against American victual imperialism and its Native collaborators.

In the aftermath of the War of 1812, federal Indian policy transformed food aid into a tool of destruction. Americans halted their attempts to reduce food distributions during the conflict—some 5,257 Indians received provisions at American posts in 1814, for example, and a Chippewa speaking for Chippewa, Ottawa, Potawatomi, Seneca, and Wyandot Indians in 1815 could still request "plenty of food" and receive it—but this response became unusual. Benjamin Hawkins reported Creek complaints that the U.S. government had withheld their annual annuity payments in 1812, 1813, and 1814. More significant still was that in 1817, Creeks whose annuities had been reinstated and who received provisions had to *pay* for their provisions using part of that annuity.[50] The United States had begun to charge for food aid and to use it in a way that encouraged Indian indebtedness. After the War of 1812 the government finally managed to quantify and standardize the amount of food required to placate Indian allies.

Some American officials even hoped that such provisions would wreak havoc on Native bodies. In 1815 Benjamin Stickney, Indian agent at Fort Wayne, wrote to the secretary of war and described the "observations" he "had the opportunity of making." Stickney had discovered "that three or four months' full feeding on meat and bread, even without ardent spirit, will bring on disease, and, in six or eight months, great mortality." Stickney joined Edinburgh doctor William Robertson, American Benjamin Rush, Mahican Hendrick Aupaumut, and other commentators on Native health, but the aims had changed. Stickney wanted to sicken Indians rather than keep them healthy. He paused long enough to wonder whether it would "be considered a proper mode of warfare" to encourage this growth of disease. But he did not ponder the question for long, because the costs compensated for his moral reservations: "more Indians might be killed with the expense of $100,000 in this way, than $1,000,000 expended in the support of armies to go against them," he concluded. Even without the destructive effects of alcohol, the writer could tell that wheat and meat had deleterious effects on Indians. By 1822 Stickney was a subagent to the Ottawas and earned $500 per year. His appointment, significantly, had been made by the War Department—rather than by the president or by one of the more knowledgeable superintendents of Indian Affairs.[51]

Stickney was a minor official in the overall structure of the U.S. government. There does not seem to be correspondence confirming that significant politicians and military strategists took his suggestions seriously. It is, however, instructive that Stickney felt comfortable making these suggestions, because they indicated how far the victual imperialistic aspects of the Plan of Civilization could be pushed. The answer to the question of whether Stickney's strategy counted as warfare was irrelevant. Federal Indian agents did not need to offer Indians food that killed them off because they had become powerful enough to lie about Indian hunger and to take land in other ways. At the same time that the U.S. government began to deemphasize food diplomacy and to distribute foodstuffs that fostered disease, it acquired Native ground.

Landgrabs may have started as individual state actions, but they gradually became federal policy that hungrily consumed Indian land. The states acquired territory, to be sure. The Creeks knew Governor Blount of Georgia as Fusse Mico, or the Dirt King. The Cherokees called him the Dirt Captain. But representatives for the United States won land cessions from Indians at Fort Stanwix in 1784, Fort McIntosh in 1785, Galphinton in 1785, Hopewell in 1785, Fort Finney in 1786, Shoulderborne in 1786, Fort Harmar in 1789, New York in 1790, Holston in 1791, Greenville in 1795, Colerain in 1796, Big Tree in 1797, Fort Wilkinson in 1802, Fort Wayne in 1803, Washington in 1805, and at the Treaty of Fort Jackson in 1814.[52]

Although this was a period of sweeping policy changes, these decades were also characterized by continuity in the form of Indian resistance. In an 1805 speech to a Christian missionary at Buffalo Creek, the Seneca Red Jacket offered *his* interpretation of early American history.

> There was a time when our forefathers owned this great island. . . . The Great Spirit had made it for the use of Indians. He had created the buffalo, the deer, and other animals for food. He had made the bear and the beaver. . . . He had scattered them over the country, and taught us how to take them. He had caused the earth to produce corn for bread. . . . But an evil day came upon us. Your forefathers crossed the great water, and landed on this island. Their numbers were small. They found friends and not enemies. . . . We gave them corn and meat, they gave us poison (alluding, it is supposed to ardent spirits) in return. . . . Yet we did not fear them. We took them to be friends. They called us brothers. We believed them, and gave them a larger seat. At length their numbers had greatly increased. They wanted more land; they wanted our country. . . . Wars took place. Indians were hired to fight against Indians, and many of our people were destroyed. They also brought strong liquor amongst us. It was strong and powerful, and has slain thousands.[53]

The history that Red Jacket narrated stood in sharp contrast to the one that Timothy Pickering recited to Cornplanter in 1791 and may even explain why Red Jacket was so critical of Pickering's recitation at the time.[54] Pickering's Englishmen were self-sufficient husbandmen who fed starving Indians. Red Jacket's Indians were self-sufficient hunters *and* farmers who offered food to starving English even when those invaders asked for land. The man who heard this speech assumed that the poison to which Red Jacket referred was liquor—he glossed *poison* with the parenthetical phrase "alluding, it is supposed to ardent spirits"—but Red Jacket mentioned "strong liquor" as a separate commodity a few lines later.[55] It seems likelier that Red Jacket was describing actual poison, which early English colonists employed against Indians. Colonists, and then white American inhabitants, reciprocated food gifts with poison, land hunger, and eventually war.

By the 1810s the U.S. government had won power over Indians by engaging in victual imperialism—specifically, by implementing the Plan of Civilization: a federal food policy that reduced Indian hunting, encouraged cattle ranching, fixed prices, interfered with grain production, reworked gender roles, and reduced food aid. These methods reveal the unrelenting, daily erosion of Indian food sovereignty, which occurred alongside American landgrabs. It was this interference with Native food systems that facilitated Indian land losses.

Some of these customs were more transferable than others. U.S. Indian agents were not the only people to practice victual imperialism by fixing prices for food, and Native Americans were not the only people to lose the fight against hunger because they lost the authority to fight hunger themselves. When black colonists left Nova Scotia, ideas about food laws and hunger prevention traveled with them to Africa. The process of colonization in Nova Scotia sent people across the ocean to Sierra Leone with collective ideas about the new, less compromising iteration of British food aid, and about the type of victual imperialism people practiced by institutionalizing colonial laws. Strategies for confronting hunger changed again in Africa. It was access to food that would shape black Loyalists' relationships with white leaders in Sierra Leone, it was hunger prevention that would foster their sense of political identity, and it was food laws that would ultimately create conflict with Africans and spark a food riot with drastic results.

CHAPTER 8

Black Loyalist Hunger Prevention in Sierra Leone

Cato Perkins and Isaac Anderson were hungry, and they were not alone. In October 1793 their hunger drove them from Freetown, Sierra Leone, to London, England. They had lived in Freetown for just over a year. Before moving to that small British colony on the upper Guinea coast, Anderson and Perkins had been enslaved in Revolutionary South Carolina, where they declared allegiance with their feet by running to the British during the war. Isaac Anderson threw in with the British as early as 1775, and in 1776 left for New York with Lord William Campbell. A man named John Perkins had enslaved Cato Perkins in Charleston, South Carolina—Perkins probably ran to the British during the siege of Charleston and possibly made it to New York with General Clinton. Thereafter the two men had lived free in Nova Scotia, before the Sierra Leone Company offered them the opportunity to migrate. In Freetown, Anderson, Perkins, and their fellow free black colonists distrusted the white people who now ruled them. In a move that bypassed the authority of their governor, the two men had traveled to England to directly petition the Sierra Leone Company. In London, they sent a draft of their petition to John Clarkson, their former governor in Sierra Leone, who now lived in England; they hoped he would listen to them and offer advice about approaching the company.[1]

Anderson and Perkins disliked their prospects in Africa. The Freetown colony was faltering, and although they hoped for "Land and [to] *be able to make a Crop to support us"* before the advent of *"the rainy Season,"* the company had not yet allotted land. This problem echoed their experiences in Nova Scotia. Then as now, "Health and Life" remained "very uncertain," and the government was hampering their abilities to be useful to themselves and to the colony.[2] Their petition would go unanswered; less than a month later they complained to John Clarkson that the Sierra Leone Company intended to ignore them without providing "any answer" and instead planned to send them "back like Fools" to Freetown. The Sierra Leone Company's decision to treat Perkins and Anderson as powerless supplicants would fuel a swift campaign that convinced formerly enslaved black colonists to advocate for the right to prevent their own hunger as political insiders in Sierra Leone.[3]

From 1792 to 1800 Freetown's black colonists—also referred to hereafter as "black Loyalists" and "Nova Scotians"—won several battles in the fight against black hunger.[4] The Nova Scotians arrived in Africa in 1792 imbued with a sense of how to use food laws to exert dominance, and within half a decade they had learned to behave as British subjects entitled to enforce that power. Whereas in Nova Scotia white Loyalists' food laws had controlled former bondpeople's access to food, in Sierra Leone black colonists gained the right to enact their own antihunger rules, which white colonists uniformly approved, beginning in 1793. These Nova Scotians fought famine first by regulating their trade in alcohol, bread, fish, and meat. Later, the black Loyalists tried to regulate the trade of Africans, particularly Susu and Temne. These laws enabled former victual warriors to try to become victual imperialists by altering African food sales while occupying African land. This attempt failed because violent Temne and Susu reactions to colonists' price-fixing encouraged white councilmen in Sierra Leone to curtail black Loyalist lawmaking; those councilmen would later try to interfere with Africans' trade.

Black Loyalists won important victories, but they lost the war, which was a shorter, more condensed affair than the conflict Native Americans had fought. Indians had been fighting the war against hunger before colonists arrived in North America in the fifteenth century, preventing famine with extensive crop production and seasonal hunting. The black colonists were latecomers to autonomous hunger-prevention efforts; during the colonial period their cash-crop production had fed white slave masters, who regulated when, what, and how enslaved people ate, and during the war self-liberated bondpeople's roles as victual warriors largely focused on dealing with white hunger. Formerly enslaved people had witnessed the political power of food laws during the 1780s in Nova Scotia, but these Nova Scotians had not won the right to independently pass legislation. They gained that right in Sierra Leone.

In the space of eight years, power waxed and waned as black Loyalists claimed, exercised, and lost their right to legislate against hunger at the end of the eighteenth century—and suffered the dramatic, violent consequences. In September 1800 black colonists in Freetown engaged in an event that resembled early modern food riots, with one exception: black colonists protested in 1800 not to urge the government to fix food prices, but to reclaim their right to fix prices and address hunger themselves. Their riotous actions in 1800 began with price-fixing, and this decision was not different from the previous few years. But between 1796 and 1800—once tensions appeared between black colonists and Africans—white officials who had grown anxious about black colonists' power had tried to limit black price-fixing. Other food riots began when officials could not protect the rights of ordinary people, but in Sierra Leone black colonists had already earned the political and legal power to prevent hunger. The 1800 event was also notable because white officials misrepresented it as a significant break with past behavior. They called it a "rebellion" rather than a riot, which made it seem as if the previous decade of black Loyalist petitioning and lawmaking had been illegitimate. Black colonists lost power as white officials seized control of the historical narrative.

This particular historical narrative has multiple beginnings and a sprawling chronology that stretches before and after the years of the Revolutionary War. It begins with enslaved people's lack of access to food during the colonial period, their flight to the British during the Revolutionary War, their reemergence as free victual warriors, and their escape from the former American colonies. It begins in Nova Scotia, where, during the late 1780s, British failures to apportion land, coupled with restrictive food laws, motivated discontented black colonists to leave Nova Scotia. It begins in London, where a group of British reformers examined their most recent failure to build an antislavery colony on the upper Guinea coast: the Granville Town colony settled by London's Black Poor (people of African descent who migrated to London in the last quarter of the eighteenth century). That last group of colonists had reckoned with hunger in London itself during the harsh winters of 1784–1785 and 1785–1786. Their experiences with food aid resembled David George's: charitable bakers in London used private funding to bake quarter loaves of bread for them.[5]

It begins in Africa, on the upper Guinea coast itself. The Granville Town colonists there were victims of the same sort of bad planning that characterized settlement in Nova Scotia. Olaudah Equiano, the former slave and antislavery writer, lived in London before the Granville Town colonists' departure and worked as a government commissary. He reported "the flagrant abuses committed by the agent," Joseph Irwin, who was in charge of making provisions arrangements for the emigrants. Such corruption impeded migration. The first Granville Town colonists sailed from England to the upper Guinea coast in the spring of 1787. Once there they obtained land from an African subruler, a Temne man named King Tom (also known as Pa Kokelly).[6] They died in huge numbers from disease. In 1789 they sealed their fate by goading a passing ship into burning the town of another leader named King Jimmy. Jimmy gave the colonists three days to vacate and torched the town to cinders, scattering the colonists.[7]

The first colonists' experiences demonstrated the uncertain success of colonial projects and emphasized to the Sierra Leone Company that new colonists would require more government structure and careful planning to thrive. When a thousand black colonists, led by the Reverend John Clarkson, sailed from Nova Scotia to Sierra Leone in January 1792, they landed at the former Granville Town colony. They renamed it Free Town, which became Freetown. They built Freetown in the shadow of mountains that appeared "to rise gradually from the sea to a stupendous height, richly wooded and beautifully ornamented." David George, who with the majority of his Baptist congregation, sailed on one of the ships in a voyage that took seven weeks, wrote that one of the mountains "appeared like a cloud to us." Boston King also undertook the voyage with his wife, Violet, who caught "a putrid fever" and died at the start of April, less than a month after the couple arrived.[8]

During these early years, hungriness characterized colonists' existence; they tried to avoid it but also came to expect it during certain months. The name "Sierra Leone" came from a Portuguese term meaning "lion mountain"—so named to denote the sound of thunder during the seasonal rains. The rainy season began in May or June, visited daily downpours on the colony until August, and decreased by September or October. During that time it became tricky to produce crops and shelter animals. That summer of 1792 was said to be "One of the wettest rainy seasons in West African history." In addition, colonists worried about the aggressive predators surrounding the colony. It was not uncommon for large leopards to carry off livestock, such as goats, but small insects also posed huge problems. When he was governor in 1796, Zachary Macaulay awakened at two in the morning to find that "an army of black Ants . . . had Spread over the whole room, blackening the walls, the floor & the bed Curtains." These pests wreaked havoc on poorly constructed structures for storing food, and two of the colonists burned their house down after a failed

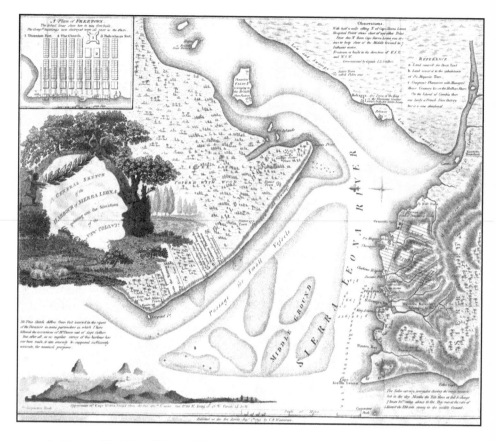

Carl Bernhard Wadström, "A General Sketch of the Harbour of Sierra Leona, pointing out the Situation of the New Colony," in *An essay on colonization, particularly applied to the western coast of Africa, with some free thoughts on cultivation and commerce; also brief descriptions of the colonies already formed, or attempted, in Africa, including those of Sierra Leone and Bulama* (London: Printed for the author, by Darton and Harvey, 1794–1795). Courtesy of the Library Company of Philadelphia.

attempt to eradicate them.[9] Unstable relations with Africans, council corruption, and storage issues resulted in additional provisioning problems.

By the eighteenth century the upper Guinea coast was populated by Limba, Bullom, Temne, Baga, Loko, Susu, Mandingo, Koranko, and Fula peoples. Beginning in 1727 the Fula extended their dominance from Fouta Djallon coastward, subjecting the peoples of the Nunez River and the Susu of the Pongo River to a tributary alliance. This expansion was driven by a jihad, which started as a reaction against the slave trade and as an attempt to spread Islam but gradually became bound up in the economies and politics of slavery. Mande and Fula marabouts, or learned men, also spread Islam peacefully throughout Sierra Leone.[10]

By 1792 Freetown's colonists interacted most frequently (and sometimes aggressively) with the Temne. The Koya Temne lived along the coast of Freetown and further inland, where they ran into the Masimera Temne. To the north of the Masimera were the Marampa Temne, and to the south were the Yoni Temne. Many Susu intermarried with the Temne and settled peacefully among them. The Bai Farma was the top Temne ruler and governed at Robaga. The Naimbana, whom the British called King Naimbana, ruled from Robana and was next in the hierarchy. The Sierra Leone Council obtained land from him, which Naimbana viewed as a rental but which Sierra Leone councilmen believed was a permanent purchase.[11] These obstacles blocked black colonists' abilities to grow crops and fueled resentment against Africans.

At first a few white men were responsible for the colony's internal and external policies and relations. The colony's all-white council not only struggled with the Temne but fought among themselves. British-Temne relations were often tense and characterized by mutual suspicion. At one point Temne leaders even accused a British sailor of poisoning one of Naimbana's sons, Henry Granville Naimbana, with a cup of chamomile tea. Alexander Falconbridge, a white slave ship surgeon turned abolitionist, complained that the Sierra Leone Company chose John Clarkson over him as superintendent. Falconbridge likely died of alcoholism. Falconbridge's wife, Anna Maria, remarked that of the remaining councilmen, "never were characters worse adapted to manage any purpose of magnitude."[12]

Upon landing in Africa, Clarkson discovered that Governor Henry Dalrymple had defected to found a rival colony at Bulama, so he took charge. As superintendent, however, Clarkson possessed no further power over fellow council members Dr. John Bell (physician), James Cocks (surveyor), Richard Pepys (works engineer), Charles Taylor (doctor), John Wakerell (storekeeper), and James Watt (plantation manager). Bell drank heavily and died in mid-March; Cocks possessed little practical experience; Pepys was a poor planner and unwilling to accept advice; and Taylor proved uninterested in tending to the sick. Councilmen allowed themselves extra food and liquor while the rest of the colonists ate reduced rations, and they sold ship's stores to Africans instead of distributing them. By March 1792 provisions were slim, and in April colonists were eating half rations. In May, Clarkson, with dismay, reported people "dying for want of food." Only in mid-1792 did John Clarkson convince the Sierra Leone Company to name him governor.[13]

Other hunger-prevention initiatives in the colony relied on inconsistent shipping patterns, which were sometimes inhibited by the maritime activities of noncolonists. From 1792 to 1801 the Sierra Leone Company sent at least sixty-seven ships to obtain produce along the coast, and between 1795 and 1801 at least ten vessels brought produce into Freetown, but over half of the outgoing voyages took place early on, in 1793. When corrupt officials could procure supplies, they possessed no place to put them. Ships struggled to land on the rocky shore. When American vessels provided beef, molasses, and pork, the casks washed away in the tide. John Clarkson complained that careless storage of "damaged cheese and biscuits, with other articles in a state of putrefaction" created "a stench" around the shoddily built storehouse that mingled with the slurry of rot "allowed to lie and soak into the ground." The French assaulted Freetown in September 1794 (a result of the French Revolutionary Wars), uprooted crops, killed one person, and wounded four. This strike was significant on its own merit for destroying supplies, but during the attack the Bai Farma also captured several colony ships, which further impeded ocean-going capabilities. Fishing may have become dangerous after the French attack, and colonists who had witnessed the circumscription of fishing activities in Nova Scotia would have found the situation familiar. Freetown's officials, by taking an antislavery stance and harboring runaways, also risked conflict with the African headmen who supplied the colony with food.[14]

Colonists traded with Africans through coastal, riverine, and overland routes but had little control over what they received. The caravan trade linked to the interior brought cattle, gold, ivory, and enslaved Africans to the coast; the trade on the coast exchanged salt and kola nuts for meat and interior trade goods; and the one across the ocean required enslaved African bodies in exchange for guns and manufactures. The landlord-stranger relationship undergirded trade in the region. Landlords were African elites, and strangers were European, Euro-African, or African foreign residents. Landlords lodged and fed caravans, served as brokers, and provided commercial information and credit. Trade alliances were bound up in other networks of kinship, age groups, royal redistribution circuits, and secret societies (or power associations: the Poro for men and the Sande for women), which the Fula established in Temne territory. The Sierra Leone Company had, since 1791, tried to enter the currents of riverine trade, which supplied goods to the Nunez and Pongo traders. This strategy took two approaches: officials tried to open negotiations with the Fula in Fouta Djallon to get them to divert commerce from the Pongo and Nunez to Freetown, and they tried to set up trading settlements at caravan terminals and to manipulate prices, which would give them control of legitimate commerce (trade in goods not associated with slavery).[15]

These trade networks yielded various provisions from the Africans who remained in control. Crucial upland-variety rice came via merchants from the Sherbro and Fouta Djallon, kola nuts from between Cape Mount and the Sierra Leone estuary, and salt (for preserving meat) from tide pools in the region north of Freetown. The Bullom Shore, on the northern estuary of the Sierra Leone River, provided rice and sugar for a limited time, before a wage disagreement between the Sierra Leone Council and the Bullom ended the arrangement. By October 1792, as many as 150 people "of the Timmany nation" came daily bearing bananas, cassava, limes, oranges, pineapples, and plantains. "Timmanies, Bullams, [and] Mandingoes" also provided rice, yams, and livestock.[16]

Because food from Africans arrived via distant networks and required daily replenishing, colonists also tried to avoid scarcity by consuming Sierra Leone Company rations and eventually growing their own produce. The Sierra Leone Company had planned for colonists to receive "full Provisions for three, and half Provisions for three other Months." The British government had promised the white Loyalists who went to Nova Scotia six months of full provisions (and six months of half provisions for children), so it seems probable that colonial planners thought that people of African descent were somehow engineered to survive on less food. They were not. During the colony's first two and a half years, the Sierra Leone Company said that it spent £20,000 on provisions.[17] Although it is difficult to find precise descriptions of black Loyalists' rations, partial data can be compared to other contemporary figures, such as those for the white Loyalists in Nova Scotia, returns for the British military, and settlement plans for the Jamaican Maroons who arrived in Sierra Leone in late 1800.

Consumption estimates changed with the weather. In the middle of the rainy season, August 1793, Zachary Macaulay said that colonists could consume half a ton of rice per day. By September, when the population stood at 1,052 (995 black men and women and 57 whites), he thought that slightly more than a third of a ton of rice was eaten daily. Using the higher figure, each member of the population would have eaten .95 pound of rice per day; using the lower estimate, each would have consumed two thirds of a pound.[18] This quantity of rice was commensurate with rations for British soldiers and the Maroons who arrived from Nova Scotia in 1800, suggesting that additional similarities probably existed in the quantities of meat, flour, and alcohol that black Loyalists received. From the Maroons' rations one could guess that black Loyalist children received no meat in their ration despite the fact that the company had originally planned that they would. When John Clarkson reduced

Table 1. Comparison of weekly rations

	BRITISH MILITARY C. 1770s					ESTIMATED RATIONS FOR MAROONS BEFORE 1800 ARRIVAL		MAROONS' RATIONS APRIL 1801				MAROONS' RATIONS AUGUST 1801			
	BEEF OR PORK	BREAD OR FLOUR	BUTTER OR CHEESE	PEAS	RICE OR OATMEAL	BEEF OR PORK	RICE OR OATMEAL OR PEAS	MEAT	FLOUR	RICE	RUM	MEAT	FLOUR	RICE	RUM
Men	7 lbs. or 4 lbs.	7 lbs. or 7 lbs.	6 oz. or 8oz.	3 pts.	½ lb. or ½ lb.	7 lbs. or 7 lbs.	7 pts. or 7 pts. or 3.5 pts.	2 lbs.	—	6 qts. (12 pts.)	1 pt.	1 lb.	1 lb.	6 qts. (12 pts.)	3 gills
Women	—	—	—	—	—	7 lbs. or 7 lbs.	7 pts. or 7 pts. or 3.5 pts.	2 lbs.	3 lbs.	4 qts. (8 pts.)	—	1 lb.	4 lbs.	4 qts. (8 pts.)	—
Children	—	—	—	—	—	3.5 lbs. or 3.5 lbs.	7 pts. or 7 pts. or 3.5 pts.	—	3 lbs.	3 qts. (6 pts.)	—	—	3 lbs.	3 qts. (6 pts.)	—

Notes: For British military rations, see the introduction to this book. For rations for the Maroons, see John Gray and T[homas] Ludlum, "Estimate of the expense likely to be incurred by the Maroons for Provisions for the first twelve months after their arrival in Africa, supposing them to be in number 560 and about an equal proportion of Men, Women & Children," Freetown, Sierra Leone, 10 June 1799, f. 195, CO 267/10, TNA; In Council, 29 April 1801, f. 156, and 21 August 1801, f. 245, CO 270/6, TNA.

rations, meat supplies decreased, and men lost their flour, but women and children retained it. People grew supplemental fruits and vegetables on the land they were able to obtain from the Temne.

Once the 1792 rainy season passed, the surviving colonists produced and stored beans, cabbages, cassava, cresses, ground nuts, maize, pumpkin, purslane, rice, tropical fruits, sweet potatoes, and yams. They raised fowls and hogs and hung "beef and pork" for smoking. John Clarkson described their craze "for building boats" and their intention to fish. By 1795 the Sierra Leone Council was trying to encourage black colonists to grow certain crops and raise certain animals—cabbages, cassava, Guinea, Indian, and Barbary corn, sugarcane, yams, pigs, and cattle—but colonists themselves also retained a say in how they fed themselves.[19]

Colonists' efforts to build a better food system began with personal negotiations with John Clarkson during his superintendency and then governorship. The Nova Scotians pushed Clarkson to regulate the sale and distribution of foodstuffs. Thomas Peters, who had successfully petitioned for the colonists' relocation from Nova Scotia and for the 1791 distribution of Christmas beef, became a vocal critic of Clarkson and tried to put himself in charge. Peters lost the authority to challenge the provisioning situation after someone accused him of stealing food—"Some hams & other articles of Diet"—from a dead man who had owed him money. This confrontation resolved itself when Peters died of a fever in June of 1792. Although some colonists, like Peters, sometimes clashed with John Clarkson, their negotiations were characterized more by accommodation than by conflict. "The people are full of complaints at the method of serving their provisions; some of them getting too much, others too little, and some nothing at all," Clarkson observed in April 1792. "The applications to me from such people are very distressing, for I have not the comforts they require," he worried.[20]

Colonists urged Clarkson to consider ways to ameliorate the situation. In August, Nova Scotians again petitioned Clarkson and complained "of the extravagant charge made by the fishermen"—their fellow colonists in Freetown. They made this complaint before the French attack in 1794, at a time when the fishing was good. Clarkson solved the problem by meeting with one Robert Horton, making him promise to lower prices and to sell fish within the colony "before he offered them for sale to other people."[21] This compromise established migrants' ability to challenge prices, led to additional regulation in distribution patterns (sales to colonists now took precedence over sales to outsiders), and enabled the Nova Scotians to broaden access to fish harvests. It also increased black migrants' political participation by giving them some say in colonywide food regulations, which in turn opened the door to additional interventions in Freetown's food system.

Clarkson was willing to address black Loyalists' complaints by instituting fixed prices, but he decried the Sierra Leone Company's rationing. He argued that "vice and every species of wickedness and discontent are spreading in the colony from so many people living together, having nothing to do, *and their provisions found them.*" He thought it wrong that lazy colonists knew they could expect provisions, though he admitted that the problem existed because land distributions had stalled. Boston King might have agreed with Clarkson, who seemed to be saying that people should work to receive charitable food assistance. Clarkson changed the company's provisioning structure by requiring people to labor for food. In May 1792, at a time when people were dying from hunger, he set wages at two shillings per day. Everyone had to work two days out of the week, and colonists bought full rations for six pence or half rations for three pence.[22] Because it was difficult to obtain money from anyone except company officials, Clarkson's decision meant that those who refused to work could not buy rations, and even those who *did* work were still expected to pay to feed themselves.

The Nova Scotians seized the first opportunity to refine Clarkson's system of exchanging labor for rations; their actions signaled more readiness to institutionalize their food-related rights. When in November 1792 Clarkson halved rations, Nova Scotian John Strong proposed that if Clarkson did not possess enough stored provisions, he and others would "work one day for the half raisions" rather than the two days originally mandated. Clarkson could pay the remaining wages in company credit, Strong said. Other black Loyalists argued that if Clarkson decreased their provisions he should reduce their workload and warned that a failure to do so would create conflict. They indicated that Clarkson had commodified their labor by fixing a price for food, and that a change in work conditions mandated an adjustment to the cost of provisions. Clarkson, who worried that extra pay would encourage drunkenness, compromised by crediting each Loyalist's account.[23]

These agreements in 1792 established significant standards. People learned that their abilities to fight hunger fluctuated with the rainy season, the availability of ships, trade with Muslim merchants and the Temne, Susu, and Bullom who provided provisions, and Nova Scotians' abilities to produce and store meat and vegetables and to fix prices for fish and labor. Although colonists sometimes critiqued John Clarkson's policies, he was willing to work with them to modify the food system. Together they fixed food prices, managed distribution networks, and readjusted rates of working for food. Colonists also requested the right to sit on juries. Clarkson sailed for London in December 1792, planning to return, but the Sierra Leone Company fired him—shortly before his wedding—when he was in England. Governorship would pass back and forth between several new officials. From afar, Clarkson received word that by January land surveying had ceased, and "there [was] neither beef, Pork, flower or any kind of provision sufficient to last the colony a week."[24] When Cato Perkins and Isaac Anderson approached Clarkson in 1793, he may have possessed the desire to help them, but he had no authority to do it. Nevertheless, his governorship had taught colonists to demand freedom from scarcity.

When food shortages continued, the Nova Scotians traveled to London, wrote letters and petitions, and then pushed for greater representation.[25] In 1792, the Freetown government changed to include elected positions that came with the right to legislate against hunger, and representatives began doing so in 1793. The act of fixing prices became one of colonists' most effective hunger-avoiding strategies, which offered the additional benefit of enlarging colonists' political rights. Given the fact that humans must eat to survive, laws about food would have pervaded political participation in the colony on a daily, visceral level. These regulations, which granted more freedom to black Loyalists, also created conflict with the Temne and Susu by interfering with *their* food system. Black Loyalists, in trying and failing to become victual imperialists, precipitated conflict with Africans, clashes with the white Sierra Leone Council, and, ultimately, a riot in 1800.

After John Clarkson left Freetown, William Dawes became governor. Even some white colonists thought that this leadership change boded poorly. Anna Maria Falconbridge contrasted his "austere, reserved conduct" with Clarkson's "sweet manners," and his "rigid military education" left little room for flexibility. Dawes was not widely liked, and colonists lost faith in his ability to represent them. When in October 1793 the colonists went over Dawes's head and sent Isaac Anderson and Cato Perkins to London to make their petition, the men talked about political economy.[26]

In addition to highlighting the absence of land and their inability to grow crops, the colonists complained about their lack of control over prices. They associated this disorder with debt and slavery, just as they had in Nova Scotia. The company store charged "extortionate" prices, they complained. Perkins and Anderson stated that Governor Dawes dishonestly *put thirty Gals. of water into a Peck of rum . . . & then* [sold] *it to us for a Shilling a Galln. more than we ever paid before.*" Anna Maria Falconbridge confirmed that Dawes was exerting his control over "almost every kind of provisions in the neighbourhood." "We must either get into debt or be starved," Clarkson recorded the Nova Scotians saying. In 1794 the colonists wrote that in Clarkson's absence they had dubbed Freetown "A town of Slavery."[27] The black Loyalists accused Dawes not only of withholding their right to set prices, but also of setting unfair prices himself. Falconbridge's observations suggested that this tendency extended beyond rum to encompass other edible commodities. Black colonists argued that they faced an unwelcome choice: they could go into debt by paying exorbitant prices, or they could go hungry. Their petition foreshadowed new efforts to legally combat famine.

Various white leaders disliked many of the would-be famine fighters. But Freetown was an antislavery colony, and even if white officials complained about some black migrants, they had to reconcile their feelings with reformers' mission to establish a home where formerly enslaved peoples could become self-governing—thus convincing observers that freed slaves would not become useless. At one point in 1796 Zachary Macaulay might have written a thesaurus entry on disagreeable people. He described elected black representatives as "artful," "busy, bold, & blind," "disaffected," "factious," "hot," "ignorant," "irresolute," "noisy," "passionate," "pestilent," "Selfish," "timid," and "void of principle." These men came to office because abolitionist Granville Sharp, in discussions about the first Sierra Leone colony settled by the Black Poor, had proposed a system of colonial self-governance. After 1792 Governor Dawes and Zachary Macaulay implemented a similar system by encouraging colonists to elect representatives. These men, called Hundredors and Tythingmen, appear in council minutes in December 1792. Every ten householders formed a tithing, every ten tithings formed a hundred, ten freeholders elected a Tythingman, and every ten Tythingmen elected a Hundredor. Collectively, the Hundredors and Tythingmen proposed regulations that the Sierra Leone Council usually approved, even in 1793, when Anderson and Perkins petitioned the Sierra Leone Company, and throughout 1796, when Macaulay complained about elected legislators.[28]

As the black Loyalists continued to experience scarcity, they bound the legal system more firmly to the food system. Evidence of black colonists' intervention became visible in the courts, where colonists had won the right to sit on juries. By 1793, when three white sailors came on shore and "killed a duck belonging to one of the Settlers," the thieves were tried "by *Judge* McAuley and a *Jury of twelve blacks*." The jury sentenced one man to a lashing and imposed fines on the other two. Although the master of the sailors' ship dubbed the court "a mockery on all law and justice," one of the sailors was nevertheless "whipped by a black man." Had the black Loyalists remained in the United States, they would have been disallowed from holding office or serving on juries.[29] In Freetown, they enjoyed both of these rights. The incident's focus on poultry was significant, first, because it punished an attack on edible poultry, and second, because it played out in the sort of legal space that had previously worked against black colonists in Nova Scotia.

Less than a year after taking office, in 1793, the Hundredors and Tything-men enacted food laws that regulated the prices of black Loyalist–produced commodities, and they tried to control Africans' abilities to sell meat in the colony. These legislators were not reacting to or battling the state; they were working with and helping to constitute the government. Having witnessed Clarkson and then Dawes fixing prices during their governorships, the black Loyalists asked their Hundredors and Tythingmen to set colonywide prices for bread and meat, and to control alcohol distribution, just as white colonists had done when fighting hunger in Nova Scotia. In 1793, the Hundredors and Tythingmen, with the Sierra Leone Council's approval, proposed laws that standardized prices for beef, goat, pork, and sheep mutton. Zachary Macau-lay had conducted experiments with colonist Pompey Young to price bread at three pence in 1794, but a 1795 resolution of the Hundredors and Tything-men introduced additional regulations that raised the price to four pence half penny per pound. When the Hundredors and Tythingmen proposed fining anyone in the colony convicted of selling liquor or wine without a license, the governor and council went so far as to deem their resolution "highly proper & expedient" before passing it. By this point in time, black Loyalists and white councilmen were collaborating to build the colony's food system.[30]

By 1795 black Loyalists' food laws also aimed to control the prices of edible goods that Africans brought into the colony, thus prompting conflict—despite initial good relations.[31] In 1795, the Hundredors and Tythingmen recommended that the governor and council "issue an order to prevent strang-ers selling Meat in the Colony by Retail." Susu men had brought "some fine Cattle" into Freetown but refused to sell them unless the Nova Scotians al-lowed them "to kill them and sell them out by the Pound." The Nova Sco-tians did "not think that is proper" and requested "that no strangers or People that doth not belong to the Colony should bring live stock here and kill them."[32] In this context, "by Retail" meant sales of prebutchered meat—likely cattle and goats slaughtered according to Muslim dietary laws. Colonists wanted the Susu to sell only live animals because it became difficult to regulate prices for butch-ered meat.

The Nova Scotians' use of the word *strangers* evoked and also revised the landlord-stranger relationship. Within Sierra Leone, Temne elite offered pro-tection as landlords of British and Nova Scotian strangers. At the same time that Freetown's residents were strangers, early Muslim immigrants in Free-town were *also* strangers. Africans initially implemented the landlord-stranger relationship to allow foreigners to influence African social structures in ways that fostered accommodation and assimilation rather than control.[33] By calling Susu traders "strangers," the Nova Scotians claimed landlord status over them, but in passing a regulation that ignored strangers' food practices, they refused to compromise. It is clear that the council voiced no objections.

It is difficult to know what Loyalists intended by enacting these laws. Maybe they meant to try to exercise power by claiming the legal muscle denied to them in Canada, and maybe they only wanted to avoid hunger. So much of their intentions remains unrecoverable from the archival record; historians can only turn to African reactions to understand the laws' effects. In the late 1790s Temne words and actions indicate dissatisfaction. In 1798 a ruler named King Tom—likely a different leader than the first King Tom associated with Granville Town colonists—appeared at a *palaver* (or meeting) and claimed that Zachary Macaulay "had spoiled the Country . . . by lowering the Price of Produce." He cited the decreased cost of rice and argued "that if Mr. Macaulay wished to do good to the Country, he must again give the same." Macaulay refused and was told that he had to agree or leave the country. Macaulay "could not do the one, nor yet would he do the other," and so King Tom "departed in great Anger." It is unclear whether prices really had decreased. The colony could not have retained much control over prices outside of Freetown, given their dependency on African trade networks for food. In 1802, Freetown suffered because slave ship captains were demanding *high* prices for produce.[34] Macaulay's interaction with King Tom thus becomes difficult to explain, but the important point is that King Tom held the colony responsible for shifting prices.

Other incidents indicate additional, more widespread conflict between colonists and Africans. In 1797 Macaulay reported a great "Mortality among the Settlers hogs." No one could detect a cause until an unidentified "Native was caught in the very act of laying Ratsbane enclosed in Cassada near some Hogs, evidently for the purpose of killing them." Macaulay speculated that had the man succeeded, "the Natives wd. have . . . begged the dead body of the owner, and thus have had a Supply of fresh meat at very little expence." It is possible that the poisoner planned to sell the carcass back to the colonists. In 1798 a storekeeper in Freetown reported "that Several of the Company's cattle had recently disappeared." He conjectured "from various circumstances it was probable they had been drawn into the woods by Natives & there Slaughtered."[35] Africans drew suspicion when domesticated cattle went missing, suggesting a larger history of animal theft and reciprocal mistrust. Perhaps colonists wanted to disallow Temne sales because they possessed no way to identify stolen animals if the animals were already dead, and perhaps fears about contaminated produce prompted regulations about meat sales.

Black Loyalists aimed these food regulations at Africans during a time when they sought Temne land, which raises the question of whether their reform of Freetown's food system involved victual imperialism. Africans' poisoning and theft of animals certainly counted as victual warfare. In Nova Scotia victual imperialism limited black colonists' access to food and land; in Sierra Leone those migrants tried to become victual imperialists themselves. Black Loyalists in Freetown prevented their own hunger by controlling access to food, which involved self-regulation—but it also involved attempting to regulate African food distribution while living in Temne territory. As Nova Scotians became dissatisfied with their lands on the coast of Freetown and built into the mountains, they encroached on Temne lands. As late as 1798 the Nova Scotians complained that because "the land allotted to them" was "Still the Subject of dispute with King Tom, they were wholly deprived of the means of engaging in cultivation."[36] Therefore it might be said that the Temne resisted black Loyalist victual imperialism by maintaining control of land, while both Temne and Susu people used victual warfare to push back against black Loyalists' animal regulations. The Nova Scotians struggled to be effective imperialists not only because the Susu and Temne objected to black Loyalists' food laws, but also because the Sierra Leone Council began to ignore them too.

When Temne-Nova Scotian conflict became obvious in the late 1790s, the Sierra Leone Council stopped approving of the Hundredors' and Tythingmen's laws and scaled back the self-governance that legitimized black Loyalists' hunger prevention. An encounter in December 1796 presents one of the first instances of a white official challenging an elected black Loyalist's policies. Zachary Macaulay described his discovery of Hundredor Ishmael York "Selling rum to the Natives at . . . a Sixpence more [per] Gallon from *Natives*." York argued that "He did not See why any one Shd. interfere in his trade with the natives." Macaulay, unmoved by York's logic, revoked his liquor license.[37] York was implying that colonists should enjoy more preferential prices than Africans. In his meeting with Macaulay York specifically averred his right to fix his own prices—though he did not attempt to introduce this price differentiation as a colonywide law. York would join the group of men who in 1800 became protestors.

Not only did the Sierra Leone Council curtail black Loyalists' abilities to set prices; it also stopped enforcing Nova Scotian animal codes. "Many cattle belonging to the Colony were killed by the Natives" in 1799. When some of the culprits had been identified, "a serious complaint was made to King Tom, who promised redress." Before he could remedy the matter, however, "another Cow . . . was stolen in the same manner." In an act of Nova Scotian–imposed justice, the colonists "armed themselves, went in to King Tom's Territory," and seized several suspects. Governor Thomas Ludlum reported that King Tom gained "an advantage" by capturing three colonists and then arguing that the council's lack of consent for colonists' actions negated his obligation to pay for the animals. Councilmen sought no reparation, and indeed Ludlum's report of the incident indicated a growing divide between the council and the Nova Scotians with respect to their ideas about government.[38]

It seems likely that colonists used extralegal violence to solve the matter because they doubted the council's willingness to administer their laws. This was not just an episode of one white councilman forbidding a Nova Scotian politician to charge what he wanted; it was a record of disintegrating cooperation between black citizens and the council. The most persuasive explanation for this reversal in policy is that councilmen deemed it expedient to acquiesce to elite landlords' power in order to avoid more serious violence.

In 1798 the black Loyalists again asserted their political rights. They appointed Methodist preacher Mingo Jordan as judge, and Isaac Anderson and John Cuthbert became justices of the peace. These actions were not radical; they merely built on the government that the Hundredors and Tythingmen established after 1792. Jordan, Anderson, and Cuthbert assumed elected positions because of a precedent in the appointment of an all-black jury and in the formulation of Hundredor- and Tythingmen-conceived (and council-approved) laws. In 1800 it was their positions as officeholders and their history of lawmaking that should have legitimized the Hundredors' and Tythingmen's revived attempt to fix food prices during the so-called rebellion.[39]

In September 1800 elected black Loyalists in Freetown posted laws that fixed prices. But those laws provoked a much different response: by December the men had been accused of rebellion and banished, bayonetted, sentenced to hard labor, or hanged. According to the Sierra Leone Council, on 10 September elected leaders Isaac Anderson, James Robertson, Nathaniel Wansey, and Ansel Zizer revealed a document that has come to be known as the "code of laws"—which fixed prices for foodstuffs—at the house of Abraham Smith. The men encouraged others to join them, reposting a revised code on the 25th. The laws set prices for butter, cheese, salt beef, salt pork, rice, rum, and sugar, and declared that anyone who refused to sell foodstuffs to other black Loyalists and who was then "found carrying" such commodities "out of the Colony" would incur a fine. The document also delineated punishments for adultery, stealing, and Sabbath breaking, denied the white governor and Sierra Leone Council the authority to interfere in domestic affairs, and warned that black Loyalists had to abide by the code or leave Freetown.[40]

When Governor Thomas Ludlum learned of the laws, he accused the elected men of rebellion. He armed company employees and amenable black

Loyalists and sent them after the "rebels," which precipitated a scuffle. David Edmonds, who had once joined Thomas Peters in petitioning John Clarkson for Christmas beef, was wounded in the head. Robertson was captured, Zizer surrendered, and Anderson and Wansey (though stabbed with a bayonet) escaped to rally about fifty of the three hundred colonists. By the 27th "intelligence was received that the Hundredors & Tythingmen . . . were in a state of open rebellion." Posted at a bridge, they "cut off all communication between Freetown & the Country . . . and were receiving hourly supplies of men & provisions from both." They stole one gun, as well as shot, powder, money, mats, hides, liquor, sugar, tea, and clothing from councilmembers' houses. King Tom may have suggested that he would become involved. After a weeklong standoff the British ship *Asia* arrived, carrying forty-five British soldiers plus Jamaican Maroons from Nova Scotia, who captured enough black Loyalists to force a peace between black colonists and the councilmen in October. By December, armed with a new royal charter, the Sierra Leone Council convened a military tribunal, meted out punishment, and revoked all black colonists' rights to elect representatives.[41]

On the one hand it could be argued that the event was a rebellion. It was the culmination of a fight—evident throughout the 1790s in disagreements over a quitrent tax—over land. White leaders certainly disapproved of many of the black Loyalists who won office in the 1798 elections. The black Loyalists were armed, and their pilfering from the houses of white councilmen resembled the victual warfare of the Revolutionary War. King Tom's willingness to lend support implies black Loyalist–Temne cooperation rather than friction. The council suggested that many colonists denounced their fellow black Loyalists' actions by recording the "general indignation at the power assumed by the Hundredors and Tythingmen in pretending to bind them by new laws." In executing and banishing the Loyalists, and in the language used in post-September accounts, the white council treated the event as a rebellion. It must also be admitted that eighteenth-century people did not always distinguish between riot and rebellion.[42]

Yet previous black Loyalists' political involvement, the actions of those colonists in 1800, and the delay between land fights and the 1800 event should make readers pause before accepting that the 1800 event was a rebellion. This protest was an act of hunger avoidance that represented continuity with the early 1790s rather than a sudden departure from the past. The Nova Scotians had spent most of the 1790s claiming their right to fight hunger as British colonists. "If we are his [King George III's] subject[s]," they had reasoned in 1798, they possessed the "right to appleyed to government to see ourselves righted in all the wrongs which are Done to us here." In 1800 the black Loyalists were restrained in the face of Ludlum's reaction to their price-fixing, probably because they maintained faith in their ability to use the government to obtain redress. They attacked no towns, burned no farm buildings or plantations, and killed, decapitated, and maimed no whites. The men were armed, but it is unclear how many guns they possessed and whether the middle-aged rioters could commit physical violence. The elections took place in 1798, and the council resolved to abolish the quitrent in 1799, meaning that colonists—who were allowed into office—would have waited almost a year to rebel over land or political issues that had seemingly been resolved. Although the authors of the code did not obtain unanimous support, it seems odd that colonists would object to the *idea* of the code of laws because lawmakers had been legislating for seven years. With respect to King Tom, descriptions of his willingness to intervene are varied—the Sierra Leone Council claimed that "intelligence was received" that the colonists obtained assistance from the interior, but did not state who supplied the information or where the assistance originated.[43]

A real rebellion close to Freetown and the biases of the Sierra Leone Company and Council provide additional support for refusing to call the event a rebellion. Nearby events in the years before the Loyalists' arrival were perhaps more appropriately dubbed rebellions. Between 1783 and 1796 a slave uprising of Temne, Baga, and Bullom people had occurred in the Mandingo and Muslim state of Moria, to the north of Freetown. Those rebels *had* set fire to crops. The black Loyalists did deny the white Sierra Leone Council the authority to intervene in domestic affairs, but they did not seem to expect white officials to vacate their positions as mediators between Crown and colony. To call the event a rebellion is to replicate the language of the white councilmen, who may have obscured details. An 1802 report stated its intention to explain the Sierra Leone Company's financial failures, and the council and company needed a scapegoat to avoid blaming themselves for poor management.[44]

Although the word *riot* carries problematic connotations today, understanding food riots on their own terms makes apparent the similarities between food riots and the Freetown event. Between 1550 and 1820 two-thirds of all riots in England were food riots. Between 1776 and 1779 protesting crowds in America gathered on more than thirty different instances. In eighteenth-century English riots, price-fixing was the most noticeable unifying factor, constituting 35 percent of riotous behavior between 1782 and 1812. A spate of English food riots occurred at the exact same time as the one in Freetown—154 from 1800 to 1801. As in Sierra Leone, many began in September of 1800.

Hunger-fighting black Loyalists were similar in these ways to many other eighteenth-century British subjects, and similar, too, to other nonwhite communities that drew upon European influences in their nation-building efforts.[45]

The 1800 protest fits into patterns of riotous behavior—the *entrave* or blockage; the agrarian demonstration; the price riot or *taxation populaire*; and the market riot. In the *entrave*, people prevented the export of grain from a rural area, whereas in an agrarian demonstration farmers destroyed their produce before it could depart. In the price riot, people seized food, set what they deemed a "just" price, and sold it. In a market riot, urban crowds acted against local magistrates, commercial bakers, butchers, or millers to force a price reduction. Nova Scotians tried to prevent food from leaving Freetown, as in the *entrave*; they set prices, as in the price riot; and they criticized government officials, as in the market riot. Black Loyalists, in regulating prices and preventing foodstuffs from leaving the colony, demanded political rights by behaving like food rioters, even though the council called them rebels.[46] When hunger was concerned, price-fixing could be a legally sanctioned action, or it could be an act of political protest.

The black Loyalists resembled other food rioters, but they also differed from them because they rioted not to push for new rights but to *reclaim* old ones: life, liberty from a state resembling bondage, and freedom from want. The commodities the rioters targeted, the composition of participants, and the punishments they incurred also make Freetown unusual. Nova Scotians, like Europeans, tried to regulate prices of staple commodities, but they also policed meat, alcohol, and butter consumption, and in 1800 they did not try to fix bread or flour prices. In many riots women started things because they remained unlikely to face capital punishment. Women in Freetown do not seem to have participated in the riot, possibly because they were excluded from voting for Hundredors and Tythingmen in 1797. They do appear in the records as shopkeepers, and riot leaders requested protection for their women and children. Most food riots were leaderless and carried out without arms.[47] At least according to the council, the Sierra Leone riot had leaders, some of whom possessed arms.

The riot also differed from those in England in the severity of its repercussions—death rates were higher in Freetown. Cato Perkins survived by offering to negotiate between the council and the rioters, the majority of whom came from his Huntingdonian Methodist congregation. Isaac Anderson was hanged.[48] The 1800 event was remarkable not only because the protestors had already learned what it was like to be granted the authority to legislate against hunger, and not only because they were fighting to win back that right, but because the white Sierra Leone Council was so determined to use a different word to erase those efforts from history.

"Whites live better perhaps than you do," Governor Zachary Macaulay admitted to the black Loyalists in 1795. To colonists who asked, "why should not we have the same[?]" Macaulay responded that when black colonists could "Write as well, figure as well, Act as well, think as well as they do . . . you shall have a preference." That year, however, he thought there was not "an office in the Colony filled by a white, which a Black could fill with any propriety."[49] By initially establishing prices for alcohol, bread, and fish, and regulating the sale of meat, free black Loyalists did what they could to claim authority using the lower political offices granted to them. They privileged their ability to fight hunger over their relationships with Africans—and despite Macaulay's reservations about black politicians, at first they did so with the blessings of the Sierra Leone Council.

John Clarkson and then the Sierra Leone Council opened the door to changes in government by approving the creation of black-Loyalist politicians, price-fixing, jury service, and legislation. Only in the late 1790s did whites question these decisions. Colonists did not riot just because they were hungry. During and after the Revolutionary War, black people had ignored, caused, and embraced scarcity. Their food-related protest in 1800 was a political, organized act that gave shape to black colonists' anger and quest for British subjecthood. Even if readers wish to call the 1800 Freetown incident a rebellion, considering its similarities to food riots contextualizes the laws that black Loyalists enacted to avoid hunger. They lost the fight against hunger not because the laws were ineffective, but because a lifetime of enslavement had slowed their abilities to pen their own history.

Hunger-prevention attempts altered victual imperialism in Sierra Leone, which began as a black-Loyalist effort to change the food system while infringing on land use and transformed into white leaders' attempts to change food production while interfering with trade. Black Loyalists, like their contemporaries in Britain and the American colonies, sought more control of their local economy through price-fixing. While eyeing Temne land, they favored laws that regulated the edible commodities that they daily produced, bought, and sold. The political authority to fight hunger became just as crucial as the ability to actually do so. The Sierra Leone Council overruled them. Councilmen called protestors rebels and executed them, likely because they thought it more strategic to privilege good relations with Africans. In August 1808 the British Crown assumed formal rule of Freetown. After the Crown took control, the colony shifted its position on victual imperialism by trying to change the state of trade in the region. Officials focused their efforts on convincing Africans that commercial cash crops, rather than the slave trade, presented a profitable alternative.[50]

At the very end of the eighteenth century, the fight against hunger became nearly inseparable from the intellectual and political questions that peopled asked when they crossed the Atlantic. In making and then unmaking black victual imperialists, the white Sierra Leone Council first legitimized and then erased a decade of black-Loyalist lawmaking. The council's description of the 1800 "rebellion" becomes a significant contradiction, because it was not a deviation from the colony's history. Calling the 1800 event a riot recognizes that the Loyalists were acting not as rebellious slaves but as emancipated political participants. Although these colonists gained only transient freedoms through their food laws, their narrative offers an opportunity to look forward and backward in time to consider how hunger prevention in Sierra Leone brought people together—and drove them apart.

Conclusion

Why Native and Black Revolutionaries
Lost the Fight

No Useless Mouth is a study of hunger during the American Revolution in Indian country and the original thirteen colonies, with Atlantic World nodes that look outside the theater of war. In turning from Native Americans to formerly enslaved people, it follows the people whose participation in the conflict meant that they had to flee further afield if they wanted to survive. I have adopted this Atlantic perspective that includes Nova Scotia and Sierra Leone—what scholars would call a circum-Atlantic approach—because I think it helps us to see the War for Independence differently in terms of power relationships, to make comparisons between food policies, and to distinguish between people who benefited and people who suffered from hunger-prevention efforts in the British Atlantic World.[1]

Scholarship on the Atlantic World has taught historians that they should look beyond the concept of the nation or state when assessing power relationships. The notion of nations was still developing in the eighteenth century, but questions about who sought, won, and lost power were much older. If readers are willing to move past the idea of the nation and its institutions as the foundations of power—as people at the time had to do—then it is hard to ignore the Native American polities that wielded power over Europeans during the sixteenth, seventeenth, eighteenth, and nineteenth centuries. This book is not the first to consider formerly enslaved people's flight to Nova Scotia and Sierra Leone alongside other events in the American Revolution or the Age of Revolutions more broadly—but it is the first to explore how the people who lived in this dynamic world experienced hunger. After the Revolutionary War it was not certain that the United States would last beyond a generation. This state of instability made the United States similar to precarious British colonies in Nova Scotia and Sierra Leone, not different from them.[2]

Adopting an Atlanticist approach to this period makes clear the similarities and differences between food policies that emerged before, during, and after the Revolutionary War. Both the British and American officials who distributed food aid during the War for Independence did so in a disorganized manner—Americans to a greater extent—and they did so in response to Native expectations that had cohered during the colonial period. During the postwar era U.S. food aid was preemptive, in British Nova Scotia it was reactive, and in Sierra Leone it was largely unnecessary after the colony's first year. Native Americans intervened in the theorization of food policies earlier than black people, and for a more extended period of time, which encompassed centuries of Native sovereignty, diplomacy, and independent political and legal systems. During the later years considered in this book, however, white Indian agents privileged their food laws over Native practices, sometimes at the request of Indians themselves. Formerly enslaved colonists, by contrast, demanded the political rights to create their own legal frameworks to regulate the food system.

It is clear that some folks prevented hunger earlier than historians have claimed, but it is also apparent that hunger prevention was just one small battle in the fight against hunger; hunger endurance and creation often mattered more. Native women controlled the provisions necessary for war. Chickamauga Cherokees and Creeks fed themselves by stealing cattle and horses during the 1770s. When, in 1779, American soldiers invaded Iroquoia and set fire to huge amounts of Seneca and Cayuga corn, they created a period of starvation that no one could prevent but some could endure. Throughout the war self-liberated former slaves filled British stomachs by stealing grain and cattle, and occasionally lost their appetites. After the War for Independence, more people began to treat hunger as something avoidable. U.S. Indian officials set food prices and centralized markets to protect the corn, beef, and pork that Native Americans raised. Ex-bondpeople who escaped to present-day Canada and starved there, and then migrated to a new colony in Sierra Leone, created a government that allowed them to circumvent famine. The costs of trying to stop its deadly effects were sometimes too high.

Indians and formerly enslaved people lost the fight against hunger not because they became bad at stopping it but because imperial officials gathered enough information to circumscribe Native Americans' and black colonists' abilities to prevent hunger themselves. Knowledge acquisition gave these white officials a specific kind of power over Native and black revolutionaries: the power to reinterpret histories of hunger.

Before the American Revolution, Edinburgh doctors like William Robertson and British generals like Jeffery Amherst knew too little; during the colonial period non-Native observers could not with accuracy assess Indian hunger. Native Americans knew how to fight famine by drawing on deep reserves of the grain that Native women produced, relying on specific famine foods, and dispersing into small bands during long winters and years of crop failure. British and American officials never managed to interpret black and Native hunger accurately because discourses of hunger were ever changing. What mattered was that after the Revolutionary War, they gained the know-how to say that they could evaluate hunger and to argue that they were better placed to prevent it. British officials began learning these lessons before the Revolutionary War. American agents improved their knowledge during the 1790s because their power struggles with state officials over Native American affairs had forced them to work hard to practice food diplomacy. They had received education about Native appetites and how to satisfy and then manipulate those appetites as they implemented a policy of victual imperialism. Black colonists gained the power to prevent their own hunger through observation and knowledge acquisition: first, they watched white colonists draw on previous colonization attempts to learn how to pass food laws in Nova Scotia, and then they reproduced similar laws in Sierra Leone. Once white officials in Sierra Leone realized how much conflict those black colonists' laws caused, they stopped black colonists from dealing with hunger on their own and then acted as if they had not in the past sanctioned the passage of similar legislation.

Government officials who delegitimized Native and black hunger-prevention efforts interfered with other people's food sovereignty.[3] They decided that Indians and formerly enslaved people were unqualified to decide what to grow, sell, cook, and eat, and they made it harder for those communities to feed themselves. Their actions ignored centuries of Native hunger prevention and erased a short decade of free black colonists' efforts to act similarly. Though scholars should be cautious about drawing a solid line from the eighteenth century to the present, it is arresting that today, black women's lifetime risk of being diagnosed with diabetes is over 50 percent, and Native Americans are much likelier than white Americans to develop diabetes and obesity.[4] A historian cannot help but be informed and influenced by the contemporary issues unfolding as she writes.

In the opening pages to *No Useless Mouth*, I noted that my periodization for this book—taking a long view of the American Revolution and distinguishing the era from the military conflict itself—was a choice I made that was determined by the school where I teach.[5] Having recently moved to Cardiff University, I am struck by the degree to which my colleagues think about history in practice. My predecessor edited an award-winning collection about teaching history, to which many of my colleagues contributed, and I inherited her team-taught class (or *module*, in British academia) that emerged alongside that volume.[6] In the United Kingdom our teaching must be driven by our research. These observations are not meant to imply that other historians fail to consider how history is used, but to admit that *I* had not thought about our discipline as extensively as I might have done until I reached the final stages of revising this book. Revision is a never-ending process; historians come back to arguments they have made in decades past and adjust them, and other scholars challenge and reinterpret other historians' earlier publications. I have made peace with the state of this book by drawing on the British meaning of the term *revision*, which my students invoke to mean that they are *studying* for final exams. This book is nearing its end, but I may never stop revising its subject matter.

No Useless Mouth concludes that white officials in the United States and the British Empire won the fight against hunger by seizing control of history to rewrite past and present representations of Native American and black hunger.[7] History does affect practice, and practice will shape history.

This book began as a study of food, and its only argument was that food was important—often more important than other historians had conceded. Over time that argument changed as the focus shifted to hunger, or food's absence, and how people characterized it before, during, and after the American Revolutionary War. I set out to write an antideclension narrative because I thought that too many histories characterized the American Revolution as a disaster for Native American and enslaved communities, and my reading of food exchange and destruction during the war contradicted these interpretations.

Upon reflection, I realize that I have also written a declension narrative, but my history offers a different chronology of the shifts in Native American power, and finds parallels between these shifts and the gains and losses in power that formerly enslaved peoples experienced in Nova Scotia and Sierra Leone. This book thus recasts an Iroquois Civil War as a time when the Haudenosaunee retained and then expanded their power. It shows that the Revolution in Creek and Cherokee country was a period of immense confusion and disorganization that contributed to a fear of powerful, starving, and violent Indians. Black colonists had to wait until they had relocated to Africa to intervene in food policies, but once in Sierra Leone they enjoyed nearly a decade of political participation built on protective food legislation before losing the power that they too had gained.

This book takes as its starting point the conviction that the American Revolution cannot be limited to the years or the geography of the military conflict, nor can it be comprehensible without considering the enslaved people and Native Americans whose lives that conflict disrupted. *No Useless Mouth*'s expansive periodization and willingness to cross traditional national boundaries invites comparison of how Americans and Britons treated the peoples who had allied with them during the war. The British government supported and then failed its black allies, who would come to identify as British subjects. Lord Dunmore offered them freedom, but then other officials changed the state of affairs, first with inadequate wartime provisioning and protection, then in the government's cessation of food aid during famine in Nova Scotia, and finally in the Sierra Leone Council's revocation of rights that had given black colonists the ability to address these failures. Native Americans were not British subjects, and Britons tried harder to accommodate them—even if Indians required no such accommodation. At first blush it seems that the early years of the war did not substantively change Indian country; kinship networks, intertribal alliances, intratribal conflict, and negotiations with non-Natives from a position of strength remained the order of the day. But the four decades after the war witnessed foreign policy decisions that rearranged Native Americans' relationships with the United States.

I have written this book for readers interested in food and in history. To food-studies scholars I have offered a study of Native American and black hunger during the American Revolution, which seemed to me to be absent from studies of food during the colonial period, the American Revolutionary War, and the Early Republic. I have also tried—by positioning food diplomacy, victual imperialism, and victual warfare on a scale from accommodating to violent behavior—to provide a model for understanding peaceful and violent food-related actions and events from the 1750s to the 1810s. I will refrain from claiming that I do not want people to use this model; I hope that people do begin to use these terms, but I also insist that they will require adjustment. My own research has shown that food diplomacy, victual warfare, and victual imperialism were different across time and space. I want people to experiment with these terms in other regions of the Atlantic World, and perhaps beyond it, so that scholars can continue to think through ways of understanding how people dealt with scarcity.

In the hope that even more scholars will wish to write about histories of food and hunger, I would like to offer some suggestions for research and writing themes that I think worthy of pursuit. These include accommodation and violence, food policy, and the project of contextualizing hunger. Hunger prevention can involve cooperation, as when people at Thanksgiving sit down to share a family feast. But when hunger is not about cooperation, it is often about violence. The first Thanksgiving meal was a fraught affair between Pilgrims and Wampanoags.[8] During the American Revolution people stole animals and burned crops when peaceful food exchanges failed, and some forms of food diplomacy themselves involved the wrecking of provisions. Hunger-prevention programs—which people portrayed as positive efforts—also enabled subtle and more overt forms of violence, from attempts to control what people could eat to distributions of debilitating foodstuffs.

Hunger prevention informed food policies, which also merit further comparisons and careful thinking. Such policies might be better understood by considering distributions of food aid, interventions in production methods, uses of the marketplace, and policy's relationship with the legal system. Writers need to ask when food aid was distributed, who took charge of distribution, and who received the foodstuffs and under what conditions. They should know who won the authority to approve or reject production methods, and whether those declarations accompanied other initiatives, like landgrabs. Scholars should observe when governments, states, and cities centralized their marketplaces, but they should not assume the benevolence or malevolence of such centralization. If there were food laws about aid, production, or marketplace sales, then it is worth asking who was responsible for passing those laws, whom the laws helped, and who suffered under them.

Last and most important is the theme of contextualizing what hunger meant during different times around the Atlantic World. To contextualize hunger, writers must try to have a sense of the baseline state of being adequately fed for the periods and places that interest them. They should know what foods people ate on a normal day in a year of unremarkable weather, what provisions they consumed during leaner times, and how often they had to resort to this diet.[9] It is acceptable for the baseline to be ineffable, but writers should talk about what makes it that way. They should investigate how people described hungriness: With exaggeration? In formal diplomatic settings? By referencing deaths by starvation? It is worth trying to separate peckishness, hunger, starvation, and famine. Writers must remain willing to see real hunger in the historical sources, but their first reading should be performed with a healthy level of skepticism, especially if the people whose hunger is described are not the same people writing the records. Authors should try as much as possible to cross-reference claims about hunger with the supposedly hungry people's actions, with reports of the environment at the time, and with interdisciplinary research on the plants and animals that lived in those places.

Any discussion of hunger must contextualize what that state of being meant to the people who grappled with it, because without this context it is impossible to assess power relations between parties who negotiated over their right to food. During the American Revolution people used the three related behaviors of food diplomacy, victual warfare, and victual imperialism in their preparations for and reactions to hunger, which allowed them to create food systems that everyone could—at varying times, and for different reasons—shape to claim power. Ideas about, countermeasures against, and reactions to deprivation all shaped food policies—from the settled Iroquois territory beneath Lake Ontario, to the mountains, rivers, swamps, and valleys of Creek and Cherokee country, to a field in the Ohio Valley where trees lay scattered by tornadoes, to the cold, rocky soils of Nova Scotia, and to the rain-soaked colony of Freetown, Sierra Leone.

What is so arresting about the American Revolution is that in the decades that followed the war, white officials working for the U.S. and British governments chose to act as if only their abilities to prevent hunger counted. U.S. Indian agents took one of many Native claims about hunger at face value and then imposed on Indians a static, unchanging notion of Native appetites that required more and more stringent intervention from the government. In Sierra Leone, British officials panicked about the freedom they had given to black legislators to deal with hunger. The Revolutionary War, the new country it created, and the exodus it encouraged were disruptive, and people wrote dishonestly about these events and institutions because the world was watching.

When Timothy Pickering told Cornplanter that early colonists thrived while Native Americans wanted food, when Andrew Pickens recalled a campaign against the Cherokees in which the Americans benevolently decided to refrain from destroying Cherokee corn, when federal officials elided Native women's labor by pretending that Indians did not farm, and when the Sierra Leone Council characterized normal price-fixing behavior by black Loyalists as evidence of rebellion, these men were trying their best to control the historical narrative by misrepresenting hunger prevention in history. Pickering's Englishmen were supposedly able husbandmen, Pickens's soldiers were concerned about Cherokee abilities to provision themselves, U.S. officials were unable to recall an entire war in which the American army destroyed Native cornfields, and the black Loyalists' decision to pass food legislation in 1800 was a rebellious deviation from past activities. These acts of willful forgetfulness or outright mendacity, call it what you will, turned out to be key pivot points in the telling of history and the courses of nations and peoples.

Historians are not fortune-tellers. We are incapable of predicting the future with any certainty, and our ability to assess the past with accuracy is a skill that we are constantly developing. But our capacity to write with confidence about the past is one of the best services we can offer in the interest of good citizenship. Until a country reckons with its history—recognizing that the birth of empires and nations involved conquest, colonization, contradictory trade policies, displacement, enslavement, land seizures, and refugee crises—its citizens cannot be good citizens because they labor under delusions about their country's past benevolence. I therefore think it of the utmost importance to expose those moments in the histories of the United States and Great Britain when government agents actively worked to distort history. That is what they did after the American Revolution, and that is the story that *No Useless Mouth* tells.

ACKNOWLEDGMENTS

As a food enthusiast, I have found that the company and conversation often matter more than what's eaten. On the lonely path to writing a book, there were luckily intervals when I had to pull my head away from sources, and eat with smart friends. I am indebted to many people and institutions for providing intellectual and physical sustenance.

I thank the David Library of the American Revolution, the Huntington Library, the Colonial Williamsburg Foundation, the Massachusetts Historical Society, the New York Public Library, the William L. Clements Library, the History Department at the University of Texas at Austin, the Faculty of Humanities and the History Department at the University of Southampton, the McNeil Center for Early American Studies, and International Security Studies at Yale for supporting this project. This work would have been impossible without help from archivists, librarians, and reading room staff at these institutions. I am grateful to my colleagues at Cardiff University for welcoming me into the department, and I thank the Cardiff Open Access Support Team for generous funding to make this monograph open access. People offered helpful feedback at meetings and seminars hosted by the American Historical Association, the Association for the Study of Food and Society, the British Group in Early American History, the Forum on European Expansion and Global Interaction, the Institute of Historical Research, the McNeil Center for Early American Studies, American Studies at the University of Manchester, History at the University of Nottingham, the Omohundro Institute of Early American History and Culture, the History Department at Queen Mary University, the Society of Early Americanists, the Société d'Etudes Anglo-Américaines des XVIIème et XVIIIème siècles, the Society for Historians of the Early American Republic, and the Yale Early American History seminar. I acknowledge *Diplomatic History* and *Slavery and Abolition* for publishing some of my first thoughts on this topic, and allowing me to revise and expand upon my ideas in chapters 2 and 8 of this book. I also thank the anonymous peer reviewers who read and provided comments on this book when I submitted it to Cornell University Press.

No Useless Mouth started growing roots over a decade ago. At Vassar College, Sasha Litwin was the first to suggest that I write about food and history. She and Chelsea Backer, Kofi James, Anna Rogers, and Kathryn Wilbert were the best brunch partners, fierce friends, and devoted eaters of multiple pieces of cake per day. I thank Lisl Prater-Lee for too many swim-meet sandwiches to count, and for cheering me on in and out of the pool. The history and English departments helped me figure out how to think and to write. Classes with Bob Brigham, Miriam Cohen, Rebecca Edwards, Priscilla Gilman, Lydia Murdoch, and Everett Weedin were foundational. Special thanks go to James Merrell, who taught me a few crucial matters of form and style as I began to study food in early America, and who continued to provide feedback when it came time to revise this book.

At the University of Texas at Austin, Carolyn Eastman offered vital support, first as I thought about cannibalism and then as I began to write about food. Erika Bsumek, Elizabeth Engelhardt, Neil Kamil, Robert Olwell, and James Sidbury offered some of the first commentaries on these pieces of work. Marilyn Lehman was a graduate coordinator extraordinaire. I owe gratitude to Rachel Ozanne for her excellent taste in polka dots, for her willingness to eat my cookies, and for constituting one-half of the House of Rachels. Ben Breen, Felipe Cruz, and Alexis Harasemovitch Truax conjure grilled sausages around a camp grill, floating conversations in Krause Springs, and early afternoon trips to the Salt Lick. Libby Nutting and Dharitri Bhattacharjee were there to catch up over coffee when we were all in town. Angela Smith made an excellent bicycling companion. I am also obliged to the Subalterns for facilitating work/life balance through poorly played soccer, and for Draught House gatherings with José Adrián Barragán, Juandrea Bates, Chris Dietrich, Jonathan Hunt, Renata Keller, Sarah Steinbock-Pratt, Claudia Rueda, Kyle Shelton, Cameron Strang, Sundar Vadlamudi, and Susan Zakaib.

I did a lot of eating on the road. On return visits to Austin, Rebekah Brewer, Richard Huey, their kids Sophia and Hendrix, Jimmy Myers, Caroline Foley, and Jay Wiltshire were always willing to meet on Sundays for dim sum. Josh Keidaish and Krisna Wymore provided a fabulous home away from home; thank you for (finally) taking me to Polvos. Rachel Laudan provided a thoughtful, generous sounding board over cups of coffee. In New Haven, Alejandra Dubcovsky did the same. Jamie Miller and Sarah Kinkel's knowledge of beer and sushi vastly improved life there. Amanda Behm knew the best places to eat cheese. Kristina Poznan and Leslie Waters fed me incredible Hungarian food in Williamsburg. Tater tots with Ted Andrews in Providence fueled me almost as well as the conversation. In Boston and then Philadelphia and Baltimore, Chelsea Backer and Nick Lekow offered excellent company for Szechuan, and delightful home-brewed beverages. Christopher Heaney was there to talk writing and weird history in Austin and Philadelphia. In New York, Kofi and Whitney James never failed to host dinner with enchiladas, or to meet for amazing Turkish food. Chris Dietrich and Verónica Jiménez Vega provided dinners of fish tacos, trekked to the East Side for breakfasts of scones and tea, and to the West Side for Hungarian pastries.

Meals at conferences have yielded opportunities to talk through ideas in progress. I had so much fun eating Mexican in London with Kelly Watson and Caroline Dodds Pennock, and discussing (but not practicing) cannibalism. I remember catching up over drinks—at the AHA with Laurie Wood, and at the Britain and the World conference with Mikki Brock. I ate far too much Indian food with Jessica Hower in Southampton. I am indebted to Christian Ayne Crouch for a London breakfast over which she shared a great deal of practical book writing tips and valuable opinions about ways to supplement my spice cabinet. Claire Jowitt has been generous with her time and willing to share strategic advice, and I will remember several delicious dinners in Paris. I always look forward to meals at conferences with Kate Grandjean, and I think of a long walk to the Green Goddess in New Orleans.

I acknowledge all members of *The Junto: A Group Blog on Early American History*, and particularly Benjamin Park for starting the whole thing, and for meeting me for a Tex-Mex breakfast on a Houston-to-Austin trip. I admire Juntoists Sara Georgini and Tom Cutterham for insisting at yearly BGEAH meetings that food should always come on plates. I thank Christopher Jones for grilling inspiration and conversations about black voyagers, Sara Damiano for tacos and her thoughts on women's history, and Joe Adelman for talking teaching and for giving me major pancake goals.

Many scholars have a temporary academic center or home that shaped their thinking and writing, and the McNeil Center was mine. I thank Daniel Richter for being the best of directors, and for providing tough and honest feedback during this foundational year. Amy Baxter-Bellamy and Barbara Natello ensured that their doors were always open, and alerted hungry fellows when seminar leftovers were available. I cannot overstate the value of lunches from various food trucks with the entire 2011–2012 cohort, especially Sari Altschuler, Chris Parsons, Nenette Luarca-Shoaf, Dael Norwood, Seth Perry, Nic Wood, and next-door office mates Whitney Martinko and Matt Karp. Jessica Roney and Adam Choppin supplied many expertly crafted cocktails and dinners, and a place to stay in Philadelphia. It was an honor to cook for them; a simple chicken soup with dumplings shared with them, Lexi, Glenda Goodman, and Mitch Fraas will stick with me for a long time.

Moving to England has been such an adventure in teaching, thinking, and eating. In Exeter, I think of Richard Toye and Kristine Vaaler having us over for fish suppers, and meeting for dinners out in town. Fish and chips always tasted better after bike rides to Dart's Farm and the Turf Locks with David Thackery. I have good memories of Chinese takeaway shared with Tehyuhn Ma and Andrew Heath, and am glad that they introduced me to the Peak District in Sheffield. Exploring Somerset's cideries was much more fun with Katrina Gulliver alongside me. In Wales my Cardiff colleagues, especially Padma Anagol, Lloyd Bowen, Emily Cock, David Doddington, Federica Ferlanti, Mary Heimann, James Ryan, Bronach Kane, Eve MacDonald, Jan Machielsen, Angela Muir, Helen Nicholson, Kevin Passmore, Ian Rapley, Shaun Tougher, Stephanie Ward, Keir Waddington, and Mark Williams, provided friendship, advice, coffee, crisps, pints, and necessary lunches at Aberdare Hall. It's been a blast living in Bristol. I thank Billy Davis for nights of red wine, Spanish hampers, and the occasional barbecue. I'm so glad that Ryan Hanley and Jessica Moody moved to town, and I look forward to many more Thanksgiving and Christmas dinners, harborside drinks, and picnics in the park. I've also enjoyed sharing pints with various Americanists who have come to visit, especially Ann Little, Drew Lipman, and Jessica Roney.

I owe a great deal to my students at the University of Southampton, particularly the 2015–2016 cohort of "America: From Revolution to Republic." Teaching the events and aftermath of the American Revolution, and hearing students' takes on those occurrences, helped give shape to this book. I am enormously grateful to my Southampton colleagues, particularly Mark Cornwall, David Cox, Chris Fuller, George Gilbert, Neil Gregor, Maria Hayward, Jonathan Hunt, Nick Karn, Claire Le Foll, Sarah Pearce, Christer Petley, Charlotte Riley, Francois Soyer, and Helen Spurling, for collegiality, friendship, and the occasional pint at the Crown. Kendrick Oliver, Chris Prior, and Mark Stoyle kindly read my work, and I hope improved it. Chris Woolgar was a model mentor; it was a privilege to share teaching and office lunches together. I thank Priti Mishra for her presence next door, and for occasionally eating far too much cheese with me. I don't know what I would do without Eve Colpus, who was always willing to catch up over Thai food. I am glad that it took less than a year to confirm our red and white wine preferences.

At Cornell, I thank Michael McGandy, first for his unflagging support on this project and then for his thoughts on all things bourbon-related. I thank Bethany Wasik for her Twitter support and wise footwear choices. I thank Kate Gibson at Westchester Publishing Services for overseeing production, and Kelley Blewster for her meticulous copyediting.

Where there is food, there is family. I write with memories of my dad, the first Dr. Herrmann. I cannot narrow down my mom's cooking to one meal, so will call up the image of everything bagels with lox and scallion cream cheese during weekends at home. Thank you for everything, Mom—but especially for teaching me to love food and cooking. I think fondly of eating with Amy and Peter Coppernoll, but nights of tapas and wine in Barcelona stand out the most. Life in England makes the prospect of Thanksgiving in Oklahoma less feasible than in past years, but during that season I always think of bowling for salami with the Nevards and Erlichs. In San Antonio, Don, Andrea, and Sean Palen provided days of excellent card games, and delicious spaghetti.

Over the course of writing this book and the search for academic jobs, dumplings and the quest to find the best of them provided grounding. I am so lucky that Marc Palen has been willing to seek them out with me. From Boston, to New York, to Sydney, Saigon, Southampton, Exeter, London, and Bristol, it's been an adventure. I thank him for loving me, even when I'm hangry.

Bibliographic Note

Various books and articles have shaped my thinking for this book, and scholars will be able to infer a lot about them from my endnotes. My approach to the primary sources requires a little bit more background.

When I started the research for this book in 2010, it would have been impossible to proceed without a car. As a New Yorker who learned to drive about a year before I moved to Austin in 2007, it always felt strange to get into my new (used) car and to drive from Austin to one coast or another. I was the fortunate recipient of fellowships on the East Coast and the West Coast of the United States, and I had funding from my department to go to London. So after a few weeks in Ottawa, I drove from Austin to Williamsburg, Virginia, and from there up and down the East Coast and throughout North Carolina, South Carolina, and Georgia. I drove back to Austin, flew to London for a summer of research, returned, and then drove east to Philadelphia for a year. After that, I drove from Austin out to San Marino, California, and back again. I ended up in New Haven, where my faithful Toyota Corolla had to be sold because it could not come with me to England.

This book's endnotes indicate where in my travels I located a particular source. Although some of these documents have by now appeared online or in printed collections, there are several stops on my archival route that I think worth visiting if scholars would like to reproduce my research. What follows is a rough description of key archives and collections in the order in which I explored them.

In Ottawa, Library and Archives Canada holds microfilm copies of documents available in Halifax. The Shelburne historical records collection was especially important for court records relating to white and black colonists, and the William A. Smy transcripts gave me a sense of which documents about Native Americans I needed to look at in London. If researchers find themselves in Ottawa, they should endeavor to eat at the ByWard Market, and the scones at the SconeWitch, right by the archives, are worth having.

At the John D. Rockefeller Library in Williamsburg, Virginia, the Cornwallis Orderly book, Dunmore's correspondence, and the Robert Carter letterbooks helped me to think about formerly enslaved people. Visitors should
check the calendar of the Omohundro Institute to see if any colloquia are
scheduled; there will be coffee, baked goods, and intellectual nourishment.

After Williamsburg, I drove to Washington Crossing, Pennsylvania, home
to the David Library of the American Revolution. This is an unmissable stop
for U.S. scholars interested in British documents, though as the library's name
indicates, historians of various stripes are welcome there. This microfilm library provided access to the British Headquarter Papers—useful for commentary on British strategy, provisioning, and Indian affairs north and south—and
some of the War Department Papers, which I used to wrap my head around
southern Indian affairs in the postwar period. Rented housing is available, but
I recommend carefully reading instructions about using the kitchen, as one
unnamed historian may or may not have broken the garbage disposal when
she put too many onion skins in it.

Following a month in Washington Crossing, I spent six weeks driving back
and forth between Georgia, North Carolina, and South Carolina. I spent the
most time at the Georgia Department of Archives and History in Morrow, but
the hours back then were limited, and I had to pass the time on the archive's
closed days with side trips to the North Carolina State Archives, the South
Carolina Department of Archives and History, the South Carolina Historical
Society, the Southern Historical Collection, the South Caroliniana Library,
the Hargrett Rare Book and Manuscript Library, and the Georgia Historical
Society—the last of which helped with the section of this book that deals with
the Treaty of Colerain. In Morrow, transcripts of Creek and Cherokee letters
reproduce documents that are otherwise scattered across the United States,
but they need to be used with some care because they are transcripts rather
than original documents. I have dealt with this problem by quoting from them
as sparingly as I could.

After this southern trip I went back to Austin to stow my car. I would like
to tell you about all the food in Austin, but my editor has given me a word
limit. Tacodeli is where readers should get their breakfast tacos (with chorizo and eggs, or eggs and steak) and their pork mole tacos; Papalote is
where they should eat turkey mole tacos and ceviche tostadas. Everyone
should drink horchata and Mexican martinis. I refuse to argue about barbecue and authenticity.

Thereafter, I flew to the East Coast. I started in Philadelphia on a recon-
naissance trip that would serve me well the following year, looking initially at
the Cadwalader papers to get to know George Croghan. A month later, in

Boston, the Massachusetts Historical Society provided access to the Sullivan Transcripts and some of Samuel Kirkland's letters, which illuminated the 1779 campaign against the Iroquois. Of real importance were the Timothy Pickering papers on microfilm, which have molded much of what I have to say in this book about history. I strongly recommend visiting Chinatown on weekends for dim sum, and Pho Basil by the MHS for very delicious bo kho.

New York came next. I depended on Maruzzella for a lot of penne alla vodka, and at the New York Public Library I consulted a mix of original manuscripts and material copied from other archives. The Philip Schuyler papers were essential for learning about Indian Affairs from the American perspective and for recovering some Six Nations' voices. Photostats of the British Headquarters Papers, which the David Library also has on microfilm, were useful for getting a head start on the research I needed to do in London.

Across the ocean, the British Library houses the voluminous Haldimand Papers, which were crucial for learning about British Indian policy. The BL also provided access to papers on Sierra Leone, and those documents could be cross-referenced with the more extensive Colonial Office records on Nova Scotia and Sierra Leone in the National Archives at Kew. I would recommend that travelers visit Brick Lane on Sunday for the street market there, and Dumplings Legend for very good soup dumplings, but trips to Borough Market are also advisable.

Once in Philadelphia and New Haven I was primarily concerned with writing up my findings. I did, however, spend a month looking at the Anthony Wayne Papers at the Historical Society of Pennsylvania. These contain commentary on the Western Confederacy War, and I was able to cross-reference them with the Wayne Papers at the Clements Library in Ann Arbor. Between academic years in Philadelphia and New Haven, I spent a month at the Huntington Library in San Marino, where I learned a lot from Zachary Macaulay's papers about those key years in Sierra Leone. In Philadelphia, researchers should head to the Italian Market for a nosh, to Han Dynasty for fiery Szechuanese (I love the eggplant and the cold noodles with chili oil), and to Dim Sum Garden for my favorite soup dumplings in the world. Frita Batidos' chorizo frita is a reasonable reward for a day in the archives in Ann Arbor. In New Haven, scholars should listen to arguments in favor of various pizza offerings, and then go to Pepe's and get a pepperoni, anchovy, and garlic pie. The fried chicken, collard greens, and candied yams at Mama Mary's are also incredible.

Manuscripts were indispensable, but I also used printed source collections to write this book. These included Vincent Carretta's *Unchained Voices* (Lexington, 1996), *The Papers of Henry Laurens*, edited by David R. Chestnutt

(Columbia, 1968–2002), Thomas H. Foster's *Collected Works of Benjamin Hawkins* (Tuscaloosa, 2003), Christopher Fyfe's *"Our Children Free and Happy"* (Edinburgh, 1991), *The Journals of Samuel Kirkland*, edited by Walter Pilkington (Clinton, 1980), *The Papers of Sir William Johnson*, edited by James Sullivan (Albany, 1921–1965), and *American State Papers*, Class II, Indian Affairs, edited by Walter Lowrie and Matthew St. Clair Clarke (Washington, 1832).

American State Papers is now available online, as are numerous other sources. Since I started the research for this book, online databases have made possible extensive primary-source research with considerably less travel. For students based in the United Kingdom or without the departmental funding to undertake expensive research trips, I would recommend exploring databases like *The Internet Archive* (where one can find all of the Johnson papers digitized and word searchable), *Documenting the American South*, *Founders Online*, and the *Papers of the War Department*.

The best advice I can offer about this research is that commentary about hunger is everywhere in the archives. As long as historians and historians in the making are prepared to recognize unconventional attitudes about it, they will find it there.

Notes

I have referenced names and places as they were spelled in the manuscripts, unless otherwise noted [in brackets].

List of Abbreviations

AWP	Anthony Wayne Papers, 0699, Historical Society of Pennsylvania, Philadelphia, PA
BHQP	British Headquarters Papers, New York Public Library, New York, NY
BL	British Library, London, UK
CL	Clements Library, Ann Arbor, MI
CRSG	*Colonial Records of the State of Georgia*, ed. Allen D. Candler (Atlanta, GA: Franklin Printing and Publishing Company, 1904–1986), 31 vols.
DLAR	The David Library of the American Revolution, Washington Crossing, PA
GDAH	Georgia Department of Archives and History, Morrow, GA
GHS	Georgia Historical Society, Savannah, GA
HL	Huntington Library, San Marino, CA
HRBML	Hargrett Rare Books and Manuscripts Library, Athens, GA
HSP	Historical Society of Pennsylvania, Philadelphia, PA
JDR	John D. Rockefeller Library, Williamsburg, VA
LAC	Library and Archives Canada, Ottawa, ON
LOC	Library of Congress, Washington, DC
MHS	Massachusetts Historical Society, Boston, MA
NCSA	North Carolina State Archives, Raleigh, NC
NYPL	New York Public Library, New York, NY
PCL	Perry Castañeda Library, University of Texas at Austin, Austin, TX
PHL	*The Papers of Henry Laurens*, ed. David R. Chestnutt (Columbia, SC: University of South Carolina Press, 1968–2002), 16 vols.
PSP	Philip Schuyler Papers, MssCol2701, New York Public Library, New York, NY
PSWJ	*The Papers of Sir William Johnson*, ed. James Sullivan (Albany: University of the State of New York, 1921–1965), 14 vols.
SCDAH	South Carolina Department of Archives and History, Columbia, SC
SCHS	South Carolina Historical Society, Charleston, SC
SCL	South Caroliniana Library, Columbia, SC

SHC   Southern Historical Collection, Louis Round Wilson Special Collections
          Library, University of North Carolina, Chapel Hill, NC
TNA   The National Archives, Kew, UK
TPP   Timothy Pickering Papers, P-31, Massachusetts Historical Society, Boston, MA

Introduction. Why the Fight against Hunger Mattered

1. [Journal of Timothy Pickering], 5 July 1791, ff. 84a–85, reel 60, TPP.

2. George H. Clarfield, *Timothy Pickering and the American Republic* (Pittsburgh: University of Pittsburgh Press, 1980), chap. 9, esp. 117–19; Alyssa Mt. Pleasant, "Independence for Whom?: Expansion and Conflict in the Northeast and Northwest," in *The World of the Revolutionary American Republic: Land, Labor, and the Conflict for a Continent*, ed. Andrew Shankman (New York: Routledge, 2014), 120–21.

3. For early colonists, see Rachel B. Herrmann, "The 'tragicall historie': Cannibalism and Abundance in Colonial Jamestown," *William and Mary Quarterly* 68, no. 1 (January 2011): 47–74; Michael A. LaCombe, *Political Gastronomy: Food and Authority in the English Atlantic World* (Philadelphia: University of Pennsylvania Press, 2012), 90–107. For Native farming, see Jane Mt. Pleasant, "A New Paradigm for Pre-Columbian Agriculture in North America," *Early American Studies* 13, no. 2 (Spring 2015): 374–412.

4. Thomas Abler, *Cornplanter: Chief Warrior of the Allegany Seneca* (Syracuse, NY: Syracuse University Press, 2007), 1–2.

5. I have drawn on several versions of this creation story, relying most on the one recorded by John Norton (an adopted Mohawk member of the Iroquois) in the early nineteenth century because I assume it is the one Pickering might have known. Norton was the nephew of Mohawk Joseph Brant, and Pickering would come to work extensively with the Iroquois, though it must be acknowledged that Norton wrote most of his version after 1810. For Norton's telling, see *The Journal of Major John Norton, 1816*, ed. Carl F. Klinck and James J. Talman (Toronto: Champlain Society, 1970), 88–91; Jeffrey Glover, "Going to War on the Back of a Turtle: Creation Stories and the Laws of War in John Norton's *Journal*," *Early American Literature* 51, no. 3 (2016): 599–622, esp. 600. For others, see "The Iroquois Creation Story," in *The Norton Anthology of American Literature*, 5th ed., ed. Nina Baym (New York: W. W. Norton, 1999), 23–27; Demus Elm and Harvey Antone, *The Oneida Creation Story*, trans. and ed. Floyd G. Lounsbury and Brian Gick (Lincoln: University of Nebraska Press, 2000), 8–9 (for Norton, and comparisons to Huron takes on the myth), 11–27 (for a comparison of the different accounts), 17 (for variant spellings of the twins' names), 30–61 (for an Oneida-language interpretation of the myth); Anthony Wonderley, *Oneida Iroquois Folklore, Myth, and History: New York Oral Narrative from the Notes of H. E. Allen and Others* (Syracuse, NY: Syracuse University Press, 2004), xix (for myths as genre), 57 (for French versions), 62–68 (for a 1915 account by James Dean).

6. For hunger experienced by Spartans in the Ancient World, see Rachel Laudan, *Cuisine and Empire: Cooking in World History* (Berkeley: University of California Press, 2013), 65. For hunger endured by female saints, see Caroline Walker Bynum, *Holy Feast and Holy Fast: The Religious Significance of Food to Medieval Women* (Berkeley: University of California Press, 1987), 2, 5. For famine, see Cormac Ó Gráda, *Famine: A Short History* (Princeton, NJ: Princeton University Press, 2009), 6–7; David Meredith and Deb-

orah Oxley, "Food and Fodder: Feeding England, 1700–1900," *Past & Present* 222, no. 1 (February 2014): 163–214, esp. 213.

7. Frederick Haldimand to Lieutenant Colonel Mason Bolton, Quebec, 29 September 1780, ff. 146–47, Add. MS 21764, BL. For the Revolution as a disaster for Indians, see Barbara Graymont, *The Iroquois in the American Revolution* (Syracuse, NY: Syracuse University Press, 1972), viii; Colin G. Calloway, *The American Revolution in Indian Country: Crisis and Diversity in North American Communities* (Cambridge, UK: Cambridge University Press, 1995), 108; Timothy Shannon, *Iroquois Diplomacy on the Early American Frontier* (New York: Viking, 2008), 192–93. For interpretations of change as a positive force in Native communities, usually during eras before the American Revolution, see Kurt A. Jordan, *The Seneca Restoration, 1715–1754: An Iroquois Local Political Economy* (Gainesville: University Press of Florida, 2008), 18, 318; David L. Preston, *The Texture of Contact: European and Indian Settler Communities on the Frontiers of Iroquoia, 1667–1783* (Lincoln: University of Nebraska Press, 2009), 13; Jon Parmenter, *The Edge of the Woods: Iroquoia, 1534–1701* (East Lansing: Michigan State University Press, 2010), xxix, xxxii–xxxiii. For limits on the experience of black revolutionaries, see Trevor Burnard, "Empire Matters? The Historiography of Imperialism in Early America, 1492–1830," *History of European Ideas* 33 (2007): 87–107, esp. 105; Manisha Sinha, "'To 'Cast Just Obliquy' on Oppressors: Black Radicalism in the Age of Revolution," *William and Mary Quarterly* 64, no. 1 (January 2007): 149–60, esp. 150.

8. Amanda Moniz, *From Empire to Humanity: The American Revolution and the Origins of Humanitarianism* (New York: Oxford University Press, 2016), esp. 171.

9. Henry Knox to Anthony Wayne, War Department, 21 June 1794, f. 23, vol. XXVI, Anthony Wayne Papers, HSP. Recent scholarship on the American Revolution disagrees about whether it is characterized more by continuity or by change. For continuity, see Jessica Choppin Roney, "1776, Viewed from the West," *Journal of the Early Republic* 37, no. 4 (Winter 2017): 655–700, esp. 659; Serena R. Zabin, "Conclusion: Writing to and from the Revolution," *William and Mary Quarterly* 74, no. 4 (October 2017): 753–64, esp. 757. For arguments in favor of change and continuity, see Alan Taylor, "Introduction: Expand or Die: The Revolution's New Empire," *William and Mary Quarterly* 74, no. 4 (October 2017): 619–32, esp. 619, 621; Paul A. Gilje, "Commerce and Conquest in Early American Foreign Relations, 1750–1850," *Journal of the Early Republic* 37, no. 4 (Winter 2017): 735–70, esp. 736.

10. For a similar point about periodization, see Taylor, "Introduction: Expand or Die," 619; Michael A. McDonnell and David Waldstreicher, "Revolution in the *Quarterly*? A Historiographical Analysis," *William and Mary Quarterly* 74, no. 4 (October 2017): 633–66, esp. 657; Alyssa Mt. Pleasant, Caroline Wigginton, and Kelly Wisecup, "Materials and Methods in Native American and Indigenous Studies: Completing the Turn," *William and Mary Quarterly* 75, no. 2 (April 2018): 207–36, esp. 227. See also Shaun Tougher, "Periodization," in *A Practical Guide to Studying History: Skills and Approaches*, ed. Tracey Loughran (London: Bloomsbury, 2017), 31–45.

11. As late as 1993, the *Cambridge History of American Foreign Relations* paid little attention to Indians, beginning instead with a discussion of George Washington, John Adams, and Thomas Jefferson and the postrevolutionary foreign policy they envisioned while facing east across the Atlantic. That volume refers to thirteen treaties that the U.S. signed with European powers between 1789 and 1815, overlooking at least sixteen additional treaties between Native Americans and the U.S. government between

1784 and 1814. Although the new 2013 edition incorporates Native American history, it is still unusual to consider Native affairs foreign affairs after the 1795 Treaty of Greenville. The newest Cambridge history of U.S. foreign relations talks briefly about Indians' involvement in the War of 1812 and their meeting with Andrew Jackson in 1814, but largely passes over the period between 1795 and the 1820s. Bradford Perkins, *The Creation of a Republican Empire, 1776–1865*, vol. 1, *The Cambridge History of American Foreign Relations*, ed. Warren I. Cohen (Cambridge, UK: Cambridge University Press, 1993), 1–6, 77 (for the thirteen treaties); William Earl Weeks, *Dimensions of the Early American Empire, 1754–1865*, vol. 1, *The New Cambridge History of American Foreign Relations*, ed. Warren I. Cohen (Cambridge, UK: Cambridge University Press, 2013), chap. 3. For two important works that do treat Native American affairs as foreign affairs, see Brian DeLay, "Indian Polities, Empire, and the History of American Foreign Relations," *Diplomatic History* 39, no. 5 (November 2015): 927–42; Gilje, "Commerce and Conquest in Early American Foreign Relations."

12. For misinterpretations, see for example the assertion that the founders "neither wanted nor expected the new government to make many treaties," the claim that the British refused aid to Native Americans after the Battle of Foreign Timbers, or the characterization of the 1780s as a hungry period of chaos for weakened Native nations. Perkins, *The Creation of a Republican Empire*, 74 (quote), 77; Weeks, *Dimensions of the Early American Empire*, 57 (for Fallen Timbers); Alan Taylor, "'The Hungry Year': 1789 on the Northern Border of Revolutionary America," in *Dreadful Visitations: Confronting Natural Catastrophe in the Age of Enlightenment*, ed. Alessa Johns (New York: Routledge, 1999), 145–81 (for the 1780s).

13. For this imperial turn in colonial history, see Trevor Burnard, "Empire Matters?" 87–107; J. H. Elliott, *Empires of the Atlantic World: Britain and Spain in America 1492–1830* (New Haven, CT: Yale University Press, 2007). For the American Revolution, see Perkins, *The Creation of a Republican Empire*; Weeks, *Dimensions of the Early American Empire*; Taylor, "Introduction: Expand or Die"; McDonnell and Waldstreicher, "Revolution in the *Quarterly*?" 662; Zabin, "Conclusion: Writing to and from the Revolution," 757; Gilje, "Commerce and Conquest in Early American Foreign Relations," 749; Roney, "1776, Viewed from the West"; A. G. Hopkins, *American Empire: A Global History* (Princeton, NJ: Princeton University Press, 2018), esp. 192–93. For settler colonialism, see Jürgen Osterhammel, *Colonialism: A Theoretical Overview*, trans. Shelley L. Frisch (Princeton, NJ: Markus Wiener Publishers, 1997), esp. 6–7, 42; Patrick Wolfe, "Settler Colonialism and the Elimination of the Native," *Journal of Genocide Research* 8, no. 4 (December 2006): 387–409; Jack P. Greene, "Colonial History and National History: Reflections on a Continuing Problem," *William and Mary Quarterly* 64, no. 2 (April 2007): 235–50, esp. 237–39; Jon Parmenter, "After the Mourning Wars: The Iroquois as Allies in Colonial North American Campaigns, 1676–1760," *William and Mary Quarterly* 64, no. 1 (January 2007): 39–76, esp. 40. For the Sullivan campaign, see chapter 2 of this book.

14. Gordon S. Wood, *Empire of Liberty: A History of the Early Republic, 1789–1815* (New York: Oxford University Press, 2009), 357–99; Eliga H. Gould, *Among the Powers of the Earth: The American Revolution and the Making of a New World Empire* (Cambridge, MA: Harvard University Press, 2012), 1–13; Bethel Saler, *The Settlers' Empire: Colonialism and State Formation in America's Old Northwest* (Philadelphia: University of Pennsylvania Press, 2014). For the argument that this turn toward empire was revolutionary,

see McDonnell and Waldstreicher, "Revolution in the *Quarterly?*" 662. For the Northwest Ordinance, see Andrew Shankman, "Toward a Social History of Federalism: The State and Capitalism to and from the American Revolution," *Journal of the Early Republic* 37, no. 4 (Winter 2017): 615–53, esp. 630; Roney, "1776, Viewed from the West," 660.

15. On land losses, see Stuart Banner, *How the Indians Lost Their Land: Law and Power on the Frontier* (Cambridge, MA: The Belknap Press of Harvard University Press, 2005), esp. chap. 4.

16. On settler colonialism, land, and sedentary non-Natives, see Wolfe, "Settler Colonialism and the Elimination of the Native," 387, 393, 395. On the need to move beyond studies of land seizures, see Katherine A. Hermes, "Native Americans, the Colonial Encounter, and the Law of Harm, 1600–1787," in *Justice without the State within the State: Judicial Self-Regulation*, ed. Peter Colin (Frankfurt am Main: Verlag Vittorio Klostermann, 2016), 266. On scholars' failures to consistently define settler colonialism, see Frederick E. Hoxie, "Retrieving the Red Continent: Settler Colonialism and the History of American Indians in the US," *Ethnic and Racial Studies* 31, no. 6 (2008): 1153–67, esp. 1158. On settled Indians, see James H. Merrell, "Second Thoughts on Colonial Historians and American Indians," *William and Mary Quarterly* 69, no. 3 (July 2012): 451–512, esp. 473.

17. For typologies of settler colonialism, see Osterhammel, *Colonialism*, 10, 20–22. For foreign policy, see Daniel H. Usner, "'A Savage Feast They Made of It': John Adams and the Paradoxical Origins of Federal Indian Policy," *Journal of the Early Republic* 33, no. 4 (Winter 2013): 607–41, esp. 623–24; DeLay, "Indian Polities, Empire, and the History of American Foreign Relations."

18. On mercantilism, see Steve Pincus, "Rethinking Mercantilism: Political Economy, the British Empire, and the Atlantic World in the Seventeenth and Eighteenth Centuries," *William and Mary Quarterly* 69, no. 1 (January 2012): 3–34, esp. 17. On free trade, mercantilism, and the ambiguity of definitions during this time, see Gilje, "Commerce and Conquest in Early American Foreign Relations," *Journal of the Early Republic* 37, no. 4 (Winter 2017): 735–70, esp. 735–36 (for definitions), and 745–46 (for free trade); Staughton Lynd and David Waldstreicher, "Free Trade, Sovereignty, and Slavery: Toward an Economic Interpretation of American Independence," *William and Mary Quarterly* 68, no. 4 (October 2011): 597–630, esp. 603. For the postwar period, see Kathy D. Matson and Peter S. Onuf, *A Union of Interests: Political and Economic Thought in Revolutionary America* (Lawrence: University Press of Kansas, 1990), 4 (for tensions), 38 (for price- and wage-fixing); Alfred E. Eckes, Jr., *Opening America's Market: U.S. Foreign Trade Policy since 1776* (Chapel Hill: University of North Carolina Press, 1995), 2, 26 (for protectionism), 10 (for external tariffs and export duties). For an argument that considers Indian policy but not Indian trade after the early 1790s, see Gilje, "Commerce and Conquest in Early American Foreign Relations," esp. 737.

19. On slavery and the Empire of Liberty, see John Craig Hammond, "Slavery, Settlement, and Empire: The Expansion and Growth of Slavery in the Interior of the North American Continent, 1770–1820," *Journal of the Early Republic* 32, no. 2 (Summer 2012): 175–206; Wood, *Empire of Liberty*, xv, 2–3, 639.

20. For overviews of food in American history, see Richard J. Hooker, *Food and Drink in America: A History* (New York: Bobbs-Merill, 1981); Evan Jones, *American Food: The Gastronomic Story* (New York: E. P. Dutton, 1975); Waverly Lewis Root and Richard de

Rochemont, *Eating in America: A History* (New York: William Morrow, 1976). For representative single-commodity histories, see Mark Kurlansky, *Cod: A Biography of the Fish That Changed the World* (New York: Penguin, 1998); Kurlansky, *Salt: A World History* (New York: Penguin, 2003); and the extensive series on single-commodity foodstuffs published by Reaktion Books Ltd. For an assessment of these works, see Kyla Wazana Tompkins, *Racial Indigestion: Eating Bodies in the 19th Century* (New York: New York University Press, 2012), 2.

21. For power, see Sidney Mintz, *Sweetness and Power: The Place of Sugar in Modern History* (New York: Viking Press, 1985); Psyche A. Williams-Forson, *Building Houses out of Chicken Legs: Black Women, Food, and Power* (Chapel Hill: University of North Carolina Press, 2006). For the eighteenth century, see Peter Thompson, *Rum Punch and Revolution: Taverngoing and Public Life in Eighteenth-Century Philadelphia* (Philadelphia: University of Pennsylvania Press, 1999); James E. McWilliams, *A Revolution in Eating: How the Quest for Food Shaped America* (New York: Columbia University Press, 2005). For the colonial period, see Sally Smith Booth, *Hung, Strung, and Potted: A History of Eating in Colonial America* (New York: Clarkson N. Potter, 1971); Robert Appelbaum, "Hunger in Early Virginia: Indians and English Facing Off over Excess, Want, and Need," in *Envisioning an English Empire: Jamestown and the Making of the North Atlantic World*, ed. Robert Appelbaum and John Wood Sweet (Philadelphia: University of Pennsylvania Press, 2005), 195–216; Marcy Norton, *Sacred Gifts, Profane Pleasures: A History of Tobacco and Chocolate in the Atlantic World* (Ithaca, NY: Cornell University Press, 2008); Trudy Eden, *The Early American Table: Food and Society in the New World* (DeKalb: Northern Illinois University Press, 2008); Sarah Hand Meacham, *Every Home a Distillery: Alcohol, Gender, and Technology in the Colonial Chesapeake* (Baltimore: Johns Hopkins University Press, 2009); David Hancock, *Oceans of Wine: Madeira and the Emergence of American Trade and Taste* (New Haven, CT: Yale University Press, 2009); LaCombe, *Political Gastronomy*. Environmental historians who have written about the colonial period have also discussed foodstuffs before and after the arrival of Europeans in North America. See Alfred W. Crosby Jr., *The Columbian Exchange: Biological and Cultural Consequences of 1492* (Westport, CT: Greenwood Press, 1972); William Cronon, *Changes in the Land: Indians, Colonists, and the Ecology of New England* (New York: Hill and Wang, 1983); Timothy Silver, *A New Face on the Countryside: Indians, Colonists, and Slaves in South Atlantic Forests, 1500–1800* (New York: Cambridge University Press, 1990). For the nineteenth century, see Sam Bowers Hilliard, *Hog Meat and Hoecake: Food Supply in the Old South, 1840–1860* (Carbondale: Southern Illinois University Press, 1972); Joseph R. Conlin, *Bacon, Beans, and Galantines: Food and Foodways on the Western Mining Frontier* (Reno: University of Nevada Press, 1986); Stephen Nissenbaum, *Sex, Diet, and Debility in Jacksonian America: Sylvester Graham and Health Reform* (Westport, CT: Greenwood Press, 1980); Adam D. Shprintzen, *The Vegetarian Crusade: The Rise of an American Reform Movement, 1817–1921* (Chapel Hill: University of North Carolina Press, 2013). For the late nineteenth and early twentieth centuries, see Laura Shapiro, *Perfection Salad: Women and Cooking at the Turn of the Century* (New York: Farrar, Straus, and Giroux, 1986); Harvey A. Levenstein, *Revolution at the Table: The Transformation of the American Diet* (New York: Oxford University Press, 1988); Donna R. Gabaccia, *We Are What We Eat: Ethnic Food and the Making of Americans* (Cambridge, MA: Harvard University Press, 1998); Hasia Diner, *Hungering for America: Italian, Irish, and Jewish Foodways in the Age of Migration* (Cambridge, MA: Harvard University Press, 2001). For the First and Sec-

ond World Wars, see Richard Pillsbury, *No Foreign Food: The American Diet in Time and Place* (Boulder, CO: Westview Press, 1998); Lizzie Collingham, *The Taste of War: World War II and the Battle for Food* (New York: Penguin Books, 2012). For the Cold War, see Kristin L. Ahlberg, "'Machiavelli with a Heart': The Johnson Administration's Food for Peace Program in India, 1965–1966," *Diplomatic History* 31, no. 4 (September 2007): 665–701; Ahlberg, *Transplanting the Great Society: Lyndon Johnson and Food for Peace* (Columbia: University of Missouri Press, 2008); Nick Cullather, *The Hungry World: America's Cold War Battle against Poverty in Asia* (New York: Harvard University Press, 2010); Alexander Poster, "The Gentle War: Famine Relief, Politics, and Privatization in Ethiopia, 1983–1986," *Diplomatic History* 36, no. 2 (April 2012): 399–425. For exceptions—histories of food that do focus on hunger—see the scholarship on food riots discussed in chapters 6 and 8.

22. Ó Gráda, *Famine*; Ó Gráda, *Eating People Is Wrong, and Other Essays on Famine, Its Past, and Its Future* (Princeton, NJ: Princeton University Press, 2015) (for a general study); Carla Cevasco, "Hunger Knowledges and Cultures in New England's Borderlands, 1675–1770," *Early American Studies* 16, no. 2 (Spring 2018): 255–81 (for the colonial period); James Vernon, *Hunger: A Modern History* (Cambridge, MA: Harvard University Press, 2007), 273–74 (for the nineteenth century); Nick Cullather, "The Foreign Policy of the Calorie," *American Historical Review* 112, no. 2 (April 2007): 337–64; Cullather, *The Hungry World* (for the twentieth). See also B. J. B. Krupadanam, *Food Diplomacy: A Case Study, Indo-US Relations* (New Delhi: Lancers Books, 1985), 16.

23. Mary Black-Rogers, "Varieties of 'Starving': Semantics and Survival in the Subarctic Fur Trade, 1750–1850," *Ethnohistory* 33, no. 4 (Autumn 1986): 353–83.

24. For definitions, see Paul Rockower, "The State of Gastrodiplomacy," *Public Diplomacy Magazine* 11 (2014): 13–17, esp. 14. For later periods, see Ahlberg, "'Machiavelli with a Heart'"; Ahlberg, *Transplanting the Great Society*; Poster, "The Gentle War." For *gastronomy*, see *Oxford English Dictionary Online*, search under "gastronomy, n.," and "culinary, adj.," accessed August 22, 2015, http://oed.com.

25. White officials often looked at white soldiers' rations as a baseline for thinking about other forms of food diplomacy—though it must be admitted that when commissaries planned to obtain rations to fill empty bellies, they often failed to get them. A British ration, which suppliers figured by the week, consisted in theory of seven pounds of bread (or seven pounds of flour), seven pounds of beef (or four pounds of pork), six ounces of butter (or eight ounces of cheese), three pints of peas, and half a pound of rice (or oatmeal). Sometimes the British army dispensed peas in lieu of oatmeal, rather than peas in addition to oatmeal. Britons included spruce beer as a safeguard against scurvy. The American ration was similar but also varied in a few ways. Some states calculated their ration by the day, rather than by the week. A white private named Joseph Plumb Martin, who fought for the American rebels, stated that he and other enlistees "were promised . . . one pound of good and wholesome fresh or salt beef, or three fourths of a pound of good salt pork, a pound of good flour, soft or hard bread, a quart of salt to every hundred pounds of fresh beef, a quart of vinegar to a hundred rations, [and] a gill of rum, brandy, or whiskey per day." Martin's ration slightly exceeded the British one for pork and made mention of other commodities such as salt and rum—the last two of which were definitely included in British planning but which commissaries dealt with separately from food rations. In addition, men were supposed to receive milk rather than cheese, as well as spruce beer

or cider. Americans enjoyed more flexibility depending on the region in which they fought; Georgians were allowed a substitution of a pound of salt fish for beef or pork, and beans or vegetables for peas. This information is compiled from a few separate contracts. For the ration, see Treasury Contract with Arnold Nesbitt, Adam Drummond, and Moses Franks, 2 April 1776, vol. 4, no. 24, photostat 153, box 1, BHQP; John Robinson to Arnold Nesbitt, Adam Drummond, Moses Franks, John Henniker, William Devaynes, and George Wombell, Whitehall, 17 April 1778, vol. 2, no. 122, photostat 1103, box 5, BHQP; John Robinson to Messrs. Nesbitt, Drummond, and Franks, Treasury Chambers, 7 November 1778, vol. 33, no. 56, photostat 1534, box 7, BHQP. For spruce beer, see John Robinson to General Howe, Whitehall, Treasury Chambers, 10 August 1776, vol. 4, no. 46, photostat 238, box 2, BHQP; John Robinson to Gen. Sir William Howe, Whitehall, Treasury Chambers, 22 October 1776, vol. 4, no. 52, photostat 292, box 2, BHQP. For Martin's ration, see Joseph Plumb Martin, *Ordinary Courage: The Revolutionary Adventures of Joseph Plumb Martin*, 2nd ed., ed. James Kirby Martin (St. James, NY: Brandywine Press, 1999), 164. For Georgia, see Georgia Council of Safety minutes, 26 June 1776, folder "Volume 3: Minutes, Aug. 1776–Feb. 1777," MS 0282, GHS.

26. William N. Fenton, *The Great Law and the Longhouse: A Political History of the Iroquois Confederacy* (Norman: University of Oklahoma Press, 1998), 7 (for forest diplomacy). For alcohol, see Peter C. Mancall, *Deadly Medicine: Indians and Alcohol in Early America* (Ithaca, NY: Cornell University Press, 1995); Maia Conrad, "Disorderly Drinking: Reconsidering Seventeenth-Century Iroquois Alcohol Abuse," *American Indian Quarterly* 23, no. 3/4 (Summer–Autumn 1999): 1–11; Jordan, *The Seneca Restoration*, 310, 315–16, 345.

27. John Grenier, *The First Way of War: American War Making on the Frontier, 1607–1814* (New York: Cambridge University Press, 2005), 24 ("feedfight"); Graymont, *The Iroquois in the American Revolution*, 213 ("warfare against vegetables").

28. For formal and informal imperialism, see John Gallagher and Ronald Robinson, "The Imperialism of Free Trade," *The Economic History Review* 6, no. 1 (1953): 1–15.

29. For a discussion of Englishness versus Britishness during the early modern period, see Jessica S. Hower, "'. . . And greedily deuoured them': The Cannibalism Discourse and the Creation of a British Atlantic World, 1536–1612," in *To Feast on Us as Their Prey: Cannibalism and the Early Modern Atlantic*, ed. Rachel B. Herrmann (Fayetteville: University of Arkansas Press, 2019), 245n5. For gifts, see C. M. Woolgar, "Gifts of Food in Late Medieval England," *Journal of Medieval History* 37, no. 1 (2011): 6–18; Felicity Heal, *The Power of Gifts: Gift Exchange in Early Modern England* (Oxford, UK: Oxford University Press, 2014).

30. For Ireland, see Wayne E. Lee, *Barbarians and Brothers: Anglo-American Warfare, 1500–1865* (New York: Oxford University Press, 2011), 34, 95, 191; Grenier, *The First Way of War*, 102–3. For animals, see Virginia DeJohn Anderson, *Creatures of Empire: How Domestic Animals Transformed Early America* (Oxford, UK: Oxford University Press, 2004), 177–8, 190.

31. On the enclosure movement, which restructured land use in England, see E. P. Thompson, *The Making of the English Working Class* (London: Penguin Books, 2013 [1963]), 217. In Scotland, see work on the Highland clearances, such as Robert Dodgshon, "The Clearances and the Transformation of the Scottish Countryside," in *The Oxford Handbook of Modern Scottish History*, ed. T. M. Devine and Jenny Wormald (New

York: Oxford University Press, 2012), 130–58, esp. 131. The enclosure movement altered food production in terms of grazing, gleaning, and livestock-rearing practices. For grazing and livestock, see Leigh Shaw-Taylor, "Labourers, Cows, Common Rights and Parliamentary Enclosure: The Evidence of Contemporary Comment c. 1760–1810," *Past and Present* 171, no. 1 (May 2001): 95–126, esp. 95–96. For gleaning, see Peter King, "Gleaners, Farmers and the Failure of Legal Sanctions in England 1750–1850," *Past and Present* 125, no. 1 (November 1989): 116–50, esp. 118. For livestock, see also Emma Hart, "From Field to Plate: The Colonial Livestock Trade and the Development of an American Economic Culture," *William and Mary Quarterly* 73, no. 1 (January 2016): 107–40, esp. 124. The clearances changed grazing and cattle- and sheep-rearing. See Dodgshon, "The Clearances and the Transformation of the Scottish Countryside," 144 (for grazing), 146 (for sheep). For barbarians, see Nicholas P. Canny, "The Ideology of English Colonization: From Ireland to America," *William and Mary Quarterly* 30, no. 4 (October 1973): 575–98, esp. 596. For pigs, see Anderson, *Creatures of Empire*, 236.

32. On this relationship, see Francis Jennings, *The Ambiguous Iroquois Empire: The Covenant Chain Confederation of Indian Tribes with English Colonies from its beginnings to the Lancaster Treaty of 1744* (New York: W. W. Norton, 1984), 314.

33. This shift to treating Indian affairs as domestic instead of foreign occurred as a result of the Marshall Trilogy of Supreme Court decisions in the 1820s and 1830s. In *Johnson v. M'Intosh* (1823), *Cherokee Nation v. Georgia* (1831), and *Worcester v. Georgia* (1832), the Supreme Court first claimed that Native Americans were "heathens" whose improper use of land legitimized the transfer of land title from Natives to non-Natives, then made Cherokees into a "domestic dependent nation," and then definitively transferred control of Indian relations to the federal government. In Patrick Wolfe's interpretation, this turn from the foreign and external to the domestic and internal began with the trilogy, but concluded much later, with the closing of the frontier in the late nineteenth century. Patrick Wolfe, "After the Frontier: Separation and Absorption in US Indian Policy," *Settler Colonial Studies* 1, no. 1 (2011): 13–51, esp. 13, 15–16. On the Supreme Court, see Gilje, "Commerce and Conquest in Early American Foreign Relations," 765.

34. Daniel K. Richter, *Trade, Land, Power: The Struggle for Eastern North America* (Philadelphia: University of Pennsylvania Press, 2013), 42–43 (for Indians' thoughts); Jill Lepore, *The Name of War: King Philip's War and the Origins of American Identities* (New York: Alfred A. Knopf, 1998), 46 (for historians' methods); Philip D. Morgan, *Slave Counterpoint: Black Culture in the Eighteenth-Century Chesapeake and Lowcountry* (Chapel Hill: University of North Carolina Press, 1998), xxi (for a similar point about interpreting behavior).

35. For primary source collections, see *Documents of the American Revolution: 1770–1783*, ed. K. G. Davies (Shannon: Irish University Press, 1972–1981), 21 vols.; *The Papers of Henry Laurens*, ed. David R. Chestnutt (Columbia: University of South Carolina Press, 1968–2002), 16 vols.; *The Papers of Sir William Johnson*, ed. James Sullivan (Albany: University of the State of New York, 1921–1965), 14 vols. For the British Navy, see Roger Knight and Martin Wilcox, *Sustaining the Fleet, 1793–1815: War, the British Navy and the Contractor State* (Woodbridge, UK: Boydell Press, 2010); Janet MacDonald, *Feeding Nelson's Navy: The True Story of Food at Sea in the Georgian Era* (London: Frontline Books, 2014); Christopher L. Pastore, *Between Land and Sea: The Atlantic Coast*

and the Transformation of New England (Cambridge, MA: Harvard University Press, 2014), esp. 183, 190.

36. On the importance of words in early Americanist scholarship, see Merrell, "Second Thoughts," esp. 473–77. I acknowledge Joel Martin's argument that the term "Creek" was an externally imposed name. However, I agree with Angela Pulley Hudson's point that by the 1790s the Creeks were "increasingly *defining themselves* as a nation and defending their sovereign rights as such" (emphasis original). Joel W. Martin, *Sacred Revolt: The Muskogees' Struggle for a New World* (Boston: Beacon Press, 1991), 6–8; Angela Pulley Hudson, *Creek Paths and Federal Roads: Indians, Settlers, and Slaves and the Making of the American South* (Chapel Hill: University of North Carolina Press, 2010), 8, 91. For loyalty, see Edward G. Gray, "Liberty's Losers," *William and Mary Quarterly* 70, no. 1 (January 2013): 184–89, esp. 186.

37. Barry Cahill, "The Black Loyalist Myth in Atlantic Canada," *Acadiensis* XXIX, no. 1 (Autumn 1999): esp. para. 3, 8, accessed December 31, 2015, http://journals.hil .unb.ca/index.php/acadiensis/article/view/10801/11587.

1. Hunger, Accommodation, and Violence in Colonial America

1. Alex White to George Croghan, Winchester, 30 August 1773, folder 38, box 203, Cadwalader Family Papers, Collection 1454, HSP (quote); Patrick Griffin, *American Leviathan: Empire, Nation, and Revolutionary Frontier* (New York: Hill and Wang, 2007), 19–20 (for this exchange); Nick Popper, "Nick Popper, BRE," *Uncommon Sense: The Blog*, 26 July 2017, accessed July 31, 2017, http://blog.oieahc.wm.edu/nick-popper-bre/ (for more on Robertson); Michael N. McConnell, *A Country Between: The Upper Ohio Valley and Its Peoples, 1724–1774* (Lincoln: University of Nebraska Press, 1992), 40, 126 (for Croghan). See also Michael J. Mullin, "Croghan, George," *American National Biography Online*, accessed June 1, 2014, http://www.anb.org/articles/02/02-00362.html.

2. For helpless hunger, see Michael A. LaCombe, *Political Gastronomy: Food and Authority in the English Atlantic World* (Philadelphia: University of Pennsylvania Press, 2012), 169. See also Mary Black-Rogers, "Varieties of 'Starving': Semantics and Survival in the Subarctic Fur Trade, 1750–1850," *Ethnohistory* 33, no. 4 (Autumn 1986): 353–83.

3. For forest diplomacy, see William N. Fenton, *The Great Law and the Longhouse: A Political History of the Iroquois Confederacy* (Norman: University of Oklahoma Press, 1998), 7. Although recent work underscores the importance of intention in the Illinois Country, this book is less focused on the Illinois region and so hews to the idea of misunderstandings. On creative misunderstandings, see Richard White, *The Middle Ground: Indians, Empires, and Republics in the Great Lakes Region, 1650–1815* (New York: Cambridge University Press, 2011), xii–xiii, xxvi. On intentional cooperation, see Robert Michael Morrissey, *Empire by Collaboration: Indians, Colonists, and Governments in Colonial Illinois County* (Philadelphia: University of Pennsylvania Press, 2015), 9. On creative misunderstandings and food, see LaCombe, *Political Gastronomy*, 70.

4. Emer de Vattel, *The Law of Nations, or, Principles of the Law of Nature, Applied to the Conduct and Affairs of Nations and Sovereigns, with Three Early Essays on the Origin and Nature of Natural Law and on Luxury*, ed. Béla Kapossy and Richard Whatmore (Indianapolis: Liberty Fund, Inc., 2008), viii, 551 (quote). For background on Vattel, see Wayne E. Lee, *Barbarians and Brothers: Anglo-American Warfare, 1500–1865* (New York: Oxford University Press, 2011), 188–91.

5. Fenton, *The Great Law and the Longhouse*, 4 (for Deganawidah and the Iroquois League), 86n3 (for the principles of the League), 95 (for the concepts of the League); José Antonio Brandão, "'Your fyre shall burn no more': Iroquois Policy towards New France and Her Native Allies to 1701" (PhD diss., York University, 1994), 130–31n116 (for Deganawidah).

6. For this neutrality policy, see Jon Parmenter, "After the Mourning Wars: The Iroquois as Allies in Colonial North American Campaigns, 1676–1760," *William and Mary Quarterly* 64, no. 1 (January 2007): 39–76, esp. 40, 46, 51. For Gayaneshagowa and Guswenta, see Alyssa Mt. Pleasant, "Independence for Whom?: Expansion and Conflict in the Northeast and Northwest," in *The World of the Revolutionary American Republic: Land, Labor, and the Conflict for a Continent*, ed. Andrew Shankman (New York: Routledge, 2014), 120; Alyssa Mt. Pleasant, "Guiding Principles: *Guswenta* and the Debate over Formal Schooling at Buffalo Creek, 1800–1811" in *Indian Subjects: Hemispheric Perspectives on the History of Indigenous Education*, ed. Brenda J. Child and Brian Klopotek (Santa Fe, NM: SAR Press, 2014), 115.

7. For mourning wars and ceremonies, see Daniel K. Richter, "War and Culture: The Iroquois Experience," *William and Mary Quarterly* 40, no. 4 (October 1983): 528–59, esp. 531–32; Daniel K. Richter, *The Ordeal of the Longhouse: The Peoples of the Iroquois League in the Era of European Colonization* (Chapel Hill: University of North Carolina Press, 1992), 39–41; Matthew Dennis, *Cultivating a Landscape of Peace: Iroquois-European Encounters in Seventeenth-Century America* (Ithaca, NY: Cornell University Press, 1993), 79; Parmenter, "After the Mourning Wars," 46; Nancy L. Hagedorn, "'With the Air and Gesture of an Orator': Council Oratory, Translation and Cultural Mediation during Anglo-Iroquois Treaty Conference, 1690–1774," in *New Trends in Translation and Cultural Identity*, ed. Micaela Muñoz-Calvo, Carmen Bueso-Gómez, and M. Ángeles Ruiz-Moneva (Newcastle upon Tyne, UK: Cambridge Scholars Publishing, 2008), 35–36. On meetings, see Hagedorn, "'With the Air and Gesture of an Orator,'" 35; Timothy J. Shannon, *Iroquois Diplomacy on the Early American Frontier* (New York: Viking, 2008), 78–102. For calumets, eagle tails, and metaphors, see Christopher M. Parsons, "Natives, Newcomers, and *Nicotania*: Tobacco in the History of the Great Lakes Region," in *French and Indians in the Heart of North America*, ed. Robert Englebert and Guillaume Teasdale (East Lansing: Michigan State University Press, 2013), 21–41; Nancy Shoemaker, *A Strange Likeness: Becoming Red and White in Eighteenth-Century North America* (New York: Oxford University Press, 2004), 66; Jane T. Merritt, *At the Crossroads: Indians and Empires on a Mid-Atlantic Frontier, 1700–1763* (Chapel Hill: University of North Carolina Press, 2003), 214; Merritt, "Metaphor, Meaning, and Misunderstanding: Language and Power on the Pennsylvania Frontier," in *Contact Points: American Frontiers from the Mohawk Valley to the Mississippi, 1750–1830*, ed. Andrew R. L. Cayton and Fredrika J. Teute (Chapel Hill: University of North Carolina Press, 1998), 60–87.

8. Conference with Cayugas, Johnson Hall, 18 February 1770, *PSWJ*, vol. 12, 778 (quote). For Onontio, see White, *The Middle Ground*, xxvii, 36. For Dutch, English, and French motivations, see Dennis, *Cultivating a Landscape of Peace*, 9, 124–25 (for brothers), 268–69; Shannon, *Iroquois Diplomacy*, 43. For the Covenant Chain, see Richter, *The Ordeal of the Longhouse*, esp. 136–38. For Iroquois-Dutch relationships, see Francis Jennings, *The Ambiguous Iroquois Empire: The Covenant Chain Confederation of Indian Tribes with English Colonies from Its Beginnings to the Lancaster Treaty of 1744* (New York: W. W. Norton, 1984), 55.

9. For paths, see Angela Pulley Hudson, *Creek Paths and Federal Roads: Indians, Settlers, and Slaves and the Making of the American South* (Chapel Hill: University of North Carolina Press, 2010), 12; Shoemaker, *A Strange Likeness*, 9. For nakedness, see Tom Hatley, *The Dividing Paths: Cherokees and South Carolinians through the Era of Revolution* (New York: Oxford University Press, 1993), 10. For hatchets, see [Indian council at Pittsburgh], 4 November 1776, f. 25, folder 9, box 204, Cadwalader Family Papers, HSP; Shoemaker, *A Strange Likeness*, 9. For Mahicans, see "Captain Hendrick's narrative of his journey in July, August, September, and October 1791," f. 11, reel 59, TPP. For Onondagas, see "At a Meeting of the Commissioners for Indian Affairs in the Northern Department," Albany, 15 August 1778, folder 57, box 23, PSP. For Atkin, see [Minutes of the Negotiations between Edmond Atkin, Superintendent of Indian Affairs, Southern Department, and Haigler, King of the Catawba], James Town Ferry, Virginia, 18 and 19 May 1757, HM 3992, HL.

10. On wampum, see Michael K. Foster, "Another Look at the Function of Wampum in Iroquois-White Councils," in *The History and Culture of Iroquois Diplomacy: An Interdisciplinary Guide to the Treaties of the Six Nations and Their League*, ed. Francis Jennings, William N. Fenton, Mary A. Druke, and David R. Miller (Syracuse, NY: Syracuse University Press, 1985), 99–114; Nancy L. Hagedorn, "'A Friend to go between Them': The Interpreter as Cultural Broker During Anglo-Iroquois Councils, 1740–70," *Ethnohistory* 35, no. 1 (Winter, 1988): 60–80, esp. 66–67; Merritt, *At the Crossroads*, 210; Ian K. Steele, *Warpaths: Invasions of North America* (New York: Oxford University Press, 1994), 89; Andrew Lipman, *The Saltwater Frontier: Indians and the Contest for the American Coast* (New Haven and London: Yale University Press, 2015), 30, 105–9; Christopher L. Pastore, *Between Land and Sea: The Atlantic Coast and the Transformation of New England* (Cambridge, MA: Harvard University Press, 2014), 7, 15, 30, 33; Shoemaker, *A Strange Likeness*, 65, 74. On speechmaking, see Carolyn Eastman, *A Nation of Speechifiers: Making an American Public after the Revolution* (Chicago: University of Chicago Press, 2009). For Johnson and the belts, see Sir William Johnson to [General] Thomas Gage, Johnson Hall, 13 November 1768, *PSWJ*, vol. 12, 636.

11. Shoemaker, *A Strange Likeness*, 43 (for medals); Hatley, *The Dividing Paths*, xiii, 194 (for Keowee); "Memorandom of necessaries Wanting to Transport Indian Goods to Pittsburgh and Build a Store House there," Fort Loudon, 27 January 1759, f. 32, Add. MS 21655, BL ("a piece" and "Horse Shoes"); [Captain Abraham] Bosomworth, "Calculations of the Expence of Indian Warriors for their Service during the Campaign," Camp at Rays Town, 23 July 1758, f. 15, Add. MS 21655, BL (for the report). On giving trade goods to procure military service, see John Clarke, *Land, Power, and Economics on the Frontier of Upper Canada* (Montreal: McGill-Queen's University Press, 2001), 95.

12. Seth Mallios, *The Deadly Politics of Giving: Exchange and Violence at Ajacan, Roanoke, and Jamestown* (Tuscaloosa: University of Alabama Press, 2006), 25–27, 29, 30 ("something-for-nothing"), 32 ("something-for-something"). See also Marcel Mauss, *The Gift: The Form and Reason for Exchange in Archaic Societies*, trans. W. D. Halls (London: Routledge, 1990), ix; Natalie Zemon Davis, *The Gift in Sixteenth-Century France* (Oxford, UK: Oxford University Press, 2000); Joseph M. Hall Jr., *Zamumo's Gifts: Indian-European Exchange in the Colonial Southeast* (Philadelphia: University of Pennsylvania Press, 2009), 7; Joel W. Martin, *Sacred Revolt: The Muskogees' Struggle for a New World* (Boston: Beacon Press, 1991), 28.

13. Alan Taylor, *American Colonies: The Settling of North America* (New York: Penguin, 2001), 96 (for sealing alliances). For fur traders, see Arthur J. Ray, *Indians in the Fur Trade: Their Role as Trappers, Hunters, and Middlemen in the Lands Southwest of the Hudson Bay, 1660–1870* (Toronto: University of Toronto Press, 1975); Calvin Martin, *Keepers of the Game: Indian-Animal Relationships and the Fur Trade* (Berkeley: University of California Press, 1978); Neal Salisbury, *Manitou and Providence: Indians, Europeans, and the Making of New England, 1500–1643* (New York: Oxford University Press, 1982); Richard White, *The Roots of Dependency: Subsistence, Environment, and Social Change among the Choctaws, Pawnees, and Navajos* (Lincoln: University of Nebraska Press, 1983); White, *The Middle Ground*, 96, 104. For payment, see Mary A. Druke, "Iroquois Treaties: Common Forms, Varying Interpretations," *The History and Culture of Iroquois Diplomacy*, 93–94.

14. Gail D. MacLeitch, *Imperial Entanglements: Iroquois Change and Persistence on the Frontiers of Empire* (Philadelphia: University of Pennsylvania Press, 2011), 34 (on demands for specific goods), 89 (for playing imperial powers off of each other), 103 ("pitied"); "Heads of the Speech to be given to the Head Warriors of the Cherokees and Catawba," n.d., f. 278, Add. MS 21655, BL ("large presents" and "Campaign").

15. For Powhatan and kinship relationships, see *Captain John Smith: A Select Edition of His Writings*, ed. Karen Ordahl Kupperman (Chapel Hill: University of North Carolina Press, 1988), 172–3; Daniel K. Richter, *Trade, Land, Power: The Struggle for Eastern North America* (Philadelphia: University of Pennsylvania Press, 2013), 3, 6, 35. For gift redistribution, see Neal Salisbury, "The Indians' Old World: Native Americans and the Coming of Europeans," *William and Mary Quarterly* 53, no. 3 (July 1996): 435–58, esp. 437; Eric Hinderaker, *Elusive Empires: Constructing Colonialism in the Ohio Valley, 1673–1800* (Cambridge, UK: Cambridge University Press, 1997), 77; James H. Merrell, *Into the American Woods: Negotiators on the Pennsylvania Frontier* (New York: W. W. Norton, 1999), 98; Cameron B. Wesson, *Households and Hegemony: Early Creek Prestige Goods, Symbolic Capital, and Social Power* (Lincoln: University of Nebraska Press, 2008), 72, 93, 135. For the Dutch and the French, see Dennis, *Cultivating a Landscape of Peace*, 125, 168, 178, 193; White, *The Middle Ground*, xxvii; Richter, *Trade, Land, Power*, 6. For Johnson's correspondent, see Myndert Wempel to William Johnson, 22 November 1755, *PSWJ*, vol. 2, 326.

16. Helen Caister Robinson, "Molly Brant: Mohawk Heroine," in *Eleven Exiles: Accounts of Loyalists of the American Revolution*, ed. Phyllis R. Blakeley and John N. Grant (Toronto: Dundurn Press Limited, 1982), 118 (for Johnson's Iroquois name); Gail MacLeitch, "Sir William Johnson (1715–1774)," in *The Human Tradition in the Atlantic World, 1500–1850*, ed. Karen Racine and Beatriz G. Mamigonian (Lanham, MD: Rowman and Littlefield, 2010), 88 (for his dress and eating habits), 92 (for his spending); MacLeitch, *Imperial Entanglements*, 55 (for kinship). See also Daniel K. Richter, "Johnson, Sir William, first baronet (1715?–1774)," *Oxford Dictionary of National Biography*, accessed July 9, 2017, http://www.oxforddnb.com/view/article/14925.

17. Captain Bosomworth to Colonel Bouquet, n.p. [probably Ray's Town], 18 June 1758, f. 12, Add. MS 21655, BL.

18. On the sixteenth and seventeenth centuries, see Mallios, *The Deadly Politics of Giving*; LaCombe, *Political Gastronomy*; Normand Mac Leod to Sir William Johnson, Ontario, 13 October 1766, *PSWJ*, vol. 12, 208 (quote); "Memorandum of Indian Presents,"

29 March 1759, *PSWJ*, vol. 3, 23; Elisabeth Tooker, "The Iroquois White Dog Sacrifice in the Latter Part of the Eighteenth Century," *Ethnohistory* 12, no. 2 (1965): 129–40 (for dogs); Thomas S. Abler, "Iroquois Cannibalism: Fact Not Fiction," *Ethnohistory* 27, no. 4 (1980): 309–16 (for cannibalism); Barbara Graymont, *The Iroquois in the American Revolution* (Syracuse, NY: Syracuse University Press, 1972), 10 (for nuts and berries). For alcohol, see Peter C. Mancall, *Deadly Medicine: Indians and Alcohol in Early America* (Ithaca, NY: Cornell University Press, 1995); Maia Conrad, "Disorderly Drinking: Reconsidering Seventeenth-Century Iroquois Alcohol Abuse," *American Indian Quarterly* 23, no. 3 / 4 (1999): 1–11, esp. 6; Kurt A. Jordan, *The Seneca Restoration, 1715–1754: An Iroquois Local Political Economy* (Gainesville: University Press of Florida, 2008), 310, 315–16, 345; David L. Preston, *The Texture of Contact: European and Indian Settler Communities on the Frontiers of Iroquoia, 1667–1783* (Lincoln: University of Nebraska Press, 2009), 105, 130, 159.

19. Joseph T. Glatthaar and James Kirby Martin, *Forgotten Allies: The Oneida Indians and the American Revolution* (New York: Hill and Wang, 2006), 150 (for Oneidas); Alan Taylor, *The Divided Ground: Indians, Settlers, and the Northern Borderland of the American Revolution* (New York: Vintage Books, 2006), 52 (for Mohawks); Joshua Aaron Piker, *Okfuskee: A Creek Indian Town in Colonial America* (Cambridge, MA: Harvard University Press, 2004), 123–24 (for Creeks). For cattle and Christian Indians, see MacLeitch, *Imperial Entanglements*, 197–98; Jordan, *The Seneca Restoration*, 278–79, 292. For plow absences and soil, see Jane Mt. Pleasant, "A New Paradigm for Pre-Columbian Agriculture in North America," *Early American Studies* 13, no. 2 (Spring 2015): 374–412, esp. 378–79, 382, 392, 411. For animals, see Virginia DeJohn Anderson, *Creatures of Empire: How Domestic Animals Transformed Early America* (New York: Oxford University Press, 2004), 6, 39, 185; Claudio Saunt, *A New Order of Things: Property, Power, and the Transformation of the Creek Indians, 1733–1816* (Cambridge, UK: Cambridge University Press, 1999), 67–135; MacLeitch, *Imperial Entanglements*, 198.

20. H. Watson Powell to Captain Mathews, Niagara, 29 May 1782, f. 49, Add. MS 21762, BL ("that no" and "avoid feeding"); Thomas Gage to William Johnson, New York, 10 February 1766, *PSWJ*, vol. 12, 15 ("the Quantity"); *Journal of Indian Affairs*, Johnson Hall, 6–26 September 1767, *PSWJ*, vol. 12, 362 ("Provisions to carry"). For a broad overview of how food functioned diplomatically, see Shannon, *Iroquois Diplomacy*, 78–102; MacLeitch, *Imperial Entanglements*, 67.

21. Shoemaker, *A Strange Likeness*, 85–89. See also Lisa Brooks, *The Common Pot: The Recovery of Native Space in the Northeast* (Minneapolis: University of Minnesota Press, 2008), xl, xli, 3–4; Gilles Havard, *The Great Peace of Montreal of 1701: French-Native Diplomacy in the Seventeenth Century*, trans. Phyllis Aronoff and Howard Scott (Montreal: McGill-Queen's University Press, 2001), 147, 149.

22. Deposition of Jean Nerban, 27 June 1757, *PSWJ*, vol. 2, 717–18.

23. Mt. Pleasant, "A New Paradigm," 381–82 (for crop yields); Anya Zilberstein, "Inured to Empire: Wild Rice and Climate Change," *William and Mary Quarterly* 72, no. 1 (January 2015): 127–58 (for rice); LaCombe, *Political Gastronomy*, 90–107 (for Indians in Virginia); Joshua Piker, "Colonists and Creeks: Rethinking the Pre-Revolutionary Southern Backcountry," *Journal of Southern History* 70, no. 3 (August 2004): 503–40, esp. 516 (for Creeks).

24. For Thanksgiving, see LaCombe, *Political Gastronomy*, 88–89. For corn destroyed in Denonville's attack, see Dennis, *Cultivating a Landscape of Peace*, 27. For Indian dis-

persal, see Fenton, *The Great Law and the Longhouse*, 259. For the 1741–42 famine, see Jordan, *The Seneca Restoration*, 82.

25. "Proceedings at a Meeting & Treaty held with the Six Nations at Johnson Hall," April 25, 1762, *PSWJ*, vol. 3, 707–8 ("Women"); Major H[enry] Basset to Frederick Haldimand, Detroit, 10 January 1774, f. 15, Add. MS 21731, BL ("the Custom," "a few," "an exceeding," and "bring in"); "Speech of a Six Nation Indian," Fort Pitt, 6 June 1761, f. 113, Add. MS 21655, BL (for Otchinneyawessahawe).

26. MacLeitch, *Imperial Entanglements*, 90 (Indian descriptions of hunger); Taylor, *The Divided Ground*, 24 (twice as much); Johnson's "Account of Indian Expenses," November 1758 to December 1759, *PSWJ*, vol. 3, 152 (for Oneidas and Tuscaroras); George Armstrong to Henry Bouquet, Drownding Creek, 2 August 1758, f. 169, Add. MS 21643, BL ("eat more"); Henry Bouquet to George Croghan, Fort Bedford, 10 August 1759, f. 78, Add. MS 21655, BL ("Idle People"); Johnson's "Account of Indian Expenses," March 1755 to October 1756, *PSWJ*, vol. 2, 567 ("complained much").

27. William Johnson to Cadwallader Colden, Johnson Hall, 29 May 1765, *PSWJ*, vol. 4, 748.

28. Nicholas P. Canny, "The Ideology of English Colonization: From Ireland to America," *William and Mary Quarterly* 30, no. 4 (October 1973): 575–98, esp. 582 (for Gilbert), 586 (for barbarism), 592 (for law). For Cromwell, Drogheda, and Hewson, see Micheál Ó. Siochrú, "Atrocity, Codes of Conduct and the Irish in the British Civil Wars 1641–1653," *Past and Present* 195, no. 1 (May 2007): 55–86, esp. 57, 67, 75–77, 82.

29. Lee, *Barbarians and Brothers*, 188 (for Grotius), 189 (for Vattel); Jill Lepore, *The Name of War: King Philip's War and the Origins of American Identities* (New York: Alfred A. Knopf, 1998), 107–8 (for *jus ad bello* and *jus in bellum*).

30. Lee, *Barbarians and Brothers*, 34, 95, 188.

31. John Grenier, *The First Way of War: American War Making on the Frontier, 1607–1814* (New York: Cambridge University Press, 2005), 102–3.

32. Lee, *Barbarians and Brothers*, 191.

33. Emer de Vattel, *The Law of Nations*, iii, 472, 570 (quote).

34. Lepore, *The Name of War*, 111 (for Christians and non-Christians); Lee, *Barbarians and Brothers*, 223 ("law of retaliation" and "savage nation"); Shoemaker, *A Strange Likeness*, 100 (for Locke's influene on Vattel); Peter Silver, *Our Savage Neighbors: How Indian War Transformed Early America* (New York: W. W. Norton, 2008), 58 (for the treatment of dead bodies); Canny, "The Ideology of English Colonization," 596 (for Native noncombatants).

35. MacLeitch, *Imperial Entanglements*, 27 (for French invasions); Steele, *Warpaths*, 43 (for Jamestown), 232 (for the 1761 attack); Katherine A. Grandjean, "New World Tempests: Environment, Scarcity, and the Coming of the Pequot War," *William and Mary Quarterly* 68, no. 1 (January 2011): 75–100, esp. 92–93 (for the Pequot War).

36. Lepore, *The Name of War*, 96 (for King Philip's War). For the Cherokee War, see Hatley, *The Dividing Paths*, 145. For Dunmore's War, see Colin G. Calloway, *The Shawnees and the War for America* (New York: Viking, 2007), 54; Patrick Griffin, *American Leviathan: Empire, Nation, and Revolutionary Frontier* (New York: Hill and Wang, 2007), chap. 4.

37. For animals, see Anderson, *Creatures of Empire*. For animals and Indians in the Dutch Hudson Valley, see Taylor, *American Colonies*, 253. For targeting of farms, see

Silver, *Our Savage Neighbors*, 44. For Shawnees, see "By Henry Bouquet Esqr. &ca: &ca," Fort Pitt, 13 May 1761, f. 199, Add. MS 21655, BL. For Delawares, see Merritt, *At the Crossroads*, 42. For the Seven Years' War, see MacLeitch, "Sir William Johnson (1715–1774)," 94. For Indian farmers, see MacLeitch, *Imperial Entanglements*, 101. For Creeks, see Ja[mes?] Hendrie to [Tayler?], Mobile, 29 August 1766, f. 37, Add. MS 21671, BL.

38. Grenier, *The First Way of War*, 13 (for tactics); Silver, *Our Savage Neighbors*, xxv, xxvi (for Indian-hating).

39. On gender divisions, see Ann M. Little, *Abraham in Arms: War and Gender in Colonial New England* (Philadelphia: University of Pennsylvania Press, 2007), 13–14, 99. On Oneidas, see Glatthaar and Martin, *Forgotten Allies*, 48. For Mohawks, see Robert W. Venables, "'Faithful Allies of the King': The Crown's Haudenosaunee Allies in the Revolutionary Struggle for New York," in *The Other Loyalists: Ordinary People, Royalism, and the Revolution in the Middle Colonies, 1763–1787*, ed. Joseph S. Tiedemann, Eugene R. Fingerhut, and Robert W. Venables (Albany: State University of New York Press, 2009), 136. For breaking into gardens, see MacLeitch, *Imperial Entanglements*, 179. Plowing did not increase Indians' agricultural production. See Jane Mt. Pleasant, "The Paradox of Plows and Productivity: An Agronomic Comparison of Cereal Grain Production under Iroquois Hoe Culture and European Plow Culture in the Seventeenth and Eighteenth Centuries," *Agricultural History* 85, no. 4 (Fall 2011): 460–92, esp. 461–62.

40. John Moultrie to Eleanor Austin, Fort Prince George, 10 July 1761, in M. C. B. Gubbins, Transcripts and abstracts of Moultrie family papers, 1746–1965 (43/36), SCHS.

41. For background reading, see Richard Follett, "The Demography of Slavery," in *The Routledge History of Slavery*, ed. Gad Heuman and Trevor Burnard (London: Routledge, 2011), 119–37; Daniel H. Usner Jr., *Indians, Settlers, and Slaves in a Frontier Exchange Economy: The Lower Mississippi Valley before 1783* (Chapel Hill: University of North Carolina Press, 1992), 277–78; Robert L. Hall, "Food Crops, Medicinal Plants, and the Atlantic Slave Trade," in *African American Foodways: Explorations of History and Culture*, ed. Anne L. Bower (Urbana: University of Illinois Press, 2007), 17–44; William C. Whit, "Soul Food as Cultural Creation," in *African American Foodways*, 45–58. For the marketplace, see Robert Olwell, *Masters, Slaves, and Subjects: The Culture of Power in the South Carolina Low Country, 1740–1790* (Ithaca, NY: Cornell University Press, 1998), 145; Psyche A. Williams-Forson, *Building Houses Out of Chicken Legs: Black Women, Food, and Power* (Chapel Hill: University of North Carolina Press, 2006), 20. For hucksters, see Dylan C. Penningroth, *The Claims of Kinfolk: African American Property and Community in the Nineteenth-Century South* (Chapel Hill: University of North Carolina Press, 2003), chap. 2, esp. 46–49; Philip D. Morgan, *Slave Counterpoint: Black Culture in the Eighteenth-Century Chesapeake and Lowcountry* (Chapel Hill: University of North Carolina Press, 1998), 240, 242, 252. For differences between the Lowcountry and the Chesapeake, see Morgan, *Slave Counterpoint*, 134, 145. Bryan Edwards, an eighteenth-century Jamaican writer, used the term *peliculum* to refer to "land held by a slave as private property." The word "continued to appear in descriptions of the slaves' customary, not legal, claim on resources in which their own labor had been invested." I am grateful to Marc-William Palen for helping me to sort out the Latin. For these garden plots, see Sidney W. Mintz, *Three Ancient Colonies: Caribbean Themes and Variations* (Cambridge, MA: Harvard University Press, 2010), 53 (quote).

42. Kyla Wazana Tompkins, *Racial Indigestion: Eating Bodies in the 19th Century* (New York: New York University Press, 2012), 4–5; Rachel B. Herrmann, "'The black people were not good to eat': Cannibalism, Cooperation, and Hunger at Sea," in *To Feast on Us as Their Prey: Cannibalism and the Early Modern Atlantic*, ed. Rachel B. Herrmann (Fayetteville: University of Arkansas Press, 2019), chap. 11.

43. Herrmann, "'The black people were not good to eat.'"

44. George Croghan to Henry Bouquet, Croghan's House, 27 March 1762, f. 178, Add. MS 21655, BL ("the Expence," "it will be," and "but travel"); George Croghan to William Johnson, Fort Pitt, 21 March 1765, folder 26, box 201, Cadwalader Family Papers, HSP ("So Sevair" and "butt fewe").

45. William Robertson, *The Works of William Robertson, D.D. Fellow of the Royal Society, and Principal of the University, of Edinburgh, Historiographer to His Majesty for Scotland, and Member of the Royal Academy of History at Madrid. To which is Prefixed, An Account of His Life and Writings, by Dugald Stewart, F. R. S. Edin*, vol. IX (London: Printed for Cadell and Davies; F. C. and J. Rivington; G. Wilkie; J. Nunn; J. Cuthell; Clarke and Sons; Longman, Hurst, Rees, Orme, and Brown; E. Jeffery; J. Booker; J. and A. Arch; S. Bagster; Black, Parbury, and Allen; J. and T. Gray; John Richardson; J. M. Richardson; Carpenter and Son; R. H. Evans; J. Murray; W. Phillips; W. Stewart; J. Mawman; Baldwin, Cardock, and Joy; Ogle and Co.; Gale and Fenner; R. S. Kirby; W. H. Reid; and W. Ginger, 1817), 86.

2. Iroquois Food Diplomacy in the Revolutionary North

1. Frederick Haldimand to Lieutenant Colonel Mason Bolton, Quebec, 29 September 1780, ff. 146–47, Add. MS 21764, BL.

2. Robert S. Allen, *His Majesty's Indian Allies: British Indian Policy in the Defence of Canada, 1774–1815* (Toronto: Dundurn Press, 1992), 44.

3. Recent histories of the Iroquois during other time periods have underscored moments of resilience. A similar observation might be made about the American Revolution. For standard works on the War for Independence, see Barbara Graymont, *The Iroquois in the American Revolution* (Syracuse, NY: Syracuse University Press, 1972); Colin G. Calloway, *Crown and Calumet: British-Indian Relations, 1783–1815* (Norman: University of Oklahoma Press, 1987); Allen, *His Majesty's Indian Allies*; Calloway, *The American Revolution in Indian Country: Crisis and Diversity in North American Communities* (Cambridge, UK: Cambridge University Press, 1995); Edward Countryman, "Indians, the Colonial Order, and the Social Significance of the American Revolution," *William and Mary Quarterly* 53, no. 2 (April 1996): 342–62; Alan Taylor, *The Divided Ground: Indians, Settlers, and the Northern Borderland of the American Revolution* (New York: Vintage, 2006). For the Revolution as a disaster for the Iroquois, see Graymont, *The Iroquois in the American Revolution*, viii; Calloway, *The American Revolution in Indian Country*, 108; Timothy Shannon, *Iroquois Diplomacy on the Early American Frontier* (New York: Viking, 2008), 192–93. For current Iroquois history, see Joseph T. Glatthaar and James Kirby Martin, *Forgotten Allies: The Oneida Indians and the American Revolution* (New York: Hill and Wang, 2006); Kurt A. Jordan, *The Seneca Restoration, 1715–1754: An Iroquois Local Political Economy* (Gainesville: University Press of Florida, 2008); David L. Preston, *The Texture of Contact: European and Indian Settler Communities on the Frontiers of Iroquoia, 1667–1783* (Lincoln: University of Nebraska Press, 2009); Jon Parmenter,

The Edge of the Woods: Iroquoia, 1534–1701 (East Lansing: Michigan State University Press, 2010); Karim M. Tiro, *The People of the Standing Stone: The Oneida Nation from the Revolution through the Era of Removal* (Amherst: University of Massachusetts Press, 2011); Edward Countryman, "Toward a Different Iroquois History," *William and Mary Quarterly* 69, no. 2 (April 2012), 347–60. Karim Tiro's scholarship is an exception in that it has highlighted resilience among Revolutionary Iroquois, but his work does not focus on food. For resilience during other periods, see Jordan, *The Seneca Restoration*, 18, 318; Preston, *The Texture of Contact*, 13; Parmenter, *The Edge of the Woods*, xxix, xxxii–xxxiii; J. A. Brandão and William A. Starna, "The Treaties of 1701: A Triumph of Iroquois Diplomacy," *Ethnohistory* 43, no. 2 (1996): 209–44; Gilles Havard, *The Great Peace of Montreal of 1701: French-Native Diplomacy in the Seventeenth Century,* trans. Phyllis Aronoff and Howard Scott (Montreal, QC: McGill-Queen's University Press, 2001), 180.

4. For the Mourning Wars, see Daniel K. Richter, "War and Culture: The Iroquois Experience," *William and Mary Quarterly* 40, no. 4 (October 1983): 528–59; Merritt, *At the Crossroads: Indians and Empires on a Mid-Atlantic Frontier, 1700–1763* (Chapel Hill: University of North Carolina Press, 2003), 22. For the 1701 treaty and Pennsylvania, see Francis Jennings, *The Ambiguous Iroquois Empire: The Covenant Chain Confederation of Indian Tribes with English Colonies from Its Beginnings to the Lancaster Treaty of 1744* (New York: W. W. Norton, 1984), 196–99, 290–97; Merritt, *At the Crossroads*, 22, 46; Brandão and Starna, "The Treaties of 1701," 209–44; Leonard J. Sadosky, *Revolutionary Negotiations: Indians, Empires, and Diplomats in the Founding of America* (Charlottesville: University of Virginia Press, 2009), 36. For the debate over the Iroquois empire, see Jennings, *The Ambiguous Iroquois Empire*, esp. 229, 296–97; Daniel K. Richter and James H. Merrell, "Introduction" in *Beyond the Covenant Chain: The Iroquois and their Neighbors in Indian North America, 1600–1800,* ed. Daniel K. Richter and James H. Merrell (Syracuse, NY: Syracuse University Press, 1987), esp. 6–7; Matthew Dennis, *Cultivating a Landscape of Peace: Iroquois-European Encounters in Seventeenth-Century America* (Ithaca, NY: Cornell University Press, 1993), 257–58.

5. For the population estimate of sixty-four hundred, see Wayne E. Lee, *Barbarians and Brothers: Anglo-American Warfare, 1500–1865* (New York: Oxford University Press, 2011), 322n26. For nine thousand, see Taylor, *The Divided Ground*, 108. For ten thousand, see "Report of Governor William Tryon, of the State of the Province of New-York, 1775," in *The Documentary History of the State of New-York*, ed. E. B. O'Callaghan, vol. 1 (Albany, NY: Weed, Parsons, 1850), 518. For their locations, see Colonel Guy Johnson, "A General Review of the Northern Confederacy and the Department for Indian Affairs," 3 October 1776, vol. 10, no. 204, photostat 280, box 2, BHQP; Graymont, *The Iroquois in the American Revolution*, 5–6, 14, 55; Taylor, *The Divided Ground*, 4; Francis Jennings, "The Indians' Revolution," in *The American Revolution: Explorations in the History of American Radicalism*, ed. Alfred F. Young (Dekalb: Northern Illinois University Press, 1976), 324.

6. For the Seven Years' War, see Fred Anderson, *Crucible of War: The Seven Years' War and the Fate of Empire in British North America, 1754–1766* (New York: Vintage, 2001); Matt Schumann and Karl Schweizer, *The Seven Years War: A Transatlantic History* (New York: Routledge, 2008). For the war called Pontiac's and the reasons for its confused terminology, see Gregory Evans Dowd, *War under Heaven: Pontiac, the Indian Nations, and the British Empire* (Baltimore, MD: The Johns Hopkins University Press, 2002), 5. For work on the Seven Years' War as a European conflict, see Anderson, *Crucible of*

War, esp. 176–79. For the war as a global conflict, see Daniel A. Baugh, *The Global Seven Years War, 1754–1763: Britain and France in a Great Power Contest* (Harlow, UK: Pearson Education Limited, 2011). On British and French policies, see Alan Taylor, *American Colonies: The Settling of North America* (New York: Penguin, 2001), 430; Christian Ayne Crouch, *Nobility Lost: French and Canadian Martial Cultures, Indians, and the End of New France* (Ithaca, NY: Cornell University Press, 2014), 32, 87–91. On trade relationships, see Shannon, *Iroquois Diplomacy*, 44; Gail D. MacLeitch, *Imperial Entanglements: Iroquois Change and Persistence on the Frontiers of Empire* (Philadelphia: University of Pennsylvania Press, 2011), 67.

7. D. S., Articles of Agreement, 26 April 1765, *PSWJ*, vol. 4, 726 (quotes); John Lottridge to [William Johnson], Montreal, 12 December 1762, *PSWJ*, vol. 3, 970 (for Mohawk reports). See also Sir William Johnson, Indian Trade Regulations at Fort Pitt, [c. September 1761], *PSWJ*, vol. 3, 530–32. On the fur trade, see Ian K. Steele, *War- paths: Invasions of North America* (New York: Oxford University Press, 1994), 179; Eric Hinderaker, *Elusive Empires: Constructing Colonialism in the Ohio Valley, 1673–1800* (Cambridge, UK: Cambridge University Press, 1997), 68, 181; Colin G. Calloway, *The Shawnees and the War for America* (New York: Viking, 2007), 50; Gail D. MacLeitch, *Im- perial Entanglements*, 194–95; Maia Conrad, "Disorderly Drinking: Reconsidering Seventeenth-Century Iroquois Alcohol Abuse," *American Indian Quarterly* 23, no. 3/4 (Summer–Autumn 1999): 1–11, esp. 8; José António Brandão, *"Your fyre shall burn no more": Iroquois Policy toward New France and Its Native Allies to 1701* (Lincoln: University of Nebraska Press, 1997), 69, 85–88, 120; Havard, *The Great Peace of Montreal*, 50, 146; Jordan, *The Seneca Restoration*, 278, 299.

8. For the French presence, see Gail MacLeitch, "Sir William Johnson (1715–1774)," in *The Human Tradition in the Atlantic World, 1500–1850*, ed. Karen Racine and Beatriz G. Mamigonian (Lanham, MD: Rowman and Littlefield, 2010), 91. See also Steele, *Warpaths*, 179. For New York exports, see MacLeitch, *Imperial Entanglements*, 195. For gender divisions, see Tiro, *The People of the Standing Stone*, 11; Claudio Saunt, "'Do- mestick . . . Quiet being broke': Gender Conflict among Creek Indians in the Eigh- teenth Century," in *Contact Points: American Frontiers from the Mohawk Valley to the Mis- sissippi, 1750–1830*, ed. Andrew R. L. Cayton and Fredrika J. Teute (Chapel Hill: University of North Carolina Press, 1998), 151–74, esp. 157; Saunt, *A New Order of Things: Property, Power, and the Transformation of the Creek Indians, 1733–1816* (Cam- bridge, UK: Cambridge University Press, 1999), 148–9. For overhunting, see Tiro, *The People of the Standing Stone*, 7.

9. Richard White, *The Middle Ground: Indians, Empires, and Republics in the Great Lakes Region, 1650–1815* (New York: Cambridge University Press, 2011), 199, 257 (for the *Pays d'en Haut*); Taylor, *American Colonies*, 428 (for French shipping); Merritt, *At the Cross- roads*, 174 (for the French inland); "A conference held by Colonel Bouquet with the chiefs of the Delaware Indians at Pittsburgh," 4 December 1758, f. 19, Add. MS 21655, BL ("can't send"); William Johnson to Henry Bouquet, Detroit, 18 September 1761, f. 170, Add. MS 21655, BL ("the dearness").

10. For Johnson's reforms, see Johnson, "Regulations for the Trade at Fort Pitt," n.d., ff. 283–84; Johnson, "Regulations for the Trade at Sandusky," n.d., f. 285; John- son, "Regulations for the Trade at Miamies," n.d., f. 288, all in Add. MS 21655, BL. See also "By the Honorable Brigadier General Monckton commanding His Majestys forces in the southern district of North America," n.d., f. 199, Add. MS 21655, BL.

11. Jeffery Amherst to Sir William Johnson, Albany, 9 April 1761, *PSWJ*, vol. 3, 515 ("to avoid"). See also MacLeitch, *Imperial Entanglements*, 189; Daniel K. Richter, *Trade, Land, Power: The Struggle for Eastern North America* (Philadelphia: University of Pennsylvania Press, 2013), 3, 174, 183; Calloway, *The Shawnees and the War for America*, 32; Hinderaker, *Elusive Empires*, 181.

12. For Amherst, see Richter, *Trade, Land, Power*, 174. For Neolin, see Dowd, *War under Heaven*, 3; Gregory Evans Dowd, *A Spirited Resistance: The North American Indian Struggle for Unity, 1745–1815* (Baltimore: The Johns Hopkins University Press, 1992), 33.

13. Gregory Evans Dowd, "'Insidious Friends': Gift Giving and the Cherokee-British Alliance in the Seven Years' War," in *Contact Points*, 114–50 (for the Cherokees); Calloway, *The Shawnees and the War for America*, 34 (for other Native participants).

14. Richter, *Trade, Land, Power*, 177–78 (for Johnson's policy), 196 (for Stuart). For Johnson's redistribution of gifts, see Taylor, *American Colonies*, 436. For the Board of Trade, see MacLeitch, "Sir William Johnson (1715–1774)," 95.

15. For Amherst's policies, see Hinderaker, *Elusive Empires*, 181. For debt, see MacLeitch, "Sir William Johnson (1715–1774)," 98; Steele, *Warpaths*, 225.

16. For land seizures, see Sadosky, *Revolutionary Negotiations*, 55–56. For the King's Proclamation, see Daniel K. Richter, "Johnson, Sir William, first baronet (1715?–1774)," *Oxford Dictionary of National Biography*, accessed July 9, 2017, http://www.oxforddnb .com/view/article/14925; Calloway, *The American Revolution in Indian Country*, 21; Graymont, *The Iroquois in the American Revolution*, 49. For the southern line, see Tom Hatley, *The Dividing Paths: Cherokees and South Carolinians through the Era of Revolution* (New York: Oxford University Press, 1993), 180. For Dunmore's War, see Calloway, *The Shawnees and the War for America*, 52–57; Hinderaker, *Elusive Empires*, 189–95; Shannon, *Iroquois Diplomacy*, 169.

17. Mary Archibald, "Sir John Johnson: Knight of the Revolution," in *Eleven Exiles: Accounts of Loyalists of the American Revolution*, ed. Phyllis R. Blakeley and John N. Grant (Toronto, ON: Dundurn Press, 1982), 202. On Guy Johnson, see Calloway, *The American Revolution in Indian Country*, 137, 146–47. On his relationship to William Johnson, see Taylor, *The Divided Ground*, 72.

18. Robert W. Venables, "'Faithful Allies of the King': The Crown's Haudenosaunee Allies in the Revolutionary Struggle for New York," in *The Other Loyalists: Ordinary People, Royalism, and the Revolution in the Middle Colonies, 1763–1787*, ed. Joseph S. Tiedemann, Eugene R. Fingerhut, and Robert W. Venables (Albany: State University of New York Press, 2009), 138.

19. For British strategy, see Allen, *His Majesty's Indian Allies*, 44; Taylor, *The Divided Ground*, 87–90. For the use of food to win the Iroquois to the British side, see Graymont, *The Iroquois in the American Revolution*, 120. For the American departments, see James H. O'Donnell III, *Southern Indians in the American Revolution* (Knoxville: University of Tennessee Press, 1973), 22; Patrick Griffin, *American Leviathan: Empire, Nation, and Revolutionary Frontier* (New York: Hill and Wang, 2007), 132. For warriors and clan mothers, see Sarah M. S. Pearsall, "Recentering Indian Women in the American Revolution," in *Why You Can't Teach United States History without American Indians*, ed. Susan Sleeper-Smith, Juliana Barr, Jean M. O'Brien, Nancy Shoemaker, and Scott Manning Stevens (Chapel Hill: University of North Carolina Press, 2015), 57–70, esp. 61.

20. For food distribution, see Joseph Plumb Martin, *Ordinary Courage: The Revolutionary Adventures of Joseph Plumb Martin*, 2nd ed., ed. James Kirby Martin (St. James,

NY: Brandywine Press, 1999), viii, 12n2; James Kirby Martin, "A 'Most Undisciplined, Profligate Crew': Protest and Defiance in the Continental Ranks, 1776–1783," in *Arms and Independence: The Military Character of the American Revolution*, ed. Ron Hoffman and Peter J. Albert (Charlottesville: University Press of Virginia, 1984), 122–25. For adulterated bread, see Martin, *Ordinary Courage*, 95 ("some villainous"); Thomas Wileman, deposition to John Potts, Philadelphia, 18 February 1778, vol. 3, no. 126, photostat 948, box 4, BHQP. For "impassable" roads, see Jeremiah Wadsworth to Henry Laurens, Philadelphia, 29 September 1778, *PHL*, vol. 14, 369. For the Hessian fly, see Brooke Hunter, "Creative Destruction: The Forgotten Legacy of the Hessian Fly," in *The Economy of Early America: Historical Perspectives and New Directions*, ed. Cathy Matson (University Park: Pennsylvania State University Press, 2006), 236–62, esp. 242–43.

21. *The American Rebellion: Sir Henry Clinton's Narrative of His Campaigns, 1775–1782, with an Appendix of Original Documents*, ed. William B. Willcox (New Haven, CT: Yale University Press, 1954), xxxiii (for the British Army); Mason Bolton to Frederick Haldimand, Niagara, 4 March 1779, f. 96, Add. MS 21760, BL (for British beliefs about planting); Preston, *The Texture of Contact*, 107 (for hospitality); Frederick Haldimand to Guy Johnson, Quebec, 22 July 1781, f. 203, Add. MS 21767, BL ("devoured by"). See also Robert Mathews to John Butler, Quebec, 21 July 1781, f. 227, Add. MS21765, BL.

22. For types of provisions, see John Robinson to General William Howe, Whitehall Treasury Chambers, 24 June 1776, vol. 25, no. 71, photostat 220, box 2, BHQP. For a good summary of these concerns, see Brigadier-General Augustine Prevost to Sir Henry Clinton, St. Augustine, 16 September 1778, vol. 8, no. 140, photostat 1361, box 6, BHQP. For "American Flour," see John Robinson to General Howe, 1 May 1776, vol. 4, no. 21, photostat 171, box 1, BHQP. For "got wet" and "sold & bought," see John Robinson to General Sir William Howe, Treasury Chambers, Whitehall, 8 April 1777, vol. 4, no. 76, photostat 482, box 3, BHQP. For Cork, see Mr. Gordon, Commissary at Corke, to John Robinson, 20 August 1776, vol. 4, no. 56, photostat 249, box 2, BHQP. For the southern campaign, see Brigadier-General John Campbell to General Sir Henry Clinton, Pensacola, 10 February 1779, vol. 13, no. 1, photostat 1737, box 8, BHQP.

23. John Butler to [Francis Le Maistre], Niagara, 1 May 1778, f. 27, Add. MS 21765, BL (quote). For Saratoga, see Graymont, *The Iroquois in the American Revolution*, 156–57, 167–68. On Claus and Butler, see Allen, *His Majesty's Indian Allies*, 53; Taylor, *The Divided Ground*, 86–96. For combined rations given to Indians and British soldiers, see Mason Bolton, "Return of Provisions issued out of the King's Store at Niagara between the 25 Decemr. 1778 & the 24th Jany. 1779 inclve.," f. 87, Add. MS 21760, BL.

24. On Brant's volunteers, see John Butler to Frederick Haldimand, Niagara, 1 December 1778, f. 75, Add. MS 21765, BL; Taylor, *The Divided Ground*, 91. On women's crop production, see Pearsall, "Recentering Indian Women in the American Revolution," 60. For Iroquois crop yields, see Jane Mt. Pleasant and Robert F. Burt, "Estimating Productivity of Traditional Iroquoian Cropping Systems from Field Experiments and Historical Literature," *Journal of Ethnobiology* 30, no. 1 (Spring/Summer 2010): 52–79, esp. 60–61; Jane Mt. Pleasant, "The Paradox of Plows and Productivity: An Agronomic Comparison of Cereal Grain Production under Iroquois Hoe Culture and European Plow Culture in the Seventeenth and Eighteenth Centuries," *Agricultural History* 85, no. 4 (Fall 2011): 460–92, esp. 462; Dennis, *Cultivating a Landscape of Peace*, 27–28.

25. John Butler to [Frederick Haldimand], Niagara, 17 September 1778, f. 34, Add. MS 21765, BL ("almost all," "in a distressed," and "neglected"); Mason Bolton to [unknown], Niagara, 31 January 1778, f. 5, Add. MS 21760, BL ("all the Beef"); Mason Bolton to Sir Guy Carleton, Niagara, 12 May 1778, f. 18, Add. MS 21760, BL ("this Garrison").

26. "A Speech To the Six Confederate nations Mohawks, Oneidas, Tuscarora's, Onondage's, Cayugae's, Seneka's. From the twelve United Colonies convened in Council at Philadelphia," 18 July 1775, ff. 3–4, folder 26, box 22, PSP. For a description of this conference, see Graymont, The Iroquois in the American Revolution, 71–72.

27. [Speech by Abraham of the Lower Mohawk Castle], 2 May 1776 ("the shops"), and [speech by Volkert Douw and Timothy Edwards], n.d., but c. May 1776 ("You Brothers"), in unlabeled bound journal, 2–10 May 1776, folder 63, box 22, PSP; "A Speech To the Six Confederate nations Mohawks, Oneidas, Tuscarora's, Onondage's, Cayugae's, Seneka's. From the twelve United Colonies convened in Council at Philadelphia," 18 July 1775, f. 7, folder 26, box 22, PSP ("to remain"). For the Americans' bargaining position, see Calloway, Crown and Calumet, 6; Allen, His Majesty's Indian Allies, 46.

28. [Volkert Douw] to Jellis Fonda, Caughnawaga, 6 January 1776, folder 63, box 22, PSP; "At a Board of Commissioners of Indian Affairs of the Northern Department held at Albany," 13 April 1778, folder 57, box 23, PSP (quotes). For later, more organized distributions, see General Schuyler Folkert P. Douw and the other commissioners of Indian Affairs to Jelles Fonda, June 1778 to March 1780, folder 27, box 23, PSP.

29. "At a Meeting of the Commissioners of Indian Affairs for the Northern Department with a Number of Sachems and Warriors of the Six Nations for the purpose of holding a conference pursuant to the orders of Congress, held at John's-Town," 10 March 1778, folder 57, box 23, PSP (quote); Jon Parmenter, "After the Mourning Wars: The Iroquois as Allies in Colonial North American Campaigns, 1676–1760," William and Mary Quarterly 64, no. 1 (January 2007): 39–76, esp. 40 (for the nonaggression pact).

30. Daniel Claus to Frederick Haldimand, Montreal, 15 September 1778, f. 1, Add. MS 21774, BL ("provision to," "Irondequoit Bay," and "nearest to"); "At a meeting of the Commissioners for Indian Affairs in the Northern Department, Albany," 15 August 1778, folder 57, box 23, PSP ("to remain" and "great many").

31. Mason Bolton to [Sir Guy Carleton], Niagara, 31 January 1778, f. 5, Add. MS 21760, BL (quote). For Johnson's efforts to challenge gender roles, see MacLeitch, Imperial Entanglements, 22, 39, 96, 143. For Cooper, see Tiro, The People of the Standing Stone, 39; Glatthaar and Martin, Forgotten Allies, 205. Tiro's book contains a good discussion about the reliability of the Cooper story.

32. 2 May [1778], "Extract from the Journal of Richard McGinnis," vol. IV, William A. Smy Collection, Butler Papers, R3779-0-7-E, LAC.

33. For "insulted & robbed," see Daniel Claus to Frederick Haldimand, Montreal, 30 August 1779, f. 57, Add. MS 21774, BL. For all other quotes, see 20 April 1778, "Depositions against persons stealing from the Canajohary Indian Castle, taken at Palatine, New York, Tryon County, before Jelles Fonda, Justice of the Peace" [enclosed in Jelles Fonda to the Honorable Board of Commissioners of Indian Affairs, Palatine, 21 April 1778], folder 57, box 23, PSP. For the background to these actions and on Deygart, see Graymont, The Iroquois in the American Revolution, 146–47; Helen Caister Robinson, "Molly Brant: Mohawk Heroine," in Eleven Exiles, 117.

34. Captain Brehm to [Frederick Haldimand], Montreal, 16 April 1779, f. 23, Add. MS 21759, BL. It was Brehm who reported Brant's warning.

35. John Butler to Captain William Caldwell, Tioga, 12 July 1778, f. 9, Add. MS 21771, BL.

36. Lieutenant Colonel Daniel Claus to General Frederick Haldimand, Montreal, 13 October 1778, vol. IV, William A. Smy Collection, the Butler Papers, LAC ("in the glory"); John Butler, memorial to Brigadier General Powell, Niagara, 1 October 1781, f. 224, Add. MS 21874, BL ("To serve"). For the removal of the phrase, see Robert Mathews to Brigadier General Powell, Quebec, 1 November 1781, f. 250, Add. MS 21764, BL.

37. "Depositions against persons stealing from the Canajohary Indian Castle, taken at Palatine, New York, Tryon County, before Jelles Fonda, Justice of the Peace" [enclosed in Jelles Fonda to the Honorable Board of Commissioners of Indian Affairs, Palatine, 21 April 1778], 20 April 1778, folder 57, box 23, PSP (quotes); Graymont, *The Iroquois in the American Revolution*, 142–47; Tiro, *The People of the Standing Stone*, 49.

38. Martin, *Ordinary Courage*, 109.

39. John Butler to Frederick Haldimand, Canadasango, 21 July 1779, ff. 115–16, Add. MS 21765, BL (quotes); Jordan, *The Seneca Restoration*, 45 (for famine foods).

40. [George Washington] to John Sullivan, Head Quarters, Middle Brook, 31 May 1779, HM 1590, HL ("immediate objects," "Settlements," "in their distress," and "supplies of," "the total"); George Washington to John Sullivan, Head Quarters, West Point, 15 September 1779, f. 23, vol. 5, box 2, John Sullivan Transcripts, MHS ("throwing").

41. Graymont, *The Iroquois in the American Revolution*, 192–223; John Grenier, *The First Way of War: American War Making on the Frontier*, 1607–1814 (New York: Cambridge University Press, 2005), 102–3, 166–67; Taylor, *The Divided Ground*, 98; Venables, "'Faithful Allies of the King,'" 142–49; Jordan, *The Seneca Restoration*, 187.

42. Pearsall, "Recentering Indian Women in the American Revolution," 60.

43. F. Barber to Governor Clinton, Praoga, 15 August 1779, f. 79, folder "John Sullivan Letters in the Rolls Office, Washington, 1775–1791. John L. Sullivan / T.C. Amory, 1856–. Extracts from N.H. Materials re John Sullivan, 1772–. Journal of West Expedition 18 June 1779–. General Orders, Campaign on RI, 1778," box 4, John Sullivan Transcripts, MHS ("very fine"); [Lieutenant John Jenkins], "A Journal of the West Expedition Commanded by the Honble Major General Sullivan began at Easton, June 18 1779," 13 August ("a glorious" and "about 40"), 13 September ("called Kanegsae"), 14 September (for Genesee Flats), 15 September ("large fires" and "piling"), 1779, ff. 169, 184, 187, folder "John Sullivan Letters . . . ," box 4, John Sullivan Transcripts, MHS; Andrew Hunter, War Diary, 1776–1779, 20 August and 8 September 1779, M 2097, JDR ("destroyed all," "girdled the," and "destroyed the").

44. Emer de Vattel, *The Law of Nations, or, Principles of the Law of Nature, Applied to the Conduct and Affairs of Nations and Sovereigns, with Three Early Essays on the Origin and Nature of Natural Law and on Luxury*, ed. Béla Kapossy and Richard Whatmore (Indianapolis: Liberty Fund, 2008), iii, 570; Lee, *Barbarians and Brothers*, 228.

45. John Butler to Frederick Haldimand, Niagara, 20 September 1779, f. 140, Add. MS 21765, BL ("the Genesee"); Peter Gansevoort to John Sullivan, Albany, 8 October 1779, f. 31, vol. 5, box 1, John Sullivan Transcripts, MHS ("great plenty"). On the word *reavers*, see James H. Merrell, "Second Thoughts on Colonial Historians

and American Indians," *William and Mary Quarterly* 69, no. 3 (July 2012): 451–512, esp. 476.

46. Venables, "'Faithful Allies of the King,'" 149 (for the bushels); Mt. Pleasant and Burt, "Estimating Productivity of Traditional Iroquoian Cropping Systems from Field Experiments and Historical Literature," 60–61 (for stored and standing grain); Alan Taylor, "'The Hungry Year': 1789 on the Northern Border of Revolutionary America," in *Dreadful Visitations: Confronting Natural Catastrophe in the Age of Enlightenment*, ed. Alessa Johns (New York: Routledge, 1999), 167 (for dietary estimates).

47. Extract of a letter from Major Butler to Colonel Bolton, Camp, Buffaloe Creek, 14 September 1779, in Lieut. Col. Mason Bolton and Major John Butler, 14, 16, and 20 September 1779, vol. 11, nos. 93 and 94, photostat 2308, box 10, BHQP (quote). For similar British sentiments, see Lieutenant Colonel Mason Bolton to General Haldimand, Niagara, 7, 8, and 10 September 1779, vol. 11, no. 83, photostat 2260, box 10, BHQP; General Haldimand to General Sir Henry Clinton, Quebec, 2 November 1779, vol. 11, no. 97, photostat 2400, box 11, BHQP. For a description of Six Nations refugees at Niagara, see Calloway, *The American Revolution in Indian Country*, chap. 5, esp. 136–37; Venables, "'Faithful Allies of the King,'" 149. For deaths that winter, see Taylor, *The Divided Ground*, 99.

48. General Haldimand to General Sir Henry Clinton, Quebec, 29 August 1779, vol. 11, nos. 45 and 60, photostat 2234, box 10, BHQP (quote); Calloway, *The American Revolution in Indian Country*, 61 (for the effects of the campaign further afield).

49. Major Butler to General Haldimand, 20 September 1779, in Lieut. Col. Mason Bolton and Major John Butler, 14, 16, and 20 September 1779, vol. 11, nos. 93 and 94, photostat 2308, box 10, BHQP (quote); Taylor, *The Divided Ground*, 99 (for the Johnsons).

50. General Haldimand to General Sir Henry Clinton, Quebec, 28 September 1779, vol. 11, no. 78, photostat 2334, box 10, BHQP (for Haldimand's proposal); General Haldimand to General Sir Henry Clinton, Quebec, 19 July 1779, vol. 11, no. 43, photostat 2129, box 9, BHQP ("the quantity"); General Frederick Haldimand to Lieutenant Colonel Mason Bolton, Quebec, 23 July 1779, vol. 5, William A. Smy Collection, LAC ("that all"); Frederick Haldimand to Major Butler, Quebec, 3 September 1779, f. 136, Add. MS 21765, BL ("make demands").

51. Frederick Haldimand to Major Butler, Quebec, August [no day] 1779, f. 134, Add. MS 21765, BL ("far Exceeds"); General Frederick Haldimand to Major Butler, Quebec, 3 September 1779, f. 136, Add. MS 21765, BL ("obliged to abandon").

52. General Haldimand to General Sir Henry Clinton, Quebec, 29 August 1779, vol. 11, nos. 45 and 60, photostat 2234, box 10, BHQP ("the Necessity"); Frederick Haldimand to Lieutenant Colonel Mason Bolton, Quebec, 29 September 1780, ff. 146–47, Add. MS 21764, BL ("that no useless").

53. Lieutenant Colonel Mason Bolton to General Haldimand, Niagara, 7 September 1779, photostat 2260, box 10, BHQP.

54. H. Watson Powell to Frederick Haldimand, Niagara, February 18, 1781, f. 7, Add. MS 21761, BL.

55. Mason Bolton to Frederick Haldimand, Canadasagoe, 24 June 1779, f. 145, Add. MS 21760, BL (for the cattle); Lieutenant Colonel Mason Bolton to General Haldimand, Niagara, 16 August 1779, vol. 11, no. 72, 2202, box 10, BHQP (all other quotes).

56. For example, see Dowd, *A Spirited Resistance*, 113.

57. "Proceedings with the Indians at Niagara," 31 October 1779, f. 60, Add. MS 21779, BL ("a sufficient"); Daniel Claus to Frederick Haldimand, Montreal, 30 September 1779, f. 72, Add. MS 21774, BL (for Montreal); Guy Johnson to Frederick Haldimand, Niagara, 12 November 1779, f. 51, Add. MS 21767, BL ("prevailed on").

58. "Proceedings with the Indians at Niagara," 3 November 1779, f. 61, Add. MS 21779, BL.

59. For riotous soldiers, see Martin, "A 'Most Undisciplined, Profligate Crew,'" 119–40.

60. Major John Butler to Lieutenant Colonel Mason Bolton, Shechquago, 31 August 1779, vol. 11, no. 85, photostat 2238, box 10, BHQP.

61. [Captain William Caldwell] to [Brigadier General Henry Watson Powell], Ochquago, 19 August 1781, f. 148, Add. MS 21762, BL.

62. [Captain William Caldwell] to [Brigadier General Henry Watson Powell], Ochquago, 19 August 1781, ff. 148–49, 152, Add. MS 21762, BL.

63. Henry Bird to Major Arent Schuyler De Peyster, Ohio, opposite Licking Creek, 1 July 1780, f. 316, Add. MS 21760, BL (quotes); John Sugden, *Blue Jacket: Warrior of the Shawnees* (Lincoln: University of Nebraska Press, 2000), 60–62 (for variations on the fort name); White, *The Middle Ground*, 407 (for the Indians as Shawnees and Great Lakes Indians).

64. Frederick Haldimand to Mason Bolton, Quebec, 10 August 1780, f. 130, Add. MS 21764, BL; Virginia DeJohn Anderson, *Creatures of Empire: How Domestic Animals Transformed Early America* (New York: Oxford University Press, 2004).

65. Frederick Haldimand to Daniel Claus, Quebec, 6 September 1779, f. 61, Add. MS 21774, BL (quote); H. Watson Powell to Frederick Haldimand, Quebec, 5 December 1782, f. 589, Add. MS 21734, BL (for distributions).

66. H. Watson Powell to Frederick Haldimand, Niagara, 17 May 1782, f. 46, Add. MS 21762, BL ("as the Indians"); extract of a letter from Captain Fraser, Carleton Island, 21 February 1780, enclosed in Frederick Haldimand to Mason Bolton, Quebec, 16 April 1780, f. 96, Add. MS 21764, BL (for baked bread); [Daniel Bliss], "Pork Issued to Indians from 24th June 1780 to 24th September 1781 at Niagara," ff. 165–67, Add. MS 21761, BL (for pork); Daniel Claus to Frederick Haldimand, Montreal, 26 October 1778, f. 7, Add. MS 21774, BL ("the Effect," "getting sickly," and fresh and salted provisions in 1778); Daniel Claus to Robert Mathews, Montreal, 23 March 1780, f. 98, Add. MS 21774, BL; Robert Mathews to Daniel Claus, Quebec, 27 March 1780, f. 99, Add. MS 21774, BL (for fresh and salted provisions in 1780); Calloway, *The American Revolution in Indian Country*, 133 (for increased spending).

67. "Distribution of Corn, and Hoes for the Indians of Colonel Johnson's Department, planting at Buffaloe Creek," 13 May 1781, f. 120, Add. MS 21769, BL; John Butler to Robert Mathews, Niagara, 7 December 1781, ff. 263–64, Add. MS 21765, BL.

68. Chris Evans, "The Plantation Hoe: The Rise and Fall of an Atlantic Commodity, 1650–1850," *William and Mary Quarterly* 69, no. 1 (January 2012): 71–100, esp. 75, 80–81; James Stanely Goddard to [John Cambell], Montreal, 8 March 1784, f. 221, Add. MS 21772, BL.

69. Extract of a letter from Colonel Guy Johnson to Frederick Haldimand, 11 January 1783, f. 134, Add. MS 21770, BL.

70. "The Answer of the Commissioners of Indian Affairs for the Northern Department to the Speech of the Oneidas & Tuscaroras," [n.d., c. 1779], folder 53, box 23, PSP.

71. [Unknown men] of the great Council of the United States and the Board of War, talk to the Oneidas, Tuscaroras, and Cochnawagas, 13 September 1781, folder 27, box 23, PSP.

72. Cornplanter's speech to the President of the United States, 1 December 1790, enclosed in Henry Knox to Timothy Pickering, Philadelphia, 2 May 1791, f. 8, reel 60, TPP ("When your army"); Colin G. Calloway, *The Indian World of George Washington: The First President, the First Americans, and the Birth of the Nation* (New York: Oxford University Press, 2018), 7 (for Washington's name and its meanings).

73. For 150,000, see James H. Merrell, "'The Customes of Our Countrey': Indians and Colonists in Early America," in *Strangers within the Realm: Cultural Margins of the First British Empire*, ed. Bernard Bailyn and Philip D. Morgan (Chapel Hill: University of North Carolina Press, 1991), 124. See also his discussion of population numbers, 123n14.

3. Cherokee and Creek Victual Warfare in the Revolutionary South

1. William Tennent to Henry Laurens, Bullock's Creek, 20 August 1775, *PHL*, vol. 10, 339 (quote). On Tennent, see Marion C. Chandler, "Tennent, William III," *American National Biography Online*, accessed February 9, 2015, http://www.anb.org/articles/01/01–01156.html. For standard works on southern Indian affairs, see James H. O'Donnell III, *Southern Indians in the American Revolution* (Knoxville: University of Tennessee Press, 1973); Gregory Evans Dowd, *A Spirited Resistance: The North American Indian Struggle for Unity, 1745–1815* (Baltimore: Johns Hopkins University Press, 1992); Tom Hatley, *The Dividing Paths: Cherokees and South Carolinians through the Era of Revolution* (New York: Oxford University Press, 1993); Claudio Saunt, *A New Order of Things: Property, Power, and the Transformation of the Creek Indians, 1733–1816* (Cambridge, UK: Cambridge University Press, 1999); Wayne E. Lee, *Crowds and Soldiers in Revolutionary North Carolina* (Gainesville: University Press of Florida, 2001); Joshua Aaron Piker, *Okfuskee: A Creek Indian Town in Colonial America* (Cambridge, MA: Harvard University Press, 2004); Andrew K. Frank, *Creeks and Southerners: Biculturalism on the Early American Frontier* (Lincoln: University of Nebraska Press, 2005); John Grenier, *The First Way of War: American War Making on the Frontier, 1607–1814* (New York: Cambridge University Press, 2005); Jim Piecuch, *Three Peoples, One King: Loyalists, Indians, and Slaves in the Revolutionary South, 1775–1782* (Columbia: University of South Carolina Press, 2008); Angela Pulley Hudson, *Creek Paths and Federal Roads: Indians, Settlers, and Slaves and the Making of the American South* (Chapel Hill: University of North Carolina Press, 2010).

2. Leonard J. Sadosky, *Revolutionary Negotiations: Indians, Empires, and Diplomats in the Founding of America* (Charlottesville: University of Virginia Press, 2009), 46–47.

3. Piker, *Okfuskee*, 98, and Hudson, *Creek Paths and Federal Roads*, 3–4 (for Creek populations); Colin G. Calloway, *The American Revolution in Indian Country: Crisis and Diversity in North American Communities* (Cambridge, UK: Cambridge University Press, 1995), 182 (for a twelve thousand-person Cherokee population); Piecuch, *Three Peoples, One King*, 28 (for twelve to fourteen thousand Cherokees); Saunt, *A New Order of Things*, 11–14 (for the emergence of the Creek confederacy); Steven C. Hahn, *The Invention of the Creek Nation, 1670–1763* (Lincoln: University of Nebraska Press, 2004), 4, 272 (for triple-nation diplomacy and trade embargoes).

4. For Creek attacks, see Piker, *Okfuskee*, 65; Saunt, *A New Order of Things*, 34. For the attacks of 1760 and 1761, see Hatley, *The Dividing Paths*, 119; Calloway, *The American Revolution in Indian Country*, 182. For land sales, see O'Donnell, *Southern Indians in the American Revolution*, viii. For Georgia's population, see Saunt, *A New Order of Things*, 46.

5. O'Donnell, *Southern Indians in the American Revolution*, vii–ix, 23–24 (for Galphin); Piecuch, *Three Peoples, One King*, 67 (for South Carolina); Saunt, *A New Order of Things*, 48 (for Stuart); Brigadier-General John Campbell to General Sir Henry Clinton, Pensacola, 10 February 1779, vol. 13, no. 1, photostat 1737, box 8, BHQP (quote).

6. John Stuart to General Gage, St. Augustine, 3 October 1776, in *Extracts of Letters, &c. Published by Order of CONGRESS* (Charles Town: Printed by Peter Timothy, 1776), 8, in Provincial Congress, Extracts of Intercepted Letters, 1775–1776, S165248, SCDAH ("necessaries" and "a supply"); John Stuart to General Sir William Howe, Pensacola, 4 February 1778, vol. 10, no. 171, photostat 925, box 4, BHQP ("Many of the Creeks," "about five," and "a very great"). On Creek-Cherokee conflict, see Piker, *Okfuskee*, 45–46, 49. For Cameron, see Alexander Cameron to George Germain, Pensacola, 18 December 1779, photostat 2489, f. 5, vol. 20, reel 7, British headquarters (Sir Guy Carleton) papers, 1747–1783, film 57, DLAR.

7. At a Council, 5 July 1776, folder "Volume 2: Minutes, Apr.–July 1776," Georgia Council of Safety minutes, MS 0282, GHS (for the Georgia Council of Safety); At a Council held at Kingston, 29 September 1777, in folder "1777," Council Minutes, 1777–1780, G.O. 119, NCSA (for North Carolina); "A Talk Delivered at Augusta in May by his Honor the Governor to the Headmen and Warriors of the Cherokee Nation Met During the war," [May 1783?], folder "Treaty of Augusta between Commissioners of Indian Affairs [of Georgia] and the Cherokee," box 1807, Governor's Subject Files, 1781–1802, GDAH (for Lyman Hall). For a similar moment see "At a Board of Commissioners for Treating with the Indians," Augusta, 25 May 1783, folder "Treaty of Augusta between Commissioners of Indian Affairs [of Georgia] and the Cherokee," box 1807, Governor's Subject Files, 1781–1802, GDAH.

8. John Stuart to Brigadier-General Augustine Prevost, Pensacola, 24 July 1777, vol. 10, no. 180, photostat 629, box 3, BHQP.

9. "A talk given by the Tallasee King and head men of the Upper and Lower Creek Nation," 28 May 1782, folder 12, box 78, Telamon Cuyler Collection, HRBML (for the Tallassee King's speech); Hatley, *The Dividing Paths*, 10–11 (for nakedness and hungriness).

10. "Articles of Convention held at Augusta, in the Country of Richmond and State aforesaid," 31 May 1783, folder "Treaty of Augusta between Commissioners of Indian Affairs [of Georgia] and the Cherokee," box 1807, Governor's Subject Files, 1781–1802, GDAH.

11. John Stuart to General Gage, St. Augustine, 3 October 1776, in *Extracts of Letters*, 4–6, 7.

12. Mr. [George] Milligen's Report of the state of South Carolina, 15 September 1775, reel 11, vol. 35, Records of the British Public Records Office Relating to South Carolina, 1663–1782, PCL ("Arms, Ammunition"); at a Council, 5 July 1776, folder "Volume 2: Minutes, Apr.–July 1776," Georgia Council of Safety minutes, MS 0282, GHS ("if the communication" and "& our Enemies"). On the deerskin trade,

see Claudio Saunt, "'Domestick . . . Quiet being broke': Gender Conflict among Creek Indians in the Eighteenth Century," in *Contact Points: American Frontiers from the Mohawk Valley to the Mississippi, 1750–1830*, ed. Andrew R. L. Cayton and Fredrika J. Teute (Chapel Hill: University of North Carolina Press, 1998), 151–74.

13. Copy of a letter from Charles Lee to Edmund Pendleton, Charleston, 20 July 1776, f. 30, Charles Lee Letterbook, 1776 July 2–Aug. [27?], SCL ("a Corps," "the destruction," and "necessary terror"); Henry Laurens to John Laurens, Charleston, 14 August 1776, *PHL*, vol. 11, 229 ("the only possible"). For Dragging Canoe, see Cristina Snyder, "Native Nations in the Age of Revolutions," in *The World of the Revolutionary American Republic: Land, Labor, and the Conflict for a Continent*, ed. Andrew Shankman (New York: Routledge, 2014), 85. For rumors of Cherokee attacks, see Lee, *Crowds and Soldiers in Revolutionary North Carolina*, 159. For Cherokee attacks, see O'Donnell, *Southern Indians in the American Revolution*, ix, 42; Hatley, *The Dividing Paths*, 194. For colonists' attacks against the Cherokees, see Lee, *Crowds and Soldiers in Revolutionary North Carolina*, 160; Armstrong Starkey, *European and Native American Warfare, 1675–1815* (Norman: University of Oklahoma Press, 1998), 123; Grenier, *The First Way of War*, 152.

14. Lee, *Crowds and Soldiers in Revolutionary North Carolina*, 160.

15. John Stuart to General Sir William Howe, Pensacola, 6 October 1777, vol. 10, no. 175, photostat 695, box 3, BHQP (quote); J. Glasgow to Waightstill Avery and William Sharp, Hewington, 15 August 1777, folder 1, Revolutionary War Papers, 1774–1782, 02194-z, SHC (for Holston). For the Cherokee split, see Dowd, *A Spirited Resistance*, 54; Hatley, *The Dividing Paths*, 223.

16. Jos. Vann to Alexander Cameron, n.d., vol. 10, no. 188, photostat 587, enc. in John Stuart to General Sir William Howe, Pensacola, 16 June 1777, vol. 10, no. 189, photostat 586, box 3, BHQP.

17. For Dragging Canoe's followers, see Dowd, *A Spirited Resistance*, 54; Hatley, *The Dividing Paths*, 223. For the Cherokee split and blocked food aid, see Calloway, *The American Revolution in Indian Country*, 202.

18. For Smithfield Market, see Emma Hart, "From Field to Plate: The Colonial Livestock Trade and the Development of an American Economic Culture," *William and Mary Quarterly* 73, no. 1 (January 2016): 107–40, esp. 109. For the Act of Union, see Fredrik Albritton Jonsson, "Climate Change and the Retreat of the Atlantic: The Cameralist Context of Pehr Kalm's Voyage to North America, 1748–51," *William and Mary Quarterly* 72, no. 1 (January 2015): 99–126, esp. 124. For the Chesapeake, see Cary Carson, Joanne Bowen, Willie Graham, Martha McCartney, and Lorena Walsh, "New World, Real World: Improvising English Culture in Seventeenth-Century Virginia," *Journal of Southern History* 74, no. 1 (February 2008): 31–88, esp. 45. For horses, see Piker, *Okfuskee*, chap. 4, esp. 111, 124. For cattle and slavery, see Saunt, *A New Order of Things*, 49–51, 62–63, 67–135, 148–49. For the Treaty of Dewitt's Corner, see "Articles of the Definitive Treaty of Peace, concluded on and signed at Dewitt's Corner the 20th day of May 1777 between the State of South Carolina and the Cherokee Indians," enc. in William Blount to John Steele, Augusta, 5 May 1789, folder 4, John Steele Papers, 1716–1846, Collection 00689, Series 1.2, SHC.

19. Frank, *Creeks and Southerners*, 71 (for McGillivray's bequest); Piker, *Okfuskee*, 100 (provisions when traveling); "At a Meeting of the Head Men of the upper Creek Nation held at the Okchoys," 5 April 1763, *CRSG*, vol. 9, 71 (for the Mortar's talk).

20. *Journals of the Proceedings of the Commons House of Assembly,* 3 November 1769, *CRSG,* vol. 15, 20 (for the 1769 bill); "AN ACT for maintaining the Peace with the Indians in the Province of GEORGIA," March 1733, *CRSG,* vol. 1, 40 (for the 1733 law); "Letter from the President and assistants to Benjamin Martyn Esq. Secretary to the honourable trustees for establishing the colony of Georgia at their office in Queen Square Westminster," Savannah, 25 July 1750, *CRSG,* vol. 26, 38 (for Yuchis plundering); [Talk by George Galphin sent to the Creeks, reproduced in] "At a Council held in the Council Chamber at Savannah," 9 December 1771, *CRSG,* vol. 12, 151 (for Galphin's talk).

21. For the letter to Laurens, see John Houstoun to Henry Laurens, Savannah, 1 October 1778, *PHL,* vol. 14, 375. For attacks in Georgia, see Copy of a letter, Charles Lee to Richard Peters, Charleston, 2 August 1776, f. 52, Charles Lee Letterbook, 1776 July 2–Aug. [27?], SCL.

22. General William Howe to John Stuart, n.p., 23 May 1776, vol. 1, no. 121, photostat 191, box 1, BHQP; Lord George Germain to Colonel John Stuart, Whitehall, 31 March 1779, vol. 10, no. 111, photostat 1871, box 8, BHQP. For continued attacks during the 1770s, see Joseph Clay to Henry Laurens, Savannah, 29 September 1777, *PHL,* vol. 11, 532. The 1780s feature later in this chapter.

23. For reports of famine, see Calloway, *The American Revolution in Indian Country,* 57, 261–62.

24. Brigadier-General John Campbell to Sir Henry Clinton, Pensacola, 25 March 1779, vol. 13, no. 12, photostat 1856, box 8, BHQP ("in the greatest"); Snyder, "Native Nations in the Age of Revolutions," 81 (for Stuart's marriage); Lord George Germain to Colonel [Thomas] Brown, Whitehall, 25 June 1779, vol. 12, no. 76, photostat 2079, box 9, BHQP ("allowance for"); Alexander Cameron to Governor Chester, Pensacola, 25 December 1779, photostat 2499, vol. 20, reel 7, British headquarters (Sir Guy Carleton) papers, 1747–1783, film 57, DLAR ("barely sufficient").

25. For critiques of Stuart before and after the March 1779 letter, see General Sir William Howe to John Stuart, New York, 3 May 1777, vol. 1, no. 118, photostat 512, box 3, BHQP; Lord George Germain to General Sir Henry Clinton, Whitehall, 1 April 1779, vol. 10, no. 107, photostat 1875, box 8, BHQP. For "the Cherokees will," see Alexander Cameron to Major General Augustine Prevost, 15 October 1779, Creek Nation, Little Tallassie, vol. 15, no. 217, photostat 2372, box 10, BHQP. For "in confusion," see Major General John Campbell to General Sir Henry Clinton, Pensacola, 14 September 1779, vol. 3, no. 38, photostat 2289, box 10, BHQP.

26. Major General John Campbell to General Sir Henry Clinton, Pensacola, 14 September 1779, vol. 3, no. 38, photostat 2289, box 10, BHQP ("laden with" and "for want"); Alan Taylor, *American Revolutions: A Continental History, 1750–1804* (New York: W. W. Norton, 2016), 266 (for Gálvez); John Campbell to Henry Clinton, Head Quarters, 10 February 1780, photostat 2565, vol. 20, reel 7, British headquarters (Sir Guy Carleton) papers, 1747–1783, film 57, DLAR (for the pork).

27. Alexander Cameron to George Germain, Pensacola, 18 December 1779, photostat 2489, vol. 20, reel 7, British headquarters (Sir Guy Carleton) papers, 1747–1783, film 57, DLAR.

28. Alexander Cameron to George Germain.

29. Alexander Cameron to George Germain.

30. This account varies a bit from another letter that Cameron sent to Prevost, in which he said that Williamson offered the Indians peace "provided they would not

oppose him, or give me any Assistance." Alexander Cameron to George Germain, Pensacola, 18 December 1779, photostat 2489, vol. 20, reel 7, British headquarters (Sir Guy Carleton) papers, 1747–1783, film 57, DLAR; Alexander Cameron to Major General Augustine Prevost, 15 October 1779, Creek Nation, Little Tallassie, vol. 15, no. 217, photostat 2372, box 10, BHQP.

31. Alexander Cameron to George Germain, Pensacola, 18 December 1779, photostat 2489, vol. 20, reel 7, British headquarters (Sir Guy Carleton) papers, 1747–1783, film 57, DLAR.

32. Alexander Cameron to Major General Augustine Prevost, 15 October 1779, Creek Nation, Little Tallassie, vol. 15, no. 217, photostat 2372, box 10, BHQP ("to treat," "into his Hands," and "that if he would"); Alexander Cameron to George Germain, Pensacola, 18 December 1779, photostat 2489, vol. 20, reel 7, British headquarters (Sir Guy Carleton) papers, 1747–1783, film 57, DLAR ("Burned Six").

33. Alexander Cameron to Major General Augustine Prevost, 15 October 1779, Creek Nation, Little Tallassie, vol. 15, no. 217, photostat 2372, box 10, BHQP (quote). For the Chickamauga population, see Calloway, *The American Revolution in Indian Country*, 43–44. Exact counts of the Chickamaugas remain elusive, and I thank Lance Greene, Tyler Barrett Howe, Kathryn Sampeck, and Gregory Smithers for their thoughts on this matter. For bushel weights, see Russ Rowlett, "U.S. Commercial Bushel Sizes," *How Many? A Dictionary of Units of Measurement*, accessed December 6, 2016, https://www.unc.edu/~rowlett/units/scales/bushels.html. For Iroquois bushel consumption, see chapter 2 of this book. For fifty thousand bushels of Cherokee corn destroyed, see Calloway, *The American Revolution in Indian Country*, 50.

34. Alexander Cameron to Major General Augustine Prevost, 15 October 1779, Creek Nation, Little Tallassie, vol. 15, no. 217, photostat 2372, box 10, BHQP.

35. Alexander Cameron to Governor Chester, Pensacola, 25 December 1779, vol. 13, no. 64, photostat 2499, box 11, BHQP.

36. Alexander Dickson to General [Frederick Haldimand], Pensacola, 9 May 1774, f. 139, Add. MS 21731, BL (for Chester's refusal to provide ammunition and provisions); Kathleen DuVal, *Independence Lost: Lives on the Edge of the American Revolution* (New York: Random House, 2015), 108 (for Germain on funds); John Campbell to Henry Clinton, Head Quarters, 10 February 1780, photostat 2565, vol. 20, reel 7, British headquarters (Sir Guy Carleton) papers, 1747–1783, film 57, DLAR (for Chester refusing to see Creeks); Lieutenant Colonel Thomas Brown to General Sir Henry Clinton, Savannah, 29 May 1780, vol. 30, nos. 147 and 190, photostat 2778, box 12, BHQP (quote).

37. Alexander Cameron to Sir Henry Clinton, Pensacola, 18 July 1780, vol. 13, no. 113, photostat 2919, box 13, BHQP ("them with," "being disatisfyed," "sold most," "when drunk," and "very insolent"); John Campbell to Henry Clinton, Head Quarters, 10 February 1780, photostat 2565, vol. 20, reel 7, British headquarters (Sir Guy Carleton) papers, 1747–1783, film 57, DLAR ("his Favorets" and "Plundering").

38. Phillip Hamilton, *The Making and Unmaking of a Revolutionary Family: The Tuckers of Virginia, 1752–1830* (Charlottesville: University of Virginia Press, 2003), 8, 47–48.

39. "Ode on the capture of the British Army under Lord Cornwallis, at York, in Virginia October 19: 1781," Poetry copybook, bound volume, 144–46, St. George Tucker Collection, 1771–1821, MS 1942.4, JDR.

40. Frank, *Creeks and Southerners*, 24 (quote). This line of argument has been influenced by *Fear and the Shaping of Early American Societies*, ed. Lauric Henneton and L. H.

Roper (Leiden, Netherlands: Brill, 2016); Bertie Mandelblatt, "'A Land where Hunger is in Gold and Famine is in Opulence': Plantation Slavery, Island Ecology, and the Fear of Famine in the French Caribbean," *Fear and the Shaping of Early American Societies*, chap. 11.

41. Daniel McMurphy to John Martin, Augusta, 22 September 1782, 30, Creek Indian Letters Talks and Treaties, 1705–1839, Part 1, 1705–1793, Transcripts, GDAH (quotes); Lee, *Crowds and Soldiers in Revolutionary North Carolina*, 197 (for violence during this part of the war).

42. Piecuch, *Three Peoples, One King*, 300 (for Cameron's death); Saunt, *A New Order of Things*, 54 (for Galphin's death).

43. Arthur Campbell to [unknown], Washington, 10 July 1781, folder 3, Revolutionary War Papers, 1774–1782, 02194-z, SHC.

44. Jonathan Cunningham to Elijah Clark, Wilkes County, 4 March 1782, 1, vol. I, Cherokee Indian Letters, Talks and Treaties, 1786–1838, Transcripts, GDAH.

45. "A Message sent to the Middle Grounds by Charles Reaman a half breed and by a fellow called the Horn to the Vallies," Long Swamp on High Tower River, 25 September 1782, enclosed in Andrew Pickens to John Martin, Long Canes, 26 October 1782, folder 9, Joseph Vallence Bevan Papers, MS 0071, GHS.

46. "A Talk delivered by General Pickens to the Head Men of the Cherokee Nation," High Towner River, 17 October 1782, enclosed in Andrew Pickens to John Martin, Long Canes, 26 October 1782, folder 9, Joseph Vallence Bevan Papers, MS 0071, GHS.

47. "A Talk deliver'd at Savannah by Governor Martin of the state of Georgia & Sent to the Tallasee King & the head men & Warriors of the upper & Lower Creek Nation," 19 July 1782, John Martin letter book and letters, MS 0543, GHS.

48. John Martin to Andrew Pickens, Augusta, 27 May 1782, 25, Creek Indian Letters Talks and Treaties, 1705–1839, Part 1, 1705–1793, Transcripts, GDAH (for the warning); Colonel Clarke to John Martin, Fort Wators, 21 May 1782, 22, Creek Indian Letters Talks and Treaties, 1705–1839, Part 1, 1705–1793, Transcripts, GDAH (for the attack); "A talk given by the Tallasee King and head men of the Upper and Lower Creek Nation," 28 May 1782, folder 12, box 78, Telamon Cuyler Collection, HRBML (for the meeting and the talk); Saunt, *A New Order of Things*, 61 (for factions); "Copy of Colonel Murphy's Instructions, & Sent by him to Mr. Richard Henderson, Assistant Deputy Superintendent for Indian Affairs," Savannah, 4 October 1782, John Martin letter book and letters, MS 0543, GHS (for Georgians' lack of goods).

49. "A Talk delivered by Governor Martin at Savannah, To the Tallesee King and the head Men & Warriors of the upper & Lower Creek Nations," 29 October 1782, folder 84, box 38F, Telamon Cuyler Collection, HRBML (for Martin's speech); John Martin to Richard Henderson, Savannah, 7 October 1782, John Martin letter book and letters, MS 0543, GHS (for Martin's limitations on visitors); James Rae to Lyman Hall, Augusta, 29 January 1783, 47, Creek Indian Letters Talks and Treaties, 1705–1839, Part 1, 1705–1793, Transcripts, GDAH (for "chearfully gave" and "the Publick").

50. Grenier, *The First Way of War*, 160 (for events in 1780 and 1781); John Crawford to Alexander Irwin, n.p., 3 March 1782, 170, Creek Indian Letters Talks and Treaties, 1705–1839, Part 1, 1705–1793, Transcripts, GDAH (quote); Colonel Clarke to John Martin, Fort Wators, 21 May 1782, 22, Creek Indian Letters Talks and Treaties, 1705–1839, Part 1, 1705–1793, Transcripts, GDAH (for injuries and casualties).

51. On noses, see Kenneth S. Greenberg, *Honor and Slavery: Lies, Duels, Noses, Masks, Dressing as a Woman, Gifts, Strangers, Humanitarianism, Death, Slave Rebellions, the Pro-slavery Argument, Baseball, Hunting, and Gambling in the Old South* (Princeton, NJ: Princeton University Press, 1996), chap. 1.

52. As a lawyer who would eventually advocate for gradual emancipation and the colonization of formerly enslaved people abroad, it is not impossible to imagine that he might have written such a poem. Hamilton, *The Making and Unmaking of a Revolutionary Family*, 150–51.

4. Black Victual Warriors and Hunger Creation

1. Benjamin Quarles, *The Negro in the American Revolution* (New York: W.W. Norton, 1961), xi (for the 1781 Dinah); Michael E. Groth, "Black Loyalists and African American Allegiance in the Mid-Hudson Valley," in *The Other Loyalists: Ordinary People, Royalism, and the Revolution in the Middle Colonies, 1763–1787*, ed. Joseph S. Tiedemann, Eugene R. Fingerhut, and Robert W. Venables (Albany: State University of New York Press, 2009), 91 ("by 'softening'"); Psyche A. Williams-Forson, *Building Houses out of Chicken Legs: Black Women, Food, and Power* (Chapel Hill: University of North Carolina Press, 2006), 19 ("thwarted an assassination"); Adrian Miller, *The President's Kitchen Cabinet: The Story of the African Americans Who Have Fed Our First Families, from the Washingtons to the Obamas* (Chapel Hill: University of North Carolina Press, 2017), 36–37 (for Phoebe). On chicken, see also Doris Witt, *Black Hunger: Soul Food and America* (Minneapolis: University of Minnesota Press, 2004), esp. 3–4.

2. For standard work, see Quarles, *The Negro in the American Revolution*; Winthrop D. Jordan, *White over Black: American Attitudes toward the Negro, 1550–1812* (Chapel Hill: University of North Carolina Press, 1968); Alan Kulikoff, "Uprooted Peoples: Black Migrants in the Age of the American Revolution, 1790–1820," in *Slavery and Freedom in the Age of the American Revolution*, ed. Ira Berlin and Ronald Hoffman (Urbana: University of Illinois Press, 1986 [1983]), 143–71; Sylvia R. Frey, *Water from the Rock: Black Resistance in a Revolutionary Age* (Princeton, NJ: Princeton University Press, 1991); Betty Wood, *The Origins of American Slavery: Freedom and Bondage in the English Colonies* (New York: Hill and Wang, 1997); Ira Berlin, *Many Thousands Gone: The First Two Centuries of Slavery in North America* (Cambridge, MA: The Belknap Press of Harvard University Press, 1998); Philip D. Morgan, *Slave Counterpoint: Black Culture in the Eighteenth-Century Chesapeake and Lowcountry* (Chapel Hill: University of North Carolina Press, 1998); Robert Olwell, *Masters, Slaves, and Subjects: The Culture of Power in the South Carolina Low Country, 1740–1790* (Ithaca, NY: Cornell University Press, 1998). For current scholarship, see Gary B. Nash, *The Forgotten Fifth: African Americans in the Age of Revolution* (Cambridge, MA: Harvard University Press, 2006); Cassandra Pybus, *Epic Journeys of Freedom: Runaway Slaves of the American Revolution and Their Global Quest for Liberty* (Boston: Beacon Press, 2006); Simon Schama, *Rough Crossings: Britain, the Slaves and the American Revolution* (New York: HarperCollins, 2006); Philip D. Morgan and Andrew Jackson O'Shaughnessy, "Arming Slaves in the American Revolution," in *Arming Slaves: From Classical Times to the Modern Age*, ed. Christopher Leslie Brown and Philip D. Morgan (New Haven, CT: Yale University Press, 2006), 180–208; Judith L. Van Buskirk, "Claiming Their Due: African Americans in the Revolutionary War and Its Aftermath," in *War and Society in the American Revolution: Mobilization and Home*

Fronts, ed. John Resch and Walter Sargent (DeKalb: Northern Illinois University Press, 2007), 132–60; Douglas R. Egerton, *Death or Liberty: African Americans and Revolutionary America* (New York: Oxford University Press, 2009); Maya Jasanoff, *Liberty's Exiles: American Loyalists in the Revolutionary World* (New York: Alfred A. Knopf, 2011). For this British military strategy, see Jim Piecuch, *Three Peoples, One King: Loyalists, Indians, and Slaves in the Revolutionary South, 1775–1782* (Columbia: University of South Carolina Press, 2008).

3. "The humble ADDRESS of the Mayor, Recorder, Aldermen, and Common Council of the city of *Williamsburg*," *Virginia Gazette*, 22 April 1775, no. 1237 ("Some wicked"); Earl of Dartmouth to Dunmore, Whitehall, 2 August 1775, 603, TR13.2, Dunmore Correspondence, 1771–1778, JDR ("with a Supply").

4. "By his Excellency the Right Honourable John Earl of Dunmore . . . ," *American Memory*, Library of Congress, accessed July 12, 2017, http://memory.loc.gov/cgi-bin/ampage?collId=rbpe&fileName=rbpe17/rbpe178/17801800/rbpe17801800.db&recNum=0; "Williamsburg, *Nov. 25*," *Virginia Gazette*, 25 November 1775, no. 1268 (for the proclamation).

5. Cassandra Pybus, "Henry 'Harry' Washington (1750s–1790s): A Founding Father's Slave," in *The Human Tradition in the Atlantic World, 1500–1850*, ed. Karen Racine and Beatriz G. Mamigonian (Lanham, MD: Rowman and Littlefield Publishers, 2010), 103 ("Ethiopian regiment"). On the relationship between Dunmore's proclamation and its effects on rebels' sentiments against Great Britain, see Frey, *Water from the Rock*, 326; Piecuch, *Three Peoples, One King*, 10. See also Quarles, *The Negro in the American Revolution*, 18; Schama, *Rough Crossings*, 7; Egerton, *Death or Liberty*, 71; Ellen Gibson Wilson, *The Loyal Blacks* (New York: Capricorn Books, 1976), 24–25; Olwell, *Masters, Slaves, and Subjects*, 238.

6. Robert Carter to Messrs. Thomas and Rowland Hunt, Merchants London, 18 April 1777, Robert Carter Letter Book, vol. III, TR 07.2, Robert Carter Papers 1760–1793, JDR ("availed themselves"); Major-General Robert Pigot to General Sir William Howe, Newport, 10 April 1778, vol. 9, no. 180, photostat 1083, box 5, BHQP (for the British in Boston); Major General Augustine Prévost to Sir Henry Clinton, Savannah, 2 November 1779, vol. 15, no. 219, photostat 2402, box 11, BHQP ("did wonders"); General Sir Henry Clinton, Proclamation, Head Quarters, Philipsburg, 30 June 1779, vol. 15, no. 132, photostat 2094, box 9, BHQP (for the Philipsburg proclamation); Frey, *Water from the Rock*, 141, and James W. St. G. Walker, *The Black Loyalists: The Search for a Promised Land in Nova Scotia and Sierra Leone 1783–1870* (New York: Africana Publishing Company, 1976), 2 (for support for the rebels); Egerton, *Death or Liberty*, 6 (for fifteen thousand); Jasanoff, *Liberty's Exiles*, 8 (for twenty thousand); Morgan, *Slave Counterpoint*, 666 (for South Carolina and Georgia); Kulikoff, "Uprooted Peoples," 144 (for Maryland, North Carolina, and Virginia).

7. "In the Council of Safety," Charles-Town, 8 December 1775, *Collections of the South Carolina Historical Society*, vol. III, 66 ("continue[d] to receive" and "be discontinued"); "In the Council of Safety," 18 December 1775, *Collections of the South Carolina Historical Society*, vol. III, 95 ("less reason," "robberies and depredations," "white and black," and "to cut"); Henry Laurens to Archibald Bulloch, Charles Town, 2 January 1776, *PHL*, vol. 10, 607 ("Since the practice," "we have refused," and "to obtain"). The same letter appears in "Extract of a Letter from Henry Laurens to Archibald Bullock," 2 January 1776, vol. I, Georgia Council of Safety minutes, MS 0282, GHS.

8. Henry Laurens to Georgetown Committee, Charles Town, 25 January 1776, *PHL*, vol. 11, 70 ("to Supply" and "be deemed"); "Conversation & information to the Town of Savannah from Govr. Wright by Doctr. Jones & Jos. Clay," 18 January 1776, folder 7, Joseph Vallence Bevan Papers, MS 0071, GHS ("That if," "if in their power," and "destroy it"); John C. Fredriksen, *Revolutionary War Almanac* (New York: Facts on File, 2006), 55 (for Wright); Andrew Barclay to James Wright, Scarborough, 19 February 1776, vol. I, Georgia Council of Safety minutes, MS 0282, GHS ("his Majesty" and "the Market").

9. John Penn to Richard Caswell, Philadelphia, 25 June 1777, folder "Correspondence, 1770–1786," Richard Caswell Papers, 1733–1790, P.C. 242.1, NCSA; John Laurens to Henry Laurens, Valley Forge, 11 April 1778, *PHL*, vol. 13, 101; Jeremiah Wadsworth to Henry Laurens, Philadelphia, 29 September 1778, *PHL*, vol. 14, 368.

10. W. R. Jones, "Purveyance for War and the Community of the Realm in Late Medieval England," *Albion* 7, no. 4 (January, 1975): 300–16, esp. 301; Emer de Vattel, *The Law of Nations, or, Principles of the Law of Nature, Applied to the Conduct and Affairs of Nations and Sovereigns, with Three Early Essays on the Origin and Nature of Natural Law and on Luxury*, ed. Béla Kapossy and Richard Whatmore (Indianapolis, IN: Liberty Fund, 2008), ii, 320 (for fair prices), vii, 533 (for neutrality), iii, 516 ("no moral obligation"), ii, 266 (for refusals to supply).

11. William Earl Weeks, *Dimensions of the Early American Empire, 1754–1865*, vol. 1, *The New Cambridge History of American Foreign Relations*, ed. Warren I. Cohen (Cambridge, UK: Cambridge University Press, 2013), 23–24.

12. "Pitt County, copies of records of the County Committee dealing with taxation and other matters," 8 July 1775, folder 1, Revolutionary War Papers, 1774–1782, 02194-z, SHC.

13. "*An ORDINANCE for establishing a MODE of PUNISHMENT for the ENEMIES in AMERICA in this colony, passed at a CONVENTION held in the city of WILLIAMS-BURG on Friday the 1st of December, 1775*," *Virginia Gazette*, 27 January 1776, no. 1277 (for the Committee of Safety); *Virginia Gazette*, 16 December 1775, no. 1271 (for the General Assembly).

14. Morgan, *Slave Counterpoint*, 192, 203.

15. Joseph Clay to Henry Laurens, Savannah, 16 October 1777, *PHL*, vol. 11, 560 (for Georgians); "Losses of Arnoldus Vanderhorst by the British," 1780, folder "12/194/33," Arnoldus Vanderhorst papers, 1763–1817, 1169.02.01, SCHS; Paul Trapier, "Losses sustained during the British war in America, c. 1783," 43/508, SCHS.

16. For antipathy, see Kathryn E. Holland Braund, "The Creek Indians, Blacks, and Slavery," *The Journal of Southern History* 57, no. 4 (November 1991): 601–36; James H. Merrell, "The Racial Education of the Catawba Indians," *The Journal of Southern History* 50, no. 3 (August 1984): 363–84, esp. 364; Morgan, *Slave Counterpoint*, 477; Colin G. Calloway, *The American Revolution in Indian Country: Crisis and Diversity in Native American Communities* (Cambridge, UK: Cambridge University Press, 1995), 263; Daniel H. Usner Jr., *Indians, Settlers, and Slaves in a Frontier Exchange Economy: The Lower Mississippi Valley before 1783* (Chapel Hill: University of North Carolina Press, 1992), 9; Tom Hatley, *The Dividing Paths: Cherokees and South Carolinians through the Era of Revolution* (New York: Oxford University Press, 1993), 72–75; Piecuch, *Three Peoples, One King*, 63; Piecuch, "Incompatible Allies: Loyalists, Slaves, and Indians in Revolutionary South Carolina," *War and Society in the American Revolution*, 195; April Lee Hatfield, "Colo-

nial Southeastern Indian History," *Journal of Southern History* 73, no. 3 (April 2007): 567–78. For Catawbas, see "In the Council of Safety," 20 February 1776, *Collections of the South Carolina Historical Society* (Charleston: Published by the South-Carolina Historical Society, 1859), vol. III, 263–64. For Bull, see Stephen Bull to Henry Laurens, Savannah, 14 March 1776, *PHL*, vol. 11, 163. For "alarming incursions," see "Copy of a letter, Charles Lee to Richard Peters," Charleston, 2 August 1776, f. 52, Charles Lee Letterbook, 1776 July 2–Aug. [27?], SCL.

17. Braund, "The Creek Indians, Blacks, and Slavery," 622 (for Indian slavery); "An Account of the Life of Mr. DAVID GEORGE, from Sierra Leone in Africa; given by himself in a Conversation with Brother RIPPON of London, and Brother PEARCE of Birmingham" (London, 1793–1797), in *Unchained Voices: An Anthology of Black Authors in the English-Speaking World of the Eighteenth Century*, ed. Vincent Carretta (Lexington: University Press of Kentucky, 1996), 334; Benjamin Hawkins, "A Sketch of the Creek Country in the Years 1798 and 1799," in *The Collected Works of Benjamin Hawkins, 1796–1810*, ed. Thomas Foster II (Tuscaloosa: University of Alabama Press, 2003), 48 (for Creeks in the 1790s); Robbie Ethridge, *Creek Country: The Creek Indians and Their World* (Chapel Hill: University of North Carolina Press, 2003), 116 (for enslaved crop production in Creek country); Joel W. Martin, *Sacred Revolt: The Muskogees' Struggle for a New World* (Boston: Beacon Press, 1991), 73 (for formerly enslaved children).

18. "At a Council held at Newbern," 7 April 1778, folder "1778 Apr–Aug," Council Minutes, 1777–1780, G.O. 119, NCSA (for North Carolina); Major General Horatio Gates to George Washington, Boston, 4 March 1779, n. 6, *Founders Online*, accessed January 26, 2017, http://founders.archives.gov/documents/Washington/03-19-02-0369 (for South Carolina); From Thomas Jefferson to the Commissioners of the specific tax for Albemarle County, in Council, 26 June 1780, *Founders Online*, accessed January 26, 2017, http://founders.archives.gov/documents/Jefferson/01-15-02-0561 (for the broadside); Horatio Gates to Thomas Jefferson, Camp at Mask Ferry, on the West Bank of Pee-dee, 3 August 1780, *Founders Online*, accessed January 26, 2017, http://founders.archives.gov/documents/Jefferson/01-03-02-0604 (for Gates's report).

19. Samuel Massey to [Henry Laurens (no address, docketed by HL, received 30 June, p. 307)], Charles Town, 12 June 1780, *PHL*, vol. 15, 305–6 (quotes). For initial work on slave foodways, see Robert William Fogel and Stanley L. Engerman, *Time on the Cross: The Economics of American Negro Slavery* (Boston: Little, Brown and Company, 1974), esp. 111. For this estimate of what enslaved people ate, see Richard Follett, "The Demography of Slavery," in *The Routledge History of Slavery*, ed. Gad Heuman and Trevor Burnard (London: Routledge, 2011), 130. See also Jessica B. Harris, *High on the Hog: A Culinary Journey from Africa to America* (New York: Bloomsbury, 2011).

20. Robert Carter Day Book, vol. XIII (1773–1776), TR 07.2, Robert Carter Papers 1760–1793, JDR.

21. Wilson, *The Loyal Blacks*, 26–27 (for people staying put); James Sidbury, *Ploughshares into Swords: Race, Rebellion, and Identity in Gabriel's Virginia, 1730–1810* (Cambridge, UK: Cambridge University Press, 1997), 27 (for escapees from Robert Carter's plantation); Rhys Isaac, *Landon Carter's Uneasy Kingdom: Revolution and Rebellion on a Virginia Plantation* (New York: Oxford University Press, 2004), 3–4 (for people who ran from Landon Carter).

22. John Lewis Gervais to Henry Laurens, Charles Town, 26 July 1777, *PHL*, vol. 11, 407 (for March); *Virginia Gazette*, 6 January 1776, no. 1274 (for the self-amputation); Egerton, *Death or Liberty*, 275 (for branding).

23. Van Buskirk, "Claiming Their Due," 137 (for battles); Frey, *Water from the Rock*, 79, and Quarles, *The Negro in the American Revolution*, 12, 74–75 (for black service on the American side).

24. Quarles, *The Negro in the American Revolution*, 13–19 (for changing American strategy); Michael McDonnell, "'Fit for Common Service?': Class, Race, and Recruitment in Revolutionary Virginia," *War and Society in the American Revolution*, 108 (for Virginia); John Laurens to Henry Laurens, Head Quarters, 14 January 1778, and John Laurens to Henry Laurens, Head Quarters, 2 February 1778, *The Army Correspondence of Colonel John Laurens*, vol. II, 108, 116. The first letter also appears in *PHL*, vol. 12, 305 (for John Laurens's proposal); Henry Laurens to John Laurens, York, 6 February 1778, *PHL*, vol. 12, 412 (for his father's reaction); John Lewis Gervais to Henry Laurens, Charles Town, 16 March 1778, *PHL*, vol. 13, 5 (for the Gervais proposal); Nathanael Greene to Governor Mathews, n.p., 11 February 1782, f. 76, reel 1, Nathanael Greene papers, MSS24026, microfilm shelf no. 13,421, LOC (for Mathews).

25. Egerton, *Death or Liberty*, 81–83 (for the Continental Congress); 4 February 1782, folder "General Assembly Committee Reports 1782, #11–13," box 27, South Carolina General Assembly Committee Reports, 1776–1879, S165005, SCDAH (quote).

26. "An Account of the Life of Mr. DAVID GEORGE," 336.

27. Jane G. Landers, *Atlantic Creoles in the Age of Revolutions* (Cambridge, MA: Harvard University Press, 2010), 9, 24–25.

28. Dunmore to Lord George Germain, Ship Dunmore in Elizabeth River, Virginia, 30 March 1776, TR 13.1, Dunmore Correspondence, 1771–1778, JDR; John Lewis Gervais to Henry Laurens, Charles Town, 16 March 1778, *PHL*, vol. 13, 5; Sir Henry Clinton, "Memoranda for the Commondant of Charleston and Earl Cornwallis," Head Quarters, Charles Town, 3 June 1780, vol. 19, no. 11, photostat 2800, box 13, BHQP ("those Negroes"). For the Black Pioneers as companies, see *Moving On: Black Loyalists in the Afro-Atlantic World*, ed. John W. Pulis (New York: Garland Publishing, 1999), xv. Scholars disagree about whether or not the Black Pioneers bore arms. For the Pioneers as noncombatants, see Todd W. Braisted, "The Black Pioneers and Others: The Military Role of Black Loyalists in the American War for Independence," in *Moving On*, 12. For the Black Pioneers receiving arms, see Pybus, "Henry 'Harry' Washington (1750s–1790s)," 104.

29. Head Quarters, York, 4 September 1781, f. 36 (for peas), and 13 September 1781, f. 44 ("Grat abusses"), Charles Cornwallis, Orderly book, 28 June to 19 October 1781, PH 02 24, JDR. For kettle shortages, see Brigadier General Augustine Prévost to Sir Henry Clinton, Ebenezer, 15 March 1779, vol. 15, no. 173, photostat 1829, box 8, BHQP; Brigadier General Augustine Prévost to Sir Henry Clinton, Savannah, 16 April 1779, vol. 15, no. 179, photostat 1925, box 8, BHQP; See also Egerton, *Death or Liberty*, 86.

30. Augustine Prévost to Henry Clinton, Savannah, 2 November 1779, vol. 15, no. 219, photostat 2402, box 11, BHQP (quote). On rations and white Loyalists, see Pybus, *Epic Journeys of Freedom*, 32. On plunder, see Braisted, "The Black Pioneers and Others," 23.

31. "WILLIAMSBURG, *December* 2," *Virginia Gazette*, 2 December 1775, no. 1269 ("Dunmore's banditti"); Egerton, *Death or Liberty*, 67 (for Titus); Augustine Prévost to

Henry Clinton, Savannah, 2 November 1779, vol. 15, no. 219, photostat 2402, box 11, BHQP (for Prévost's assessments). See also Quarles, *The Negro in the American Revolution*, 29.

32. For roles during the war, see Frey, *Water from the Rock*, 169; Pybus, "Henry 'Harry' Washington (1750s–1790s)," 106. For Furman, see Quarles, *The Negro in the American Revolution*, 91. For Allen, see "Book of Negroes Registered & certified after having been Inspected by the Commissioners appointed by His Excellency Sr: Guy Carleton K.B. General & Commander in Chief, on Board Sundry Vessels in which they were Embarked Previous to the time of sailing from the Port of New York between the 23d April and 31st July 1783 both Days Included," f. 67, photostat 10427, box 43, BHQP. For the Georges, see "An Account of the Life of Mr. DAVID GEORGE," 336. For Liele, see John W. Pulis, "Bridging Troubled Waters: Moses Baker, George Liele, and the African American Diaspora to Jamaica," *Moving On*, 194–95.

33. "An Account of the Life of Mr. DAVID GEORGE," 336 (quote). For a similar point about the Revolution scattering families, see Sara T. Damiano, "Writing Women's History through the Revolution: Family Finances, Letter Writing, and Conceptions of Marriage," *William and Mary Quarterly* 74, no. 4 (October 2017): 697–728, esp. 702, 706.

34. Boyrereau Brinch (Jeffrey Brace), *The Blind African Slave, or Memoirs of Boyrereau Brinch, Nick-named Jeffrey Brace. Containing an Account of the Kingdom of Bow-Woo, in the Interior of Africa; with the Climate and Natural Productions, Laws, and Customs Peculiar to That Place. With an Account of His Captivity, Sufferings, Sales, Travels, Emancipation, Conversion to the Christian Religion, Knowledge of the Scriptures, &c. Interspersed with Strictures on Slavery, Speculative Observations on the Qualities of Human Nature, with Quotation from Scripture* (St. Albans, VT: Printed by Harry Whitney, 1810), 157–58; *Documenting the American South*, accessed December 4, 2015, http://docsouth.unc.edu/neh/brinch/menu.html (quote); Van Buskirk, "Claiming Their Due," 155 (for the hog); "The Life and Confession of JOHNSON GREEN, Who is to be Executed this Day, August 17th, 1786, for the Atrocious Crime of Burglary; Together with his LAST and DYING WORDS," 17 August 1786, *Unchained Voices*, 135 (for Green); Quarles, *The Negro in the American Revolution*, 91 (for Grandison, Burns, and Coopers); Pybus, *Epic Journeys of Freedom*, 21 (for Handley). On hunger in Brinch's narrative, see Lynn R. Johnson, "Narrating an Indigestible Trauma: The Alimentary Grammar of Boyrereau Brinch's Middle Passage," in *Journeys of the Slave Narrative in the Early Americas*, ed. Nicole N. Aljoe and Ian Frederick Finseth (Charlottesville: University of Virginia Press, 2014), 127–42.

35. Schama, *Rough Crossings*, 88 (for the island's inhabitants); "General orders," 7 December 1775, f. 17, Orderly books of William Moultrie, 1775, June 20–1780, December 15, HM 681, HL (for plans of the expedition); "Major Pinkney's Instructions," 9 December 1775, Signed Wm. Moultrie, Charles Town, 7 December 1775, f. 17, Orderly books of William Moultrie, 1775, June 20–1780, December 15, HM 681, HL (for Moultrie's instructions); Henry Laurens to Col. Richardson, Charles Town, 19 December 1775, in "Journal of the Council of Safety, Appointed by the Provisional Congress," November 1775, *Collections of the South Carolina Historical Society*, vol. III, 102 (for Laurens's report).

36. Messers. Stedman and Booth, Commissaries, "A General Abstract of Provisions, Issued to His Majesty's Army, late under the Command of the Right Honourable Lieutenant-General Earl Cornwallis, on the March of that Army through the

Provinces of North-Carolina and Virginia, in the Years 1780 and 1781," f. 5, part 1, CO 5/8, TNA.

37. "The Life and Confession of JOHNSON GREEN," 135.

38. Daniel Claus to Frederick Haldimand, Montreal, 16 September 1779, f. 69, Add. MS 21774, BL ("every thing was" and "he heard"); Groth, "Black Loyalists and African American Allegiance in the Mid-Hudson Valley," 91 ("Blacks in the Kitchen").

39. Daniel Claus to Frederick Haldimand, Montreal, 16 September 1779, f. 69, Add. MS 21774, BL.

40. For "the daring," "carry off," "The free booty," "their numbers," and "daily increasing," see James Jackson to the Governor of South Carolina, n.p., 1787, Joseph Vallence Bevan Papers, MS 0071, folder 10, GHS. This letter is simply dated 1787, so Jackson could have been writing to William Moultrie or to Thomas Pinckney. For "left six" and "Their baggage," see James Gunn to James Jackson, n.p., 6 May 1787, Joseph Vallence Bevan Papers, MS 0071, folder 10, GHS. See also Merrell, "The Racial Education of the Catawba Indians," 371.

41. "Memoirs of the Life of BOSTON KING, a Black Preacher. Written by Himself, during his Residence at Kingswood-School" (London, 1798), *Unchained Voices*, 356.

42. General Frederick Haldimand to [unknown], Quebec, 21 April 1783, vol. VIII, William A. Smy Collection, LAC ("are not considered"); Brigadier General Allan Maclean to General Frederick Haldimand, Niagara, 2 May 1783, vol. VIII, William A. Smy Collection, LAC ("the Indians"); Barbara Graymont, *The Iroquois in the American Revolution* (Syracuse, NY: Syracuse University Press, 1972), 259 (for the treaty's terms).

5. Fighting Hunger, Fearing Violence after the Revolutionary War

1. James Seagrove to [Henry Knox], Rock Landing on Oconee, 5 July 1792, 172, reel 1, Correspondence of the War Department Relating to Indian Affairs, Military Pensions, and Fortifications, 1791–1799, film 455, DLAR. I thank Kathie Ludwig at the David Library of the American Revolution for sending a scan of this document.

2. Robbie Ethridge, *Creek Country: The Creek Indians and Their World* (Chapel Hill: University of North Carolina Press, 2003), 61–62, 75, 152.

3. For works on this period, see James H. Merrell, "Declarations of Independence: Indian-White Relations in the New Nation," in *The American Revolution: Its Character and Limits*, ed. Jack P. Greene (New York: New York University Press, 1987), 197–223; Reginald Horsman, "The Indian Policy of an 'Empire for Liberty,'" in *Native Americans and the Early Republic*, ed. Frederick E. Hoxie, Ronald Hoffman, and Peter J. Albert (Charlottesville: University Press of Virginia, 1999), 37–61; Stuart Banner, *How the Indians Lost Their Land: Law and Power on the Frontier* (Cambridge, MA: Belknap Press of Harvard University Press, 2005), esp. chaps. 4 and 5; Kathleen DuVal, "Independence for Whom?: Expansion and Conflict in the South and Southwest," in *The World of the Revolutionary American Republic: Land, Labor, and the Conflict for a Continent*, ed. Andrew Shankman (New York: Routledge, 2014), 97–115; Alyssa Mt. Pleasant, "Independence for Whom?: Expansion and Conflict in the Northeast and Northwest," *The World of the Revolutionary American Republic*, 116–33.

4. Collin G. Calloway, *The American Revolution in Indian Country: Crisis and Diversity in North American Communities* (Cambridge, UK: Cambridge University Press, 1995),

153 (for migrations); "Substance of Captain Brant's Wishes respecting forming a Settlement of Mohawk & others of the Six Nation Indians upon the Grand River &ca.," n.d., f. 67, Add. MS 21829, BL ("about Six Miles"); Alan Taylor, *The Divided Ground: Indians, Settlers, and the Northern Borderland of the American Revolution* (New York: Vintage, 2006), 119–20 (for Iroquois locations), 122–23 (for Brant and Grand River), 160 (for Stanwix).

5. Allan Maclean to Frederick Haldimand, Niagara, 19 July 1783, f. 197, Add. MS 21763, BL ("Continue to Victuall"); Allan Maclean to Ephraim Douglass, Niagara, 16 July 1783, folder 27, box 23, PSP (for Niagara rations); Daniel Claus to Frederick Haldimand, Montreal, 19 January 1784, f. 348, Add. MS 21774, BL (for Montreal Mohawks).

6. "Substance of Captain Brant's Wishes respecting forming a Settlement of Mohawk & others of the Six Nation Indians upon the Grand River &ca.," n.d., f. 67, Add. MS 21829, BL ("assist them"); Copy of a letter from P. Langan to Lt. Governor Hamilton, Montreal, 18 November 1784, f. 633, Add. MS 21735, BL ("Commissioners from" and "report the same"); Taylor, *The Divided Ground*, 124 (for rent in provisions).

7. Allan Maclean to Frederick Haldimand, Niagara, 1 August 1783, ff. 214–15, Add. MS 21763, BL.

8. 12 October 1784, f. 30, Indian Treaties, 1778–1795, AWP. NB: Unlike most of the Wayne Papers, this volume consists of different sections of unlabeled documents with more than one set of folio numbers, which are sometimes placed at the top of the page and sometimes at the bottom. For ease of reference, the folio numbers cited here refer to the numbers at the bottom pages of the volume. All other citations to Wayne Papers volumes refer to folio numbers at the top right of the volume.

9. 20 October 1784, f. 37, Indian Treaties, 1778–1795, AWP ("You are" and "You have"); 15 January 1785, f. 49, Indian Treaties, 1778–1795, AWP ("we claim").

10. Bradford Perkins, *The Creation of a Republican Empire, 1776–1865*, vol. 1, *The Cambridge History of American Foreign Relations*, ed. Warren I. Cohen (Cambridge, UK: Cambridge University Press, 1993), 55 (for the Department of Foreign Affairs), 74 (for the Secretary of State); Max Edling, *A Revolution in Favor of Government: Origins of the U.S. Constitution and the Making of the American State* (New York: Oxford University Press, 2008), 83 (for domestic taxes), 129–206 (for economic and military considerations under the Articles). See also Horsman, "The Indian Policy of an 'Empire for Liberty,'" 38.

11. *The Collected Works of Benjamin Hawkins, 1796–1810*, ed. Thomas Foster II (Tuscaloosa: University of Alabama Press, 2003), 7–8 (for Congress's appointments).

12. See for example George Handley to William Few and Abraham Baldwin, 26 April 1788, Governor's Letter Book, 20 October 1786–31 May 1789, 167–68, Transcripts, GDAH.

13. Taylor, *The Divided Ground*, 153, 155, 159, 246–47. See also Kathy D. Matson and Peter S. Onuf, *A Union of Interests: Political and Economic Thought in Revolutionary America* (Lawrence: University Press of Kansas, 1990), 2, 4.

14. Taylor, *The Divided Ground*, 163, 165 (quote). For northern crop failures and the Hessian fly, see Alan Taylor, "'The Hungry Year': 1789 on the Northern Border of Revolutionary America," in *Dreadful Visitations: Confronting Natural Catastrophe in the Age of Enlightenment*, ed. Alessa Johns (New York: Routledge, 1999), 145–81, esp. 145–47. For crop failures among Creeks and Cherokees, see [James Seagrove] to the Kings & Chiefs of the Cussetas & Cowettas with all other Chiefs of the Creek Nation, St. Mary's in Georgia, 6 October 1791, 221, and James Seagrove to [Henry Knox], Rock Landing

on Oconee, 5 July 1792, 172, reel 1, Correspondence of the War Department Relating to Indian Affairs, Military Pensions, and Fortifications, 1791–1799, film 455, DLAR.

15. For food aid from New York, see Taylor, *The Divided Ground*, 198. On the fly's diet, see Kathy L. Flanders, Dominic D. Reisig, G. David Buntin, Matthew Winslow, D. Ames Herbert Jr., and Douglas W. Johnson, "Biology and Management of Hessian Fly in the Southeast," *Entomology at the University of Kentucky*, January 2013, accessed February 16, 2017, https://entomology.ca.uky.edu/files/efpdf1/ef155.pdf. I am grateful to Kathy Flanders for confirming via email on February 27, 2017, that Hessian flies will not attack corn.

16. Christopher Densmore, *Red Jacket: Iroquois Diplomat and Orator* (Syracuse, NY: Syracuse University Press, 1999), xv, 23.

17. Mt. Pleasant, "Independence for Whom?," 120–21 (for the murders); Taylor, *The Divided Ground*, 236 (for Pennsylvania); [Journal of Timothy Pickering], 30 October 1790, f. 43, reel 61, TPP ("provisions prepared"); Horatio Jones to Timothy Pickering, [Geneseo], 24 October 1790, f. 50, reel 61, TPP ("hang[ing] some," "Antiant customs," "a little Staff," and "walking staff"). Pickering called him "Tishkaaga . . . usually called Seneca Billy." Granville Ganter calls him Gissehhacke, or Little Billy. *The Collected Speeches of Sagoyewatha, or Red Jacket*, ed. Granville Ganter (Syracuse, NY: Syracuse University Press, 2006), 1–3. For the kettles, see Daniel K. Richter, *Trade, Land, Power: The Struggle for Eastern North America* (Philadelphia: University of Pennsylvania Press, 2013), 59. For the walking staff, see Timothy Pickering to Captain William Ross, Tioga Point, 30 October 1790, f. 58a, reel 61, TPP.

18. [Journal of Timothy Pickering], 30 October 1790, f. 44, reel 61, TPP.

19. Bezaleel Seely to Timothy Pickering, Chemung, 28 September 1790, f. 30, reel 61, TPP (for Seely's message); [Journal of Timothy Pickering], 9 November 1790, f. 47, reel 61, TPP (for the rumors and Pickering's change of strategy).

20. [Journal of Timothy Pickering], 15 November 1790, f. 64, reel 61, TPP (quotes); Sarah M. S. Pearsall, "Recentering Indian Women in the American Revolution," in *Why You Can't Teach United States History without American Indians*, ed. Susan Sleeper-Smith, Juliana Barr, Jean M. O'Brien, Nancy Shoemaker, and Scott Manning Stevens (Chapel Hill: University of North Carolina Press, 2015), 57–70, esp. 60 (for Johnson). See also Jane T. Merritt, "Metaphor, Meaning, and Misunderstanding: Language and Power on the Pennsylvania Frontier," in *Contact Points: American Frontiers from the Mohawk Valley to the Mississippi, 1750–1830*, ed. Andrew R. L. Cayton and Fredrika J. Teute (Chapel Hill: University of North Carolina Press, 1998), 77; Claudio Saunt, "'Domestick . . . Quiet being broke': Gender Conflict among Creek Indians in the Eighteenth Century," in *Contact Points*, 151–74; Theda Perdue, *Cherokee Women: Gender and Culture Change, 1700–1835* (Lincoln: University of Nebraska Press, 1998).

21. Timothy Pickering to George Washington, 4 December 1790, Wilkes barre, [Pennsylvania], in *Founders Online*, accessed April 5, 2015, http://founders.archives.gov/documents/Washington/05-07-02-0014 (quote). For their numbers, see Timothy Pickering to George Washington, 23 December 1790, Philadelphia, in *Founders Online*, accessed April 5, 2015, http://founders.archives.gov/documents/Washington/05-07-02-0065. For the cost, see "Enclosure: Estimate of the expense of necessaries for the meeting of the Seneca Indians at Tioga," 25 October 1790, *Founders Online*, accessed April 5, 2015, http://founders.archives.gov/documents/Washington/05-06-02-0191-0002.

22. "Questions relative to the proposed Indian Treaty and Hendrick's Answers," 24 February 1793, f. 55, reel 59, TPP (for Aupaumut's information); Benjamin Rush, "Questions to be asked of the Indians by Col. Pickering," Philadelphia, 2 May 1791, ff. 184–86a, reel 61, TPP ("tying their," "Spikenard," "often," and "excretions"); [Journal of Timothy Pickering], 9 November 1790, f. 47, reel 61, TPP ("two or three"). On Aupaumut, see also Alan Taylor, "Captain Hendrick Aupaumut: The Dilemmas of an Intercultural Broker," *Ethnohistory* 43, no. 3 (Summer 1996): 431–57.

23. Richard Winn to Henry Knox, Winnsborough, 25 June 1788, sec. F, vol. 3, box 3, Henry Knox Papers II, 1736–1803, Ms. N-198, MHS. See also Richard Winn to General Knox, Winnsborough, 25 June 1788, *American State Papers*, Class II, Indian Affairs, ed. Walter Lowrie and Matthew St. Clair Clarke, vol. 1 (Washington, DC: Gales and Seaton, 1832), 26.

24. [Journal of Timothy Pickering], 21 June 1791, ff. 73–74, reel 60, TPP ("to hang"); "Letter sent from Timothy Pickering by the Oneida Runners to the Senecas, &c.," 21 June 1791, f. 74, reel 60, TPP ("be exceedingly," "the lowness," "the goods and provisions," "beef & corn," and "walking Staff"); [Journal of Timothy Pickering], 25 June 1791, ff. 74–74a, reel 60, TPP ("that the business").

25. [Journal of Timothy Pickering], 25 June 1791 (for Pickering's payment), 14 July 1791 (for Red Jacket's critique), ff. 74–74a, 106, reel 60, TPP.

26. [Journal of Timothy Pickering], 17 July 1791, f. 111a (for Iroquois numbers), f. 112 ("one barrel" and "hanging on"), and 10 August 1791, f. 117 ("the great expences"), reel 60, TPP.

27. [Journal of Timothy Pickering], 17 July 1791, f. 111a, reel 60, TPP (quote). For additional food exchanges see Timothy Pickering to the Secretary of War, Kanandaigua, 15 October 1794, f. 204, reel 60, TPP. For the Senecas' visit, see Daniel K. Richter, "Onas, the Long Knife: Pennsylvania and the Indians, 1783–1794," *Native Americans and the Early Republic*, 144. For the larger Iroquois delegation, see Densmore, *Red Jacket*, 36–37.

28. [Samuel Elbert?] to William Houstoun, John Habersham, and Abraham Baldwin, Savannah, 9 June 1785, 34, Force Transcripts, Georgia Records, Council Correspondence 1782–1789 & Governors Correspondence, GDAH ("boundary line"); [Anonymous] to Elijah Clarke, Savannah, 9 June 1785, 33, Force Transcripts, Georgia Records, Council Correspondence 1782–1789 & Governors Correspondence, GDAH (other quotes).

29. William Blount to John Steele, Greenville, 11 January 1789, folder 4, John Steele Papers, 1716–1846, Collection 00689, Series 1.2, SHC ("the only," "such as," and "a better"); John Steele to Alexander Martin, Salisbury, 19 February 1789, folder 4, John Steele Papers, 1716–1846, Collection 00689, Series 1.2, SHC ("absolutely forbidden").

30. George Handley to John Sevier, n.p., 19 February 1788, 139, Governor's Letter Book, 20 October 1786–31 May 1789, Transcripts, GDAH (quote). For these state campaigns, see George Mathews to Jared Irwin, n.p., 28 November 1795, 46, Governor's Letter Book of George Walton, Governor, 10 August 1795–17 January 1796, and James Jackson, Governor, 24 January 1798–3 January 1799, GDAH. For the Intercourse Act, see Banner, *How the Indians Lost their Land*, 135.

31. Anthony Bledsoe to Richard Caswell, Nashville, 12 May 1786, folder "Governor Richard Caswell (2nd Administration), Correspondence, January 14–December 21, 1786," box 3, Governor's Papers, Series 2, NCSA; Anthony Bledsoe to John Sevier, Sum-

ner County, 5 August 1787, 158, Creek Indian Letters Talks and Treaties, Part 1, GDAH. See also Thomas Evans to Richard Caswell, Nashville, 25 November 1787, Governor's Papers, Series 2, folder "Governor Richard Caswell (2nd Administration), Correspondence, January 7–November 25, 1787," NCSA. For additional reports of violence, see Brigadier General Clark to [George Walton], Washington, 29 May 1789, folder 4, John Steele Papers, 1716–1846, Collection 00689, Series 1.2, SHC; James Seagrove to [Henry Knox], St. Mary's, 14 June 1792, 160, reel 1, Correspondence of the War Department Relating to Indian Affairs, Military Pensions, and Fortifications, 1791–1799, film 455, DLAR. For Seagrove's letter, see James Seagrove to [Henry Knox], Rock Landing on Oconee, 5 July 1792, 172, reel 1, Correspondence of the War Department Relating to Indian Affairs, Military Pensions, and Fortifications, 1791–1799, film 455, DLAR. For reports about Cherokees, see Joseph Blackwell to George Mathews, Woffort Fort, 7 June 1794, 15, Cherokee Indian Letters, Talks and Treaties, 1786–1838, Transcripts, GDAH. For Seagrove's relocation see [Henry Knox] to James Seagrove, n.p., 31 August 1792, 95, reel 1, Correspondence of the War Department Relating to Indian Affairs, Military Pensions, and Fortifications, 1791–1799, film 455, DLAR.

32. Benjamin Hawkins, Andrew Pickens, and Jos. Martin to John Hancock, Hopewell, 4 January 1786, *American State Papers*, Class II, Indian Affairs, ed. Walter Lowrie and Matthew St. Clair Clarke, vol. 1 (Washington, DC: Gales and Seaton, 1832), 49–50 (quote, 50).

33. [James Seagrove] to the "Kings & Chiefs of the Cussetas & Cowettas with all other Chiefs of the Creek Nation, St. Mary's in Georgia," 6 October 1791, 221, reel 1, Correspondence of the War Department Relating to Indian Affairs, Military Pensions, and Fortifications, 1791–1799, film 455, DLAR.

34. Extract of a letter from James Seagrove to [Henry Knox], Rock Landing on the Oconee, 27 July 1792, 204, reel 1, Correspondence of the War Department Relating to Indian Affairs, Military Pensions, and Fortifications, 1791–1799, film 455, DLAR.

35. George Washington, [communication to the senate], 25 June 1795, *American State Papers*, Class II, Indian Affairs, ed. Walter Lowrie and Matthew St. Clair Clarke, vol. 1 (Washington: Gales and Seaton, 1832), 560 (for Seagrove's invitation and the names of other federal officials); "A talk from James Seagrove to the Creek Chiefs, submitted to Governor Irwin," folder "Ca. 1796," box 1807, Governor—Executive Dept.—Governor's Subject Files—1781–1802, GDAH (quote). See also "A talk from James Seagrove to the Kings, Chiefs, Headmen & Warriors of the Upper and Lower Creeks, Simanolias, and all other Tribes living in the Creek Land," [9 April 1796], 472, Creek Indian Letters Talks and Treaties, 1705–1839, Part 2, Transcripts, GDAH. For the Yazoo Sale, see Joel W. Martin, *Sacred Revolt: The Muskogees' Struggle for a New World* (Boston: Beacon Press, 1991), 91; Angela Pulley Hudson, *Creek Paths and Federal Roads: Indians, Settlers, and Slaves and the Making of the American South* (Chapel Hill: University of North Carolina Press, 2010), 28, 46.

36. James Hendricks to Jared Irwin, Savannah, 18 May 1796, f. 20, Georgia Commission to Attend a Treaty with the Creek Indians journal, 1796, MS 280, GHS (for seven thousand attendees); 7 June 1796, f. 54, Georgia Commission to Attend a Treaty with the Creek Indians journal, 1796, MS 280, GHS (for accounts of what Indians ate); James Hendricks to Jared Irwin, Savannah, 18 May 1796, f. 21, Georgia Commission to Attend a Treaty with the Creek Indians journal, 1796, MS 280, GHS (for Georgia's

contractor); James McHenry to Governor Jared Irwin, War Office, 3 March 1796, PC 39, Pickens Papers, HL (for treaty costs paid by Georgia). Georgia commissioners recorded, "Twenty two Kings, seventy five principal Chiefs, and 150 Warriors present," spread out among twenty different towns, but a return by James Seagrove reveals that the Georgia commissioners did not include the 126 young men, 31 women, and 29 children also present. See 17 June 1796, f. 64, Georgia Commission to Attend a Treaty with the Creek Indians journal, 1796, MS 280, GHS; James Seagrove, "A Return of Creek Indians at Colerain," 14 June 1796, EA 517, Papers of William Eaton, 1792–1829, EA 1–555, FAC 385–, HL. Note that the folio numbers of the manuscripts in the GHS disappear toward the end of this volume; I have cited those that I have.

37. James Hendricks to the Commissioners of the United States, Coleraine, 31 May 1796, f. 37, Georgia Commission to Attend a Treaty with the Creek Indians journal, 1796, MS 280, GHS (for the denunciation); Benjamin Hawkins and George Clymer to [James Hendricks, James Jackson, and James Simms], 26 May 1796, f. 39, Georgia Commission to Attend a Treaty with the Creek Indians journal, 1796, MS 280, GHS (for other regulations); James Hendricks to the Commissioners of the United States, Coleraine, 31 May 1796, f. 37, Georgia Commission to Attend a Treaty with the Creek Indians journal, 1796, MS 280, GHS ("under the actual"); Benjamin Hawkins, George Clymer, and Andrew Pickens to the Commissioners of the State of Georgia, Coleraine, 1 June 1796, f. 40, Georgia Commission to Attend a Treaty with the Creek Indians journal, 1796, MS 280, GHS (for Hawkins's response).

38. 18 June 1796, f. 72, Georgia Commission to Attend a Treaty with the Creek Indians journal, 1796, MS 280, GHS (for the proofreading); 28 June 1796, Georgia Commission to Attend a Treaty with the Creek Indians journal, 1796, MS 280, GHS ("where the Commissioners"). The only portion of the talk that the federal commissioners rejected outright was Georgia's definition of *slaves*, which Hawkins tried to define more narrowly.

39. For slaves, cattle, hogs, and horses, see James Hendricks, James Jackson, and James Simms to Jared Irwin, Louisville, 24 April 1796, ff. 3–4; James Hendricks to Jared Irwin, Savannah, 18 May 1796, f. 20; James Hendricks to Jared Irwin, Savannah, 24 May 1796, f. 31, all in Georgia Commission to Attend a Treaty with the Creek Indians journal, 1796, MS 280, GHS. For the speech, see 18 June 1796, f. 77, Georgia Commission to Attend a Treaty with the Creek Indians journal, 1796, MS 280, GHS.

40. Ethridge, *Creek Country*, 102 (*tcoko-thlako*), 104 (for square etiquette); 18 June 1796, f. 81, Georgia Commission to Attend a Treaty with the Creek Indians journal, 1796, MS 280, GHS ("not one").

41. [James Hendricks, James Jackson, and James Simms] to Jared Irwin, 22 June 1796, f. 89, Georgia Commission to Attend a Treaty with the Creek Indians journal, 1796, MS 280, GHS (quotes). See also Claudio Saunt, *A New Order of Things: Property, Power, and the Transformation of the Creek Indians, 1733–1816* (Cambridge, UK: Cambridge University Press, 1999), 80–81.

42. [James Hendricks, James Jackson, and James Simms] to Jared Irwin, 22 June 1796, f. 93, Georgia Commission to Attend a Treaty with the Creek Indians journal, 1796, MS 280, GHS.

43. 24 and 25 June 1796, Georgia Commission to Attend a Treaty with the Creek Indians journal, 1796, MS 280, GHS.

44. For the budget, see William Earl Weeks, *Dimensions of the Early American Empire, 1754–1865*, vol. I of *The New Cambridge History of American Foreign Relations*, ed. Warren I. Cohen (Cambridge, UK: Cambridge University Press, 2013), 56.

45. For representative works on this period, see Gregory Evans Dowd, *A Spirited Resistance: The North American Indian Struggle for Unity, 1745–1815* (Baltimore: Johns Hopkins University Press, 1992), chap. 5; Colin G. Calloway, *The Shawnees and the War for America* (New York: Viking, 2007); Calloway, *The American Revolution in Indian Country*, 160; Harvey Lewis Carter, *The Life and Times of Little Turtle: First Sagamore of the Wabash* (Urbana: University of Illinois Press, 1987); Sami Lakomäki, *Gathering Together: The Shawnee People through Diaspora and Nationhood, 1600–1870* (New Haven, CT: Yale University Press, 2014), 102–31. For Shawnee-Miami relationships, see Laura Keenan Spero, "'Stout, Bold, Cunning, and the greatest Travellers in America': The Colonial Shawnee Diaspora" (PhD diss., University of Pennsylvania, 2010), 288. For Creeks, Delawares, and Shawnees, see Martin, *Sacred Revolt*, 50, 116; Hudson, *Creek Paths and Federal Roads*, 21. For Chickamaugas, see Dowd, *A Spirited Resistance*, xviii, 52, 91, 93. For Gnadenhütten, see John Sugden, *Blue Jacket: Warrior of the Shawnees* (Lincoln: University of Nebraska Press, 2000), 52; Calloway, *The Shawnees and the War for America*, 72. For Bird, Elliott, McKee, and Girty, see Elizabeth Mancke, *The Fault Lines of Empire: Political Differentiation in Massachusetts and Nova Scotia, ca. 1760–1830* (New York: Routledge, 2005), 26; John Clarke, *Land, Power, and Economics on the Frontier of Upper Canada* (Montreal: McGill-Queen's University Press, 2001), 58, 60, 93–154. For rumors of the confederacy, see William Grayson, Richard Henry Lee, and Edward Carrington to [Edmund Randolph], New York, 22 July 1787, box 6, Robert Alonzo Brock Collection, mssBR, HL. For the triumvirate, see Calloway, *The Shawnees and the War for America*, 86–87.

46. 26 January 1786, f. 80, Indian Talks and Treaties, 1778–1795, AWP (quote). For the treaties, see Calloway, *The Shawnees and the War for America*, 78, 80, 83, 89; Sugden, *Blue Jacket*, 84. For Chillicothe, see Calloway, *The American Revolution in Indian Country*, xiii, 39, 55, 164–70.

47. For preemptive burning, see Jean François Hamtramck to Josiah Harmar, Fort Knox, 28 November 1790, vol. 13, Josiah Harmar Papers, CL; Sugden, *Blue Jacket*, 100; Calloway, *The Shawnees and the War for America*, 90. For warriors' hunting, see Carter, *The Life and Times of Little Turtle*, 105, 125; Sugden, *Blue Jacket*, 162, 164.

48. Richard White, *The Middle Ground: Indians, Empires, and Republics in the Great Lakes Region, 1650–1815* (New York: Cambridge University Press, 2011), 454 (for stuffed mouths); William Blount to [Henry Knox], 11 September 1792, f. 311, reel 1, Correspondence of the War Department Relating to Indian Affairs, Military Pensions, and Fortifications, 1791–1799, film 455, DLAR (quote); [Henry Knox] to [Charles Pinckney], 27 October 1792, ff. 104–5, reel 1, Correspondence of the War Department Relating to Indian Affairs, Military Pensions, and Fortifications, 1791–1799, film 455, DLAR (for Upper Creeks); Dowd, *A Spirited Resistance*, 105–6 (for the 1792 meeting).

49. John C. Kotruch, "The Battle of Fallen Timbers: An Assertion of U.S. Sovereignty in the Atlantic World along the Banks of the Maumee River," in *Between Sovereignty and Anarchy: The Politics of Violence in the American Revolutionary Era*, ed. Patrick Griffin, Robert G. Ingram, Peter S. Onuf, and Brian Schoen (Charlottesville: University of Virginia Press, 2015), 270.

50. James Wilkinson to Messrs Elliot & Williams, Contractors, Camp on Deer Creek, 18 November 1793, f. 118, vol. XXX, AWP ("I am here"); Carter, *The Life and Times of Little Turtle*, 128 (for stockpiling); Copy of a Contract for supplying the Western Posts with provisions for the year 1792 made and concluded in Philadelphia, 24 September 1791, f. 195, Indian Treaties, 1778–1795, AWP ("losses sustained").

51. William Wells, Deposition to Anthony Wayne, Hobsons Choice, 16 September 1793, f. 46, vol. XXIX, AWP; Major Strong to [James Wilkinson], Fort Jefferson, 25 June 1792, f. 60, vol. XX, AWP (for the hay); Anthony Wayne to Henry Knox, Camp SW Branch of Miami, Six Miles advanced of Fort Jefferson, 23 October 1793, f. 35, vol. XXX, AWP (for the corn and "the Savages"). On Wells see also Carter, *The Life and Times of Little Turtle*, 121.

52. Henry Knox to Anthony Wayne, War Department, 2 March 1793, f. 57, vol. XXV, AWP; Henry Knox to Anthony Wayne, War Department, 2 February 1793, f. 121, vol. XXIV, AWP (for the commissioners); Henry Knox to Benjamin Lincoln, 9 [March] 1792, f. 24, reel 10, Benjamin Lincoln Papers, P-40, MHS (for the commissioners and treaty location); White, *The Middle Ground*, 461 (for background); Anthony Wayne to Brigadier General James Wilkinson, Head Quarters, Legion Ville, 19 February 1793, f. 47, vol. XXV, AWP (for plans to supply provisions); Sebastian Bairman to [Timothy Pickering], New York, 27 April 1793, f. 89, reel 59, TPP (for articles provided); Estimate of the Supplies for the Commissioners and their attendants, on the proposed treaty with the Indians at Sandusky, [1793], and Estimate for the Supplies of the Commissioners & their Attendants On the intended Treaty with the Indians at Sandusky, ff. 276–78, reel 59 (for costs); Timothy Pickering to Sebastian Bairman, Philadelphia, 23 March 1793, f. 137a, reel 60, TPP (for requests for specific articles).

53. William Hull to [Alexander Hamilton], Niagara, 6 February 1793, ff. 47–48, reel 59, TPP (quote). On Simcoe see Larry L. Nelson, *A Man of Distinction Among Them: Alexander McKee and the Ohio Country Frontier, 1754–1799* (Kent, OH: The Kent State University Press, 1999), 149; Taylor, *The Divided Ground*, 279. On the Confederacy at McKee's see Calloway, *The Shawnees and the War for America*, 99; Carter, *The Life and Times of Little Turtle*, 120; Reginald Horsman, *Matthew Elliott, British Indian Agent* (Detroit: Wayne State University Press, 1964), 77.

54. Memo. of Instructions given to Captain Hendrick by Colonel Pickering, Niagara, 4 June 1793, f. 146, reel 60, TPP ("a large" and "hunt on"); 16 August 1793, At the Mouth of the Detroit River, ff. 173–173a, reel 60, TPP (for the Shawnees' answer); Extracts from the Journal of the Commissioners of the United States, appointed to hold a Treaty at Sandusky, with the western Indians, in the year 1793, f. 260, Indian Treaties, 1778–1795, AWP (for the Shawnees' suggestions). For the commissioners' response see Nelson, *A Man of Distinction among Them*, 143, 156, 164–66; Horsman, *Matthew Elliott, British Indian Agent*, 83, 88; Sugden, *Blue Jacket*, 498; Carter, *The Life and Times of Little Turtle*, 60, 418, 420.

55. [Captain Hendrick's narrative of his journey in July, August, September, and October 1791], f. 8a, reel 59, TPP ("three years"); [Diary of Thomas Proctor], to Henry Knox, 12 May 1791, *American State Papers*, Class II, Indian Affairs, ed. Walter Lowrie and Matthew St. Clair Clarke, vol. 1 (Washington: Gales and Seaton, 1832), 159 ("great quantities"); Horsman, *Matthew Elliott, British Indian Agent*, 70 (for Elliott's boat), 93; Memorandum of John Heckewelder for the information of the Commissioners, River

La Frenchée, 17 to 23 June 1793, f. 186, reel 59, TPP; Horsman, *Matthew Elliott, British Indian Agent*, 79; Sugden, *Blue Jacket*, 146 (for provisions at McKee's storehouse).

56. Anthony Wayne to Henry Knox, Hobson's Choice near Fort Washington, 2 July 1793, f. 87, vol. XXVII, AWP (for June 1); John Heckewelder, Memorandum, for the information of the Commissioners, River La Frenchée, from 17 June to 23 June 1793, f. 184, reel 59, TPP (quote).

57. Nicholas Rosencrantz to Anthony Wayne, Fort Franklin, 23 September 1793, f. 71, vol. XXIX, AWP ("ordered three" and "sais we shall"); Benjamin Lincoln, Beverly Randolph, and Timothy Pickering to Anthony Wayne, Fort Erie, 23 August 1793, f. 96, vol. XXVIII, AWP; Henry Knox to Anthony Wayne, War Department, 3 September 1793, f. 120, vol. XXVIII, AWP ("be adequate").

58. Anthony Wayne to Henry Knox, Head Quarters, Greene Ville, 25 January 1794, f. 62, vol. XXXII, AWP ("put a period"); Anthony Wayne, Speech to the Six Nations, Greene Ville, 26 March 1794, f. 81, vol. XXXIII, AWP ("some Angry," and "eat or drank").

59. Anthony Wayne, Speech to the Six Nations, Greene Ville, 26 March 1794, f. 81, vol. XXXIII, AWP ("in consequence," "this mode," and "is Cowardly"); Anthony Wayne to Nicholas Rosencrantz, Head Quarters, Greene Ville, 26 March 1794, f. 82, vol. XXXIII, AWP ("cool"); Proceedings of a council holden at Buffaloe Creek, 9 February 1794, enclosed in Israel Chapin to Henry Knox, Canadaraqua, 25 February 1794, f. 13, vol. XXXIII, AWP ("in such"); Sugden, *Blue Jacket*, 157 (for Brant's faction); Anthony Wayne to Henry Knox, Head Quarters, Greene Ville, 14 December 1794, box 9, Anthony Wayne Papers, CL.

60. For Buchanan's Station see Dowd, *A Spirited Resistance*, 96, 110. For Fort Recovery see "The Examination of a Potawatime Woman who was in the Attack upon Fort Recovery, & taken prisoner by Mr. Wells," 23 July 1794, f. 101, vol. XXVI, AWP. Initial accounts of the Indians' numbers ranged from 500 to 2,000 men. For 500, see Alexander Gibson to Anthony Wayne, Fort Recovery, 30 June 1794, f. 52, vol. XXVI. For 1,000 and 1,500 see Anthony Wayne to Messrs Elliot & Williams, Head Quarters, Greene Ville, 4 July 1794, f. 68. For 2,000 see Extract of a letter from Anthony Wayne to Henry Knox, Head Quarters, Greene Ville, 7 July 1794, f. 77, vol. XXVI, AWP.

61. Calloway, *The Shawnees and the War for America*, 102 (for the Ottawas); Alexander Gibson to Anthony Wayne, Fort Recovery, 30 June 1794, f. 52, vol. XXVI, AWP (for horses and cattle); Alexander Gibson to [Anthony Wayne?], Fort Recovery, 5 July 1794, f. 72, vol. XXVI, AWP ("killed & eat"); Calloway, *The Shawnees and the War for America*, 102–3 (for Ottawas, Ojibwas, Potawatomis, and Little Turtle); Examination of a Shawanoe Prisoner taken by Cap. Wells, 12 August 1794, f. 4, vol. XXXVII, AWP (for the Confederacy's numbers in August).

62. Anthony Wayne to Henry Knox, Head Quarters, Grand Glaize, 28 August 1798, f. 15, vol. XXXVII, AWP ("cover'd with" and "It is with"); John Caldwell to Charles Scott, n.p., 1 September 1794, f. 31, vol. XXXVII, AWP ("to pieces" and "destroyed all"); Anthony Wayne to Henry Knox, Head Quarters, Grand Glaize, 28 August 1794, f. 15, vol. XXXVII, AWP ("waste the villages"). See also Carter, *The Life and Times of Little Turtle*, 135, 137; Dowd, *A Spirited Resistance*, 113.

63. General Orders, Head Quarters, Banks of the Miami, 23 August 1794, f. 10, vol. XXXVII, AWP ("produce a conviction"). For assertions about Indians' faith in the British, see Calloway, *The Shawnees and the War for America*, 104; Weeks, *Dimensions of the Early American Empire, 1754–1865*, 57.

64. Narrative of Lassell, 16 October 1794, f. 92, vol. XXXVII, AWP ("well & regularly"); Thomas Hunt to Anthony Wayne, Fort Defiance, 9 June 1795, f. 57, vol. XLI, AWP ("large Feasts"). See also Sugden, *Blue Jacket*, 181; Nelson, *A Man of Distinction among Them*, 172–73; Andrew R. L. Cayton, "'Noble Actors' upon 'the Theatre of Honour': Power and Civility in the Treaty of Greenville," in *Contact Points*, 238; Patrick Griffin, *American Leviathan: Empire, Nation, and Revolutionary Frontier* (New York: Hill and Wang, 2007), 250.

65. Kotruch, "The Battle of Fallen Timbers," 275 (for geopolitics after Fallen Timbers); Cayton, "'Noble Actors' upon 'the Theatre of Honour,'" 238; Griffin, *American Leviathan*, 250 (for Jay's Treaty); Snyder, "Native Nations in the Age of Revolutions," *The World of the Revolutionary American Republic: Land, Labor, and the Conflict for a Continent*, 89 (for the Treaty of San Lorenzo); "Proceedings of a council held at Fort Knox by Capt. Pasteur with the Potawatomis," Fort Knox, 19 April 1795, f. 58, vol. XL, AWP ("something to eat"); Thomas Hunt to Anthony Wayne, Fort Defiance, 9 May 1795, f. 104, vol. XL, AWP (for the Delawares' request); John Hamtramck to Anthony Wayne, Fort Defiance, 7 May 1795, f. 98, vol. XL, AWP ("Bring his Nation" and "Supply them").

66. For the treaty grounds, see Griffin, *American Leviathan*, 248–49; Cayton, "'Noble Actors' upon 'the Theatre of Honour,'" 255. For the boundary, see Sugden, *Blue Jacket*, 205.

67. "Minutes of a treaty with the tribes of Indians called the Wyandots, Delawares, Shawanoes, Ottawas, Chipewas, Putawatimes, Miamis, Eel River, Kickapoos, Piankashaws, and Kaskaskias; begun at greene Ville on the 16th day of June, and ending on the 10th day of August 1795," 16 June 1795, f. 262, Indian Talks and Treaties, 1778–1795, AWP ("a little drink"); "Minutes of a treaty . . . ," 30 June 1795, f. 265, Indian Talks and Treaties, 1778–1795, AWP ("We expect," "You have told," and "would like").

68. "Minutes of a treaty . . . ," 30 June 1795, f. 266, Indian Talks and Treaties, 1778–1795, AWP.

69. "Minutes of a treaty . . . ," 30 June 1795, f. 266, Indian Talks and Treaties, 1778–1795, AWP ("alone complains," "to consult," "really [did] not," "are for the Comfort," "shall most," "with pleasure," and "with your Chiefs"); "Minutes of a treaty . . . ," 23 July 1795, ff. 284–85, Indian Talks and Treaties, 1778–1795, AWP ("my plate" and "to see").

70. "Minutes of a treaty . . . ," 29 July 1795, f. 294, Indian Talks and Treaties, 1778–1795, AWP (quote); White, *The Middle Ground*, 494 (for poison).

71. Snyder, "Native Nations in the Age of Revolutions," 89 (for Nickajack and Running Water); Anthony Wayne to the "Cherokees, now settled on the Head Waters of Sciota," 3 August 1795, f. 314, Indian Treaties, 1778–1795, AWP (for Wayne and the Cherokees); Anthony Wayne to Margaretta Atlee, Head Quarters, 12 September 1795, f. 112, vol. XLII, AWP (for Wayne's Christmas dinner).

72. Benjamin Hawkins to [George Washington], Senate Chamber, 10 February 1792, folder 9, Hawkins Family Papers, Collection 00322, Series 1.1, SHC (quotes).

6. Learning from Food Laws in Nova Scotia

1. St. George Tucker, Journal of the Siege of Yorktown and Surrender of Cornwallis, 4 October 1781, 1781, PH 02 31, JDR; 1 October 1781, St. George Tucker, Journal of the Siege of Yorktown and Surrender of Cornwallis, 1781, PH 02 31, JDR (quote);

John Ferling, *Almost a Miracle: The American Victory in the War of Independence* (New York: Oxford University Press, 2007), 508 (for provisions shortages), 538 (for smallpox).

2. For dogs and limbs, see Cassandra Pybus, *Epic Journeys of Freedom: Runaway Slaves of the American Revolution and their Global Quest for Liberty* (Boston: Beacon Press, 2006), 51, 53. For King, see Boston King, "Memoirs of the Life of Boston King, a Black Preacher. Written by Himself, during his Residence at Kingswood-School" (London, 1798), in *Unchained Voices: An Anthology of Black Authors in the English-Speaking World of the Eighteenth Century*, ed. Vincent Carretta (Lexington: University Press of Kentucky, 1996), 351–68, esp. 356. For an excellent exploration of the help King received in penning his narrative, see Ryan Hanley, *Beyond Slavery and Abolition: Black British Writing, c. 1770–1830* (Cambridge, UK: Cambridge University Press, 2019), chap. 5, esp. 142. For George, see David George, "An Account of the Life of Mr. David George, from Sierra Leone in Africa; given by himself in a Conversation with Brother Rippon of London, and Brother Pearce of Birmingham" (London, 1793–1797), in *Unchained Voices*, 333–50 (see 332n21 for Rippon as editor). For standard works on black colonists in Nova Scotia, see Robin W. Winks, *The Blacks in Canada: A History* (New Haven, CT: Yale University Press, 1971); James W. St. G. Walker, *The Black Loyalists: The Search for a Promised Land in Nova Scotia and Sierra Leone 1783–1870* (New York: Africana Publishing Company, 1976); Ellen Gibson Wilson, *The Loyal Blacks* (New York: Capricorn Books, 1976); Wilson, *John Clarkson and the African Adventure* (London: Macmillan Press, 1980); Neil MacKinnon, *This Unfriendly Soil: The Loyalist Experience in Nova Scotia 1783–1791* (Kingston, ON: McGill-Queen's University Press, 1986); Mary Louise Clifford, *From Slavery to Freetown: Black Loyalists after the American Revolution* (Jefferson, NC: McFarland and Company, 1999); W. Bryan Rommel-Ruiz, "Colonizing the Black Atlantic: The African Colonization Movements in Postwar Rhode Island and Nova Scotia," *Slavery and Abolition* 27, no. 3 (December 2006): 349–65.

3. [Anonymous], [untitled], n.d., ff. 84, 86–87, CO 5/8, part I, TNA (quotes); Maya Jasanoff, *Liberty's Exiles: American Loyalists in the Revolutionary World* (New York: Alfred A. Knopf, 2011), 88–91; Winks, *The Blacks in Canada*, 31–32; James Sidbury, *Becoming African in America: Race and Nation in the Early Black Atlantic* (New York: Oxford University Press, 2007), 81; Henry Wiencek, *An American God: George Washington, His Slaves, and the Creation of America* (New York: Farrar, Straus, and Giroux, 2003), 256–58.

4. Maya Jasanoff, "The Other Side of the Revolution: Loyalists in the British Empire," *William and Mary Quarterly* 65, no. 2 (April 2008): 205–32, esp. 208, 220–22; Elizabeth Mancke, *The Fault Lines of Empire: Political Differentiation in Massachusetts and Nova Scotia, ca. 1760–1830* (New York: Routledge, 2005), 35.

5. Alexandra L. Montgomery, "The River Belongs Exclusively to the Passamaquoddy Tribe: Borderlands, Borderseas, and the Creation of an International Boundary Line," draft essay (for Mi'kmaqs); Michael Francklin to General Sir Henry Clinton, Halifax, Nova Scotia, 2 August 1779, vol. 21, no. 102, photostat 2158, box 9, BHQP (quote); Kathleen DuVal, *Independence Lost: Lives on the Edge of the American Revolution* (New York: Random House, 2015), 66–67 (for Acadians).

6. "Recapitulation of the number of Negroes who have availed themselves of the Late Commanders in Chiefs Proclamations by comming in within the British Lines in North America . . . ," photostat 10427, f. 257, box 43, BHQP; "Book of Negroes Registered & certified after having been Inspected by the Commissioners appointed by

His Excellency Sr: Guy Carleton K.B. General & Commander in Chief, on Board Sundry Vessels in which they were Embarked Previous to the time of sailing from the Port of New York between the 23d April and 31st July 1783 both Days Included," photostat 10427, f. 47, box 43, BHQP; King, "Memoirs of the Life of Boston King," 367n21.

7. Winks, *The Blacks in Canada*, 33 (for the 165 people); "Recapitulation of the number of Negroes . . . ," photostat 10427, f. 257, box 43, BHQP (for the population breakdown); Wilson, *The Loyal Blacks*, 69 (for their places of origin).

8. Joseph Pynchon to Gentlemen, Halifax, Nova Scotia, 23 January 1783, Minutes of the Proceedings of the Port Roseway Associates, 1782, ff. 61, 64, Shelburne historical records collection, reel H-984, MG 9 B9-14, LAC. This microfilm reel only sometimes contains page numbers. I have attempted to cite them when they were legible and seemed consistent with the overall numbering style. The numbering in the Court Records is very irregular.

9. For Liverpool, see Mancke, *The Fault Lines of Empire*, 16–17; for "servants," see Winks, *The Blacks in Canada*, 37–38; Walker, *The Black Loyalists*, 40; Jasanoff, "The Other Side of the Revolution," 220n21. For shipboard provisions, see Minutes of the Proceedings of the Port Roseway Associates, 8 March 1783, f. 83, Shelburne historical records collection, LAC. For six months of provisions, see Report, 20 March 1783, f. 89, Minutes of the Proceedings of the Port Roseway Associates, Shelburne historical records collection, LAC. For "that each member," see Minutes of the Proceedings of the Port Roseway Associates, 8 March 1783, f. 81, Shelburne historical records collection, LAC.

10. On Parr, see Wilson, *The Loyal Blacks*, 71.

11. Captain Durfee's Report, New York, 26 [?] March 1783, Minutes of the Proceedings of the Port Roseway Associates, f. 94, Shelburne historical records collection, LAC (quotes). For Durfee, see Mary Archibald, "Joseph Durfee: Shelburne Pioneer," in *Eleven Exiles: Accounts of Loyalists of the American Revolution*, ed. Phyllis R. Blakeley and John N. Grant (Toronto: Dundurn Press Limited, 1982), 13. For the absence of provisions for black colonists upon arrival, see Winks, *The Blacks in Canada*, 35–36; MacKinnon, *This Unfriendly Soil*, 50.

12. Captain Durfee's Report, New York, 26 March 1783, Minutes of the Proceedings of the Port Roseway Associates, f. 94, Shelburne historical records collection, LAC. Durfee reproduced Carleton's quotes.

13. Historians disagree about Shelburne population numbers; some books estimate eighty-six hundred, others ten thousand, and others sixteen thousand. They agree that by 1784, Shelburne ranked as the fourth-largest English-speaking city within North America, and the biggest in British North America. Winks, *The Blacks in Canada*, 36–38; Walker, *The Black Loyalists*, 22, 28; MacKinnon, *This Unfriendly Soil*; John N. Grant, ". . . those in General called Loyalists," Archibald, "Joseph Durfee: Shelburne Pioneer," and Blakely, "Boston King: A Black Loyalist," *Eleven Exiles*, 15, 108, 276; Laird Niven and Stephen A. Davis, "Birchtown: The History and Material Culture of an Expatriate African American Community," in *Moving On: Black Loyalists in the Afro-Atlantic World*, ed. John W. Pulis (New York: Garland, 1999), 60.

14. George, "An Account of the Life of Mr. David George," 336; Muster Book of Free Black Settlement at Birchtown, ff. 132–33 (Roberts), 136–37 (Laurence), 138–39 (Wilkinson), 144–45 (Cooper and Darling), 148–49 (Donaldson and Freeman), 150–51 (Williams), 156–57 (Jarrat), 164–65 (Davis), 168–69 (Fortune), 170–71 (Daniel), Shelburne historical records collection, LAC.

15. Muster Book of Free Black Settlement at Birchtown, ff. 120–21 (Brown), 128–29 (Post), 130–31 (Thomas), 132–33 (Kane), 136–37 (Virginia), 148–49 (Jones), 156–57 (Taylor), 158–59 (Glass), 162–63 (Rivers), 173–74 (George), Shelburne historical records collection, LAC.

16. For Quebec, see Jasanoff, "The Other Side of the Revolution," 214. For potatoes, see Walker, *The Black Loyalists*, 43, 46. My analysis of this food system has been influenced by Robert Olwell, *Masters, Slaves, and Subjects: The Culture of Power in the South Carolina Low Country, 1740–1790* (Ithaca, NY: Cornell University Press, 1998), esp. 178–79, 219; Dylan C. Penningroth, *The Claims of Kinfolk: African American Property and Community in the Nineteenth-Century South* (Chapel Hill: University of North Carolina Press, 2003), chap. 2, esp. 46–49.

17. Daniel H. Usner Jr., *Indians, Settlers, and Slaves in a Frontier Exchange Economy: The Lower Mississippi Valley before 1783* (Chapel Hill: University of North Carolina Press, 1992), 197 (for Mississippi), 215 (for New Orleans); David Shields, *Southern Provisions: The Creation and Revival of a Cuisine* (Chicago: University of Chicago Press, 2015), 178 (for Savannah).

18. John Wentworth to the Duke of Portland, Halifax, Nova Scotia, 24 May 1800, f. 203, CO 217/73, TNA ("Several markets," "Butchers and Fishmongers," "for want," "shops and stands," and "hawk[ed] their meat"); John Wentworth to the Duke of Portland, Halifax, Nova Scotia, 5 May 1799, f. 31, CO 217/70, TNA ("contributed"); Alexander Howe to W. D. Quarrell, Maroon Hall, 9 August 1797, f. 173, CO 217/68, TNA ("great profit"); Walker, *The Black Loyalists*, 43, 46 (for the price of potatoes). For the types of fish available in Shelburne, see Stephen Kimber, *Loyalists and Layabouts: The Rapid Rise and Faster Fall of Shelburne, Nova Scotia: 1783–1792* (Toronto: Doubleday Canada, 2008), 163.

19. For Marston, see Blakely, "Boston King: A Black Loyalist," *Eleven Exiles*, 273–74. For land issues in Nova Scotia, see Christopher Fyfe, *A History of Sierra Leone* (London: Oxford University Press, 1962), 34–47; Walker, *The Black Loyalists*, 18; Winks, *The Blacks in Canada*, 35–9; MacKinnon, *This Unfriendly Soil*, 50; Pybus, *Epic Journeys of Freedom*, 148; Blakely, "Boston King: A Black Loyalist," 276. For economies of time and land, see Penningroth, *The Claims of Kinfolk*, 47.

20. "A Sketch of Shelburnian Manners, Anno 1787," f. 213, Shelburne historical records collection, LAC (quote). The authorship of this piece is uncertain but is usually ascribed to Scotsman James Fraser, district judge of New Brunswick in 1788. See *A Few Acres of Snow: Documents in Pre-Confederation Canadian History*, 3rd ed., ed. Thomas Thorner and Thor Frohn-Nielsen (North York, ON: University of Toronto Press, 2009), 81. For comparisons between provisions for white and black colonists, see Walker, *The Black Loyalists*, 44–45.

21. Clifford, *From Slavery to Freetown*, 48 (for government rations), 62 (for Digby); Winks, *The Blacks in Canada*, 37 (for distance); Wilson, *The Loyal Blacks*, 87 (for distribution).

22. E. P. Thompson, "The Moral Economy of the English Crowd in the Eighteenth Century," *Past and Present* 50, no. 1 (February 1971): 76–136. John Bohstedt argues that Thompson's model was one focused on how governments managed the economy, rather than on a whole economic system of production, extraction, trade, distribution, and services. Bohstedt's newer model, the "politics of provisions," is concerned with the "political practices and contexts that afforded crowds a rioter's franchise." I use "moral economy" here because this chapter is less concerned with food riots. John

Bohstedt, *The Politics of Provisions: Food Riots, Moral Economy, and Market Transition in England, c. 1550–1850* (Surrey, UK: Ashgate Publishing, 2010), 8–9 (quote, 9).

23. J. Davis, "Baking for the Common Good: A Reassessment of the Assize of Bread in Medieval England," *Economic History Review* 57 (2004): 465–502 (for the medieval period); Andy Wood, *Riot, Rebellion and Popular Politics in Early Modern England* (Hampshire, UK: Palgrave Macmillan, 2002), 97 (for the *Book of Orders*); Cynthia A. Bouton, *The Flour War: Gender, Class, and Community in Late Ancien Régime French Society* (University Park: Pennsylvania State University Press, 1993), 10 (for France); Bohstedt, *The Politics of Provisions*, 1, 261 (for riotous Englishmen); Kathy D. Matson and Peter S. Onuf, *A Union of Interests: Political and Economic Thought in Revolutionary America* (Lawrence: University Press of Kansas, 1990), 4, 38 (for North America).

24. For the late eighteenth-century example of Newfoundland, for instance, see Peter E. Pope, *Fish into Wine: The Newfoundland Plantation in the Seventeenth Century* (Chapel Hill: University of North Carolina Press, 2004), 429–30. On county courts, see Mancke, *The Fault Lines of Empire*, 27, 139, 149. On Durfee's role, see Archibald, "Joseph Durfee: Shelburne Pioneer," *Eleven Exiles*, 109.

25. For court records, I have provided a date and volume number—several volumes appear on each microfilm reel. Court Records, 17 February 1785, 7 July 1785, vol. 6, Shelburne historical records collection, LAC.

26. Court Records, 12 May 1785, vol. 6, Shelburne historical records collection, LAC; Court Records, 18 March 1800, vol. 6, Shelburne historical records collection, LAC.

27. King, "Memoirs of the Life of Boston King," 360; Court Records, 10 April 1786, vol. 6, Shelburne historical records collection, LAC.

28. For fish lots in Liverpool, see Mancke, *The Fault Lines of Empire*, 49. For black Loyalists' remembrances of land restrictions, see Cassandra Pybus, "Henry 'Harry' Washington (1750s–1790s): A Founding Father's Slave," in *The Human Tradition in the Atlantic World, 1500–1850*, ed. Karen Racine and Beatriz G. Mamigonian (Lanham, MD: Rowman and Littlefield, 2010), 110. David George was one of the few black Loyalists who was awarded land by the water, but he used it for baptisms. George, "An Account of the Life of Mr. David George," 337.

29. Wilson, *The Loyal Blacks*, 104; Sidbury, *Becoming African in America*, 83; Niven and Davis, "Birchtown: The History and Material Culture of an Expatriate African American Community," 59–84, esp. 63–64, 72.

30. Winks, *The Blacks in Canada*, 39 (for the stop in provisioning); Mancke, *The Fault Lines of Empire*, 17 (for Liverpool); "Memorial of Robert Ross, Samuel Campbell, and Alexander Robertson, to Governor Parr," n.d., f. 307, Shelburne historical records collection, LAC (quote).

31. Mancke, *The Fault Lines of Empire*, 17; "A petition from the Overseers of the poor to the magistrates of Shelburne for the relief of Negroes," 3 February 1789, ff. 209–10, Shelburne historical records collection, LAC (quote).

32. Although Nova Scotia earned this nickname in the late 1780s, Americans were calling it by that name on the eve of Loyalist departure from the colonies. For this early nickname, see Wilson, *The Loyal Blacks*, 71. For other uses of the term, see Walker, *The Black Loyalists*, 52; John N. Grant, "John Howe, Senior: Printer, Publisher, Postmaster, Spy," *Eleven Exiles*, 25. For overseers of the poor, see Simon P. Newman, *A New World of Labor: The Development of Plantation Slavery in the British Atlantic* (Philadelphia: University of Pennsylvania Press, 2013), 243.

33. For Senegambia, see Paul E. Lovejoy, "Forgotten Colony in Africa: The British Province of Senegambia (1765–83)," in *Slavery, Abolition and the Transition to Colonialism in Sierra Leone*, ed. Paul E. Lovejoy and Suzanne Schwarz (Trenton, NJ: Africa World Press, 2015), 109–25. For Bulama, see Deirdre Coleman, *Romantic Colonization and British Anti-Slavery* (Cambridge, UK: Cambridge University Press, 2005), 88. For Granville Town, see Sidbury, *Becoming African in America*, 53. For the Black Poor, see George E. Brooks, *Eurafricans in Western Africa: Commerce, Social Status, Gender, and Religious Observance from the Sixteenth to the Eighteen Century* (Athens: Ohio University Press, 2003), 306.

34. Quotes are from John Clarkson's notebook that he kept upon arrival in Halifax, which is mostly undated and unnumbered. "Remarks Halifax," ff. 1 (for Coffee and Jones), 8 (other quotes), Add. MS 41262B, BL. See also John Clarkson to William Dawes, Freetown, 5 October 1792, "Diary of Lieutenant J. Clarkson, R.N. (governor, 1792)" (Freetown, Sierra Leone), *Sierra Leone Studies*, no. VIII (March 1927): 34.

35. George, "An Account of the Life of Mr. David George," 337 (for Parr), 338 (quote).

36. King, "Memoirs of the Life of Boston King," 360.

37. King, "Memoirs of the Life of Boston King," 360.

38. George, "An Account of the Life of Mr. David George," 339.

39. King, "Memoirs of the Life of Boston King," 363.

40. [Memorial of Thomas Peters], enclosed in [Unknown] to Governor Parr, Whitehall, 6 August 1791, f. 80, CO 217/72, TNA (quote). See also Petition of Thomas Peters, 1791, enclosed in John Clarkson to William Wilberforce, [c. after August 18, 1815], f. 156, Add. MS 41263, BL. On Peters, see Wilson, *The Loyal Blacks*, 178; Winks, *The Blacks in Canada*, 63; Wilson, *John Clarkson and the African Adventure*, 54, 93–94, 97; Jasanoff, *Liberty's Exiles*, 282; Pybus, *Epic Journeys of Freedom*, 23; Clifford, *From Slavery to Freetown*, 61; Fyfe, *A History of Sierra Leone*, 32. On similar patron-client relationships during the Revolution itself, see Alexander X. Byrd, *Captives and Voyagers: Black Migrants across the Eighteenth-Century British Atlantic World* (Baton Rouge: Louisiana State University Press, 2008), 177–78.

41. [Various inhabitants of Birch Town, Shelburne] to John Parr, n.p., 1 November 1791, f. 86, CO 217/72, TNA (quote). On Blucke, see Wilson, *John Clarkson and the African Adventure*, 66, 85, 87. For other leaders, see Winks, *The Blacks in Canada*, 35–40, 60, 78. For religion, see Mancke, *The Fault Lines of Empire*, 61. For free rations, see Fyfe, *A History of Sierra Leone*, 34; Wilson, *John Clarkson and the African Adventure*, 66.

42. Contrary to the company's plans for Sierra Leone (which Clarkson probably did not know about), Clarkson promised the colonists that they would owe no quitrents on their lands in Sierra Leone. This promise made migration much more enticing. A quitrent was a single monetary payment collected annually. It traditionally allowed English peasants to avoid paying their landlords in labor or produce. Usually it was low, but in the American colonies colonial administrators struggled to successfully collect it. In Nova Scotia no quitrents had been collected since 1772. The black Loyalists would avoid paying it in Nova Scotia, and in Sierra Leone, the Sierra Leone Company would refuse to honor Clarkson's promise. Wilson, *The Loyal Blacks*, 73–74.

43. Sometimes Edmonds is written as "Edmons" in the archives. Thomas Peters and David Edmons, "In behalf of the Black People of at Halifax bound to Sierra Leone," Halifax, 23 December 1791, f. 24, Add. MS 41262A, BL.

44. James Vernon, *Hunger: A Modern History* (Cambridge, MA: Harvard University Press, 2007), 12.

45. P. J. Marshall, *The Making and Unmaking of Empires: Britain, India, and America c. 1750–1783* (Oxford, UK: Oxford University Press, 2005), 148.

46. [Journal of Timothy Pickering], 5 July 1791, f. 86, reel 60, TPP.

47. For race, see Nancy Shoemaker, "How Indians Got to be Red," *American Historical Review* 102, no. 3 (1997): 625–44; Jane T. Merritt, *At the Crossroads: Indians and Empires on a Mid-Atlantic Frontier, 1700–1763* (Chapel Hill, NC: University of North Carolina Press, 2003), 254; Nancy Shoemaker, *A Strange Likeness: Becoming Red and White in Eighteenth-Century North America* (New York: Oxford University Press, 2004), 130.

7. Victual Imperialism and U.S. Indian Policy

1. [Journal of Timothy Pickering], 5 July 1791, ff. 84a, 85 (quote), reel 60, TPP. On Pickering, see George H. Clarfield, *Timothy Pickering and the American Republic* (Pittsburgh, PA: University of Pittsburgh Press, 1980), esp. chap. 9. Various scholars have discussed the Plan of Civilization. James Merrell dates the plan's inception to 1790, and Theda Purdue to the 1791 Treaty of Holston with the Cherokees. Daniel Richter has discussed some of the plan's implications among Indians and Quakers in 1795, and Claudio Saunt has focused on the period from 1797 to 1811. Paul Gilje interprets the emphasis on civilization as a shift in U.S. Indian affairs from commerce to conquest. James H. Merrell, "Second Thoughts on Colonial Historians and American Indians," *William and Mary Quarterly* 69, no. 3 (July 2012): 451–512, esp. 471; Theda Perdue, *Cherokee Women: Gender and Culture Change, 1700–1835* (Lincoln: University of Nebraska Press, 1998), 110–11; Daniel K. Richter, "'Believing That Many of the Red People Suffer Much for the Want of Food': Hunting, Agriculture, and a Quaker Construction of Indianness in the Early Republic," *Journal of the Early Republic* 19, no. 4 (Winter 1999): 601–28; Claudio Saunt, *A New Order of Things: Property, Power, and the Transformation of the Creek Indians, 1733–1816* (Cambridge, UK: Cambridge University Press, 1999), 139–232; Paul A. Gilje, "Commerce and Conquest in Early American Foreign Relations, 1750–1850," *Journal of the Early Republic* 37, no. 4 (Winter 2017): 735–70, esp. 737. See also Gregory Evans Dowd, *A Spirited Resistance: The North American Indian Struggle for Unity, 1745–1815* (Baltimore, MD: Johns Hopkins University Press, 1992), 114; Lori J. Daggar, "The Mission Complex: Economic Development, 'Civilization,' and Empire in the Early Republic," *Journal of the Early Republic* 36, no. 3 (Fall 2016): 467–91.

2. Dowd, *A Spirited Resistance*, 116.

3. For these contradictions about farming, see Richter, "'Believing That Many of the Red People Suffer Much for the Want of Food,'" 602–3, 611; Robbie Ethridge, *Creek Country: The Creek Indians and Their World* (Chapel Hill: University of North Carolina Press, 2003), 15; Stuart Banner, *How the Indians Lost Their Land: Law and Power on the Frontier* (Cambridge, MA: Belknap Press of Harvard University Press, 2005), 151–60; Merrell, "Second Thoughts," 469–73; Karim Tiro, "'We Wish to Do You Good': The Quaker Mission to the Oneida Nation, 1790–1840," *Journal of the Early Republic* 26, no. 3 (Fall 2006): 353–76, esp. 356. My use of *collaboration* recognizes that it is an enormously complicated idea. In some works, such as Robert Michael Morrissey's, collaboration is an intentional way of claiming power, and the cessation of collaboration is fairly lamentable. In other scholarship, *collaboration* is considered a dirty word. Given the his-

tory of warfare against Native Americans throughout the 1790s and the decreasing ability to bargain with imperial powers besides the United States, however, I am not convinced that Indians had other choices. This chapter employs the term to illustrate that it was an imperfect choice that many Indians were forced to make. For work on collaboration in Native American history, see Robert Michael Morrissey, *Empire by Collaboration: Indians, Colonists, and Governments in Colonial Illinois County* (Philadelphia: University of Pennsylvania Press, 2015), 10, 232. For comparative work on collaboration, see John Gallagher and Ronald Robinson, "The Imperialism of Free Trade," *Economic History Review* 6, no. 1 (1953): 1–15, esp. 10; Ronald Robinson, John Gallagher, and Alice Denny, *Africa and the Victorians: The Official Mind of Imperialism* (London: Macmillan and Company, 1961), 468; Paul Kramer, *The Blood of Government: Race, Empire, the United States, and the Philippines* (Chapel Hill: University of North Carolina Press, 2006), esp. 29. For a critique of collaboration as a form of analysis, see Jürgen Osterhammel, *Colonialism: A Theoretical Overview*, trans. Shelley L. Frisch (Princeton, NJ: Markus Wiener Publishers, 1997), 64.

4. The work on victual imperialism in this chapter has been informed by work on settler colonialism and food sovereignty. For food sovereignty, see Jennifer Cockrall-King, *Food and the City: Urban Agriculture and the New Food Revolution* (Amherst, NY: Prometheus Books, 2012), 319; Charlotte Coté, *Spirits of Our Whaling Ancestors: Revitalizing Makah and Nuu-chah-nulth Traditions* (Seattle: University of Washington Press, Capell Family Book Series, 2010), 204; John C. Super, *Food, Conquest, and Colonization in Sixteenth-Century Spanish America* (Albuquerque: University of New Mexico Press, 1988); Kristin L. Hoganson, *Consumers' Imperium: The Global Production of American Domesticity, 1865–1920* (Chapel Hill: University of North Carolina Press, 2007); Enrique C. Ochoa, *Feeding Mexico: The Political Uses of Food since 1910* (Wilmington, DE: Scholarly Resources, 2000). For settler colonialism, see the introduction to this book.

5. In 1753 Benjamin Franklin was one of the first to connect civilization to hunger, and he worried that the reduction of Native lands by treaties had begun to affect Indians' abilities to hunt game and feed themselves—but he also conveyed Indians' critiques of non-Native education programs, which produced educated Indians incapable of proper hunting techniques. Henry Knox wrote at the same time as Samuel Kirkland and Timothy Pickering (discussed below) in 1789, but he did not theorize hunger prevention extensively in his letters. For earlier commentaries on civilization and civilization initiatives, see "From Benjamin Franklin to Peter Collinson," 9 May 1753, *Founders Online*, accessed June 21, 2018, https://founders.archives.gov/documents/Franklin/01-04-02-0173; "Address from the Delaware Nation," [Princeton, N.J.], 10 May 1779, *Founders Online*, accessed June 21, 2018, https://founders.archives.gov/documents/Washington/03-20-02-0361; V: Lady Huntingdon's Plan for Settlement, 8 April 1784, *Founders Online*, accessed June 21, 2018, https://founders.archives.gov/documents/Washington/04-02-02-0161–0006; "From Henry Knox to George Washington," War Office, 7 July [1789], *Founders Online*, accessed June 21, 2018, https://founders.archives.gov/documents/Washington/05-03-02-0067. On antecedents to such civilization programs, see, for example, Nicholas P. Canny, "The Ideology of English Colonization: From Ireland to America," *William and Mary Quarterly* 30, no. 4 (October 1973): 575–98, esp. 586–92. On Kirkland, see Alan Taylor, *The Divided Ground: Indians, Settlers, and the Northern Borderland of the American Revolution* (New York: Vintage, 2006), 3.

6. *The Journals of Samuel Kirkland: 18th-Century Missionary to the Iroquois, Government Agent, Father of Hamilton College*, ed. Walter Pilkington (Clinton, NY: Hamilton College, 1980), 161 ("on account"), 164 (for dispersal), 167 (other quotes).

7. *The Journals of Samuel Kirkland*, 157 ("To make provision" and "The other kind"), 181 ("your wandering" and civility).

8. [Undated entry], ff. 39–41, Journal of Samuel Kirkland, "Missionary from the Society in Scotland & Corporation of Harvard College to the Oneidas & other tribes of the Six United nations of Indians from February 16 to May 30 1791," Society for Propagating the Gospel among the Indians and Others in North America Records, 1752–1948, Ms. N-176, MHS (quotes); *The Journals of Samuel Kirkland*, 189 (for women's education).

9. *The Journals of Samuel Kirkland*, 125 (for 1785), 158 (for 1789).

10. Taylor, *The Divided Ground*, 209, 212–13, 368 (for individual land speculators, Massachusetts, and New York), 242, 248 (for passing messages); *The Journals of Samuel Kirkland*, 193 (for the fire).

11. Timothy Pickering to [George Washington], n.p., 7 January 1791, f. 164, reel 61, TPP ("the means"); Timothy Pickering to Samuel Kirkland, Philadelphia, 4 December 1791, f. 304, reel 61, TPP (for their correspondence); "Cornplanter, half Town, and the Great Tree's speech to the President of the United States," Philadelphia, 10 January 1791, enclosed in Henry Knox to Timothy Pickering, Philadelphia, 2 May 1791, f. 25a, reel 60, TPP (for women); Timothy Pickering to [George Washington], n.p., 7 January 1791, f. 164, reel 61, TPP ("Indian youths," "to their own," and "mere Savages").

12. Timothy Pickering to [George Washington], n.p., 7 January 1791, ff. 164a–65, reel 61, TPP (quotes); "Estimate of the Expence in making Three Establishments for the purpose of introducing among the Six Nations the art of Civil Life," n.d., 135, reel 60, TPP (for the budget).

13. For maize, plows, soil, tobacco, and wheat, see Chris Evans, "The Plantation Hoe: The Rise and Fall of an Atlantic Commodity, 1650–1850," *William and Mary Quarterly* 69, no. 1 (January 2012): 71–100, esp. 93–94; Ethridge, *Creek Country*, 144; Virginia DeJohn Anderson, "Animals into the Wilderness: The Development of Livestock Husbandry in the Seventeenth-Century Chesapeake," *William and Mary Quarterly* 59, no. 2 (April 2002): 377–408, esp. 408; Stephen Nissenbaum, *Sex, Diet, and Debility in Jacksonian America: Sylvester Graham and Health Reform* (Westport, CT: Greenwood Press, 1980), 5–7; Stephen Mennell, *All Manners of Food: Eating and Taste in England and France from the Middle Ages to the Present* (Urbana: University of Illinois Press, 1995), 342; Adam D. Shprintzen, *The Vegetarian Crusade: The Rise of an American Reform Movement, 1817–1921* (Chapel Hill: University of North Carolina Press, 2013), 24. For landowning, see Steven Sarson, "Yeoman Farmers in a Planters' Republic: Socioeconomic Conditions and Relations in Early National Prince George's County, Maryland," *Journal of the Early Republic* 29, no. 1 (Spring 2009): 63–99, esp. 65, 69, 99. For Franklin, see Mark McWilliams, "Distant Tables: Food and the Novel in Early America," *Early American Literature* 38, no. 3 (2003): 365–93, esp. 372. For Rush, see Benjamin Rush to James Craik, n.p., 26 July 1798, in *Letters of Benjamin Rush*, ed. L. H. Butterfield, vol. II (Princeton, NJ: Published for the American Philosophical Society by Princeton University Press, 1951), 801; Sari Altschuler, *The Medical Imagination: Literature and Health in the Early United States* (Philadelphia: University of Pennsylvania Press, 2018), 27–35. For Barlow, see Joel Barlow, "The Hasty Pudding: A Poem, in Three Cantos," in *The*

Works of Joel Barlow, ed. Harry Warfel, vol. II (Gainesville, FL: Scholars' Facsimiles and Reprints, 1970), 87–101; William Earl Weeks, *Dimensions of the Early American Empire, 1754–1865*, vol. I, *The New Cambridge History of American Foreign Relations*, ed. Warren I. Cohen (Cambridge, UK: Cambridge University Press, 2013), 35.

14. Jane Mt. Pleasant, "The Paradox of Plows and Productivity: An Agronomic Comparison of Cereal Grain Production under Iroquois Hoe Culture and European Plow Culture in the Seventeenth and Eighteenth Centuries," *Agricultural History* 85, no. 4 (Fall 2011): 460–92, esp. 462; Erin Pawley, "The Point of Perfection: Cattle Portraiture, Bloodlines, and the Meaning of Breeding, 1760–1860," *Journal of the Early Republic* 36, no. 1 (Spring 2016): 37–72, esp. 50–51.

15. [Journal of Timothy Pickering], 5 July 1791, f. 84, reel 60, TPP (quotes); Clarfield, *Timothy Pickering and the American Republic*, 122 (for Knox and Washington).

16. For "submit wholly," see *The Journals of Samuel Kirkland*, 182. For "teach us," see "Cornplanter, half Town, and the Great Tree's speech to the President of the United States," Philadelphia, 10 January 1791; for "nine Seneka boys," see "Cornplanter, Half Town, and the Big tree to the Great Councilor of the Thirteen Fires," 7 February 1791— both are enclosed in Henry Knox to Timothy Pickering, Philadelphia, 2 May 1791, ff. 25, 29, reel 60, TPP. For "one or two," see [Henry Knox's] reply to Cornplanter's speech, 8 February 1791, enclosed in Henry Knox to Timothy Pickering, Philadelphia, 2 May 1791, ff. 30–31, reel 60, TPP. For "clothing, domestic animals," see "In Senate," 26 March 1792, f. 13, reel 62, TPP. For the annuity, see Timothy Pickering to James McHenry, Philadelphia, 10 March 1796, f. 68, reel 2, James McHenry Papers, 1775–1862, MSS32177, microfilm 19,006, LOC.

17. Kathryn E. Holland Braund, "The Creek Indians, Blacks, and Slavery," *Journal of Southern History* 57, no. 4 (November 1991): 601–36, esp. 623, 627 (for Creeks and the plan); Saunt, *A New Order of Things*, 80 (for previous treaties); "Treaty of New York," 7 August 1790, 224–32, Creek Indian Letters Talks and Treaties, Part 1, GDAH ("furnish gratuitously"); Timothy Pickering to [George Washington], n.p., 7 January 1791, f. 164, reel 61, TPP ("from hunters").

18. Saunt, *A New Order of Things*, chaps. 3–5 (for the rise of this "new order"); Ethridge, *Creek Country*, 161 (for pricing).

19. "Treaty of New York," 7 August 1790, 227, Creek Indian Letters Talks and Treaties, Part 1, GDAH (quote); Saunt, *A New Order of Things*, 46 (for the 1750s).

20. The Bloody Fellow, King Fisher, the Northward, the Disturber, the Prince, and George Miller are the men listed in the records.

21. [Henry Knox] to William Blount, n.p., 31 January 1792, ff. 2–3, reel 1, Correspondence of the War Department Relating to Indian Affairs, Military Pensions, and Fortifications, 1791–1799, DLAR (for Cherokees in 1792); Joseph Blackwell to George Mathews, Woffort Fort, 7 June 1794, 15, Cherokee Indian Letters, Talks and Treaties, 1786–1838, Transcripts, GDAH (for Cherokees in 1794); Dowd, *A Spirited Resistance*, 96 (for Dragging Canoe's death); Perdue, *Cherokee Women*, 111 (for the 1796 talk).

22. "Cornplanter's speech to the President of the United States," 1 December 1790, enclosed in Henry Knox to Timothy Pickering, Philadelphia, 2 May 1791, ff. 8 ("town-destroyer"), 15 ("The game," "intended," and "mean to"), reel 60, TPP. On Cornplanter, see Thomas Abler, *Cornplanter: Chief Warrior of the Allegany Seneca* (Syracuse, NY: Syracuse University Press, 2007), 1–2.

23. "President's reply to the Speech of the Cornplanter, Half Town and Great Tree, Chiefs and Counselors of the Seneca Nation of Indians," 29 December 1790, enclosed in Henry Knox to Timothy Pickering, Philadelphia, 2 May 1791, ff. 19–19a, reel 60, TPP.

24. "Cornplanter, half Town, and the Great Tree's speech to the President of the United States," Philadelphia, 10 January 1791, enclosed in Henry Knox to Timothy Pickering, Philadelphia, 2 May 1791, f. 23, reel 60, TPP (for Stanwix and Washington's refusal); Samuel Kirkland to Timothy Pickering, Oneida, 31 May 1792, ff. 45–46, reel 62, TPP ("cool reception" and "cared nothing"); Henry Knox to Timothy Pickering, Philadelphia, 2 May 1791, ff. 4–4a, reel 60, TPP ("attachment and fidelity"); Henry Knox to Anthony Wayne, War Department, 3 August 1792, Box 5, Anthony Wayne Papers, CL (for 1792). For background on the second Stanwix Treaty, see Colin G. Calloway, *The Shawnees and the War for America* (New York: Viking, 2007), 78. For Brant and Red Jacket, see Taylor, *The Divided Ground*, 247.

25. Hendrick Aupaumut, [Captain Hendrick's Narrative of his journey to the Niagara & Grand River, in February 1792], f. 19, reel 59, TPP (for Brant's comments); Richard White, *The Middle Ground: Indians, Empires, and Republics in the Great Lakes Region, 1650–1815* (New York: Cambridge University Press, 2011), 441 (for Brant and the Western Confederacy); Anthony Wayne to William Irvine, Pittsburgh, 20 July 1792, f. 88, vol. XX, AWP.

26. [George Washington], "talk sent to the headmen and warriors of the tribes of Indians of the Miami Towns and its neighborhood, and inhabiting the waters of the Miami River, of Lake Erie, and to the tribes inhabiting the waters of the River Wabash," 11 March 1791, enclosed in Henry Knox to Timothy Pickering, Philadelphia, 2 May 1791, f. 41, reel 60, TPP; Henry Knox to Alexander Freeman, War Department, 3 April 1792, f. 209, Indian Treaties, 1778–1795, AWP.

27. Hendrick Aupaumut, [Captain Hendrick's narrative of his journey in July, August, September, and October 1791], f. 8a, reel 59, TPP.

28. John C. Kotruch, "The Battle of Fallen Timbers: An Assertion of U.S. Sovereignty in the Atlantic World along the Banks of the Maumee River," in *Between Sovereignty and Anarchy: The Politics of Violence in the American Revolutionary Era*, ed. Patrick Griffin, Robert G. Ingram, Peter S. Onuf, and Brian Schoen (Charlottesville: University of Virginia Press, 2015), 275; Andrew R. L. Cayton, "'Noble Actors' upon 'the Theatre of Honour': Power and Civility in the Treaty of Greenville," in *Contact Points: American Frontiers from the Mohawk Valley to the Mississippi, 1750–1830*, ed. Andrew R. L. Cayton and Fredrika J. Teute (Chapel Hill: University of North Carolina Press, 1998), 238; Patrick Griffin, *American Leviathan: Empire, Nation, and Revolutionary Frontier* (New York: Hill and Wang, 2007), 250; Christina Snyder, "Native Nations in the Age of Revolutions," in *The World of the Revolutionary American Republic*, ed. Andrew Shankman (New York: Routledge, 2014), 89.

29. "Questions relative to the proposed Indian Treaty and Hendrick's Answers," 24 February 1793, f. 55, reel 59, TPP (quote); Ian Mosby, "Administering Colonial Science: Nutrition Research and Human Biomedical Experimentation in Aboriginal Communities and Residential Schools, 1942–1952," *Histoire sociale/Social History* 46, no. 91 (May 2013), 170 (for anemia).

30. Saunt, *A New Order of Things*, 67–89 (for McGillivray), 196 (for the Treaty of New York); [James Seagrove to Alexander McGillivray], St. Mary's, 8 October 1792, f.

227, reel 1, Correspondence of the War Department Relating to Indian Affairs, Military Pensions, and Fortifications, 1791–1799, DLAR (quote). On Cornplanter's fall from favor, see Henry Knox to Anthony Wayne, War Department, 9 March 1793, f. 74, vol. XXV, AWP; "To George Washington from Timothy Pickering," 14 November 1795, *Founders Online*, accessed June 21, 2018, https://founders.archives.gov/documents/Washington/05-19-02-0106.

31. On the publication of this work, see "Hawkins, Benjamin," *American National Biography Online*, accessed July 18, 2017, http://anb.org. For Hawkins and gender, see Claudio Saunt, "'Domestick . . . Quiet being broke': Gender Conflict among Creek Indians in the Eighteenth Century," *Contact Points*, 151–74, esp. 166. For his relationship with the Creeks, see Ethridge, *Creek Country*, 5.

32. Benjamin Hawkins, *A Sketch of the Creek Country in the Years 1798 and 1799*, in *The Collected Works of Benjamin Hawkins, 1796–1810*, ed. Thomas Foster (Tuscaloosa: University of Alabama Press, 2003), 56s.

33. Ethridge, *Creek Country*, 143.

34. Hawkins, *A Sketch of the Creek Country*, 56s.

35. Hawkins, *A Sketch of the Creek Country*, 60s (for quotes about Creeks); Benjamin Hawkins, *A Viatory or Journal of Distances and Observations*, in *The Collected Works of Benjamin Hawkins, 1796–1810*, 3j (for quotes about Cherokees). See also Perdue, *Cherokee Women*, 127.

36. Benjamin Hawkins to James McHenry, Coweta, 6 January 1797, *Letters of Benjamin Hawkins*, in *The Collected Works of Benjamin Hawkins, 1796–1810*, 57.

37. Hawkins, *A Sketch of the Creek Country*, 30s (for Toolk-au-bat-che Haujo), 36s ("Coo-sau-dee").

38. Hawkins, *A Sketch of the Creek Country*, 59s (quotes); Benjamin Hawkins to Edward Price, Fort Wilkinson, 6 January 1798, folder 10, 1795–1799, Hawkins Family Papers, Collection 00322, SHC (for corn and salt); Ethridge, *Creek Country*, 182 (for cabbages).

39. Hawkins, *A Sketch of the Creek Country*, 61s. A gross hundredweight of pork was priced at three dollars, and at net for four dollars. A hundredweight of net bacon was ten dollars; beef, three dollars. Corn was priced at a half dollar per bushel. See also Saunt, "'Domestick . . . Quiet being broke,'" 164.

40. Ethridge, *Creek Country*, 163 (for white traders); *Letters of Benjamin Hawkins, 1796–1806* (Savannah: Published by the Georgia Historical Society, 1916), 38 ("accustomed to," "the same," and "making no"). I have consulted several versions of the Hawkins letters. This citation is the only one that draws on the volume published by the Georgia Historical Society; all other citations in this chapter are to the volume edited by Foster. For the Creeks in 1799, see Hawkins, *A Sketch of the Creek Country*, 61s. For Baltimore, Boston, Charleston, New York, and Philadelphia in 1795 and 1800, see *History of Wages in the United States from Colonial Times to 1928*, U.S. Bureau of Labor Statistics Bulletin no. 604. Revision of Bulletin No. 499, with Supplement, 1929–1933 (Washington: United States Printing Office, 1934), 21. I have only made comparisons of foodstuffs when weight or bulk measurements were the same.

41. E. P. Thompson, "The Moral Economy of the English Crowd in the Eighteenth Century," *Past and Present* 50, no. 1 (February 1971): 76–136; Braund, "The Creek Indians, Blacks, and Slavery," 608–9.

42. "Questions relative to the proposed Indian Treaty and Hendrick's Answers," 24 February 1793, f. 54, reel 59, TPP; [Unlabeled journal], 24 April 1797, *Letters of Benjamin Hawkins*, 159.

43. Extract from a talk delivered by the Little Turtle to the President of the United States, 4 January 1802, in *American State Papers*, Class II, Indian Affairs, ed. Walter Lowrie and Matthew St. Clair Clarke, vol. 1 (Washington, DC: Gales and Seaton, 1832), 655; Benjamin Hawkins to James McHenry, Coweta, 6 January 1797, *Letters of Benjamin Hawkins*, 57 (for flax and cotton); Benjamin Hawkins to Henry Dearborn, Chickasaw Bluffs, 28 October 1801, *Letters of Benjamin Hawkins*, 393–94 (for Creeks in 1801).

44. Benjamin Hawkins to Edward Price, Flint River, 10 February 1797, *Letters of Benjamin Hawkins*, 77.

45. Timothy Pickering to James McHenry, Philadelphia, 10 March 1796, ff. 68–69, reel 2, James McHenry Papers, LOC (quotes). For changes at Niagara, see Taylor, *The Divided Ground*, 297, and for a source confirming that Indians were receiving considerably less than soldiers, see David Thompson, A Statement of Commissary at Fort Niagara, 1 October 1798, box 3, James McHenry Papers, CL.

46. Extract from James McHenry to Major General Hamilton, 21 May 1799, *American State Papers*, Class II, Indian Affairs, vol. 1, 645–46 ("great and unnecessary"); "Communicated to the House of Representatives," 5 May 1800, *American State Papers*, Class II, Indian Affairs, vol. 1, 644 ("the usual supply" and "know how much").

47. [Unlabeled journal], 15 July [1805], *Letters of Benjamin Hawkins*, 442 (quotes). On Tecumseh and Tenskwatawa, see Dowd, *A Spirited Resistance*, 33, 39. For the Red Sticks, see Saunt, *A New Order of Things*, 249–72. For this period, see Angela Pulley Hudson, *Creek Paths and Federal Roads: Indians, Settlers, and Slaves and the Making of the American South* (Chapel Hill: University of North Carolina Press, 2010), 87; Ethridge, *Creek Country*, 155.

48. Weeks, *Dimensions of the Early American Empire, 1754–1865*, 95 (for Creeks starving); M. Hardin to David B. Mitchell, Travelars Hotel, 20 August 1812, 760, Creek Indian Letters Talks and Treaties, 1705–1839, Part 2, GDAH (quotes); Calloway, *The Shawnees and the War for America*, 131 (for Tenskwatawa).

49. Benjamin Hawkins to General Armstrong, Creek Agency, 7 June 1814, *American State Papers*, Class II, Indian Affairs, vol. 1, 858. See also M. Hardin to David B. Mitchell, Travelars Hotel, 20 August 1812, 760, Creek Indian Letters Talks and Treaties, 1705–1839, Part 2, GDAH.

50. For 5,257, see Benjamin Hawkins to Major General Armstrong, Fort Hawkins, 13 July 1814, *American State Papers*, Class II, Indian Affairs, vol. 1, 860. For "plenty of food," see "Journal of the proceedings of the commissioners appointed to treat with the Northwest Indians at Detroit," Spring Wells, 25 August 1815, *American State Papers*, Class II, Indian Affairs, vol. 2, 18 (quote), 19. For withheld annuity payments, see Benjamin Hawkins to James Monroe, Creek Agency, 5 October 1814, *American State Papers*, Class II, Indian Affairs, vol. 1, 861. For Indian payments for provisions, see D. B. Mitchell to J. C. Calhoun [Secretary of War], Creek Agency, 28 January 1818, *American State Papers*, Class II, Indian Affairs, vol. 2, 153.

51. B[enjamin] F. Stickney to William H. Crawford [Secretary of War], Indian Agency Office, Fort Wayne, 1 October 1815, *American State Papers*, Class II, Indian Affairs, vol. 2, 86 (quotes). For more on Stickney, see "Statement showing the number

of Superintendents, Agents, Sub-Agents, Interpreters, and Blacksmiths, employed in the Indian Department, with their names, by whom appointed, and their respective compensations," *American State Papers*, Class II, Indian Affairs, vol. 2, 365; "To James Madison from William Bentley," 11 December 1809, *Founders Online*, accessed July 11, 2017, http://founders.archives.gov/?q=Benjamin%20F.%20Stickney&s=1111311111& sa&r=1&sr.

52. Richard Thomas, "Translations of Creek expressions used in the foregoing" [translated by Timothy Barnard, Cusseta, 24 November 1797], *Letters of Benjamin Hawkins*, 250 (for Blount); Ethridge, *Creek Country*, 13 (for federal landgrabs).

53. Christopher Densmore, *Red Jacket: Iroquois Diplomat and Orator* (Syracuse, NY: Syracuse University Press, 1999), 137–38.

54. For additional context on this speech, see Granville Ganter, "Red Jacket and the Decolonization of Republican Virtue," *American Indian Quarterly* 31, no. 4 (Fall 2007): 559–81, esp. 560.

55. Densmore echoes the assertion that the poison in Red Jacket's speech referred to alcohol. Densmore, *Red Jacket*, xiii.

8. Black Loyalist Hunger Prevention in Sierra Leone

1. For background on Anderson and Perkins, see Christopher Fyfe, *A History of Sierra Leone* (London: Oxford University Press, 1962); Robin W. Winks, *The Blacks in Canada: A History* (New Haven, CT: Yale University Press, 1971), 51; Cassandra Pybus, *Epic Journeys of Freedom: Runaway Slaves of the American Revolution and their Global Quest for Liberty* (Boston: Beacon Press, 2006), 23, 209, 215. For their London journey, see Ellen Gibson Wilson, *John Clarkson and the African Adventure* (London: Macmillan Press, 1980), 134.

2. "Cato Pirkins and Isaac Anderson to the Hble the Chairmain & Court of Directors of the Sierra Leone Company London" [sent to John Clarkson 30 October 1793], 13 October 1793, ff. 98–99, Add. MS 41263, BL; Isaac Anderson and Cato Perkins to John Clarkson, London, 9 November 1793, f. 105, Add. MS 41263, BL. Many of the manuscript letters that follow can be found in *"Our Children Free and Happy": Letters from Black Settlers in Africa in the 1790s*, ed. Christopher Fyfe (Edinburgh: Edinburgh University Press, 1991). Clarkson, who retained a copy of the petition, seems to have punctuated their complaints with underlining in much the same way that he underlined his own correspondence. I believe that the underlining in the letters is Clarkson's because the printed copies in Christopher Fyfe's edited volume make no indication of underlining. In keeping with common practices, I have silently edited all underlining into italics.

3. Standard works on black colonists in Sierra Leone focus on land problems, Freetown's place within the context of other colonization movements, and works on diaspora, migration, and the Revolutionary Atlantic. For the first, see Fyfe, *A History of Sierra Leone*; Winks, *The Blacks in Canada*; James W. St. G. Walker, *The Black Loyalists: The Search for a Promised Land in Nova Scotia and Sierra Leone 1783–1870* (New York: Africana Publishing Company, 1976); Ellen Gibson Wilson, *The Loyal Blacks* (New York: Capricorn Books, 1976); Wilson, *John Clarkson and the African Adventure*; Neil MacKinnon, *This Unfriendly Soil: The Loyalist Experience in Nova Scotia 1783–1791* (Kingston, ON: McGill-Queen's University Press, 1986); Mary Louise Clifford, *From Slavery to*

Freetown: Black Loyalists after the American Revolution (Jefferson, NC: McFarland and Company, 1999). For the second, see Deirdre Coleman, *Romantic Colonization and British Anti-Slavery* (Cambridge, UK: Cambridge University Press, 2005); W. Bryan Rommel-Ruiz, "Colonizing the Black Atlantic: The African Colonization Movements in Postwar Rhode Island and Nova Scotia," *Slavery and Abolition* 27, no. 3 (December 2006): 349–65; Emma Christopher, "A 'Disgrace to the very Colour': Perceptions of Blackness and Whiteness in the Founding of Sierra Leone and Botany Bay," *Journal of Colonialism and Colonial History* 9, no. 3 (Winter 2008), accessed January 28, 2016, http://muse.jhu.edu/journals/journal_of_colonialism_and_colonial _history/v009/9.3.christopher.html; Bronwen Everill, *Abolition and Empire in Sierra Leone and Liberia* (Basingstoke, UK: Palgrave Macmillan, 2013). For the third, see *Moving On: Black Loyalists in the Afro-Atlantic World*, ed. John W. Pulis (New York: Garland, 1999); Barry Cahill, "The Black Loyalist Myth in Atlantic Canada," *Acadiensis* XXIX, no. 1 (Autumn 1999), accessed December 31, 2015, http://journals.hil.unb.ca/index .php/acadiensis/article/view/10801/11587; Maya Jasanoff, *Liberty's Exiles: American Loyalists in the Revolutionary World* (New York: Alfred A. Knopf, 2011); Pybus, *Epic Journeys of Freedom*; James Sidbury, *Becoming African in America: Race and Nation in the Early Black Atlantic* (New York: Oxford University Press, 2007); Alexander X. Byrd, *Captives and Voyagers: Black Migrants across the Eighteenth-Century British Atlantic World* (Baton Rouge: Louisiana State University Press, 2008); Isaac Land and Andrew M. Schocket, ed., "Special Issue: New Approaches to the Founding of the Sierra Leone Colony, 1786–1808," *Journal of Colonialism and Colonial History* 9, no. 3 (Winter 2008), accessed January 28, 2016, http://muse.jhu.edu/journals/journal_of_colonialism _and_colonial_history/toc/cch.9.3.html; *Slavery, Abolition and the Transition to Colonialism in Sierra Leone*, ed. Paul E. Lovejoy and Suzanne Schwarz (Trenton, NJ: Africa World Press, 2015); Janet Polasky, *Revolutions without Borders: The Call to Liberty in the Atlantic World* (New Haven, CT: Yale University Press, 2015). Little work exists on food in the early years of the colony, and what does emphasizes the Sierra Leone Company's interest in cash crops for legitimate commerce, or white colonists' interactions with the Temne. For cash crops, see Coleman, *Romantic Colonization*, 132; Suzanne Schwarz, "From Company Administration to Crown Control: Experimentation and Adaptation in Sierra Leone in the Late Eighteenth and Early Nineteenth Centuries," *Slavery, Abolition and the Transition to Colonialism in Sierra Leone*, 173–74; Everill, *Abolition and Empire in Sierra Leone and Liberia*, 19. For white colonists' interactions with the Temne, see Rachel B. Herrmann, "'If the King had really been a father to us': Failed Food Diplomacy in Eighteenth-Century Sierra Leone," in *The Routledge History of Food*, ed. Carol Helstosky (New York: Routledge, 2014), 92–112. For food in Freetown between 1792 and 1803, see Philip R. Misevich, "On the Frontier of 'Freedom': Abolition and the Transformation of Atlantic Commerce in Southern Sierra Leone, 1790s to 1860s" (PhD thesis, Emory University, 2009); Misevich, "The Sierra Leone Hinterland and the Provisioning of Early Freetown, 1792–1803," *Journal of Colonialism and Colonial History* 9, no. 3 (Winter 2008), accessed January 28, 2016, https://muse.jhu .edu/article/255266; Rachel B. Herrmann, "Rebellion or Riot?: Black Loyalist Food Laws in Sierra Leone," *Slavery and Abolition* 37, no. 4 (2016): 680–703.

4. On terminology, see Barry Cahill, "The Black Loyalist Myth in Atlantic Canada," *Acadiensis* XXIX, no. 1 (Autumn 1999): para. 3, accessed December 31, 2015, http:// journals.hil.unb.ca/index.php/acadiensis/article/view/10801/11587.

5. George E. Brooks, *Eurafricans in Western Africa: Commerce, Social Status, Gender, and Religious Observance from the Sixteenth to the Eighteen Century* (Athens: Ohio University Press, 2003), 306; Mary Beth Norton, "The Fate of Some Black Loyalists of the American Revolution," *The Journal of Negro History* 58, no. 4 (October 1973): 402–46, esp. 407; Wilson, *John Clarkson and the African Adventure*, 53; Pybus, *Epic Journeys of Freedom*, 87, 103.

6. For "the flagrant abuses," see Olaudah Equiano, "The Interesting Narrative of the Life of Olaudah Equiano, or Gustavus Vassa, *The African*. Written By Himself" (London, 1794 [1789]), in *Unchained Voices: An Anthology of Black Authors in the English-Speaking World of the Eighteenth Century*, ed. Vincent Carretta (Lexington: University Press of Kentucky, 1996), 283–84 (quote); Norton, "The Fate of Some Black Loyalists of the American Revolution," 415; Wilson, *The Loyal Blacks*, 149. For more on Equiano, see Vincent Carretta, *Equiano, the African: Biography of a Self-Made Man* (New York: Penguin Books, 2005). For the voyage, see Byrd, *Captives and Voyagers*, 1. For King Tom, see Jasanoff, *Liberty's Exiles*, 304. Background on King Tom is contradictory. C. Magbaily Fyle states that King Tom was the subruler around the Rokel River estuary and observes that his son, Henry, studied in England. George Brooks and Christopher Fyfe say that this King Tom, known as Panabouré Forbana, died in 1788, and Cassandra Pybus suggests that it was King Naimbana's son Henry who studied in England. Fyle identifies King Tom as Pa Kokelly and says that by decision of the Bai Farma, the area's head ruler, Kokelly replaced King Jimmy in the mid-1790s. C. Magbaily Fyle, *Historical Dictionary of Sierra Leone* (Lanham, MD: Scarecrow Press, 2006), 210–11; Brooks, *Eurafricans in Western Africa*, 299; Fyfe, *A History of Sierra Leone*, 22; Cassandra Pybus, "'A Less Favourable Specimen': The Abolitionist Response to Self-Emancipated Slaves in Sierra Leone, 1793–1808," *Parliamentary History* 26, Issue Supplement S1 (June 2007): 97–112, esp. 99n12.

7. For disease, see Fyfe, *A History of Sierra Leone*, 34–47; Walker, *The Black Loyalists*, 20. For King Jimmy, see Fyfe, *A History of Sierra Leone*, 25; Sidbury, *Becoming African in America*, 53; Anna Maria Falconbridge, *Narrative of Two Voyages to the River Sierra Leone during the Years 1791–1792–1793*, ed. Christopher Fyfe (Liverpool: Liverpool University Press, 2000), 4.

8. Sidbury, *Becoming African in America*, 98 (for the renaming); Falconbridge, *Narrative of Two Voyages*, 16 ("to rise gradually"); David George, "An Account of the Life of Mr. David George, from Sierra Leone in Africa; given by himself in a Conversation with Brother Rippon of London, and Brother Pearce of Birmingham" (London, 1793–1797), in *Unchained Voices: An Anthology of Black Authors in the English-Speaking World of the Eighteenth Century*, ed. Vincent Carretta (Lexington: University Press of Kentucky, 1996), 340; "Memoirs of the Life of Boston King, a Black Preacher. Written by Himself, during his Residence at Kingswood-School" (London, 1798), *Unchained Voices*, 364.

9. Clifford, *From Slavery to Freetown*, 114 (for seasonal rains), 115 (for the burned house); Fyfe, *A History of Sierra Leone*, 20 (for animals); Wilson, *John Clarkson and the African Adventure*, 95 ("one of the wettest"); Journal of Zachary Macaulay, 18 August 1796, mssMY 418 (13), Macaulay Papers, HL ("an army").

10. Ismail Rashid, "Escape, Revolt, and Marronage in Eighteenth and Nineteenth Century Sierra Leone Hinterland," *Canadian Journal of African Studies/Revue Canadienne des Études Africaines* 34, no. 3 (2000): 656–83, esp. 662 (for the population), 663 (for the

jihad). For Fouta Djallon, see Bruce L. Mouser, "Landlords-Strangers: A Process of Accommodation and Assimilation," *International Journal of African Historical Studies* 8, no. 3 (1975): 425–40, esp. 428; Brooks, *Eurafricans in Western Africa*, xxiii, 200–1, 293; C. Magbaily Fyle, *The History of Sierra Leone: A Concise Introduction* (London: Evans, 1981), 27. For the Mande and Fula, see Brooks, *Eurafricans in Western Africa*, 249, 295; Fyle, *The History of Sierra Leone*, 31.

11. Fyfe, *A History of Sierra Leone*, 1–10, 16–19, 31, 47, 54; Kenneth C. Wylie, *The Political Kingdoms of the Temne: Temne Government in Sierra Leone, 1825–1910* (New York: Africana Publishing Company, 1977), xiii, xv, 3.

12. For British weakness in Africa generally, see Trevor Burnard, "The British Atlantic," in *Atlantic History: A Critical Appraisal*, ed. Jack P. Greene and Philip D. Morgan (New York: Oxford University Press, 2008), 122; Philip D. Morgan, "Africa and the Atlantic, c. 1450 to c. 1820," *Atlantic History*, 225. For the tea incident, see Rachel Herrmann, "Death by Chamomile?: The Alimentary End of Henry Granville Naimbana," *The Appendix: A New Journal of Narrative and Experimental History* 1, no. 1 (December 2012), accessed July 20, 2017, http://theappendix.net/issues/2012/12/death-by-chamomile-the-alimentary-end-of-henry-granville-naimbana. For Alexander Falconbridge's alcoholism, see Falconbridge, *Narrative of Two Voyages*, 1, 4, 74 ("never were worse"), 95.

13. For Clarkson's role, see Winks, *The Blacks in Canada*, 74–75; Wilson, *John Clarkson and the African Adventure*, 106, 113; Rev. E. G. Ingham, *Sierra Leone after a Hundred Years* (London: Frank Cass and Co., [1894] 1968), 74 ("dying"), 76; Walker, *The Black Loyalists*, 146 (for half rations). For other councilmen, see Wilson, *John Clarkson and the African Adventure*, 85–86; Wilson, *The Loyal Blacks*, 191–92.

14. Misevich, "The Sierra Leone Hinterland and the Provisioning of Early Freetown, 1792–1803"; Misevich, "On the Frontier of 'Freedom,'" 109, 115 (for ships); Falconbridge, *Narrative of Two Voyages*, 76 (for the shore); [Isaac DuBois], "Journal from my Departure from the Colony [31 December 1792] to 16 February 1793," 12 January 1793, f. 5, Add. MS 41263, BL (for casks); Ingham, *Sierra Leone after a Hundred Years*, 91–92 (for the storehouse). For the French attack, see Zachary Macaulay and James Watt to the Chairman and Court of Directors of the Sierra Leone Company, Freetown, 15 November 1794, f. 1, Journal of Zachary Macaulay, mssMY 418 (7), Macaulay Papers, HL; Ad[am] Afzelius to the Governor and Council of Sierra Leone, n.p., 27 November 1794, ff. 186–87, Add. MS 12131, BL. For the wounded, see George, "An Account of the Life of Mr. David George," 344. For the Bai Farma, see Journal of Zachary Macaulay, 18 October 1794, mssMY 418 (4), HL. For runaways and antislavery, see Philip Misevich, "Freetown and 'Freedom?': Colonialism and Slavery in Sierra Leone, 1790s to 1861," *Slavery, Abolition and the Transition to Colonialism in Sierra Leone*, 190.

15. For trade, see Bruce L. Mouser, "Rebellion, Marronage and Jihād: Strategies of Resistance to Slavery on the Sierra Leone Coast, c. 1783–1796," *Journal of African History* 48 (2007): 27–44, esp. 32; Mouser, "Landlords-Strangers," 431. For landlords and strangers, see Mouser, "Landlords-Strangers," 425; Allen M. Howard, "The Relevance of Spatial Analysis for African Economic History: The Sierra Leone-Guinea System," *Journal of African History* 17, no. 3 (1976): 365–88, esp. 373. For secret societies, see Howard, "The Relevance of Spatial Analysis for African Economic History," 374; Fyle, *The History of Sierra Leone*, 9, 23.

16. Misevich, "On the Frontier of 'Freedom,'" 31 (for rice), 36–37 (for kola nuts and salt); Allen M. Howard, "Nineteenth-Century Coastal Slave Trading and the British Abolition Campaign in Sierra Leone," *Slavery and Abolition* 27, no. 1 (April 2006): 23–49, esp. 28 (for rice); Schwarz, "From Company Administration to Crown Control," 173–74 (for the Bullom Shore); 17 March 1792, f. 13, Add. MS 41264, BL; "Diary of Lieutenant J. Clarkson, R.N. (governor, 1792)," 23 October 1792, *Sierra Leone Studies* (Freetown, Sierra Leone), no. VIII (March 1927): 91 ("of the Timmany"); Zachary Macaulay to Henry Thornton, Thornton Hill, 7 June 1797, Journal of Zachary Macaulay, mssMY 418 (21), Macaulay Papers, HL ("Timmanies, Bullams").

17. Thomas Clarkson to John Clarkson, 2 January 1792, f. 67, Add. MS 41262A, BL (quote); *Report from the Committee on the Petition of the Court of Directors of the Sierra Leone Company*, 1802. *House of Commons Parliamentary Papers Online*, 8, accessed January 28, 2016, http://gateway.proquest.com/openurl?url_ver=Z39.88-2004&res_dat=xri:hcpp&rft_dat=xri:hcpp:rec:1801-000196 (for money spent on provisions).

18. For the first estimate, see Journal of Zachary Macaulay, 8 August 1793, f. 118, mssMY 418 (1), Macaulay Papers, HL. For the second estimate, see Misevich, "On the Frontier of 'Freedom,'" 145. For the population count, see Clifford, *From Slavery to Freetown*, 136.

19. Ingham, *Sierra Leone after a Hundred Years*, 122; "Diary of Lieutenant J. Clarkson," 21 September and 2 November 1792, 51, 94; "Diary of Lieutenant J. Clarkson," 15 September 1792, 49. For rewards that incentivized the production of certain crops and animals, see 19 May 1795, ff. 155–61, CO 270/3, TNA; 5 February 1798, ff. 191–93, CO 270/4, TNA; 20 January 1801, f. 35, CO 270/6, TNA.

20. 1 May 1792, f. 35, Add. MS 12131, BL ("Some hams"); Jasanoff, *Liberty's Exiles*, 298 (for Peters's death); Ingham, *Sierra Leone after a Hundred Years*, 66 ("the people" and "the applications").

21. "Diary of Lieutenant J. Clarkson," 31 August and 1 September 1792, 34.

22. Ingham, *Sierra Leone after a Hundred Years*, 65 (quote). For the change in provisioning, see "Diary of Lieutenant J. Clarkson," 19 November 1792, 106; Council Minutes, 12 May 1792, ff. 37–38, CO 270/2, TNA.

23. John Strong to John Clarkson, Freetown, 19 November 1792; [Captains of companies] to John Clarkson, Freetown, 18 November 1792; all in "Diary of Lieutenant J. Clarkson," 19 November 1792, 105–6. See also Luke Jordan to John Clarkson, n.p., 18 November 1792, *"Our Children Free and Happy,"* 28.

24. Beverhout Company to John Clarkson, n.p., 26 June 1792, *"Our Children Free and Happy,"* 26 (for juries); Wilson, *John Clarkson and the African Adventure*, 127, 130–35 (for Clarkson's wedding and firing); Journal of Isaac Du Bois, sent to John Clarkson, 10 January 1793 and 14 January 1793, ff. 4 ("there [was] neither"), 6 (for land), Add. MS 41263, BL. William Dawes governed from 1792 to 1794 and 1795 to 1796, and then Zachary Macaulay from 1794 to 1795 and 1796 to 1799. John Gray governed from April to May of 1799 before Thomas Ludlum took over.

25. On petitioning, see Sidbury, "'African' Settlers in the Founding of Freetown," 132.

26. Falconbridge, *Narrative of Two Voyages*, 100 (quote).

27. "Cato Pirkins and Isaac Anderson to the Hble the Chairmain & Court of Directors of the Sierra Leone Company London" [sent to John Clarkson 30 October 1793], 13 October 1793, f. 99, Add. MS 41263, BL ("extortionate" and *"put thirty"*); Falcon-

bridge, *Narrative of Two Voyages*, 105–6 ("almost every kind"); Ingham, *Sierra Leone after a Hundred Years*, 80 ("we must either"); Moses Wilkinson, Isaac Anderson, [?] Peters, James Hutchinson, Luke Jordan, Jno. Jordan, Burbin Simmons, Amarica Tolbert, and "a Great many More the paper wont afford" to John Clarkson, Sierra Leone, 19 November 1794, f. 114, Add. MS 41263, BL ("a town").

28. Journal of Zachary Macaulay, 20 December 1796, mssMY 418 (17), Macaulay Papers, HL (quotes). For Sharp, see Fyfe, *A History of Sierra Leone*, 16, 48; Byrd, *Captives and Voyagers*, 132. For an alternate description of Sharp's plan, see Wallace Brown, "The Black Loyalists in Sierra Leone," *Moving On*, 104. For Dawes, Macaulay, and the Hundredors and Tythingmen in Sierra Leone, see 31 December 1792, f. 66, CO 270/2, TNA; Fyfe, *A History of Sierra Leone*, 16, 48.

29. Falconbridge, *Narrative of Two Voyages*, 124 (quote); Ariela J. Gross, *Double Character: Slavery and Mastery in the Antebellum Southern Courtroom* (Princeton, NJ: Princeton University Press, 2000), 53–54 (for U.S. juries).

30. 4 July 1793, f. 77, CO 270/2, TNA (for meat prices). For the experiments, see Resolutions of Council, Freetown, Sierra Leone, 23 August 1794, ff. 5–6, CO 270/3, TNA; Journal of Zachary Macaulay, 21 August 1794, mssMY 418 (3), Macaulay Papers, HL. For the higher bread price, see In Council, 9 June 1795, f. 174, CO 270/3, TNA. For "highly proper," see In Council, 12 October 1795, ff. 230–33, CO 270/3, TNA. For black Loyalists' relationship to the market, see Sidbury, *Becoming African in America*, 93–94. For reactions to state food systems, see Jeffrey M. Pilcher, *¡Que Vivan los Tamales! Food and the Making of Mexican Identity* (Albuquerque: University of New Mexico Press, 1998), 2; Nick Cullather, "The Foreign Policy of the Calorie," *American Historical Review* 112, no. 2 (April 2007): 337–64, esp. 360.

31. At first, many colonists felt driven by a religious impulse that explained their flight from North America, what they saw as their mission in Africa, and, for some, desires to forge bonds with Africans. David George and Boston King both spoke of teaching Africans Christianity and hoped for successful conversion attempts. Black Loyalists welcomed Africans into Freetown because doing so increased possibilities for Christian conversion as well as trade. In 1796 a group of Methodists even moved to Pirate's Bay with the permission of two Temne headmen, claiming identities as Christian Africans. Most of the colonists, however, would have had trouble identifying as Africans. Less than one-fourth of them were African-born. Of the 123 heads of households in Birchtown, Nova Scotia, who registered interest in migrating to Sierra Leone, 39 percent were born in the Chesapeake, 31 percent in Africa, and 24 percent in the Carolinas. Because these percentages included only adult men, who comprised a larger portion of African slaves, they inflated the African-born members of the population. Religious differences between Loyalists and Africans caused significant problems, and language barriers further impeded conversion. For black missionaries, see Edward E. Andrews, *Native Apostles: Black and Indian Missionaries in the British Atlantic World* (Cambridge, MA: Harvard University Press, 2013). For King and George, see "An Account of the Life of Mr. David George," 343, 345; "Memoirs of the Life of Boston King," 365. For Methodists, Pirate's Bay, and black Loyalists' places of origin, see Sidbury, "'African' Settlers in the Founding of Freetown," 129, 131, 134–35, 139n5. For language and conversion problems, see Falconbridge, *Narrative of Two Voyages*, 110; Brown, "The Black Loyalists in Sierra Leone," 120.

32. In Council, 9 June 1795, f. 174, CO 270/3, TNA ("issue an order"); Richard Corankapoor and Thomas Jackson to [the Governor and Council], Free Town, 8 June 1795, f. 175, CO 270/3, TNA ("some fine," "to kill," "not think," and "that no").

33. David E. Skinner, "The Incorporation of Muslim Elites into the Colonial Administrative Systems of Sierra Leone, the Gambia, and the Gold Coast," *Journal of Muslim Minority Affairs* 29, no. 1 (2009): 91–108, esp. 94 (for Muslim elites); Mouser, "Landlords-Strangers," 425 (for accommodation and assimilation).

34. 6 January 1798, ff. 184–85, CO 270/4, TNA (quotes); Misevich, "On the Frontier of 'Freedom,'" 11 (for high prices).

35. Journal of Zachary Macaulay, 12 September 1797, mssMY 418 (22), Macaulay Papers, HL; In Council, 23 March 1798, f. 196, CO 270/4, TNA. See also Clifford, *From Slavery to Freetown*, 185.

36. 5 March 1798, f. 193, CO 270/4, TNA.

37. Journal of Zachary Macaulay, 22 December 1796, mssMY 418 (17), Macaulay Papers, HL.

38. In Council, 24 June 1799, f. 269, 272, CO 270/4, TNA.

39. For Jordan's, Anderson's, and Cuthbert's offices, see Douglas R. Egerton, *Death or Liberty: African Americans and Revolutionary America* (New York: Oxford University Press, 2009), 219. For interpretations of this event, see Wilson, *The Loyal Blacks*, 388–96; Jasanoff, *Liberty's Exiles*, 304–5; Pybus, *Epic Journeys of Freedom*, 198–99; Sidbury, *Becoming African in America*, 125–28; Cassandra Pybus, "Henry 'Harry' Washington (1750s–1790s): A Founding Father's Slave," in *The Human Tradition in the Atlantic World, 1500–1850*, ed. Karen Racine and Beatriz G. Mamigonian (Lanham, MD: Rowman and Littlefield Publishers, 2010), 113.

40. "Paper of Laws stuck up at Abram Smith's house by the Hundredors and Tythingmen," Appendix, ff. 98–100, CO 270/5, TNA (quotes); "A Narrative of the Rebellion which broke out in this Colony on the 25th of Septr. 1800," Appendix, ff. 100–11, CO 270/5, TNA. The code was dated 3 September.

41. "A Narrative of the Rebellion which broke out in this Colony on the 25th of Septr. 1800," Appendix, ff. 100 (for the postings of the code), 102 (for the scuffle, the 27th, and the bridge), 104 (for pillaging), CO 270/5, TNA; Wilson, *The Loyal Blacks*, 392 (for the bayonet). For King Tom, see Jasanoff, *Liberty's Exiles*, 304; Fyle, *Historical Dictionary of Sierra*, 210–11. For the Maroons, see [John King] to John Schoolbred, Whitehall, 7 July 1796, f. 139, CO 267/10, TNA. For the soldiers, see f. 105, CO 270/5, TNA. For slightly different numbers, see Egerton, *Death or Liberty*, 220. For the tribunal, see Jasanoff, *Liberty's Exiles*, 304–5; Wilson, *The Loyal Blacks*, 388–96.

42. In 1794 the council intended to force payment of a quitrent ten times higher than any of those in America, despite many colonists remaining landless. For quitrent rates in Sierra Leone, see Wilson, *The Loyal Blacks*, 189. For primary documents, see Resolution of Council Omitted, [?] January 1794, f. 139, CO 270/2, TNA; Henry Thornton to John Clarkson, London, 30 December 1791, f. 41, Add MS. 41262A, BL; Zachary Macaulay and James Watt to the Chairman and Court of Directors of the Sierra Leone Company, Freetown, Journal of Zachary Macaulay, 15 November 1794, f. 2, mssMY 418 (7), Macaulay Papers, HL. For the elections, see Fyfe, *A History of Sierra Leone*, 68, 81–87; Wilson, *The Loyal Blacks*, 383–401; Clifford, *From Slavery to Freetown*, 189–96; Pybus, *Epic Journeys of Freedom*, 191–202; Egerton, *Death or Liberty*, 219; Jasanoff,

Liberty's Exiles, 304–7; Sidbury, *Becoming African in America*, 125–28. For "general indignation," see "A Narrative of the Rebellion which broke out in this Colony on the 25th of Septr. 1800," Appendix, f. 100, CO 270/5, TNA. For executions and post-September accounts, see "A Narrative of the Rebellion which broke out in this Colony on the 25th of Septr. 1800," Appendix, ff. 100–11, CO 270/5, TNA; *Report from the Committee on the Petition of the Court of Directors of the Sierra Leone Company*, 1802. The literature on black rebellions is vast, and the terminology related to *riot* and *rebellion* is not uniform in scholarship. Paul Gilje excludes slave rebellions from his survey of American riots because he argues that it was difficult for the enslaved to riot. Paul A. Gilje, *Rioting in America* (Bloomington: Indiana University Press, 1996), 6. For representative examples on rebellion, see Peter Wood, *Black Majority: Negroes in Colonial South Carolina: From 1670 through the Stono Rebellion* (New York: Alfred A. Knopf, 1974); Gad Heuman, *"The Killing Time": The Morant Bay Rebellion in Jamaica* (London, UK: University of Tennessee Press, 1994); James Sidbury, *Ploughshares into Swords: Race, Rebellion, and Identity in Gabriel's Virginia, 1730–1810* (New York: Cambridge University Press, 1997). In some works, only after emancipation does crowd action become "political unrest" or "riot." Other scholars have used terms like *rebellion, riot,* and *uprising* interchangeably regardless of whether dissenters were enslaved or free. For postemancipation terminology, see Michael Naragon, "From Chattel to Citizen: The Transition from Slavery to Freedom in Richmond, Virginia," *Slavery and Abolition* 21, no. 2 (2000): 93–116, esp. 112. For works that vary word usage, see Julie Saville, "Rites and Power: Reflections on Slavery, Freedom and Political Ritual," *Slavery and Abolition* 20, no. 1 (1999): 81–102, esp. 84–85; Natasha Lightfoot, "'Their Coats were Tied Up like Men': Women Rebels in Antigua's 1858 Uprising," *Slavery and Abolition* 31, no. 4 (November 2010): 527–45; Stephan Lenik, "Plantation Labourer Rebellions, Material Culture and Events: Historical Archaeology at Geneva Estate, Grand Bay, Commonwealth of Dominica," *Slavery and Abolition* 35, no. 3 (September 2014): 508–26, esp. 518–19.

43. Ishmael York, Stephen Peters, and Isaac Anderson to the Honourable Captain Ball Esq., 16 January 1798, in *"Our Children Free and Happy,"* 58 ("If we are his"); Edward A. Pearson, "'A countryside full of flames': A Reconsideration of the Stono Rebellion and Slave Rebelliousness in the Early Eighteenth-Century South Carolina Lowcountry," *Slavery and Abolition* 17, no. 2 (1996): 22–50, esp. 38–39 (for rebellious behavior); Pybus, "Henry 'Harry' Washington (1750s–1790s)," 113 (for the rioters' ages); In Council, 5 January 1799, f. 234, CO 270/4, TNA (for colonists taking office); Coleman, *Romantic Colonization*, 109 (for land and subjecthood); "A Narrative of the Rebellion which broke out in this Colony on the 25th of Septr. 1800," Appendix, f. 102, CO 270/5, TNA ("intelligence was received"). See also Jasanoff, *Liberty's Exiles*, 304; Egerton, *Death or Liberty*, 219–20; Sidbury, "'African' Settlers in the Founding of Freetown," 138; Wilson, *The Loyal Blacks*, 396.

44. Mouser, "Rebellion, Marronage and *Jihād*," 33; Rashid, "Escape, Revolt, and Marronage in Eighteenth and Nineteenth Century Sierra Leone Hinterland," 667–68; *Report from the Committee on the Petition of the Court of Directors of the Sierra Leone Company*, 1802, 4.

45. For England and September 1800, see John Bohstedt, *The Politics of Provisions: Food Riots, Moral Economy, and Market Transition in England, c. 1550–1850* (Surrey, UK: Ashgate, 2010), 2, 192, 217. For America, see Barbara Clark Smith, "Food Rioters and

the American Revolution," *William and Mary Quarterly* 51, no. 1 (January 1994): 3–38, esp. 3; Wayne E. Lee, *Crowds and Soldiers in Revolutionary North Carolina: The Culture of Violence in Riot and War* (Gainesville: University Press of Florida, 2001). For nonwhite communities, see Eliga Gould, "Independence and Interdependence: The American Revolution and the Problem of Postcolonial Nationhood, circa 1802," *William and Mary Quarterly* 74, no. 4 (October 2017): 729–52, esp. 732.

46. For types of riots, see John Walton and David Seddon, *Free Markets and Food Riots: The Politics of Global Adjustment* (Cambridge, UK: John Wiley and Sons, 1994), 25–26. For food riots elsewhere, see E. P. Thompson, "The Moral Economy of the English Crowd in the Eighteenth Century," *Past and Present*, no. 50 (February 1971): 76–136; Cynthia A. Bouton, *The Flour War: Gender, Class, and Community in Late Ancien Régime French Society* (University Park: Pennsylvania State University Press, 1993); Walton and Seddon, *Free Markets and Food Riots*; Smith, "Food Rioters and the American Revolution"; Andy Wood, *Riot, Rebellion and Popular Politics in Early Modern England* (Hampshire, UK: Palgrave Macmillan, 2002); Bohstedt, *The Politics of Provisions*.

47. For riotous women, see Thompson, "The Moral Economy of the English Crowd in the Eighteenth Century," 115; John Bohstedt, "Gender, Household and Community Politics: Women in English Riots 1790–1810," *Past and Present* 120, no. 1 (August 1988): 88–122; Lightfoot, "'Their Coats were Tied Up like Men,'" 537. For female shopkeepers, see *"Our Children Free and Happy,"* 12; John Clarkson to William Dawes, Freetown, 5 October 1792, "Diary of Lieutenant J. Clarkson," 79. For women and children during the riot, see Isaac Anderson, unsigned, n.d., in *"Our Children Free and Happy,"* 65. For the absence of leaders and arms, see Charles Tilly, "Food Supply and Public Order in Modern Europe," in *The Formation of National States in Western Europe*, ed. Charles Tilly (Princeton, NJ: Princeton University Press, 1975), 443.

48. For death rates in England and France, see Bohstedt, *The Politics of Provisions*, 224; Tilly, "Food Supply and Public Order in Modern Europe," 383. For America, see Gilje, *Rioting in America*, 25. For Perkins, see Fyfe, *"Our Children Free and Happy,"* 18. For Anderson, see Appendix, f. 110, CO 270/5, TNA.

49. In Council, Journal of Zachary Macaulay, 7 March 1795, ff. 55–56, MY 418 (3), HL.

50. For changes to pricing in Britain, see Marc-William Palen, "Adam Smith as Advocate of Empire, c. 1870–1932," *Historical Journal* 57, no. 1 (March 2014): 179–98, esp. 183. For the American colonies and United States, see Smith, "Food Rioters and the American Revolution," 24. For the 1800s, see Alfred E. Eckes Jr., *Opening America's Market: U.S. Foreign Trade Policy Since 1776* (Chapel Hill: University of North Carolina Press, 1995), 26; Marc-William Palen, "Foreign Relations in the Gilded Age: A British Free-Trade Conspiracy?" *Diplomatic History* 37, no. 2 (April 2013): 217–47, esp. 219, 247. For 1808 Sierra Leone, see Brown, "The Black Loyalists in Sierra Leone," 122; Fyfe, *A History of Sierra Leone*, 97; David Northrup, "Becoming African: Identify Formation among Liberated Slaves in Nineteenth-Century Sierra Leone," *Slavery and Abolition* 27, no. 1 (August 2006): 1–21; David Lambert, "Sierra Leone and Other Sites in the War of Representation over Slavery," *History Workshop Journal* 64, no. 1 (Autumn 2007): 103–32. For cash crops and slavery, see Schwarz, "From Company Administration to Crown Control," 181; Coleman, *Romantic Colonization*, 132; Everill, *Abolition and Empire in Sierra Leone and Liberia*, 19.

Conclusion. Why Native and Black Revolutionaries Lost the Fight

1. For circum-Atlantic history, see David Armitage, "Three Concepts of Atlantic History," in *The British Atlantic World*, ed. David Armitage and Michael J. Braddick (Basingstoke, UK: Palgrave Macmillan, 2002), 16.

2. For representative works, see Benedict Anderson, *Imagined Communities: Reflections on the Origin and Spread of Nationalism* (London: Verso, 2006 [1983]); Cassandra Pybus, *Epic Journeys of Freedom: Runaway Slaves of the American Revolution and their Global Quest for Liberty* (Boston: Beacon Press, 2006); Jane G. Landers, *Atlantic Creoles in the Age of Revolutions* (Cambridge, MA: Harvard University Press, 2010); Maya Jasanoff, *Liberty's Exiles: American Loyalists in the Revolutionary World* (New York: Alfred A. Knopf, 2011); Janet Polasky, *Revolutions without Borders: The Call to Liberty in the Atlantic World* (New Haven, CT: Yale University Press, 2015); Benjamin E. Park, *American Nationalisms: Imagining Union in the Age of Revolutions, 1783–1833* (Cambridge, UK: Cambridge University Press, 2018), esp. 1, 4.

3. For a useful definition of the term *food sovereignty*, see Jennifer Cockrall-King, *Food and the City: Urban Agriculture and the New Food Revolution* (Amherst, NY: Prometheus Books, 2012), 319.

4. Edward W. Gregg, Xiaohui Zhuo, Yiling J. Cheng, Ann L. Albright, K. M. Venkat Narayan, and Theodore J. Thompson, "Trends in Lifetime Risk and Years of Life Lost Due to Diabetes in the USA, 1985–2011: A Modelling Study," *Lancet: Diabetes and Endocrinology* 2, no. 11 (November 2014), 867–74, esp. 869; Vanessa W. Simonds, Adam Omidpanah, and Dedra Buchwald, "Diabetes Prevention among American Indians: The Role of Self-Efficacy, Risk Perception, Numeracy and Cultural Identity," *BMC Public Health* 17, no. 763 (2017): 1–11. For Black Britons, see also Anoop Dinesh Shah, Claudia Langenberg, Eleni Rapsomaniki, Spiros Denaxas, Mar Pujades-Rodrigues, Chris P. Gale, John Deanfield, Liam Smeeth, Adam Timmis, and Harry Hemingway, "Type 2 Diabetes and Incidence of Cardiovascular Diseases: A Cohort Study in 1.9 Million People," *Lancet: Diabetes and Endocrinology* 3, no. 2 (February 2015): 105–13, esp. 108.

5. When I was an undergraduate, my professors taught me not to use the first person in formal historical writing because it is "obtrusive," and I repeat this advice to my students. But as an undergraduate I also learned that it was okay to break some of the rules of writing history once I'd learned them, and nowadays I'm not sure that historians agree whether the first person "I" is allowable or forbidden anyway. James H. Merrell, "A Few Matters of Form and Style," unpublished handout, Vassar College, 7. Merrell was citing James Axtell, "Writing History," also an unpublished handout. Here I have broken another rule by not consulting this source directly, but whereas James Merrell was an undergraduate teacher of mine, James Axtell was not. I thank Seth Tannenbaum for scanning and sending me his copy of "A Few Matters," and I accept full responsibility for breaking these rules.

6. *A Practical Guide to Studying History: Skills and Approaches*, ed. Tracey Loughran (London: Bloomsbury, 2017).

7. This observation about who in the past won the right to write history has been shaped by scholarship on colonists' conflicts with Indians during other time periods. See especially Alfred A. Cave, "The Pequot Invasion of Southern New England: A Reassessment of the Evidence," *New England Quarterly* 12, no. 4 (1988): 277–97; Jill

Lepore, *The Name of War: King Philip's War and the Origins of American Identity* (New York: Vintage Books, 1998); Andrew C. Lipman, "Murder on the Saltwater Frontier: The Death of John Oldham," *Early American Studies* 9, no. 2 (2011): 268–94.

8. Michael A. LaCombe, *Political Gastronomy: Food and Authority in the English Atlantic World* (Philadelphia: University of Pennsylvania Press, 2012), 88–89; Jack Santino, *All around the Year: Holidays and Celebrations in American Life* (Chicago: University of Illinois Press, 1994), 169.

9. Most recently, David Shields has even argued that scholars need to know what varieties of foodstuffs people ate and how they tasted. David Shields, *Southern Provisions: The Creation and Revival of a Cuisine* (Chicago and London: University of Chicago Press, 2015), xi–xii, 16.

Index

Readers will find Native Americans indexed by the name I thought would be most familiar; sometimes a person appears by surname, and sometimes by the name most frequently discernible in the records. I have indexed places using modern geographical designations.

Page numbers in *italics* refer to figures.

Abeel, John. *See* Cornplanter
abolitionists, 3, 138, 149, 183, 190
Acadians, 139
accommodation, 9, 36, 75, 187, 192, 204
Act of Union (1707), 73
African Americans, 17, 100
Africans: Baga, 182, 198; Bullom, 182, 185, 188, 196; Fula, 182, 184; Koranko, 182; Limba, 182; Loko, 182; Mande, 183; Mandingo, 182, 185, 196; Susu, 14, 179, 182, 183, 188–93; Temne, 14, 179, 181–84, 187–89, 191–98; Yoruba, 151
agriculture: American colonists', 44, 48, 51, 62, 94, 107; Americans', 162; black colonists', 142, 187; changes to, 12, 157, 160, 167, 171; Europeans', 2, 34, 145; formerly enslaved peoples', 97; gender roles in, 22, 35, 161, 163, 168, 169; hoes, 61, 162, 174; Loyalists', 114, 139, 147, 149; misrepresentations about, 12, 14, 123, 154, 157, 160, 206; model farms, 169; Native American cropping systems in, 2, 28, 29, 34, 124, 125, 132, 158, 163, 169, 176; pelicula, 35; plows, 51, 162, 163, 165, 169, 170, 173, 174; soil disturbance in, 28. *See also* victual imperialism; victual warfare
Alabama, 34, 67, 84, 121
alcohol: Madeira, 27, 128; Port, 128; rum, 27, 46, 49, 75, 76, 98, 105, 113, 116, 118, 128, 132, 171, 186, 189–90, 193, 194; whiskey, 172; wine, 28, 191
Allen, William, 103
alliances: confusion about, 81, 83; disruptions to, 46, 66, 72, 75, 131; formation of, 9, 11, 45, 50, 68, 120, 125, 127; maintenance of, 9, 26–29, 42, 50, 64, 68, 71, 74; severing of,

43. *See also* Cherokee; Creek; Delaware; Iroquois; Shawnee; trade; Western Confederacy Indians
American Legion, 127–29, 131
Amherst, Jeffery, 43, 44, 116, 173, 202
animals: ants, 181; beaver, 42, 176; birds, 50, 53, 24; bulls, 31, 98; caterpillars, 46; cats, 42, 150; calves, 164; cattle, 1, 12, 27, 28, 34, 35, 46, 50, 51, 53, 57, 59, 60, 69–76, 79, 83–85, 96, 97, 104, 120, 123, 124, 127, 129, 130, 157, 162, 164, 169, 171, 174, 184, 187, 191–3; chickens, 28, 35, 39; deer, 8, 29, 42, 71, 73, 126, 164, 174, 176; dogfish, 143; dogs, 27, 53, 72, 136, 150; eel, 53, 143; flounder, 143; goats, 96, 181, 191; haddock, 143; herring, 105, 143; Hessian fly, 46, 115; horses, 28, 34, 51, 52, 54, 72–77, 83, 84, 96, 118, 120, 123, 127, 130, 136, 164, 170, 172, 173; leopards, 181; manure, 28, 170; muskrats, 42, 53; otters, 42; pigs, 1, 11, 12, 28, 34, 51, 52, 84, 96, 104, 106, 120, 123, 124, 157, 169, 170, 172, 174, 187, 192; raccoons, 42; salmon, 143; shad, 143; sheep, 1, 152, 157, 166, 191; skate, 143; steers, 103, 164; sturgeon, 143
antislavery, 3, 149, 180, 184, 190
Appalachian Mountains, 6, 44
appetite: blacks', 89, 91, 107, 136, 139, 201; non-Native knowledge about, 17, 21, 23, 31, 36, 37, 38, 47, 117, 119, 158, 162, 169, 202, 206; Native American, 13, 17, 21, 29, 31; suppressants, 117
Articles of Confederation, 114–15, 126
Atkin, Edmond, 24, 25, 67
Atlantic World, 13, 53, 200–201, 204, 205
Aupaumut, Hendrick, 117, 128, 129, 167, 171, 175

CPSIA information can be obtained
at www.ICGtesting.com
Printed in the USA
FSHW012243280919
62472FS